D0288463

THE
ADVENTUROUS
GARDENER

Where to buy the best plants in
NEW ENGLAND

THE ADVENTUROUS GARDENER

Where to buy the best plants in NEW ENGLAND

by Ruah Donnelly

The
Horticultural
Press

635

For information and permission to reproduce
selections from this book, write to:
The Horticultural Press
P.O. Box 390
Jaffrey, NH 03452

ISBN 0-9677303-1-7
Library of Congress Card Number: 00-100925

Cover photograms: Ann Parker
        Red Anemone, "Botanical Metamorphics," © Ann Parker
        Jack-in-the-pulpit, "Botanical Metamorphics," © Ann Parker
Cover design: Fionn Reilly
Editing: Mary V. Dearborn
        Doris Troy
        Naomi Rosenblatt

Printed in Canada

CONTENTS

ACKNOWLEDGMENTS

Nobody prepares a guidebook alone. This book could not have been written without the encouragement and support of my husband, Steve Dinkelaker. Although I always visited the nurseries portrayed here with legitimate gardening needs, many subjects of this guide extended me kindness, time, and attention far exceeding my value as a retail customer. Without their horticultural knowledge and generosity, there would be no book. I enjoyed the use of library resources at Tower Hill Botanic Garden, the Massachusetts Horticultural Society, and the Boston Athenaeum. I owe a debt of gratitude to countless plant professionals, state inspectors, gardening friends, relatives, writers, readers, mentors, enthusiasts, book experts, advice-givers, and good-deed-doers, all of whom contributed greatly to whatever merit this book may possess.

On the book's cover, I am honored to use two luminous works by Massachusetts artist Ann Parker, *Red Anemone* and *Jack-in-the-Pulpit*, from her photogram series, *Botanical Metamorphics*. I am also indebted to the anonymous creators of beautiful line drawings, originally printed in American nursery catalogs of the 19th century. These extraordinary images are part of New England's horticultural heritage; where possible I have selected catalog images from the vanished nurseries of New England.

People making memorable contributions to the book whom I would be swinish not to thank publicly are Mary V. Dearborn, Fionn Reilly, Doris Troy, Beth Walker and Irwin Wolf of Walker Press, Dick and Tommy Dearborn, Jean Berry, Bill and Bobby Fuller, Diane Dalton, Sally Bass, Dottie DeWitt, Jeff Steele, Libby Eustis, Miriam Scott, Pamela Esty and Whitney Beals, Margaret Miner and Hugh Rawson, Jessie Lie Farber, Kim Ciborowski, Bonnie Shershow, Rose Moss, Eva Somaripa, Ralph Helmick and Nan Niland, Steve Apple, Scott Hall, Paula Panich, Sheila Butler, John Donnelly, Naomi Rosenblatt, Tom Cooper, and John Trexler and the staff of Tower Hill Botanic Garden. Any errors or misjudgments in the book are, of course, my own.

INTRODUCTION AND OTHER DISCLAIMERS

THE ADVENTUROUS GARDENER: Where to Buy the Best Plants in New England is dedicated to our fellow gardeners. It is meant to help you find good, regionally grown plants for your garden. We hope you will use this as a travel companion, whether in search of particular plants or a horticultural romp through New England. We hope you will consult this guide when you are dreaming and planning your garden.

This book is for venturesome gardeners, weekend gardeners, enthusiasts, connoisseurs, urban gardeners, variegated-foliage nuts, garden designers, and people with green thumbs. It is for smart gardeners who know that the best plants are usually local plants, grown within 100 miles of their garden. It is for garden tourists who enjoy visiting nurseries and display gardens while traveling the byways of New England. It is for armchair gardeners who savor reading garden catalogs on cold winter nights. It is for gardeners who love the historical landscape of New England and want to reward and encourage farmers seeking viable agricultural uses for its farmland. It is for cold-climate gardeners who love exotic new plants and want to know where to find them in New England.

When we first started gardening, the task of locating good New England nurseries did not seem urgent. It took us a while to appreciate the difference between a healthy, nursery-grown plant and a juiced-up product of the horticulture industry. Once we did, we realized that there was no shortcut to gardening that did not involve buying good plants—well-selected, well-grown plants that would thrive in the grounds of our old farmhouse, in our city container garden—whatever garden we had at the moment. Good plants—who was making them in New England, for New England? We started poking around. We asked questions, sent for catalogs, talked to horti-culturists. (Professionals often know a few nurseries well, but can be as cagey as fishermen protecting their favorite trout holes.) We began to search for the best regional nurseries and growers.

This book offers help in finding regional sources for garden plants you may be looking for, whether native wildflowers, Chinese tree peonies, African violets, or plants that look good in winter. We do not pretend to proclaim the "best" sources for any particular plant, beyond some personal recommenda-tions. (See the Index to Plant Sources on page 273.) Though we have great respect for reputable commercial garden centers, most are well advertised and already known to local gardeners; instead, our focus has been on growers of plants that can't be found in garden centers—though we have included a few garden centers we think are standouts.

Being horticultural amateurs, not professionals, we had much to learn in order to write this book, and we admit to some outright prejudices. We prefer nurseries that strive for excellence and sell healthy, well-selected plants that are regionally adapted to New England. We prefer establishments that grow their own plants, because this normally produces a stronger, healthier plant than trucked-in stock or the force-fed plugs of the nursery industry. We seek interesting, unusual, and beautiful varieties of ornamental plants. We want plants that are correctly labeled. We like responsible pest management and organic growing practices. We love eloquent nursery catalogs that are fun to read. We admire hybridizers and nurserymen who expand our consciousness about what can be grown in a cold-climate garden. We oppose wild-collecting of native plants, rare or not. We have a weakness for family farms and adventurous spirits. We find the eccentricities of New England growers to be endearing. We prefer nurseries and specialty growers that contribute to preserving the rural landscape of New England. We have omitted any place where the plants are on drugs and you can smell chemical fertilizer from the driveway.

We have made every effort to present accurate information and observations in order to enliven public knowledge and encourage patronage of good plant sources in New England. We do not pretend that our information is totally free of errors, or that every single good nursery in New England is listed in this book. We have tried hard to exhaust available research sources and verify all facts. We have personally contacted (and in almost all cases, personally visited) each nursery, garden center, hybridizer, and grower listed here, as well as many others omitted from the book. Few divined our purpose, and none influenced the result. We have consciously excluded purveyors of wild-collected endangered plants, nurseries we found inferior or fishy, moribund and ho-hum enterprises, businesses changing hands, nurseries about to be closed, and growers too small to entertain the general public or impart a reasonable sense of security about their future. We have included some publicity-shy growers who might have preferred to be omitted but are too good to pass over in silence. We have erred in favor of listing nurseries offering something special or unusual, even if they do not play a good retail game. Above all, we have looked for good plants.

We warmly welcome correspondence and feedback from readers, either to help correct entries or to expand coverage in future editions. Correspondence and book orders may be addressed to The Horticultural Press (toll free 877-GARDEN-A or 877-427-3362).

Online gardeners may contact us at *www.adventurousgardener.com*. We encourage opinionated criticism, as well as suggestions for worthy New England nurseries that we may have missed in researching this book.

A Note on Plant Selection

Although we are not gardening professionals, we think it would be amiss to provide you with a guide to gardening sources without telling you what to do when you get there—that is, how to select a good plant, the right plant for your garden. According to an ancient Sufi parable, perfect action requires the right time, the right place, the right people, and the right skills.

RIGHT NURSERY. Many of the best people spending their lives in horticulture do it for love, not money. Nurseries that know and love plants will serve you, while those that don't will just sell you. Look for well-run nurseries with healthy plants and good growing practices; for an involved, reputable owner; and for knowledgeable staff who can advise you on plant-specific questions. Certified nurserymen, arborists, and people with degrees in horticulture really do know more about plants than most of us. Horticultural farmers and practiced hybridizers are keen students of their plants.

A few definitions are in order. A *nursery* is, loosely, a horticultural enterprise raising its own plant stock from cuttings, seed, or division—not just buying industry plugs and juicing them up with fertilizer in a greenhouse. Small nurseries often supplement homegrown stock with bought-in material, preferably from local growers. A *garden center* is a retailer selling a range of garden plants bought in from outside suppliers—from local growers to large commercial enterprises. Garden centers may propagate and grow some of their own stock, but not in critical mass. (For reasons given in our introduction, commercial garden centers, however meritorious, are not our primary focus here.) A *hybridizer* is a breeder of genetically new cultivars, and often a nurseryman, by either vocation or necessity.

RIGHT VALUE. Getting good ornamental plants does not require a trust fund or a six-figure income; it requires discretion and intelligence. You can get some very good deals on plants in New England, particularly if you recognize that a cheap price tag is not the ultimate indicator of value. A bargain may come as a well-filled perennial pot containing two or three individual plants; a choice hybrid for the price of an ordinary plant; an excellent older cultivar no longer carrying introduction costs; a flat of seedlings; or a healthy plant on sale in the fall planting season, when some plants actually prefer to be moved. Organic and chemical-free growers provide added value in the quality of their soil and growing conditions; even smaller plants may prove more durable. One of the best bargains are those little packets of horticultural information called seeds. We know of an impressive connoisseur's garden that originated in nothing but seeds, even the shrubs and trees.

RIGHT SOURCE. Regionally grown and adapted plants from good horticultural homes can be a bargain even at full price, for they have enhanced odds of thriving in your garden. Among native plants, research indicates that plants genetically derived from regional natives are hardier and more durable than identical species from a different climate—so much for trees trucked in from Tennessee and Oregon. As a rule of thumb, buying a plant that is proven hardy and grown within 100 miles of your home will significantly increase its odds in your garden. In almost all cases, plants that are young transplant more easily, adapt quicker, and perform better in the long run than large specimens. In perennials, look for small, stocky plants with good roots. In shrubs and trees, look for the young, sturdy, northern-grown plant with a substantial root ball and no damage to trunk and limb (lift the burlap to check out the base). Many people are surprised to learn that after a few years, an immature tree or shrub will actually catch up to its mature counterpart in height and girth. In nursery stock, perhaps the best value is a small, well-rooted, field-grown plant that is already acclimated to New England. Avoid potted plants with girdling roots that have outgrown their pots: These are the skeleton grandmothers of the nursery trade.

RIGHT PLANT. At one time or another, most gardeners waste time on banal or aggressive plant material that they later regret being involved with and have to replace. Fast-forward this process and select good ornamental plants to begin with. Insist on fine, well-behaved cultivars, and you will be surprised at how affordable they can be. Compare the cost with a good arrangement from the florist—and then consider that the live plant will last for years. Especially do not fool around with unworthy or disease-prone trees and shrubs, which take time to mature and are not easily replaced. Look for well-recommended, graceful cultivars with durable good looks and disease resistance. For flash and dazzle, stick to dalliances with gorgeous neon annuals that are fun while they last—for a season.

RIGHT TREATMENT. You can buy the greatest plant in the world from a nursery, but if you mistreat it during the critical transfer stage, you might as well donate your money to charity. Do not bake a plant in a hot car. Do not let a plant sit around in a pot or a bare-root mailing bag. If you are rushed, heel it into the ground and give it a good watering until you have time for full treatment. Bare-root plants can be saved through home baptism, that is, immersion up to their necks in a bucket of water. Many tree and shrub nurseries warn against planting too deep, which can kill a larger plant. After transplanting, make sure the plant stays well watered until it adjusts to its new home—this is especially critical for larger stock. As for planting depth, soil amendments, and the like, follow sound planting instructions—a good nursery will provide them with the plant.

RIGHT SEASON. Despite the practices of the commercial nursery industry, not all plants like being pumped up with chemicals, forced into bloom, and transplanted in the spring. Plants like to flower in their own time, not at the convenience of commercial growers who sell plants more easily when they are in bloom. A nursery plant that is not putting all its energy into producing flowers is often a better choice than one that is. Some plants, such as peonies and many wildflowers, actually prefer being planted dormant in the fall. Many hardy trees and shrubs enjoy a fall planting. A good nursery will steer you right.

RIGHT ZONE. If you know your garden's heat and cold tolerance, you can choose plants that will best survive and grow there. Adventurous gardeners may try to push a plant into a marginal zone, for plant tolerances are not ironclad. Microclimates can depart from local growing norms; conditions change somewhat from year to year; and tricks such as mulching and winter wrapping can help to defy climatic norms. In parts of New England, deep snow cover protects plants that would perish of cold if exposed. Still, pushing a plant beyond its zone of comfort is always a risk. By learning something of a plant's origins and habits, you can often tell where it will thrive: alpine plants in a rock garden, desert plants in a dry, sunny window box.

RIGHT PLACE. Take time to observe and assess your garden's patterns and characteristics—its natural allotment of sun and shade, its moisture or dryness, its directional face, wind exposure, structure, and the character of its soil. You can have the pH level of soil tested at the local USDA Extension Service (indicating alkaline, neutral, or acid soil), although in New England everyone knows that we run to acid, and not just in our political commentary. Selecting plants that do well in the native conditions of your garden will not only save frustration and headache, but also can actually tell you what type of garden will be most suited to your site. Forget sunny perennial borders if you have woodland shade. Don't force plants that want rich soil to live in gravel scree, or vice versa. If mountain laurel grows wild in the woods near you, consider planting the cultivated version in your garden. If violets have colonized your lawn, why not put together a violet collection?

Great gardeners do not defy nature, but observe it and make use of it in order to create gardens that resonate in their surroundings. Defying plant norms inevitably involves a gardener in coddling and other extraordinary measures that would not be necessary if the right plants had been invited to live there in the first place. One serious gardener we know, whose garden has won many prestigious awards, asserts that the real secret of success is laziness—choosing plants that look good and thrive without a great deal of effort. Amuse yourself with the sophisticated puzzle of finding fine cultivars that grow readily in your conditions, while providing real beauty and garden interest. Make the puzzle more interesting, if you want, by seeking plants that support wildlife, plants that extend the bloom season, plants that provide winter interest, ancient plants that were known in biblical times, fragrant evening-blooming plants, native species, or new and unusual plants that your friends and neighbors have never seen before.

RIGHT ATTITUDE. New England is blessed with an extraordinary horticultural legacy, troves of terrific plants, and a fascinating population of expert growers, farmers, and nurserymen. Gardening is an ancient activity, among the most important achievements of human culture. Even the most ordinary garden plants connect a gardener to thousands of years of human effort—to the canny toil of a long chain of gardening forebears in choosing and cultivating beneficial plants. Garden plants are an inheritance, a legacy derived from the wild order of nature and from centuries of human effort in cottage gardens, physic gardens, palaces, monasteries, and farms. Even the newest hybrids rely on ancient chains of DNA. Garden plants are at once a rich bequest and the ultimate in affordable antiques.

A garden is the dynamic result of the gardener's choices—a series of choices about timing, placement, structure, color scheme, style, ecology, and ornament—about making the kind of living room that nature provides. Gardens invite creatures into our lives, both flora and fauna, and open doors to the natural world. (Our own small urban container garden, the habitat of countless microorganisms, worms, and insects, is routinely visited by children, foreign tourists, neighbors, dogs, and butterflies.) Through the medium of the garden, each of us develops a fluency with the news of wind and water; an ear for the language of birds; a friendship with bats, worms, spiders, and ladybugs; an appreciation for the needs and habits of insects, fungi, deer, voles, and "the creatures that crawl upon the earth." A garden provides engaging physical work, food for thought, a connection with living things and their seasons, spiritual refuge, and a reminder of death and the possibilities of renewal. Making a garden is a fugitive act of human hope, organization, and genius. Considered the right way, a garden contains all the ingredients of happiness.

New England
Nurseries

CONNECTICUT

CONNECTICUT

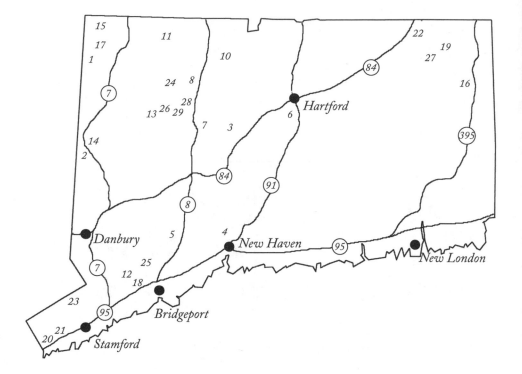

1. Beardsley Gardens
2. Bloomingfields Farm
3. Bristol Mums, Inc.
4. Broken Arrow Nursery
5. Butterbrooke Farm Seeds
6. Comstock, Ferre & Co.
7. Cricket Hill Garden
8. The Daffodil Mart
9. Gilbertie's Herb Gardens, Inc.
10. The Great Plant Company
11. Hillside Gardens
12. J&L Orchids
13. John Scheepers, Inc.
14. Kathleen Nelson Perennials
15. Lauray of Salisbury
16. Logee's Greenhouses
17. Old Farm Nursery
18. Oliver Nurseries
19. Resourceful Judith Designs
20. Sam Bridge Nursery & Greenhouses
21. Schipper & Co.
22. Select Seeds
23. Shanti Bithi Nursery
24. Shepherd's Garden Seeds
25. Twombly Nursery
26. Van Engelen Inc.
27. The Variegated Foliage Nursery
28. Walnut Hill Greenhouse
29. White Flower Farm

BEARDSLEY GARDENS

P.O. Box 1764, 157 Gay Street (Route 41), Sharon, CT 06069
(860) 364-0727; fax (860) 364-1006
Cynthia Rice

Perennials, annuals, grasses, ferns, roses, and woody plants. *Retail garden center.*
Open February through December, daily 9–5. Catalog $1.50. No mail order. Visitors
welcome. Display gardens. Lectures. Landscape architecture and design services.
Web site: www.beardsleygardens.com.

Beardsley Gardens is a stylish, upscale garden center operated by landscape
designer Cynthia Rice in northern Litchfield County. Known for its
imaginative selection of 1,500 ornamental plants, Beardsley Gardens is adept
at assisting both novice and expert gardeners in selecting plants for special
sites. A fraction of Beardsley Gardens' container-grown plants are propagated
here, and the rest raised locally. Attractive display gardens, worth seeing in
their own right, include a cottage garden, rockery, water garden, grass border,
evergreen screen, and woodland garden.

The emphasis at Beardsley Gardens is on ornamental plants of the kind
valued by landscape architects. Its diverse selection includes a bit of
everything, but is geared toward good looks, low maintenance, and wildlife
interest. For container gardeners, a range of colorful annuals and tender
perennials is stocked in spring. Gardeners spicing up a perennial border can
find superior varieties of delphinium, phlox, aster, bellflower, bee balm,
coralbells, lilies, and hostas. We noticed a number of uncommon foxgloves,
including a rare yellow Russian foxglove with woolly foliage, as well as
gentians, hellebores, and ornamental rhubarb. Cottage gardeners will like
garden pinks, bleeding hearts, and peonies. Ornate grasses and ferns round out
the designer perennials available at this attractive garden center. The shrub and
tree yard contains reliable roses and woody ornamentals of architectural
interest, though the shrub stock can get a bit dog-eared by summer's end.

With a designer's eye, Beardsley Gardens offers plants adapted to specific
sites. These include poppy, sea holly, and globe thistle for seaside and drought;
mayapple, dog-tooth violet, and variegated Solomon's seal for woodland
shade; cardinal flower, unusual iris, and montbretia for wet sites; native partridgeberry, crysogonum (green-gold), and pink and variegated lily of the
valley for ground cover; and a good smattering of sedums and alpines for the
rock garden. Aquatic plants include hardy water lilies, lotus, marginals for the
pond's edge, and tender aquatics that need to be indoors for the winter.

Beardsley Gardens' informative catalog publishes plant lists for deer
resistance, containers, water gardens, and hardy bulb displays. The nursery's

knowledgeable staff will help with selections. A charming shop offers such upscale items as border spades, alpine troughs, crevice trowels, daffodil augers, and flower presses. Hundreds of garden books are also in stock. For a small fee, regular customers can join the Beardsley "Gardener's Club" for discounts and seasonal specials.

Directions: Sharon is in northwestern Connecticut, near the New York border. From Danbury, take Route 202/7 north and stay on Route 7 when the roads diverge. In Cornwall Bridge, turn left onto Route 4 west. In Sharon, take Route 41 north; Beardsley Gardens is on your right.

BLOOMINGFIELDS FARM

P.O. Box 5, Route 55 (Sherman), Gaylordsville, CT 06755-0055
(860) 354-6951
Lee and Diana Bristol

Organically grown daylilies. *Small specialty nursery. Open June through August, Friday to Sunday noon–5, and by appointment. Catalog $1. Mail order. Display gardens. Volume discounts. E-mail: daylily@snet.net. Web site: www.bloomingfieldsfarm.com.*

Bloomingfields is a picturesque farm growing daylilies on 25 acres of bottomland in northwestern Connecticut. The nursery is a NOFA-certified organic farm founded on the kind of rich, living soil that lies deep in the longings of most gardeners. Bloomingfields Farm offers 125 kinds of daylilies, with many more occupying the growing beds. Owners Lee and Diana Bristol live in the farmhouse and hand-tend the daylily beds and trial gardens, in addition to working their sheep meadow, hayfields, vegetable garden, orchard, and woodlot. She is a weaver and artist whose paintings of prize farm animals adorn the potting shed. He is a biologist, organic nurseryman, market gardener, and former plant hunter and landscape designer. As they describe it, "our patch of earth is productive and beautiful. ... Foods grow to sustain us, flowers to cheer our spirits." To call upon Bloomingfields Farm is to visit the utopian microcosm that comprises the Bristols' daily life and work.

Bloomingfields Farm is uninvolved in any commercial hustle involving flamboyant daylily hybrids. The Bristols focus their efforts on durable classics of chaste appearance that can be combined to produce extended bloom in cold-climate gardens. According to Bloomingfields Farm, "We grow all we sell and are positive of the variety we ship." This nursery is a source for delicious pink, mulberry, and pure yellow daylilies; heirlooms such as the time-honored lemon lily; and a number of long-blooming Richards hybrids, all perfect for low-maintenance gardens. The nursery's airy yellow 'Autumn Daffodil' daylily and the apricot 'August Pioneer' each yield eight weeks of bloom in August and September. We admired lemon 'Wee Willie Winkie', white-faced 'Sweet Harmony' with its rose eyezone, and a gorgeous red-and-lime spider called 'Stoplight'.

Bloomingfields Farm offers several unique introductions bred by design or chance in its own garden. These include ever-blooming apricot 'Clementella', long-blooming 'Stella Bella', and ethereal 'Lavandelle' (which can be interplanted with its parent, 'Catherine Woodbury', to produce eight weeks of bloom). Some enduring standbys such as 'Stella de Oro' are modestly priced; others, such as 'Europa' (the common roadside daylily, escaped from pioneer homesteads and still used for erosion control), are outright bargains. A monthly special offers thrifty gardeners a collection of eight named daylily hybrids for $30. (Diana Bristol calls this aspect of organic daylily production "philanthropy, not farming.")

At dawn each day, the Bristols wade through the ground mist hovering over their fields in order to record the bloom habit of each daylily in their organic growing beds. The resulting bloom logs, of great precision and value to daylily gardeners, are printed in their catalog. Flowers are listed by color group and bloom season. All daylilies are hand-dug to order and reportedly come "blooming size" in large three-fan divisions with substantial roots. For visitors to the farm, a daylily list orients guests to each plant's location in the growing beds, well labeled for selection and display. Orders from farm visitors are added to the digging list for the following week and delivered free of charge.

Bloomingfields claims to be the "only full-livelihood farm in town," and its magnificent heirloom vegetable garden (adjacent to the daylily beds) is a perfect jubilation of organic farming methods. (Barbara Damrosch, author of *The Garden Primer,* had her first job here, and dug the well.) Depending on availability, fresh lettuces, squash, garlic, and potatoes grown for the local farmer's market may be purchased straight from the garden. At dusk, if you are lucky, Lee Bristol may lean on his hoe and discourse on diverse philosophical subjects. Diana Bristol may offer a stroll through her beautiful kitchen garden, overseen by moorhens roosting on the roof. On departure, visitors should be careful not to flatten Chanticleer, an endearing widower Guinea fowl who sometimes falls in love with people's car tires.

Directions: Sherman is in west-central Connecticut near the New York border. The Farm's driveway is in Sherman on Route 55, 1.25 miles west of Route 7 and 4.5 miles east of NY Route 22.

Nearby attractions: Elephant Trunk Flea Market, Route 7, New Milford (860-355-1448), is New England's largest trash-and-treasure flea market—haggling expected, no pets; open Sunday 6–3, late March to Christmas.

BRISTOL MUMS, INC.

50 Pinehurst Road, Bristol, CT 06010
(800) 58B-MUMS (582-6867); fax (860) 582-2434
Jerry Heresko

Potted chrysanthemums. *Specialty grower. Open April through December, daily 9–5. Free catalog. Mail order.*

Bristol Mums is a specialty hybridizer, propagator, and grower of low-growing chrysanthemums, popularly known as cushion mums. The business was founded in 1920, and still grows one of its original Korean mums, a hardy pink daisy called 'Venus' (which is making a comeback in perennial circles). Owner Jerry Heresko had a summer job here in high school, then trained and worked as a mechanical engineer before returning to the nursery.

Bristol Mums produces 45,000 container-grown cushion mums per year and sells out briskly. It offers these in a wide variety of colors and shapes, far outdistancing those normally seen at farm stands in the fall. The colors range from warm (red, bronze, gold, and yellow) to cool (purple, lavender, pink, and white). Shapes include buttons, pompons, cushions, daisies, and quills. Bristol Mums produces original hybrids in new colors such as 'Peach Parfait', 'Raspberry Parfait', and 'Rose Debutante'. The most innovative colors—ginger, terra-cotta, scarlet, and fuchsia—are on patented plants that carry small royalties. Bristol Mums also offers tall, decorative chrysanthemums suitable for cut flowers, sold as cuttings in spring; the list includes spider spoon quills in purple and red and a silky white spider, 'Shaman's Vision'.

Although the catalog is set up for wholesalers, retail customers can buy small potted plants by mail at wholesale prices; the minimum order is 10 plants. Many gardeners prefer to stop by at the nursery in the fall, when mature cushion mums sell out at the rate of 1,500 per day. Though famed for its mums, Bristol Mums grows other seasonal plants as well: poinsettias in December and geraniums and New Guinea impatiens in April.

Directions: Bristol is west of Hartford. From I-84, take exit 38/Farmington onto Route 6 west. In Bristol, turn right onto Hill Street (George's Terryville Market is on your left). Take the third right onto Pinehurst Road; the nursery is on your left.

BROKEN ARROW NURSERY

13 Broken Arrow Road, Hamden, CT 06518-1001
(203) 288-1026; fax (203) 287-1035
Dick Jaynes

Kalmia (mountain laurel). Rare woody plants. Unusual conifers. Native shrubs and trees. Small specialty nursery. Open April through October. Call for open hours. Catalog $2. Send SASE for price list and directions. Limited shipping. Display garden. Lectures. Landscape design. Christmas tree farm. Peak kalmia bloom bracketing Memorial Day. Web site: www.brokenarrownursery.com.

Richard Jaynes is the world's foremost hybridizer of kalmia, or mountain laurel, which is the Connecticut state flower. Author of the authoritative *Kalmia: The Laurel Book,* Jaynes is a botany Ph.D. who spent 25 years breeding plants at the Connecticut Agricultural Experiment Station before retiring, as he says, to "rest on his laurels." Jaynes has produced many original mountain laurel cultivars of surpassing beauty. His specialty nursery, established in 1984 on land adjacent to his home, carries 25 original mountain laurel hybrids and 50 kinds of rhododendron (some his own hybrids). Broken Arrow also grows unusual and exotic conifers and woody ornamentals, including rare Oriental and native plants. The nursery propagates and sells small, healthy shrubs, hardy to the area, offering excellent value in the garden.

Indigenous to the eastern United States, mountain laurel has been described as our most beautiful native shrub. Jaynes's work with mountain laurel transformed it from a native woodland shrub to a distinguished ornamental plant, virtually guaranteeing its future in gardens and landscapes. His hybridizing efforts favor dense, compact, and miniature varieties suited to small modern gardens. 'Elf', for example, is about one-third normal size, with full-size blooms. The first time we saw 'Raspberry Glow' we could hardly believe the richness of its bloom color, stunning against the laurel's glossy green foliage. Jaynes's breeding efforts have also produced beautiful flower innovations, such as red buds and dramatically spotted and banded flower cups. His award-winning 'Peppermint' has a candy-cane pattern; 'Olympic Wedding' has an inner band of maroon; and 'Kaleidoscope' has raspberry buds that open to cinnamon with a white edge. Jaynes's favorite pink kalmia, 'Sarah', is named for his wife. These are all neat, handsome, slow-growing shrubs that keep their foliage in winter and thrive in Zones 5 and 6 (and parts of Zone 4), making them ideal choices for many New England gardens.

Students of prestigious plant awards, and of the Garden Club of America's book *Plants That Merit Attention,* may recognize the unusual woody

ornamental plants grown at Broken Arrow. The nursery distinguished itself
with "a wide variety of lesser known and attractive trees and shrubs." Fine
ornamental shrubs include winter hazel; witch hazel; bottlebrush buckeye;
silver-bell (*Halesia* spp.), including a colleague's hybrid called 'Wedding Bells';
and drooping leucothoe, a native shrub steadily gaining in reputation. Rare
Oriental shrubs include Chinese niellia, yellowhorn, fringe tree, and seven
sons flower *(Heptacodium miconoides)*. An award-winning sweetspire, *Clethra
alnifolia* 'Ruby Spice', is an original Jaynes hybrid. Hydrangeas, andromedas,
and viburnums are well represented. Our parents bought excellent native
winterberry here; the selection of native and Asian hollies is especially good.
The nursery's box sand myrtle would make a good substitute for boxwood in
cold-threatened gardens.

Connoisseurs have long looked to Broken Arrow Nursery as a clandestine
source of the prestigious yellow magnolia, of which it grows eight varieties.
The Jaynes rhododendron and azalea collection is extraordinary for its depth
and originality. The nursery also offers stewartia and exciting cultivars of
anthracnose-resistant Chinese dogwood *(Cornus kousa)*. Broken Arrow's tree
yard contains the fragrant epaulette tree; unique dove tree; variegated giant
dogwood; hardy mimosa; golden-chain tree; Chinese tree lilac; and many
exotic maples, such as striped maple, three-flower maple, and a Balkan maple
introduced by the Arnold Arboretum. Interesting native trees include
American bladdernut, sassafras, black tupelo, and yellowwood. Conifer
fanatics will relish the exceptional Japanese, native, and dwarf forms of
conifer, including unusual Eastern larch hybrids developed by plant pioneer
Sid Waxman at the University of Connecticut. (A very dwarf Eastern larch
called 'Stubby' originated with a witches'-broom found along the
Massachusetts Turnpike.)

Visitors are welcome to the nursery, but should call ahead to make sure
that Jaynes or his staff will be present. Excellent horticultural and landscaping
advice is shared liberally with customers. Jaynes has good contacts with
breeders and academics, and grows some fascinating and unique plants in his
shrubbery. Allow time to stroll the small, naturalistic arboretum surrounding
the nursery, where many rare shrubs and trees grow in a mature state. Peak
bloom for mountain laurel takes place around Memorial Day. Visitors can
take a refreshing walk past a small pond to a plantation of Christmas trees
(sold fresh at the holidays), exposing a view east to Sleeping Giant Mountain.

*Directions: Hamden is north of New Haven. From I-91, take exit 10 onto Route 40
north. Turn right to Route 22/Ives Street (it becomes Route 10/Whitney Avenue).
Turn left onto Todd Street. Past Shepherd Avenue, turn right at the T-junction onto
Gaylord Mountain Road, then right again onto Broken Arrow Road; the nursery is on
your right.*

From Route 15/Wilbur Cross Parkway, take exit 59 to Route 63 north. Exit immediately onto Route 69 north. In 7 miles, turn right onto Gaylord Mountain Road, then left onto Broken Arrow Road; the nursery is on your right.

Nearby attractions: Sunflower Farms (203-795-6829), off Route 34 in Orange (Merritt Parkway exit 56), is the largest grower of ornamental sunflowers in Connecticut, offering spring seedlings, potted plants, and cut sunflowers (open in-season, Monday to Friday 1–6, weekends 10–6). Painters, photographers, and gardeners come to admire its 2-acre field ablaze with bronze, cream, and yellow sunflowers in summer and fall.

BUTTERBROOKE FARM SEEDS

78 Barry Road, Oxford, CT 06478-1529
(860) 888-2000
Tom Butterworth

Organic vegetable seed. *Small organic seed farm. Seed list 50 cents. Mail order only. Open by chance or appointment; call for directions. Newsletter and organic gardening video.*

Founded in 1979, Butterbrooke Farm is a small cooperative in northeastern Connecticut whose motto is SEEDS FOR PEOPLE, NOT PROFIT. Tom Butterworth, biologist, farmer, and educator, is committed to growing pure, untreated, open-pollinated vegetable seed using self-reliant biodynamic farming methods. The farm is certified organic, and every operation is said to be "performed as a craft"; seed harvesting, drying, and packaging is done by hand, without machines or chemicals, using natural methods.

Butterbrooke Farm seeds are short-season vegetable varieties that do well in New England. Its mail-order seed list includes rapidly maturing bush beans, beets, cantaloupe, lettuce, okra, popcorn, tomato, squash, watermelon, herbs, and sunflowers. The list provides only common names, presuming familiarity with the vegetable or a willingness to trust tradition. Gardeners can order seed packets from the regular list, or join the farm's Seed Co-op ($15) and receive a supplemental list of heirloom seeds grown by co-op members and seed savers. The heirloom list is brief but intriguing, with entries for rocambole garlic, a tart yellow-striped tomato from Czechoslovakia, and a rare Chinese leek. For the millennium, Butterbrooke Farm offers "Survive on Seeds," an SOS collection of some 100,000 non-hybrid seeds that are judged "sufficient to grow a year's supply of food for a family of four."

Harkening back to earlier times, Butterbrooke Farm's homemade seed lists are the product of a vintage typewriter with uneven type and no erase key. There is no Web site. Customers are expected to use and conserve seed lists for two years. According to the farmer, "You will not find Butterbrooke

Farm spending a penny on frills or wasteful practices such as advertising."
(Curiously, the farm has the ideal year-2000 telephone number.) Seed
prices are very modest. Customers can also order inexpensive organic *Garden
Guides* and a video called *How to Grow Healthy Veggies* ($19.75). Co-op
members get a subscription to *Germinations*, a newsletter setting forth the
philosophical ruminations of Tom Butterworth on gardening, homesteading,
and healthful living.

The co-op believes that its seed list can be "the key to unlocking a
beautiful relationship with the natural world which supports and nourishes
you." We plan to attend Open Farm Day, held once each summer, to see if
the farm's root cellar is all we imagine.

*Directions: Oxford is southwest of Waterbury. From Route 84, take Route 8 south to
exit 22, then Route 42 west into Oxford; call for local directions.*

COMSTOCK, FERRE & CO.

263 Main Street, Old Wethersfield, CT 06109
(800)733-3773 and (860) 571-6590; fax (860) 571-6595
Pierre Bennerup

Garden seeds. Perennials and alpine plants. *Retail seed store and perennial
plant nursery. Seed store open daily, Monday to Wednesday and Saturday
9–6, Sunday 10–5. Shorter hours in winter. Outside sales April through November.
Free seed catalog. Perennial plant list $3. Mail order for seed only.
Web site: www.comstockferre.com.*

Founded in 1820, Comstock, Ferre & Co. is the oldest seed house in New
England, still housed in 19th-century seed barns in historic Old Wethersfield.
These creaking wooden barns still display weathered ads for "Garden Seeds"
in faded red paint. Inside, visitors encounter the old-fashioned clutter of a
dry goods store (note the antique seed bins). A series of interconnected shops
purvey seeds, dried herbs, watering cans, terra-cotta pots, and garden gifts.
The seed store sells Comstock, Ferre seed in packets and bulk (also available
through the company's mail-order catalog and Web site). Original ornamental
borders printed on the seed packets, the innovation of an early owner, are in
use to this day.

Although Comstock, Ferre seed is no longer grown on Connecticut
farmland, reliable standards are maintained. All seed is tested to meet or
exceed USDA germination requirements, and almost all is untreated by
fungicides or chemicals. The seed list is extensive, and includes old and new
varieties of garden vegetables, salad greens, herbs, vines, and annual and
perennial flowers. The vegetables include open-pollinated yellow corn and an

antique German vegetable called Hamburg parsley, grown for its edible root. We counted 50 kinds of herb seed, including assorted lavenders, basils, thymes, and hard-to-find cardoon, horehound, sweet woodruff, and watercress. Flower seeds emphasize old cottage-garden varieties such as corn cockle, wallflower, and forget-me-not, and new varieties such as vanilla marigold and columnar mallow. Grass seed, wildflower mixes, garlic and onion sets, and a rich odorless fertilizer made of worm castings are also available.

By a stroke of good fortune, Comstock, Ferre was purchased in 1991 by master plantsman Pierre Bennerup, a well-known bon vivant who is one of the region's foremost nurserymen. Bennerup owns Sunny Border Nursery, a noted wholesale grower in Kensington, Connecticut, and travels internationally collecting new and unusual garden perennials. Some are sold under the Sunny Border Gold label at discriminating nurseries, but a larger number are now being retailed through Comstock, Ferre in Old Wethersfield.

Some 40 plant display tables are located outside the seed barns; open seasonally, they display a diverse selection of garden perennials and a strong collection of unusual alpine plants. On our visit we saw rare primroses, distinctive violets, enchanting saxifrages and pearlworts, and several Rocky Mountain natives. Each year, new Sunny Border introductions—its dwarf purple coneflower (*Echinacea purpurea* 'Kim's Knee High'), for example—add pizzazz to the collection. All plants are well labeled and healthy. Unlike the seeds, potted perennials are not available by mail order.

The surrounding town of Old Wethersfield, Connecticut's "most ancient town" (founded in 1634), has a remarkable legacy of 17th- and 18th-century houses flanking its broad, tree-lined streets. These and the creaky seed barns give a trip to Comstock, Ferre the delightfully spooky quality of a visit to a vanished township, a Connecticut version of Brigadoon.

Directions: Old Wethersfield is south of Hartford. From I-91, take exit 26 and follow signs into Old Wethersfield. Comstock, Ferre is on Main Street, across from the brick church with the white steeple.

Nearby attractions: Old Wethersfield retains a picturesque collection of historic houses, some operating as museums. Avoid Wethersfield Weekend in mid-May if you do not wish to be caught in a historic battle reenactment. Since 1892, the Chas. C. Hart Seed Co., 304 Main Street, Old Wethersfield (800-326-HART), has been a dependable source of short-season flower and vegetable seeds, sold by mail order in distinctive packets using the original red-heart logo (Plant HART's Seeds); a small store is sited in the Wethersfield headquarters. Gledhill Nursery, 660 Mountain Road, West Hartford, CT 06117 (860-233-5692), founded in 1922, is a fantasy garden center set on a small private estate traversed by a kid-size garden railway and diminutive millrace, complete with bridge and small functional windmill. Elizabeth Park, Prospect and Asylum Avenues, Hartford (860-242-0017), is the country's oldest municipal rose garden, growing 15,000 rosebushes, some nearly a century old; open daily from dawn to dusk.

CRICKET HILL GARDEN

670 Walnut Hill Road, Thomaston, CT 06787
(860) 283-1042; (877) PAEONIA (723-6642); fax (860) 283-5508
Kasha and David Furman

Chinese tree peonies. *Small specialty nursery. Open Thurssday to Sunday, 10–4. Catalog $3. Mail order. Display beds. Lectures. Peak bloom May 15 to early June. E-mail: kasha@treepeony.com. Web site: www.treepeony.com.*

Cricket Hill Garden, which calls itself Peony Heaven, is a small nursery specializing in imported Chinese tree peonies. Owners David and Kasha Furman founded Cricket Hill Garden on a hillside in Thomaston in 1988, after retiring from careers in advertising and graphic design. David Furman holds a degree in Chinese history and has been fascinated since childhood with Chinese culture, in which the "thousand-petal flower" peony (China's national flower) has been an important motif for more than a millennium.

Cricket Hill's gorgeous color catalog offers 55 of the 1,000 tree peony cultivars grown in China today, supplemented with a few herbaceous peonies. Plant stock is imported directly from growers in Luoyang in northern China, the same Tang Dynasty city where tree peonies were grown for Mandarin gardens in the 8th century. (The summer palace of Emperor Ming Huang was planted with 10,000 tree peonies.) Properly planted and tended, a Chinese tree peony (*mudan hua* in Chinese) can live for 400 years. All Cricket Hill stock is field-tested and sold as mature four-year plants with substantial roots, guaranteed for the next season and shipped bare-root in autumn. Because of the intricacies of importation and propagation, mature tree peonies are expensive, but not as costly as they were in the 8th century, when the Chinese poet Po Chu-i wrote, "a cluster of deep red flowers would pay the taxes on ten poor farms."

In Chinese culture, tree peonies symbolize wealth and prosperity and are popular as New Years gifts. Their covert meaning, however, is a sexual one: According to the Chinese, the stems, roots and leaves represent "the male vermillion stalk" and the flower represents the female element, "wet with dew like pearls." Such covert meanings illuminate the charm and humor of tree peony titles such as 'Tipsy Imperial Concubine' (named for a famous courtesan), and 'Princess Zhao Marries Beyond the Great Wall' (named for a Chinese princess seized in marriage by a barbarian). One needs little imagination to decipher such coy names as 'Smiling in the Thicket', 'Intoxicated Celestial Peach', 'Powdered Lotus', and 'Heaven Scented Wet with Dew'. Male pride seems reflected in 'Wei's Purple', 'Zhao's Pink', 'Number One Scholar Red', and 'Jade Seal of State'. An alchemical meaning may attach to 'Fire that Makes the Pills of Immortality' and 'Taoist Stove Filled With Pills of Immortality'. Perhaps the meanings are unknowable. As the Emperor Yang of Sui wrote in the 7th century, "All day long we have questioned the flowers, / but the flowers do not speak. / For whom will they shed their petals and leaves, / for whom do they bloom?"

Cricket Hill's tree peony selections admirably reflect the unique aesthetic of ancient Chinese horticultural tastes, known to Western gardeners as much through art as garden plants. The Chinese prize tree peonies of the opulent thousand-petal variety, but some singles do exist, such as 'Phoenix White' and 'White Screen Reflects a Blue Jewel'. Unlike Japanese varieties, Chinese tree peonies were bred for fragrance as well as looks. Rare oddities—'Pea Green' (pale green flowers), 'Twin Beauty' (red and pink blooms on the same plant), and 'Better Than Jade with Triple Magic' (a green-pink-white novelty)—suggest strong parallels between ancient Chinese tastes and those of modern gardeners. The maroon-black flowers of 'Champion Black Jade' and 'Grand Black Flower', for example, seem just as stylish now as they were 10 centuries ago.

For all the connections, Chinese tree peonies still pose some surprises. We gave 'Yellow Crane Plume' as a gift to a peony-loving friend and found that, despite modern China's political claims to Tibet, Chinese plantsmen never discovered the yellow peony of Tibet. They developed instead a pale, ethereal yellow peony, almost silvery in tone, subtle as a winter sun.

Like their Chinese counterparts, the Furmans hold a peony-viewing festival at Cricket Hill Garden during peak bloom, from mid-May to early June. Although centuries-old peony festivals continue to draw tourists to China today, gardeners who cannot travel to the East should put Cricket Hill on the calendar, for its floral display is glorious. Visitors may notice amusing touches such as the painted parasol posed at an angle near the pond, in imitation of a Chinese painting. Be sure to ask the Furmans for a Cricket Hill Garden catalog, sumptuously illustrated with flower photographs, and for their collection of Chinese peony poems. Our favorite is a verse by Ling-hu

Ch'u: "We had a drinking party to admire the peonies. / I drank cup after cup until I was drunk. / Then to my shame I heard the flowers whisper, / 'What are we doing, blooming for these old alcoholics?'"

Directions: Thomaston is 20 miles west of Hartford. From I-95 and I-84, exit onto Route 8 north. Take exit 38/Thomaston and turn left off the ramp onto Main Street. Turn left at the third light onto Route 254 north. In 0.5 mile, at a flashing yellow light, turn left onto Walnut Hill Road. The nursery is up the hill 1 mile on your right. Coming from the north on Route 8, take exit 40 and turn right off the ramp. Turn right at the third light onto Route 254 north; follow the directions above.

Nearby attractions: The birthplace of the American Episcopal Church, Glebe House and Garden, Hollow Road, Woodbury, CT 06798 (203-263-2855), is an antique rectory with the only garden in America designed by Britain's Gertrude Jekyll. Jekyll's original garden plans were shelved, and only installed after their discovery in Beatrix Ferrand's archives 60 years later. Designed in Jekyll's heyday, this small garden has a disarming simplicity: A perennial border runs along a yew hedge, connected to a cottage garden; a simple rose arbor leads to kitchen herb gardens.

THE DAFFODIL MART

30 Irene Street, Torrington, CT 06790-6668
(800) ALL-BULB (255-2852); fax (800) 420-2852
Eliot Wadsworth II

Specialty bulbs. *Bulb importer. Open weekdays 9–9, Saturday and Sunday 9–6. Fax open 24 hours. Free catalog. Mail and phone order. No display gardens. Minimum order $50. Quantity discounts. Web site: www.whiteflowerfarm.com; www.800oldbulbs.com.*

The Daffodil Mart is a large, Connecticut-based mail-order company with a national reputation for selling premium-quality flower bulbs. Previous owners Brent and Becky Heath grew the business from a small family operation into a large company, then sold the business in 1997. The Daffodil Mart is now part of a horticultural conglomerate that includes White Flower Farm (CT) and Shepherd's Garden Seeds (CT). It claims to carry "the largest selection in America" of flower bulbs for spring, summer, and fall gardens.

We would expect a company called the Daffodil Mart to offer a wide choice of daffodils, but for once, reality exceeds expectations. Touted as "the perfect perennial," daffodils are adaptable, pest-resistant, and virtually indestructible flowering bulbs, justly famous for their spring brilliance. The Daffodil Mart carries every imaginable kind and color of daffodil: trumpets, doubles, jonquils, large-cupped and small-cupped daffodils, miniatures, cyclamens (with flared-back petals), papillons (butterfly daffodils), poeticus (old-fashioned pheasant-eyes), split-coronas (with unusual divided trumpets), tazettas (with multiple blooms per stem), and triandrus (with fuchsialike flowers). Some daffodils are heirloom varieties, others are cherished for fragrance. The Daffodil Mart carries so-called "wild" or species daffodils, which are good for naturalizing. (Curiously missing from this list is the wild Lent lily, *Narcissus pseudonarcissus,* about which the English poet William Wadsworth rhapsodized in praising a "host of golden daffodils.") Daffodil mixes, including white and pink collections, are available for those paralyzed by too many choices.

As might be expected from a premium bulb specialist, the tulip collection is nearly as comprehensive as the daffodils'. Today's hybrid tulips are an affordable luxury; anyone questioning the cost should consult a history book, for tulips commanded extravagant prices during the 17th-century Dutch "tulipomania," and were equally prized by the Ottoman emperors. (In 1574, Selim II ordered "50,000 bulbs for my royal gardens from the Sherif of Aziz.") The Daffodil Mart offers a king's ransom in tulips, tested for performance in its trial gardens: Darwin hybrids; double and single tulips; early and late tulips; fringed and lily-flowered tulips; multi-flowering tulips; triumph tulips; green tulips; richly colored parrot tulips, and Rembrandt tulips. Perennial tulips include species tulips and the greigii, Kaufmanniana, and Fosteriana hybrids, all good for naturalizing. For overwhelmed customers, a useful chart depicts the color and bloom time of all tulips offered.

Besides tulips and daffodils, the Daffodil Mart sells a multitude of specialty bulbs, with an emphasis on hardy spring bulbs. Hyacinths, bluebells, anemones, and crocus (including snow crocus) are joined by grape hyacinth, winter aconite, chionodoxa, fritillaria, and dog-tooth violet. For summer and fall, the Daffodil Mart has bulbs for camassia, corydalis, oxalis, autumn crocus, lilies, and some foliage plants in the Arum family that are getting a lot of attention from landscapers. We had never even heard of native American bulb species such as *Triteleia, Dichelostemma,* and *Chalochorthus* 'Golden Orb'. Another unknown, *Bellevalia pycnantha,* sounds tempting for the rock garden, with its muscari-like flowers that "look a bit like little blue Christmas trees."

Indoor bulbs consist of popular paperwhite narcissus, fine amaryllis (including a rare yellow), and amarcrinum, the dazzling amaryllis–crinum lily hybrid. We were a bit disappointed to see only 5 demure little snowdrops, when we know of an Irish lady who grows 54 kinds in her garden. But we are quibbling. A helpful list of the catalog's heirloom bulbs will give heart to preservationists. Bargain hunters should be aware that the Daffodil Mart's less expensive bulbs are not inferior but simply bred in huge quantities in Holland.

Although mainly serving landscape designers and public gardens, the Daffodil Mart will sell to retail customers in minimum orders of $50.

Growing instructions accompany each order. All bulbs are field-propagated; wild-collected bulbs are excluded for ethical reasons. Although the Daffodil Mart conducts bulb trials to ensure superior home garden performance, it has no display garden or other facility for visitors.

GILBERTIE'S HERB GARDENS, INC.

7 Sylvan Lane, Westport, CT 06880
(203) 227-4175
Sal Gilbertie

Culinary herbs. *Specialty nursery. Open year-round, Monday to Saturday 8:30–5:30; Sunday, April to June 10–3 and December noon–5. Call ahead on Mondays. No catalog or mail order. Newsletter, lectures, and demonstrations. Display garden. Herb products. Books. Web site: www.gilbertiesherbgardens.com.*

Sal Gilbertie is an author, lecturer, and nurseryman who grew up in the family's wholesale cut-flower business, founded in the 1920s. Many years ago, his grandfather diversified into herbs at the behest of an eccentric grand dame dubbed The Countess, a perfume manufacturer who once fired a gardener on her estate for speaking the word manure to her on the telephone. Since 1973, organically raised herbs and herb products have been Gilbertie's exclusive business. More than 400 varieties of herbs are grown at the wholesale farm in Easton, the largest volume grower of potted herbs in New England. The retail greenhouses are located in Westport, right behind the senior Mrs. Gilbertie's white clapboard house, with its long pleasant lawn sloping down to Sylvan Avenue.

Some 80 percent of Gilbertie's herbs are culinary, with a growing selection of medicinal herbs. Common culinary herbs, popular since medieval times, include many varieties of basil (15 kinds), sage (18 kinds) and thyme (19 kinds). Sophisticated ornamental herbs, labeled ROYAL HERBS, include fruit-scented geranium, angelica, African blue basil, indigo, Japanese catnip, creeping rue, balm of Gilead, and a sweet herb called Aztec, useful as a sugar substitute. Gilbertie's carried 17 varieties of lavender (visible in its display borders) long before lavender was voted Herb of the Year for 1999.

Gilbertie's best-selling medicinal herbs, St.-John's-wort and echinacea, are special cultivars biologically tested for pharmaceutical value by Conrad Richter, the Ontario seedman who supplies the seed. Other medicinals include ginkgo biloba, ginseng, goldenseal, gotu kola, and throatwort. Insect-repellent herbs, which release their fragrance when bruised, include a pungent lemon thyme that tested twice as effective as Deep Woods OFF, and santolina, said to be the most effective insect repellent in horticulture.

In the greenhouse, potted herbs are arranged alphabetically on tables, in the company of descriptive placards. Large mature plants, decorative herb topiaries, and shoulder-high laurel trees (all for sale) are artfully distributed throughout the greenhouse. Flats of vegetables and flowering plants are sold each spring from an adjacent greenhouse. Organic soil laced with natural fungicide and fertilizer is used on all plants.

Gilbertie's garden shop carries herbal extracts, fragrances, dried herbs, seeds, spring bulbs, tools, trellises, and Mexican pottery. Visitors can purchase Sal Gilbertie's popular books, *Kitchen Herbs* and *Gilbertie's Herb Guide*, or sign up for the newsletter listing lectures and workshops. The staff is helpful and unusually wholesome-looking.

Outside, in back of the farmhouse, a small, slightly rumpled display garden employs culinary herbs in ornamental uses, and offers a refreshing spot to take the air.

Directions: From I-95, take exit 17/Westport and turn left onto the Post Road. In 1 mile, turn left onto Riverside Avenue, then left again at the Sunoco Station onto Sylvan Avenue; the nursery is straight ahead.

THE GREAT PLANT COMPANY

P.O. Box 1041, 208 Bruning Road, New Hartford, CT 06057
(800) 441-9788; fax (860) 379-8488
Steve Frowine and Peter Overing

Limited-edition plants. *Specialty plant merchandiser. Mail order catalog on web site only. Web site: www.greatplants.com.* [Connecticut operations discontinued in 2001.]

The Great Plant Company is a specialty merchandiser of limited-edition plants for the collector; we think of it as a virtual nursery, nominally based in Connecticut (though it could be anywhere). Co-owner Steve Frowine is an accomplished horticulturist, merchandiser, and self-confessed "plant nerd" who has been obsessed with flowering plants since childhood. Over a 30-year period, Frowine worked at various public gardens and managed public relations and merchandising for W. Atlee Burpee & Company. Most recently, as vice president of White Flower Farm (CT), he traveled extensively to locate new plants for its catalog. Frowine continues to track down specialty plants for the Great Plant Company, a business he founded in 1999 in partnership with Troppus Inc., a Canadian holding company owned by Peter Overing, described as its "very entrepreneurial CEO." (Frowine is also chairman of the National Gardening Association and an active garden writer and speaker.)

The Great Plant Company's stated goal is to be "the first on the market with the newest and the best" garden plants. In addition to glossy spring and fall catalogs, each listing more than 80 plants, the company frequently updates its Web site with Collector's Choice discoveries for discriminating gardeners. The company emphasizes what it calls "rare and very limited offerings available nowhere else." The Great Plant Company serves the important function, possible only in the computer age, of selling new and unusual plants long before they are available through ordinary commercial channels. This is accomplished by forceful marketing, which zeroes in on a select clientele, and direct fulfillment by specialty growers, which eliminates the cumbersome middlemen and long lead times of mass-market horticulture.

The Great Plant Company merchandises plants directly from individual hybridizers and small wholesale growers who lack the means or the inclination to mount a national marketing campaign for their wares. A few of these sources are listed elsewhere in this book: Siberian iris from Tranquil Lake Nursery (MA); seeds from Renee Shepherd, founder of Shepherd's Seeds (CT); and a Chinese tree peony from Cricket Hill Garden (CT).

ORINOCO BANANA.

The range of Great Plant Company stock is wide and various: It includes Asian "windowsill" orchids; Siamese lucky plants; hardy lady's slippers; rare daffodils from Oregon; lilacs from a Canadian grower; Asian wildflowers from a nursery in Appalachia; unusual woodland perennials, such as cyclamen and ginger; "elite daylilies" from hybridizer Patrick Stamile; and brilliant tropicals such as bougainvillea and hibiscus, bred in South Florida by American Hibiscus Society members.

The Great Plant Company is the only source we can think of, other than Hillside Nursery (CT) and Avant Gardens (MA), of *Veronicastrum sibericum,* a terrific garden perennial that looks something like lavender gooseneck loosestrife. It is the only source we know for *Cardiocrinum giganteum,* the "world's largest lily" (6 to 9 feet). Many company plants (such as daffodils, daylilies, tree peonies, and Asian woodlanders) grow well in New England gardens, while others require a sunny windowsill, a hothouse, or a villa in Palm Beach.

Plants are sold in limited quantities, like ball gowns, thus ensuring their relative rarity and justifying enhanced price tags. Although Frowine and company phone lines are located in Connecticut, the Great Plant Company has no special relationship to New England horticulture—no growing fields, no display garden, no retail shop, no place to visit—no "there" there, just a mail-order catalog and a Web site. [As of 2001, "there" is in California.]

HILLSIDE GARDENS

P.O. Box 614, 515 Litchfield Road (Route 272), Norfolk, CT 06058-0614
(860) 542-5345
Frederick and Mary Ann McGourty

Uncommon perennials. *Specialty nursery. Display gardens open to visitors Friday only, May through September. Group tours by arrangement. Garden workshops. Design and consultation services. McGourty books. E-mail: hillsidegardens@yahoo.com.* [Retail nursery closed in 2001.]

Located in the scenic Litchfield Hills of northwestern Connecticut, Hillside Gardens is the perennial garden and nursery of Frederick and Mary Ann McGourty, esteemed authors, lecturers, garden designers, and professional horticulturists. Fred McGourty edited the Brooklyn Botanical Garden Handbook series; authored *The Perennial Gardener;* and coauthored *Perennials: How to Select, Grow and Enjoy Them.* (Both books are sold at the nursery and by mail order.) Mary Ann McGourty edited the *Taylor Guide to Ground Covers, Vines & Grasses;* has contributed articles to *American Horticulture* magazine; and has served as horticultural consultant to several book publishers, including New York's Metropolitan Museum of Art. Both have received important horticultural awards for their achievements. Gardeners who know them confirm our impression of the McGourtys as ideal parents in the region's horticultural family: expert, generous, and as nice as can be.

Needless to say, the McGourtys' perennial garden is considered one of the region's most distinguished plant collections. Hillside is a 5-acre private garden surrounding the McGourtys' vintage farmhouse; it contains some 2,000 varieties of perennials in naturalistic beds and borders laced with old stone walls. The retail nursery at Hillside Gardens, easily accessible at the entryway to the display gardens, specializes in perennial classics, both new and old, and a few roses and hydrangeas that interplant well with perennials.

Hillside Gardens' dense, informative plant list features perennials personally selected by the McGourtys after a trial period in their garden: delightful old-timers and what are called "cream-of-the-crop" and "limited-edition" plants, accompanied by invaluable suggestions for siting and companion planting. The nursery grows superior varieties of aster, astilbe, bee balm, phlox, sedum, and cranesbill geranium (especially 'Biokovo', described as "no fuss, no nonsense").

VERGE CUTTER.

The McGourtys collect underused allium (ornamental onion), their favorite being the fall-blooming, reddish purple *A. thunbergii* 'Ozawa', which can be seen in the garden dating a purple euphorbia.

The nursery houses a valuable collection of older, hardier autumn chrysanthemums assembled by the McGourtys over many years. Other favorites are Canadian burnet, blue Siberian catmint, and a number of worthwhile ground covers such as barren strawberry, *Vancouveria hexandra,* and blue-eyed Mary (recommended as "a skirt for gawky stems"). Hillside Gardens' most requested plant is a unique 6-foot snakeroot called 'Hillside Black Beauty', a nursery original bearing stately white candles and dark purple foliage. The nursery takes pains to indicate deer-resistant perennials, a special interest of Mary Ann McGourty, on which she gives a popular lecture.

Hillside Gardens' rare plant collection features exceptional perennials that are difficult to obtain from commercial sources. Of note are the dwarf lady's mantle, fall-blooming monkshood, pink Queen Anne's lace, double pink eupatorium, white foamflower with maroon-striped foliage, Japanese forest grass, and miniature Korean goatsbeard. Many plants are valued for uncommon foliage, such as purple Japanese cryptotaenia, chocolate eupatorium, variegated sedge, and variegated moor grass (recommended as "useful for toning down nearby orange or brassy yellow flowers"). Hillside Gardens also carries many fine hosta, of which the huge, celebrated 'Sum and Substance' is touted as "the only hosta that can be identified from a helicopter." Hosta plants are "priced, like lobster, according to size."

The perennials at Hillside Gardens are nursery-grown container plants that are at their best in spring but look good even at summer's end—the litmus test of a good nursery. Many old and new perennials not on the plant list are available on request; additions are constant, for plant selection changes 25 percent each year. All are incorporated in the garden's perennial beds, where they can seen in their proper location (sun, shade, dry, wet) in the company of thoughtfully considered companion plants.

Hillside Gardens comprises a memorable, instructional display garden providing flower and foliage interest from mid–June to mid–September, peaking in mid–July. Visitors are welcome to stroll through the garden (many come repeatedly) to observe its wall borders, perennial islands, specimen trees, dry stream, shady glades, and garden seats for dreamers. The McGourtys' garden has been showcased on television on PBS's *Victory Garden,* and has the enduring tranquillity of a great, established garden. We recommend it, appreciatively and warmly, as one of the few sophisticated private gardens that actually seem within the reach of the ordinary, dedicated home gardener. [Although their retail nursery closes in 2001, the McGourtys continue to offer design services and open their garden to visitors.]

Directions: Hillside Gardens is in northwest Connecticut, 11 miles north of Torrington. From Hartford, take I-91 to exit 40/Bradley Intl. Airport. Take Route 219 south and then Route 328 south. Turn right onto Route 44 west. At the Norfolk common, take Route 272 south; the nursery is 2.5 miles on your left.
From Route 84 in Danbury, take exit 8 onto Route 7 north. Turn left onto Route 44 east. At the Norfolk common, take Route 272 south; the nursery is 2.5 miles on your left.

Nearby attractions: Picnic lovers can use Dennis Hill State Park, next to the nursery, where a stone tower (1,627 feet in elevation) provides panoramic views of the Litchfield Hills. A small local herb farm, Nobody Eats the Parsley (860-542-5479), sells 175 kinds of herbs, herb jelly, and herbal products from a barn surrounded by herb gardens (0.3 mile south of the Norfolk common on Route 272; open Wednesday to Sunday 10–5). The Pub (860-542-5716), in the brownstone castle just off the Norfolk common, serves a nice lunch and 120 kinds of beer (notice the chair made of antlers).

J&L ORCHIDS

20 Sherwood Road, Easton, CT 06612
(203) 261-3772; fax (203) 261-8730
Cordelia Head, Marguerite Webb, and Lucinda Winn

Rare and unusual miniature orchids. *Specialty greenhouses. Open Monday to Saturday 9–4. Closed Sunday except sale days. Catalog $1. Mail order. Seasonal greenhouse sales. Visitors welcome. E-mail: jlorchid@snet.net. Web site: www.orchidmall.com/jlorchids.*

For more than two decades, J&L Orchids has offered fanatics a diverse selection of rare miniature orchids, many the result of J&L's own energetic collecting and breeding efforts. This greenhouse-nursery has been owned since 1979 by three orchid experts, who began as lab assistants ("the girls") to founders Janet and Lee Kuhn. The Kuhns were avid orchid collectors and growers who amassed the nursery's original stockpile through plant-hunting expeditions and an active hybridizing program.

After being sold to "the girls," the nursery became a leader in innovative efforts to propagate orchids artificially from seed—enabling the production and distribution of many plants that are now threatened in the wild. The owners have also been at the forefront of hybridizing Masdevallia orchids, creating such noted hybrids as 'Angel Frost' and 'Copper Angel' that are still widely used in breeding programs. Certain rare orchids grown by the nursery are almost impossible to find from other sources.

The nursery's miniature orchids are a diverse and intriguing lot that spans the various orchid tribes. Most miniatures measure 6 inches or less (excluding the flower stalk) and are highly ornamental: frilled lips, ruffled edges, spotted throats, and ornamental wings, crests, markings, and margins. Larger orchids are available as well; particularly charming are the fragrant varieties. Recent J&L introductions include warm-growing African orchids and new Masdevallia hybrids, and more are added each year. Among the nursery's most popular orchids are the rare South American Dracula orchids, whose showy, sinister blossoms look like bats or flying insects. (The most scary, *Dracula vampira,* has spectacular tails and dramatic black stripes.)

J&L Orchids sells miniatures by mail order year-round. The catalog lists orchid stock by tribe and subtribe, according to Dressler's classification. For novices, J&L offers "beginner" plants, mostly pretty moth and lady's slipper orchids that require little more attention than African violets. About half of J&L's orchids are propagated at the greenhouses; others are grown from seedlings. Visitors wishing to view the lush orchid spectacle and choose plants while in bloom are welcome to visit the greenhouses in southeastern Connecticut. Considering the rarity of its plant stock, prices seem reasonable. A holiday open house is held in early December for gardeners seeking Christmas presents. Other special events are the summer sale and "January Thaw" sale, with guest vendors and good deals on orchids. E-savvy gardeners can take advantage of monthly specials offered regularly on the Web site.

Directions: Take Route 15/Merritt Parkway to exit 46, and then take Route 59 north. In 4 miles, turn right at the stop sign; Sherwood Road is the third street on your left.

JOHN SCHEEPERS, INC.

23 Tulip Drive, Bantam, CT 06750
(860) 567-0838; fax (860) 567-5323
Jan S. Ohms

Flower bulbs. *Large mail-order bulb company. Business hours Monday to Friday 8:30–9, weekends 9–5. Free color catalog. Mail, phone, and fax orders. Volume discounts. Horticultural advice. E-mail: catalog@johnscheepers.com. Web site: www.johnscheepers.com.*

John Scheepers, Inc., established by an uncle of the current owner, Jan Ohms, has been one of the country's finest bulb merchants for more than 80 years. Its founder once supplied the great estates of Long Island using a Wall Street address and a chauffeured Cadillac. Today the firm remains a reliable source of first-quality flower bulbs, in varieties both new and classic. Scheepers publishes *Beauty from Bulbs,* a gorgeous color catalog filled with flower portraits—the best bulb catalog around. Although volume discounts are offered, savvy gardeners often place small bulb orders with Scheepers and large orders with its sister company, wholesaler Van Engelen Inc. (CT).

Begin with Scheepers's premium tulips: doubles and singles, peony tulips, triumphs (good for forcing), giant Darwins, green tulips, fringed tulips, lily-flowering tulips, multi-flowering tulips (great for filling the border), parrot tulips (like the ones in Dutch still lifes), and Rembrandts. Scheepers has excellent botanical tulips: huge emperors, water-lily tulips, *T. greigii* tulips (known for their mottled foliage), and nursery-propagated wild tulips, suitable for rock gardens. Catalog photographs of brilliant, silky, exotic tulips are calculated to make modern gardeners salivate with the same plant lust that drove Dutch merchants crazy in the 17th century.

Next, Scheepers's daffodils, in more varieties than ordinary mortals know exist: singles, doubles, trumpets, pink trumpets, large-cupped daffodils, multi-flowering daffodils, cyclamen daffodils (with blown-back petals), sweet jonquils, tiny miniatures, tazetta daffodils, triandrus daffodils (fragrant, delicate, many per stem), and the old-fashioned "poet's narcissus," with its pheasant's eye. Others include split-corona daffodils with divided, ruffled cups; butterfly daffodils with red and yellow markings; and many naturalizing mixtures, including all-pink and all-white collections.

Finally, there are Scheepers's exceptional hardy lilies (mainly Asiatic and Oriental lilies); Dutch and rock-garden iris; fritillaria (14 kinds); and allium (30 kinds), including a cornflower blue flowering onion dating to 1830. The "Best of the Rest" offers miscellaneous bulbs such as camassia, calla lily, and fool's onion; indoor bulbs for forcing; and all the little carpet bulbs that make spring so rewarding: crocus, grape hyacinth, squill, snowflake, snowdrop, starflower, winter aconite, anemone—the same "flowery mede" trod by ladies in medieval tapestries.

Scheepers's vibrant color catalog obviates any need for a display garden. Those seeking live bulb displays, however, may visit the Dutch bulb growers' garden located at the International Bloembollen Centrum in the Netherlands, said to be unforgettable in spring.

KATHLEEN NELSON PERENNIALS

55 Mud Pond Road, Gaylordsville, CT 06755
(860) 355-1547
Kathleen Nelson

Perennials. Ferns, grasses, and native plants. *Small specialty nursery. Open May and June, Friday to Sunday 10–5; at other times by chance or appointment. For appointments, call from 8 A.M. to 10 P.M. and let it ring; best time is just after dark. Plants for sale April through September. Free catalog. No mail order. Display gardens. Visitors welcome "even if you don't plan to buy." Group lectures by arrangement. Landscape design services.*

Kathleen Nelson Perennials is a small, home-based nursery specializing in excellent perennial plants that grow well in the garden of its proprietor. Nelson is a landscape designer who practices tough love: She replaces difficult veronica with tough agastache, spurns Shasta daisies, and ousts mainstays such as roses and delphiniums on account of failures in garden performance. She states the case plainly: "Plants that don't do their job in the garden, that don't thrive or are disease prone ... have been removed from my sales list and relegated to the compost heap."

The perennial collection that has emerged from this winnowing process is impressive for its durability, good looks, and ease of care. Plants offered at the nursery can be seen growing in sophisticated, low-maintenance display gardens designed by Nelson around her home. These horticultural displays comprise a wall-and-gravel dry garden, a fragrant "native meadow," a perennial grass garden punctuated by giant specimens, and (our personal favorite) a shady foliage island designed to be viewed from a first-story deck, where it looks like an embroidered jacquard. We actually wished this last garden would turn into a magic carpet and take off for our house. Even visitors who do not plan to buy are invited to view these gardens for help choosing plants for their own borders. This generous offer should not be resisted by any sane gardener looking for practical ways to beautify the backyard. Succession planting and season-extending choices make Nelson's display gardens beautiful all the time.

The nursery's catalog describes more than 200 select perennials, ferns, and grasses (some with numerous cultivars). Nelson enjoys experimenting, and many plants are uncommon varieties or hard-to-find natives obtained from seed exchanges and fellow gardeners. Perennials include white asters, smooth phlox, choice bleeding hearts, *Crambe cordifolia* (a cabbage relative with a huge cloud of white flowers), a lemon black-eyed Susan, a white perennial sweet pea, a "lost label" scutellaria with tiny lavender-blue flowers, noninvasive sundrops, and numerous cranesbill geraniums, including one black-eyed magenta variety

(G. psilostemon) that grows to 4 feet and blooms all summer. Among the shade perennials are numerous hosta and heuchera, several delicate corydalis, the green-flowered *Helleborus foetidus,* Japanese kirengeshoma, Himalayan Mayapple, Korean patrinia with yellow umbels, and what is described as a "jack-in-the-pulpit from outer space" called 'Green Dragon'.

Nelson interests herself in deer-resistant plants and fragrant herbs such as mountain mint, bronze fennel, and salvia. Garden-worthy native plants include wild meadow rue *(Thalictrum polygamum),* baccharis (a shrub), aralia (a 4-foot perennial with grape-like flowers), a native astilbe *(A. biternata),* and a delicate native orchid, *(Spiranthes odorata).* A number of plants will live under maple trees, where little else will grow. Nelson's wide collection of ferns and grasses includes maidenhair fern, royal fern, wild oats, prairie dropseed, and little bluestem. Most dramatic of all is the joe-pye weed that reaches immense proportions in the display garden, with a root ball the size of a washing machine.

With the help of her husband and college-age son, Kathleen Nelson grows her own plants and pots them up from spring to fall, so that a fresh selection is available all season. Dusk is a nice time to visit the nursery, when chores are winding down and the light goes golden. "Hats for gnats" are thoughtfully provided for visitors. If Nelson has time, she may give you a guided garden tour, accompanied by astute observations and shrewd horticultural advice. Her plant list and recommendations combine to give gardeners plants that, according to her customers, simply "grow better."

Besides her accomplishments as a nurserywoman, Nelson is a zoologist, biologist, educator, and lecturer. For appreciators of Nelson's distinctive garden style and ruthless attitude toward plant performance, landscape design and renovation services are available. Take a look at the handsome metal "embracers" (great for peonies) that Nelson had fashioned by a sculptor friend. The nursery invites suggestions "for the continuing war on deer, bunnies, chucks, and voles."

Reaching the nursery involves an adventurous drive down a one-lane dirt road, appropriately called Mud Pond Road, but the trip is worth it.

Directions: Gaylordsville is in west-central Connecticut, near the New York border. From New Milford, take Route 7 north, pass the ROUTE 55 *sign in Gaylordsville, cross the bridge, and turn right and then quickly left onto South Kent Road. In 1 mile, turn right onto Long Mt. Road, cross the railroad tracks, turn left, and take the next left onto Mud Pond Road; the nursery is about 0.5 mile on the left.*

Nearby attractions: On Route 7 a mile north of Kent, the Sloan Stanley Museum (860-927-3849), located on the site of an old blast furnace, displays an oddly beautiful collection of antique farm tools, collected and arranged by New England artist/author Eric Sloan.

LAURAY OF SALISBURY

432 Undermountain Road (Route 41), Salisbury, CT 06068-1102
(860) 435-2263
Judy Becker

Orchids. Cacti and succulents. Begonias. Gesneriads. Tropical plants. *Family-run retail greenhouse. Open by appointment or chance. Catalog $2. Free orchid seedling list. Mail order. E-mail: jbecker@mohawk.net. Web site: www.lauray.com.*

Lauray of Salisbury is a greenhouse nursery that proprietor Judy Becker took over from her parents, Laura and Ray Becker (together "Lauray"). The greenhouse is attached to their home on a rural byway in northwest Connecticut. The greenhouse grows a huge variety of tropical plants, all propagated on-site and meticulously labeled. Lauray is a respected source of unusual orchids, cacti, tender succulents, begonias, and other tropical plants. A treasure trove for connoisseurs and collectors, Lauray's greenhouse is open to visitors, though much of its trade is accomplished by mail order. The plants come in 2 1/2-inch pots and are moderately priced, offering a great way to jump-start a collection of these strange little plants.

A specialty of the greenhouse is its amazing collection of gesneriads, a family of unusual tropical plants with interesting foliage and bright flowers, often with tubular throats. Lauray's catalog lists 38 gesneriad species and some 800 hybrids, with others available on request—an astonishing collection by any standards. The best-known gesneriads, other than African violets (treated separately due to their popularity) are florist plants such as gloxinia and Cape violet (*Streptocarpus* spp.). We liked the cheerful kohlerias with their mottled hairy leaves and pink spotted flowers. Equally ornamental is Lauray's collection of 400 tender begonias, including angel-wing, shrubby, rhizomatous, semi-tuberous, and trailing varieties. Newcomers should not be put off by the catalog's technical vocabulary; these are wonderful houseplants, often with ornamental foliage so baroque that it seems intended to prove the design theory of the universe.

The greenhouse has a superb miscellany of tropical plants suitable for home and conservatory. Our favorites were achimenes, a gorgeous Victorian houseplant with purple, coral, or pink blooms (great in hanging baskets), and crodendrum, a spiraling summer vine producing red-tipped white flower lanterns. The catalog lists many peperomia with colorful foliage, and numerous vining tropical plants (such as hoya and dischidia) with waxy leaves and fragrant flowers. Lauray's orchid seedlings (listed on a separate sheet) include stunning varieties of cattleya (or corsage orchids), phalaenopsis (or moth orchids), doritaenopsis, dendrobium, and other tropical orchid alliances.

Mature orchid plants are available to those who cannot wait several years for the seedlings to flower.

Lauray is a virtual living museum of desert plants. The greenhouse grows nearly 300 kinds of tender cactus, including many epiphytic (aerial-root), large-flowered, and small-flowered varieties with neon blooms. Cacti are sold bare-root. They include plants that resemble sand dollars, pincushions, crowns of thorns, Martian cities, ladyfingers, and brains; they come armed with spikes, fish hooks, pins, teeth, and bristles. We suggest that people interested in the bizarre world of desert cactus schedule themselves for a visit to Lauray's greenhouse.

AUSTRALIAN
SALT
BUSH

Lauray's collection of more than 400 tender succulents is similarly bewildering, partly because some of them actually look like cacti, or orchids, or staghorn fern. (Our own experience with succulents was limited to a window box garden crammed with hardy specimens, of which we were rather proud until we came here.) We may not know our way around the universe of succulents, but Judy Becker does. Her tender succulents include 45 species, each with many subspecies and hybrids: lithops, crassula, agave, sedum, euphorbia, and countless other oddball plants that have a curious power to evoke their own world.

Directions: Northwest Connecticut is two hours from New York City and Boston, driving fast. The nursery is on Route 41 in the northwest corner of Connecticut, near the borders of Massachusetts and New York.

Nearby attractions: The Appalachian Trail crosses Route 41 at the Mount Everett State Reservation, a few miles north in Massachusetts; the southern Berkshires are riddled with lovely walks. Harney & Sons Fine Teas, 11 Brook Street (off Route 44), Salisbury (800-TEA-TIME), has a tea-tasting room with lovely views. Some miles south in Cornwall, Cornwall Bridge Pottery (800-501-6545) makes hand-thrown garden and bulb pots. In West Cornwall, the Housatonic Anglers Fly-fishing Guide Service & Bed & Breakfast (860-672-4457) offers riverside cottages with fly-casting lessons.

LOGEE'S GREENHOUSES

Dept. 8C, 141 North Street, Danielson, CT 06239
(888) 330-8038; fax (888) 774-9932;
horticulturist hotline (860) 779-7481
Byron E. Martin

Tropical plants. Container plants. Herbs. Begonia, passionflower, geranium (pelargonium), dwarf fuchsia, viola. Family-run greenhouses. Open year-round, Monday to Saturday 9–4, Sunday 11–4. Closed major holidays. Free catalog. Collector's choice list on request. Mail order since 1936. Horticulturist hotline open Monday to Friday 9–5. Visitors welcome; groups by appointment. Membershhip newsletter and discounts. Seminars. Consulting on greenhouse installation. E-mail: logees@neca.com. Web site: www.logees.com.

Logee's Greenhouses in northeastern Connecticut is the grandmother of all New England greenhouses. Distinguished purveyors of tropical floral plants since 1892, Logee's remains a preeminent resource for unusual showy plants for the conservatory and container garden. Logee's collection comprises more than 1,500 plants, assembled by the Logee-Martin family over three generations in eight dirt-floor greenhouses comprising "a half-acre rain forest in Connecticut." A glossy color catalog lists its major holdings, and a Collector's Choice list inventories the odds and ends. Most plants are propagated on-site and sold as small, well-rooted starter plants in 2 1/2-inch pots. (Experienced gardeners sometimes quarantine Logee's plants to ensure against greenhouse pests).

Logee's expert staff regularly mans a horticultural hotline, conducts weekend seminars, and offers consulting services on home greenhouse or sunroom construction. The legendary Joy Logee Martin, family matriarch and mother of the present owner, spent her life at Logee's and still functions as Logee's "worldwide reference for plant collectors." (She was once visited by a Japanese gentleman who came, with his own interpreter, to discuss rare begonias.) Reference books are for sale at the greenhouses. Special collections can be assembled for an astonishing number of species. After more than a century, Logee's remains the richest resource for tropical plants and advice about them that can be found in New England.

Logee's Greenhouses, with its mother lode of tropical and subtropical plants, is a great supplier of innovative nurseries. Mature specimens of bougainvillea, jasmine, camellia, acacia, and brugmansia inhabit the greenhouses, many of which are more than 50 years old and seem to have made themselves quite comfortable there. Revived interest in Victorian conservatory plants makes Logee's a superior source of hot "new" tropicals with a steamy past in grandmother's day. Logee's has 18 kinds of angel's-trumpets—huge, poisonous, intoxicating plants that produce pastel "dreamsicles"; 16 varieties of passionflower in rich coral, cochineal, lavender, wine, and purple; 14 flowering maples; and 10 kinds of dwarf fuchsia, including doubles, miniatures, and a winter-bloomer. Old-fashioned sweet violets, Parma violets, camellias, gardenias, and citrus trees seem like a legacy from a rich grandmother.

Logee's is celebrated for its hoard of rare begonias: rex begonias with "painted" leaves in swirling combinations of rose, celadon, and pewter; fibrous begonias; hairy-leaved begonias, seemingly cut from velvet; trailing begonias; maple-leaf and calla-lily begonias; dwarf rhizomatous begonias, used in terrariums; and semi-tuberous begonias, good for bonsai. Balcony geraniums form another formidable plant collection, ranging from rare Victorian parlor specimens to new introductions for sunny windowsills. Among these are wonderful scented-leaf geraniums of all descriptions, and fancy-leaved, zonal, ivy, pansy-flowering, regal, and rare species geraniums. Many other strange and rare tropical plants are available to adventurous gardeners, including gesneriads, succulents, and moth orchids. Near a pretty grotto in the fern house we found some lovely tropical ferns and oxalis not even listed in the catalog.

Are we gushing? Logee's is also renowned for unusual herbs. Joy Logee Martin has been a member of the Herb Society of America for nearly 60 years and is its former horticultural chairman. Under her guidance, Logee's has gathered a distinctive herb collection containing such exotics as patchouli, true licorice, Australian mint bush, Moujean tea, agastache, cinnamon-scented pinks, sugar leaf, and every kind of mint imaginable. Logee's has scores of ornamental thyme, oregano, lavender, and annual salvia, collected well before their current fascination as container subjects. For homeopaths, Logee's also carries a miraculous "healing onion" *(Ornithogalum caudatum)* that once cured Byron Logee of blood poisoning.

Directions: Logee's is in northeast Connecticut, not far from the Rhode Island border. From Route 395, take exit 92. Coming from the south, turn right at the ramp; from the north, go left. Turn right at the light onto Route 12 and take your first left onto North Street; Logee's is 0.4 mile on the left.

Nearby attractions: Zip's Diner, at the junction of Routes 12 and 101, Dayville (860-774-6335), is an original O'Mahoney's lunch car built in 1954, with quilted aluminum walls, pink Formica bathrooms, and comfort food made from scratch; Grape Nuts pudding is the house specialty.

OLD FARM NURSERY

158 Lime Rock Road (Route 112), Lakeville, CT 06039
(860) 435-2272; fax (860) 435-0535
Judy and Pat Murphy

Perennials. Trees and shrubs. *Landscaper's nursery. Open daily 9–5. No catalog or mail order. Show gardens. Landscape design and contracting services. Web site: www.oldfarm.com.*

Old Farm Nursery is the retail facet of Judy and Pat Murphy's landscape architecture and construction firm, located on their beautiful 25-acre farm in the horse country of northwest Connecticut. The Murphys are sophisticated landscape designers with their hands in the earth. They met years ago at work, landscaping the gardens at the Greenbriar Hotel in West Virginia. The Murphys opened Old Farm Nursery in 1988, and have since designed and installed hundreds of gardens for clients (she designs, he installs). Their nursery occupies 10 acres and seven outbuildings, and specializes in choice perennials, trees, and shrubs, all bought in from outside sources (primarily in Pennsylvania, Ohio, and Canada). The nursery also supplies the Murphys' design and landscaping jobs.

Elegant garden rooms showcasing their design and landscaping talents surround the Murphys' farmhouse and offset its long view over sloping cornfields. Visitors are welcome to tour the show gardens, which include an evergreen and grass island, a rustic cottage garden with witty plant combinations, a white garden with Corinthian columns flanking a swimming pool, and a formal potager punctuated with bell jars.

Despite a warm welcome to visitors, Old Farm feels like a wholesale nursery. Plants are located in the barns and adjacent fields, and visitors must sidestep trucks and forklifts operated by the Murphys' 10-man landscaping crew. Although most plants are labeled, many have no price tag, and no catalog or plant list is available.

Old Farm's well-tended stock seems intended mainly for well-heeled, low-maintenance, and deer-resistant gardens. Perennial selections tend to focus on white, blue, and pink varieties. We noticed attractive lilies, cranesbill geranium, boltonia, globe thistle, nepeta, Russian sage, interesting vines, and mature grasses. Following the norm of better nurseries, uncommon perennials such as ornamental onion (allium), white tradescantia, and *Crambe cordifolia* are mixed among garden classics. Old Farm Nursery carries good landscape roses and an excellent selection of ornamental trees, evergreens, and shrubs, many of specimen size. We found numerous lilacs, hydrangeas, and roses stylishly pruned as standards (tree-form) for patio gardens. Uncommon annuals are available from mid–May to mid–June.

Old Farm Nursery also carries beautiful garden ornaments, new and antique, such as obelisks, tuteurs, crown chimney pots, reproduction iron urns, terra-cotta containers, and outdoor furniture. "A dangerous place," remarked a lady carrying a pair of iron swans. "I'll take them."

Directions: Lakeville is in Connecticut's northwest corner, near the New York border. From the Berkshires, take Route 7 south into Canaan and turn right at the light onto Route 44. In Lakeville, veer left at the flashing light and turn left onto Route 112 west; Old Farm is 1.5 miles on your right.
From New York, take Route 684 north to the end. Then take Route 22 north to Amenia. Take Route 44 east and turn right onto Route 112 east; Old Farm is 1.5 miles past Hotchkiss School on the left.

Nearby attractions: Founded in the 18th century, Lakeville is named for Lake Wononscopomuc, where Ethan Allen operated the Salisbury Furnace (now renovated to modern uses) as a major supplier of cast cannonballs for the Revolutionary War. Belgian author Georges Simenon, creator of the Inspector Maigret mystery novels, lived and wrote in Lakeville from 1950 to 1955; here he wrote Inspector Maigret and the Headless Body. *The pretty town of Salisbury hosts a garden tour in June (860-824-0882). Sweethaven Herb and Flower Farm, 70 Wheatogue Road, Salisbury (860-824-5765), is a small organic herb farm with a Peter Rabbit garden for children; open Friday to Sunday 10–4. Lime Rock Park in Lime Rock (899-RACE-LRP), billed as "The Road Racing Center of the East," runs a Grand Prix for Dodge dealers in May.*

OLIVER NURSERIES

1159 Bronson Road (at Sturges Road), Fairfield, CT 06430-2821
(203) 259-5609; fax (203) 254-2701
Scott Jamison

Trees and shrubs. Conifers. Alpine and perennial plants. *Nursery and garden center. Open daily February through December. Hours March through June, Monday to Saturday 8–5, Sunday 9–5; July and August, Monday to Saturday 8–4:30, Sunday 10–4; September through Thanksgiving, Monday to Saturday 8–5, Sunday 9–5; November 26 to December 24, Monday to Saturday 8–6, Sunday 9–5; February daily 9–4. Closed July 4 and Labor Day. Hours may fluctuate due to weather. Free catalog. No mail order. Display garden.*

If you had to pick one place in Connecticut for choice ornamental trees, shrubs, and rock-garden perennials, Oliver Nurseries would be on the short list. Gardeners can probably find nurseries with more on-hand stock and nominally lower prices, but few rival the quality, sophistication, and adept plant handling of this one. Oliver Nurseries has a smart horticultural staff and an informative catalog that is worth buying just for the plant descriptions and special-sites lists (enumerating plants for moist soil, poor dry soil, winter interest, deer resistance, and early bloom). We started getting the catalog years ago, and have never tired of it as an imaginative garden reference and winter reading resource. Prices are not listed in the catalog because they change constantly, depending on what comes in and how much the nursery paid for it. Supplies fluctuate and plants move fast, so if your heart is set on something particular, call ahead.

Oliver Nurseries occupies a large sloping lot in an affluent residential neighborhood in Fairfield. The site is dense with well-labeled plants that are attractively integrated into the nursery yard and expanding display gardens. The nursery has an outstanding selection of ornamental trees, woody shrubs, and evergreens, bought in from outside sources and hardy to at least Zone 6B. Most trees and evergreens are large, one-of-a-kind specimens in impressive health, with freshly balled-and-burlapped root systems.

Of special interest are the many unusual conifers and Japanese maples and the strong holdings of azalea, rhododendron, hydrangea, and holly. Most are beguiling varieties that make you want to squander the rent on rare ornamentals. We coveted a dwarf filigree Japanese maple with gold flecks on its leaves; a rare pink-flowered Chinese yellowwood; contorted pines with a windswept appearance; and a silver-needled fir that seems permanently dusted in snow. Choice shrubs include tomato-red flowering quince, hardy camellias and crape myrtles (to Zone 6), variegated enkianthus (tinged pink in autumn), and a few fig trees, just for fun. Among the azaleas are fragrant hybrids developed from a native shrub *(Rhododendron viscosum)* and vivid, late-blooming varieties bred by Polly Hill on Martha's Vineyard.

The nursery's fine collection of perennials is propagated on-site and arranged on terraces under wooden awnings. A special area is reserved for an enchanting collection of well-grown alpine plants, some of which are visible in the nursery's wall garden. These exquisite plants (none has been wild-collected) are suited to growing in rock gardens, scree, stone walls, and troughs; if you need direction, Oliver's catalog and informed staff can tell you how to plant and care for them. We could go on about these alpines—tiny violet-blue campanulas, little Corsican wildflowers, miniature pinks, alpine gentians, delicate saxifrages, mat-forming thymes, tight little sand phlox, and diminutive primroses. The list includes a rare pygmy trailer with pink flowers *(Chaenorrhinum origanifolium),* a tiny ground-hugging willow with red catkins *(Salix hylomatica),* and an adorable 3-inch erigeron called 'Goat Rocks' after the Washington mountains where it was discovered at 7,000 feet. These alpine plants are simply irresistible; the only way to avoid seduction is to avoid going near them.

One gets the feeling that a good deal of unrushed, efficient, and purposeful activity takes place at Oliver Nurseries. Staff are cordial but always moving. The nursery's energetic planting and landscaping services are headquartered on the premises. The nursery is involved in civic horticultural projects, such as historic garden renovation. It puts out a custom-blended fertilizer called Oliver's Good Stuff. A good reference library is housed on-site, and someone took the trouble to order a fine selection of horticultural books for sale in the shop. In a small renovated barn, a potter produces hand-thrown garden ceramics. Oliver Nurseries is, justifiably, a favorite haunt of horticultural society day trips. Martha Stewart sightings are reported here, along with bluebirds.

Directions: From I-95 south, take exit 20 and turn right onto Bronson Road; the nursery is 0.8 mile on your left, just after the second stop sign.
From I-95 north, take exit 21 and turn left onto Mill Plain Road. Turn right at the stop sign onto Sturges Road, and right again at the first intersection (continuing on Sturges Road). Turn left at the second stop sign; the nursery is 0.3 mile on your left. From the Merritt Parkway/Route 15, take exit 44, turn left off the ramp, and left again onto Route 58. Turn right at the first light onto Congress Street. In 2 miles, at the second stop sign, turn left onto Hillside Road. Turn left again at the T-junction onto Bronson Road; the nursery is 0.6 mile on your right.

RESOURCEFUL JUDITH DESIGNS

P.O. Box 265, 486 Scenic Route 169, Woodstock, CT 06281
(860) 928-4421 and (860) 963-7755
Judith R. Gries

Hardy and historic roses. *Garden designer's nursery. Open May through July and September through October, Thursday to Sunday 11–5:30, and by chance. Closed in August. Free rose list. No mail order. Display gardens. Guided tours by appointment. Garden ornaments. Design services. Lectures. E-mail: rjudith@earthlink.net.*

Resourceful Judith is another name for Judith Gries, a professional "garden embellisher" who keeps an uncommonly pretty English-style country garden in northeastern Connecticut. Gries's garden contains an old-fashioned rose collection, perennial borders, romantic nooks, secret rooms, *trompe l'oeuil* trellises, and a water hammer with a stone basin (*tsukubai* in Japanese). *Fine Gardening* magazine once published a special article on its small, garden-sized allées (tree-lined avenues) cleverly planted with European hornbeam, ornamental pear, and flowering crab apple. At the garden's entry, Resourceful Judith maintains a small retail nursery selling old garden roses, elegant garden statuary, shrubs, and a few choice dividends from the perennial garden.

Resourceful Judith's specialty is beautiful, fragrant roses. The nursery carries over 50 hardy rose varieties, both own-root and grafted. Many are brought in from Canada, and others propagated on the premises, where the stock is root-pruned and well tended. The nursery carries floribunda roses, including award-winning 'Sea Foam'; pillar roses and climbers, such as popular, large-flowered 'Eden'; a sampling of Dr. Griffith Buck roses; and various David Austin English roses, including 'Evelyn', a fragrant apricot rose named for the Crabtree & Evelyn firm of soap and bath products (a local success story in this area of Connecticut).

Resourceful Judith also has a good collection of Rosa rugosa hybrids and shrub roses, useful for hedges and mixed borders. Among these are the apple-scented 'Queen Margrethe', pale 'Morden Blush', and ever-blooming 'Carefree Delight', which flowered all summer for us on a city street, until one night when its planter barrel was overturned by drunken stockbrokers. Toughest of all are 'John Cabot', 'Champlain', 'William Baffin', and other Canadian Explorer roses, grown to survive in Zone 2.

Resourceful Judith offers a charming selection of antique roses, the historic offspring of wild roses having one long, lovely bloom period every year in June. Old garden roses include fragrant Gallicas, grown in Paris in the 13th century; medieval albas, used in perfumery and medicine; fragrant damasks, taken from ancient Arabic gardens and brought to America by Spanish missionaries; centifolias, the cabbage roses seen in 17th-century Flemish flower paintings; and lush Bourbon roses, the romantic offspring of early China roses and old European hybrids. Resourceful Judith's heirloom rose collection is supplemented with Victorian moss roses, Portlands, and hybrid perpetuals (the only rose we know that will tolerate shade). Interested gardeners should inquire about roses not named on the nursery's plant list, for many interesting old garden roses are grown here in small quantities.

Directions: The nursery is in Connecticut's northeast "quiet corner," 30 minutes from Worcester and Providence and 90 minutes from Boston. From Route 395, take exit 97 onto Route 44 west. In 1 mile, take Route 171 west for 3 miles, until it merges with Scenic Route 169; the nursery is on your left.

Nearby attractions: Roseland Cottage on the Woodstock common (860-928-4074) is a charming 1846 Gothic Revival summer cottage, complete with family furnishings, an indoor bowling alley, and boxwood parterre gardens; its owner, the Society for the Preservation of New England Antiquities (SPNEA), holds children's garden parties, tussie-mussie teas, and twilight lawn concerts in summer. Wright's Mill Farm, 63 Creasy Road (off North Society Road), Canterbury, CT 06331 (860-774-1455; www.wrightsmillfarm.com), is a picturesque Christmas tree farm selling tree seedlings in spring for privacy screens, boundary plantings, and "favors at our weddings;" visitors can inspect the 300-year-old millpond and the remains of an old cider mill.

SAM BRIDGE NURSERY & GREENHOUSES

437 North Street, Greenwich, CT 06830
203-869-3418
Samuel F. Bridge III

Perennials. Ornamental nursery stock. Retail nursery/greenhouse. Open daily, Monday to Saturday 8:30–5. Free catalog. No mail order. Web site: www.sambridge.com.

Located in Greenwich on an elegant road lined with mansions, Sam Bridge Nursery & Greenhouses has been a stable source of superior garden plants for two generations. Established in 1930 by owner Samuel Bridge's parents, the nursery occupies 20 acres of wooded bottomland between the town cemetery and church. In spring, its entry drive is marked by a profusion of daffodils lining the public road.

The distinguishing features of Sam Bridge Nursery are its superior cultivation practices and eye for quality. Most of the nursery's plant stock is still propagated in greenhouses on-site. This being Greenwich, one expects to pay for the pleasure, but price is not the gardener's sole criterion. Sam Bridge is a good place to reflect on garden plants as investments: on how long we live with our purchases, and how much pleasure we get from a fine, well-chosen plant.

Sam Bridge Nursery specializes in ornamental perennials grown and displayed in open hoop houses next to the parking lot. A perennial catalog, obtainable at the nursery, lists over 1,000 perennials (more are available); plant descriptions are supplemented by attractive photographs. These plants are a classy lot, stylish without being faddish. On a spring visit we found nearly 20 varieties of columbine, a white perennial gloxinia, a new loosestrife with pink-variegated foliage, and superior astilbes ranging from rock-garden dwarfs to a 3-foot 'Ostrich Plume'. Sam Bridge perennials are vigorous, and their labels give a full account of their names and horticultural needs. Gardeners must come to Greenwich to buy them, for there is no mail order.

Beside perennials, Sam Bridge Nursery sells huge technicolor pansies, attractive hanging baskets, and pots of bulbs forced in its greenhouses. One whole greenhouse is filled with gorgeous patio plants that the nursery has trained as topiary standards—tree-form geranium, heliotrope, mallow, solanum, and sweet potato vine. Early birds can also find little-leaf lilac standards and dwarf Norway spruce brought in from the West Coast. Outside, from spring to fall, a sizable selection of decorative trees and shrubs is set out under an atmospheric grove of pine trees. These include choice weeping trees, dwarf and unusual conifers, corkscrews, and espaliers. None of the trees and shrubs is grown locally, but on our visit they were all healthy and carefully tended, with root balls well buried in mulch. The staff are active and friendly, and if they do not know an answer they will get it for you.

Directions: From Route 15/Merritt Parkway, take exit 31, bear right onto North Street, and proceed south for 2 miles to the entry drive on the right. If you reach the cemetery, you have gone too far.

Nearby attractions: The Gardener's Education Center of Greenwich, Bible Street, Cos Cob, CT 06807 (203-869-9242), holds an annual Gardener's Market in early May, featuring various vendors and plants raised in the Education Center's greenhouses, and a display of festive table arrangements in October.

SCHIPPER & CO.

P.O. Box 7584, Greenwich, CT 06836-7584
(203) 625-0638; (888) TIP-TOES (847-8637); fax (203) 862-8909
Timothy P. Schipper

Tulip and bulb mixes. *Wholesale bulb importer. Open Monday to Friday 8:30–5:45. Fax open 24 hours. Catalog $2. Mail, fax, and phone orders. Minimum order $50. Free bulb food with early orders. No visitors. E-mail: schipper@colorblends.com. Web site: www.colorblends.com.*

Schipper & Co. is a large Dutch bulb importer specializing in "Colorblends," sophisticated mixtures of tulip and daffodil bulbs coordinated for color effect and simultaneous bloom. Touted as "nature's fireworks," Colorblends provide stunning visual impact in spring bulb gardens, especially when closely grouped, as they often are outside corporate office buildings. Colorblends are used by universities, estates, golf courses, and landscape professionals who want surefire results without having to do companion bulb research.

Founded in the Netherlands in 1912 and moved to the United States following World War II, Schipper & Co. is a family business currently owned by Tim Schipper, known as "the Tulip Man." Although Schipper operates as a wholesale supplier, ordinary gardeners with enough space for a large spring bulb spectacle are welcomed as customers.

Schipper offers 39 different Colorblends of hybrid tulips, priced per 100 bulbs (minimum order $50). Tulip collections include 'Double Time' (red/yellow peony tulips), 'Purple High' (purple/white two-tier tulips), 'Get Rhythm' (pink/white/lavender tulips), and 'Kings & Jesters' (black tulips/yellow jester tulips). Gardeners can also choose among daffodil naturalizing blends and bulb mixtures such as 'Milky Way' (white daffodils/blue muscari), 'Peaches and Cream' (apricot daffodils/apricot hyacinths), 'Mother and Daughter' (giant/miniature lemon daffodils), and 'Red Star' (red tulips/white anemones). Schipper also offers "deerproof bulbs for woodland and shade," such as bluebells and snowdrops, useful for naturalizing under trees. Custom mixtures can be created for specific needs.

All Colorblends and specialty bulbs are pictured in Schipper's award-winning color catalog; its centerfold is a sepia photograph of grandfather Schipper standing with his workmen in the family's Dutch bulb field in 1920. Bulbs are shipped with planting instructions and, for early customers, free bulb food.

SELECT SEEDS

180 Stickney Road, Union, CT 06076
(860) 684-9310; fax (860) 684-9224
Marilyn Barlow

CONVOLVULUS MAJOR.

Vintage flower seed. Heirloom sweet peas. Specialty seed house. Business hours Monday to Friday 9–5 daily, Saturday 9–4 from January to May. Free catalog. Mail, phone and fax orders. E-mail: select@neca.com. Web site: www.selectseeds.com.

Select Seeds is a small seed house specializing in vintage flower seed. Owner Marilyn Barlow founded the business in 1987, after restoring a forgotten garden whose survivors she noticed were fragrant perennials lost to commerce. Its flower seed has been used by historic sites, museums, and botanical gardens around the country to re-create period gardens. Using organic methods, Select Seeds grows some seed varieties long dismissed by commercial sources, and works closely with small, family-owned seed suppliers in France, Germany, and Holland that still purvey old-fashioned, open-pollinated seed.

Select Seeds is a superior seed source for perennial and annual wildflowers, edible flowers, and old-fashioned annuals such as ornamental cotton and striped hollyhock. Select Seeds has excellent seed for flowering vines and trailers, including heirloom balcony petunias, variegated hops, purple-black morning glories rescued from an abandoned farmstead, and two nasturtiums that won AAS awards in the 1930s. Here cottage gardeners can source old-fashioned straw foxgloves, cowslips, purple toadflax, and variegated honesty (a plant, not a political philosophy). Seed for vintage annuals includes double white love-in-a-mist, kiss-me-over-the-garden-gate, shoofly plant, heirloom pansies, a pre-Columbian wild tobacco, and Victorian exotics such as striped maize and black peony poppy. Virtually all of these delightful plants have extraordinary survival skills, making them wise choices for low-maintenance gardens, vintage gardens, and restored sites.

Select Seeds is an exclusive seed source for heirloom grandiflora sweet peas, bred in the 18th and 19th centuries and saved from oblivion by an English seedsman. Some have romantic literary credentials, such as 'Painted Lady', a bicolor sweet pea described by the English poet John Keats as having "wings of gentle flush o'er delicate white ... and taper fingers catching at all things." Sweet peas called 'Butterfly' and 'Blanche Ferry' were recommended for their "vivid delicacy" in Celia Thaxter's *An Island Garden* (now a garden museum, located off the coast of New Hampshire). Other antique sweet peas have aristocratic associations, such as 'Queen Alexandra', named for a Danish princess who became the Queen of England, and 'Spencer', a mutation found by the estate gardener to Earl Spencer, ancestor to Diana, the late Princess of Wales. Our own favorite is 'America', a patriotic sweet pea with silvery white stripes on a red ground, excellent for celebrating the Fourth of July.

SHANTI BITHI NURSERY

3047 High Ridge Road, North Stamford, CT 06903
(203) 329-0768; fax (203) 329-8872
Jerome Rocherolle

Japanese bonsai. Growers and importers of bonsai. Open daily, Monday to Saturday 9–5. Color mail-order catalogue $3. Supplies and classes. Japanese-style garden design. E-mail: shanti@webcom.com. Web site: www.shantibithi.com.

Shanti Bithi Nursery began importing bonsai from Japan in 1974, and now has an extensive collection, some imported and some propagated at the nursery. Bonsai, which means "potted plant" in Japanese, is the art of growing and shaping dwarfed, ornamentally shaped trees and shrubs in small shallow pots. Shanti Bithi is Japanese for "Path of Peace," a name given to the nursery by U.N. Peace Advocate and Spiritual Master Sri Chinmoy.

Shanti Bithi Nursery is located in a plain wooden house on a minor highway in North Stamford, near the New York border. The nursery exudes an Oriental atmosphere of extraordinary tranquillity. Under tall pines in the entry court are displayed specimen bonsai hardy to the outdoors. Each is unique: miniature bonsai camellia, tiny Antarctic beech, exquisite little elm and hornbeam trees. Some are living antiques that evoke animated beings, or whole landscapes. We were particularly moved by the beauty of one bonsai group, a miniature forest of 85-year-old Japanese white pine, 2 feet high. Microscopic mosses covered its roots, and the wind moved in its boughs.

In the nursery's inner courtyard, hardy bonsai are presented in classic shallow pots, along with bonsai containers and Japanese stone lanterns standing on raked gravel. A greenhouse out back contains tropical bonsai. On our visit, some large Japanese bonsai of great beauty and costliness had just arrived after completing two years in quarantine, a necessary condition for importing these plants. Inside the house are books, videos, tools, supplies, and information about bonsai classes and workshops held on the premises. Bonsai plants and supplies can be purchased at the nursery or by mail order. An air of serenity imbues everything, even the checkout counter.

Mature bonsai are often queerly shaped, impressing themselves on the imagination and evoking alternate life-forms: a tiny bald cypress bent over like an old man; a miniature red-leaf maple with one hip akimbo, like a geisha swaying. Some bonsai look amusingly like animated cartoons or pet poodle trees. Consistent with this animist view, Shanti Bithi offers kennel and clipping services for treasured bonsai plants. Inexpensive starter plants and accent grasses are also available for those seeking to be schooled in the art of patience.

Directions: From I-95, take exit 7 onto Route 137 north. At the end of Washington Boulevard, turn left (continuing on Route 137) and proceed 8 miles (under the Merritt Parkway) to the nursery on the right.
From Route 15/Merritt Parkway, take exit 35 onto Route 137 north and turn left onto High Ridge Road. In 5 miles, the nursery will be on your right.

Nearby attractions: Three miles south on Route 137, follow signs to the Bartlett Arboretum, 151 Brookdale Road, Stamford, CT 06903 (203-322-6971; www.vm.uconn.edu/~www.barad), is a 63-acre arboretum owned by the University of Connecticut, containing a natural woodland, woody ornamentals, and a bog. Collections include dwarf conifers, nut trees, pollarded trees, and witches' brooms; an educational greenhouse holds a February flower show and activities for children. United House Wrecking Co., 535 Hope Street, Stamford, CT 06903 (203-348-5371), is a 5-acre salvage yard renowned for its collection of stately-home architectural remnants, garden iron, and old gates.

Shepherd's Garden Seeds

30 Irene Street, Torrington, CT 06790-6658
(860) 482-3638; fax (860) 482-0532
Eliot Wadsworth II

Gourmet vegetable seed. Heirloom flower and herb seed. *Specialty seed house. Business hours Monday to Friday 9–9, weekends 9–6. Free catalog. Mail, fax, and phone orders. E-mail: garden@shepherdseeds.com. Web site: www.shepherdseeds.com.*

Renée Shepherd founded Shepherd's Garden Seeds in 1982 after a European seed executive told her how hard it was to market gourmet vegetable seed to American gardeners accustomed to bland, cosmetically perfect supermarket varieties. Shepherd decided to supply America with hard-to-find seed (mostly from European and Asian sources) for fine-flavored vegetables, fragrant and heirloom flowers, and unusual herbs. Shepherd's Garden Seeds was sold in 1996 and is now part of the same horticultural enterprise that owns White Flower Farm (CT) and the Daffodil Mart (CT).

Shepherd's publishes an appealing catalog containing what one horticulturist terms "a fine selection of gourmet vegetable seed, and gourmet prices to match." Seeds are imported from around the world, after first undergoing garden and kitchen trials in various locations around the country. Shepherd's office in Connecticut is basically a seed warehouse with a trial garden on the grounds (not open to visitors).

Shepherd's specializes in provisioning kitchen gardeners with a dazzling range of gourmet vegetable seed, whose diverse origin is part of its charm. Here you can find seed for French escarole, Bulgarian carrots, Italian drying tomatoes, Japanese pole beans, Thai chiles, Burmese okra, Mexican poblano peppers, and wild kale. Shepherd's carries seed for haricot vert snap beans, baby pak choi, thornless artichokes, climbing summer squash, and heirloom green slicing tomatoes. Garden gourmets can savor Shepherd's baby cabbages, golden beets, white eggplant, Italian heirloom button onions, and rocambole garlic.

This is an excellent source of salad bowl seed for 'Deer Tongue' heirloom lettuce, edible amaranth (a hot-weather substitute for spinach), broccoli sprouts, and a new 'Wrinkled Crinkled Crumpled' cress (effective as an edible edging herb). Shepherd's also sells American heirloom broad beans with names like 'Jacob's Cattle' and 'Speckled Yellow Eye'; a purple-podded soup pea called 'Blauschokkers Capucijner'; a sweet Italian striped beet, 'Chioggia'; a novelty radish, 'Easter Egg II', which produces pink, white, red, and purple radishes (beneficial for repelling bean beetles); and a 'Tamra' hybrid cucumber, sold as a thirst-quencher in the Middle East before the days of Coca-Cola. For romantics, Shepherd's carries seed for an antique French Cinderella pumpkin.

Shepherd's herb and flower seed is equally intriguing. Gardeners can order seed for lanky, pungent epazote (Mexican tea); Japanese shiso (red perilla); traditional Finnish dill; sweet-seeded bronze fennel; breadseed poppy; and a short-season dwarf lavender called 'Lavender Lady', which won an AAS award. Shepherd's flower seed collection focuses on fragrant old-fashioned flowers, annual flowering vines, and plants suitable for wildlife habitat gardens. Shepherd's offers excellent choices of antique morning glory, poppy, cosmos, and nasturtium (a Peruvian native first popularized at Louis XIV's garden at Versailles). Ornamental sunflowers include giants and dwarfs, red and bronze hybrids, and a Japanese silver-leafed variety. Shepherd's supports the revival of heritage sweet peas with such heirlooms as 'Cupani', a perfumed cultivar dating to 1699, named for the Italian monk who first discovered sweet peas in Sicily. Shepherd's has assembled special seed collections for white and evening gardens, fragrance and children's gardens, and cutting gardens of old-fashioned annuals, everlastings, and wildflowers.

In addition to seed, Shepherd's carries garlic clove sets, onion plants (including sweet Italian cipollini and Walla Wallas), saffron crocus bulbs, lily of the valley pips, and tissue-culture potato tubers. Herb seedlings (i.e., live plants) are available for alpine strawberries, lemongrass, fruit-scented mints, and various culinary herbs. Kitchen gardeners may appreciate pleasing accessories such as Tuscan garlic jars, olive oil pumps, Joyce Chen stir-fry pans, rattan garden caddies, wire compost bins, and "NOnion" metal bars for removing onion and garlic odors.

TWOMBLY NURSERY

163 Barn Hill Road, Monroe, CT 06468
(203) 261-2133; fax (203) 261-9230
Kenneth and Priscilla Twombly

Ornamental shrubs and trees. Unusual conifers. Perennials and alpine plants. Native plants. Winter-interest plants. Ground cover. Large specialty nursery. Open March through October, daily 8–5, Sunday 9–5. Closed Sunday in July and August. Open November through February by appointment. Catalog $5 (free at the nursery). No mail order. Display gardens. Lectures. Landscaping services and masonry. Web site: www.twomblynursery.com.

Twombly is a large specialty nursery growing uncommon plants of all descriptions. More than 5,000 varieties of plants are for sale here, with particular emphasis on dwarf conifers, native and ornamental shrubs, and specimen plants. Owners Ken and Priscilla Twombly are distinguished nurserymen and plant enthusiasts (he is a licensed arborist) who have specialized in growing rare and unusual plants for more than 30 years. Their fine collection, now grown to mind-boggling proportions, is constantly being enhanced with additions from influential growers around the country. Located in Zone 6, Twombly Nursery is a leading supplier of rare and unusual shrubs and trees in the Northeast.

The nursery's 25-acre site has numerous parklike display gardens, of which its award-winning Winter Garden is most celebrated. In addition to its headquarters, the nursery operates the Twombly Plant Shop at the New York Botanical Garden.

We are almost at a loss to summarize Twombly's holdings. In the shrub category, the nursery carries uncommon cotoneaster, as both ground cover and grafted patio tree; nine kinds of witch hazel; 10 shrub willows; 25 hydrangeas; 23 andromedas; countless rhododendrons and azaleas; and numerous rose and lilac hybrids, including fernleaf and little-leaf lilac (we searched for years for the latter). Twombly outdoes itself in the *Ilex* genus, which embraces holly, possum haw, inkberry, and winterberry—both male and female, native and Asian, long-stalked and short, red- and yellow-berried, you name it. Choice shrubs include such rarities as pink Japanese snowbell, golden elderberry, salt tree (*Halimodendron* spp.), and, for the outer border, fern-leaf tallhedge.

In the tree category, Twombly is a source for rare weeping zelkova, hardy crape myrtle, horizontal Persian parrotia, variegated tulip tree, double white horse chestnut, and the white-flowering dove tree, or handkerchief tree *(Davidia involucrata),* considered one of the most beautiful small ornamental trees. Twombly has excellent range in its Japanese maples, magnolias, flowering crab apples and cherries, and now, in response to customer demand, fruit-bearing trees. The conifers include a wealth of dwarf and exotic pine, spruce, fir, false cypress (*Chamaecyparis* spp.), juniper, yew, and hemlock. Any gardener whose tastes have graduated to shrubs and trees would do well to study Twombly's extraordinary stock.

Although its strength is in woody plants and evergreens, Twombly has managed to work a similar magic in the perennial yard. Few perennial specialists carry such good offerings of epimedium, gentian, oenothera (sundrops), penstemon (beardtongue), and heuchera (coralbells). Alpine and shade perennials are constantly on the increase here. We noted interesting choices of daylily, peony, iris, campanula, and ground cover such as native pachysandra and chrysogonum (gold star). Most perennials come in starter sizes (3-inch pots)—a moderately priced way to establish a choice plant collection in the border or rock garden.

Twombly's catalog is both an intelligent guide to nursery stock and a "gardeners' handbook on growing things in the Northeast." Regional gardeners should happily pay the publication cost in order to get their hands on this informative plant reference, published biannually with a "New Plants" addendum in alternate years. The catalog includes descriptions of Twombly's ornamental plants, planting instructions, a reference list, and suggested plants for deer resistance, drought resistance, wetlands, native-plant collections, and wildlife habitats. Plant prices and sizes are omitted from the catalog, as much depends on what is available from outside growers. For on-line gardeners, the nursery's Web site replicates the catalog and offers intelligent garden planning tools that far outdo anything we have seen posted on the Internet by a commercial nursery.

Twombly Nursery styles itself as "Connecticut's garden spot," with all the amenities of a destination nursery. A 41/2-acre display park contains shade, wetland, alpine, vegetable, and butterfly gardens. Based on British models, the nursery's celebrated Winter Garden is devoted to season-extending plants that enhance the cold-weather landscape. Unfolding color contrasts among foliage, flower, and berry accents lend fascination to these gardens year-round. We were even mesmerized by the mixed rug of groundcover in the parking lot island. Look out for the magnificent fearsome scarecrow—a six-armed Shiva brandishing old kitchen and garden tools, its metal head a long-nosed watering can.

Excellent advice on garden culture and pests (bring in your problem leaf or twig) is available from Twombly's educated staff. The garden shop carries good tools and books. We love Twombly's organic bug spray recipes that you can mix up in the kitchen. Educational lectures are held at the nursery from spring to fall, often with eminent speakers, including the owners.

Directions: Monroe is in central Connecticut, midway between New York City and Hartford. From the south on I-95, take exit 27A onto Route 25/8 north, staying on Route 25 when the roads split. Turn right onto Route 111 north, and after 3.3 miles turn right again onto Route 110. Take your second left after the golf course onto Barn Hill Road; the nursery is on your left.
From Route 15/Merritt Parkway, take exit 49 onto Route 25 north and proceed as above. Alternatively, from the north on I-84, take exit 11 and turn right at the light. Turn right onto Route 34 east, and in 5.2 miles right again onto Route 111 south. In 1.8 miles, turn left onto Barn Hill Road; the nursery is on your right.

Nearby attractions: A meditation on ozone posted in the Twombly rest room, taken from an ancient Indios legend: "The trees are the support of the sky; if we cut them down, the firmament will fall over us."

VAN ENGELEN INC.

23 Tulip Drive, Bantam, CT 06750
(860) 567-8734; fax (860) 567-5323
Jan S. Ohms

Flower bulbs. *Wholesale mail-order bulb company. Business hours Monday to Friday 8:30–9, weekends 9–5. Free catalog. Mail, phone, and fax orders. Volume discounts. Special orders. E-mail: catalog@vanengelen.com. Web site: www.vanengelen.com.*

Once the American branch of a huge Dutch bulb company, Van Engelen Inc. is a wholesale bulb importer that sells from the same bulb list as its sister company, John Scheepers (CT). The Scheepers's lily and amaryllis bulbs are one size larger, but otherwise, the bulbs are the same size and quality. Van Engelen specializes in filling large orders of 50, 100, or 250 premium-size bulbs per variety: tulips, daffodils, alliums, iris, and countless specialty flowers. Its collections (including tulip mixtures, all-white and all-blue mixes, and various small-garden and rock-garden assortments) are similarly geared to larger quantities.

Van Engelen's catalog is a plain bulb list, lacking entirely the glorious flower photographs of its sister catalog from John Scheepers. Since both firms offer the same bulbs, gardeners wishing to order in small and large quantities can consult both catalogs at once, as we often do, and sort out where best to order. Van Engelen remains our favorite source for naturalizing mixtures and large quantities of indoor forcing bulbs (including excellent paperwhite narcissus) to get us through the winter. Van Engelen still sells directly to estates, and can fill large bulb orders (including special orders for bulbs not listed in the catalog) at wholesale prices.

The business is basically a warehouse, so although visitors are welcome, there is not much to see. Prices are fair, with cost savings in Holland usually passed on to the customer.

Nearby attractions: Stillbrook Horticultural Supplies (800-414-4468; free catalog) is a supplier of discount garden tools and supplies operating out of Van Engelen's office. Stillbrook is owned by Bill Kennedy, Van Engelen's warehouse manager and a former estate gardener, and specializes in products he has personally tested and approved.

THE VARIEGATED FOLIAGE NURSERY

245 Westford Road, Eastford, CT 06242
(860) 974-3951 phone and fax; (860) 974-1077 orders
Stan Megos

Variegated foliage plants. Hosta. *Small specialty nursery. Open April 15 to November 15, Wednesday to Sunday noon–6, and by appointment. Phone orders Monday to Friday noon–7. Catalog $3 (deductible). Mail order. Display garden. Group tours and slide shows. Live concerts Sundays at 4 and 6 P.M. May through September. E-mail: varigatedfoliage@neca.com. Web site: www.variegatedfoliage.com.*

Stan Megos, sole proprietor of the Variegated Foliage Nursery, is a retired carpenter and self-confessed vitamin nut whose obsession with variegated foliage plants got so out of hand that he had to open a nursery in order to cover his travel and acquisition costs. Variegation, according to a noted nurseryman, "adds a welcome bit of insanity to any garden." Usually the product of virus or genetic variation, variegation reduces a plant's chlorophyll and affects its vigor, but in the right place adds multiseason interest and beauty to otherwise common plants.

Located on the hill behind Megos's home in rural northeast Connecticut,

Variegated Foliage offers 1,100 varieties of perennials, trees, and shrubs, every one of which is spotted, streaked, mottled, marbled, pied, edged, blotched, or banded with color variegation. About a third are propagated at the nursery, the rest bought in for spring. Bargain hunters may wait until fall, when much of the plant stock goes on sale; distant gardeners can use mail order. We recommend an on-site visit to the 12,000-square-foot nursery display, if only for the dizzying novelty of moving through a never-ending sea of dappled foliage.

For foliage gardeners whose equilibrium can withstand giddy color variations, the Variegated Foliage Nursery is a useful resource. Stan Megos carries more than 300 hosta, including such classics as 'Spilt Milk', an albino called 'Mostly Ghostly', and a huge blue-puckered variety called 'Mohegan' (newly introduced through this nursery). Megos carries the daphne 'Briggs Moonlight', which is the reverse of 'Carol Mackie' (green edge, cream center). His variegated perennial collection is strong in splotched heuchera (42 kinds), polka-dot pulmonaria (19 kinds), dappled ajuga, and silvered Oriental woodlanders such as Asian ginger and Japanese jack-in-the-pulpit. Mottling and veining lends interest and charm to ground cover such as lamium, lamb's ears, saxifrage, viola, lily of the valley, and cotoneaster. Banding and pin-striping add drama to the strap foliage of grass, iris, yucca, and hardy bamboo. In our opinion, however, variegation makes some phlox and lilac foliage *look* indelibly mildewed, and gives aquilegia and crab apple leaves a fevered appearance. (The nursery stock itself is mildew-free, and Phlox 'Harlequin' has a dashing stripe.) We hardly know what to think of variegated horseradish and plantain, though we loved the woodland delicacy of variegated Asian fairy bells (*Disporum sessile* 'Variegatum').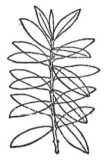

Stan Megos has managed to acquire numerous variegated dogwoods, variegated Japanese maples, and variegated forms of azalea, rhododendron, aralia, elderberry, forsythia, and weigela. At some point, though, so much variegation becomes unnerving. Picnic-table benches are available to visitors who need to sit down. We plan to come back when our stomach is settled to investigate the variegated tree collection, which includes variegated forms of ginkgo, katsura, ash, locust, redbud, bald cypress, and dawn redwood.

Directions: From I-84, take exit 71, turn left off the ramp, and go straight past the church in Westford Center. At the fork where the road becomes dirt (the paved road bears right), go straight onto Eastford Road. In about 4 miles (where Eastford Road becomes Westford Road), the nursery will be on your right.

WALNUT HILL GREENHOUSE

219 Wheeler Road, Litchfield, CT 06759
(860) 482-5832
The Richard family

Tropical houseplants. Cacti and succulents. Garden plants and vegetable flats.
*Family-run greenhouse. Open year-round, daily 8–5, closed Thanksgiving and
Christmas. No catalog or mail order. Mailing list for coupons and specials. Seasonal
plants. Group tours. Web site: www.walnuthillgreenhouse.org.*

Walnut Hill is a greenhouse nursery owned and operated by the Richard family
just outside Litchfield. It specializes in exotic houseplants and desert plants, and
is favored by collectors for cactus and succulent collections that are among the
most extensive in the Northeast. The Richards propagate all their plants and
sell them directly out of large greenhouses in back of their garden-supply shop.
A small tropical display forest and a cactus garden add charm to the plant
displays. In the warm months, nursery-grown perennials, annuals, and vegetable
flats are sold on outside tables; seasonal plants are available at the holidays.

Walnut Hill has a tantalizing range of unusual tropical plants: strikingly
patterned wax and rex begonias; pink and purple Cape primrose (*Streptocarpus*
spp.); staghorn fern; scented geraniums; tropicals from Florida; and a table full of
tender, low-light plants. These greenhouses are heaven for the houseplant
enthusiast. Of interest to us were the many botanically unrelated plants called
"ivy," including yellow and purple Swedish ivy (*Plectranthus* spp.), variegated wax
ivy *(Senecio macroglossus),* and Polynesian ivy *(Pellionia pulchra).* We also admired
the purple oxalis, beet-colored bloodleaf (*Iresine* spp.), miniature silver-nerved
(Fittonia minima), and the wonderful weird wire vine (*Muehlenbeckia* spp.).

Walnut Hill's desert plants, most in 3-inch pots, are just as engrossing. We
were confronted with a bewildering variety of rare cacti, a specialty of owner
Roseanne Richard, and well beyond our analytic skill. To us they looked like
blue fingerlings; ruby spikes; gray roses; bowls, gourds, and hydras—some netted
in white, some in bloom, all armed. The collection of rare succulents had
similar diversity; its odd forms seemed positively extraterrestrial. We noted a
variegated dwarf aloe with red stripes; a microscopic *Sedum humifusum;* a dwarf
crown-of-thorns *(Euphorbia milii);* an utterly flat table-form *Aeonium;* a strange
Andromischus with fleshy, frilled lips; and several plants called *Haworthia* that
looked like plastic wedges. We leave it to experts to say whether any of these
plants come from Mars.

*Directions: From Litchfield, take Route 202 east. In 4 miles, turn right onto Peck
Road, then left onto Russell Road; the greenhouse is 0.5 mile on your right.*

Nearby attractions: A soothing outdoor labyrinth is open to visitors at Wisdom House Retreat Center, 229 East Litchfield Road, Litchfield (860-567-3163). On Route 118, Litchfield, the Montfort Missionaries maintain a 35-acre replica of the Lourdes Grotto in France (860-567-1041), open from dawn to dusk as a place of pilgrimage.

WHITE FLOWER FARM

P.O. Box 50 (Route 63), Litchfield, CT 06759-0050
Orders (800) 503-9624; inquiries (800) 411-1659; fax (860) 567-3507
Retail store (860) 567-8789
Eliot Wadsworth II

Ornamental perennials, shrubs, bulbs, and houseplants. *Commercial mail-order house and nursery. Order phone open daily 9–9. Retail store open daily, April through October, 9–6; November to March, 10–5. Free color catalog. Mail and phone orders. Horticultural advice by telephone, Monday to Friday, 9–4. Display gardens. July open house. Web site: www.whiteflowerfarm.com and www.800oldbulbs.com.*

White Flower Farm is the country's best-known upscale nursery, where many people begin a serious interest in gardening. Based in the gracious town of Litchfield, White Flower is famed for publishing *The Garden Book*, a stylish color catalog displaying fashionable ornamental plants for aspiring gardeners.

The nursery was founded in 1950 by "Amos Pettingill," alias William Harris and Jane Grant, two successful writers from New York City with an eye for good advertising copy and professional ties to the *New York Times, Fortune* magazine, and Wall Street. These sophisticated urbanites renovated a weekend barn in Litchfield and soon became obsessed gardeners. Their all-white flower garden was fashioned after the famous British white garden at Sissinghurst Castle; it later provided the "white flower" image for their mail-order nursery, opened out of frustration with the shortcomings of postwar American nurseries. The original White Flower Farm catalogue has been described as "masterful merchandising masquerading as great journalism"—a successful formula still in use by the enterprise. Today, White Flower Farm employs hundreds of employees, including an expert horticultural staff. This is not simply a nursery; it is the centerpiece of a horticultural conglomerate that includes the Daffodil Mart (CT) and Shepherd's Garden Seeds (CT). Interested visitors can still visit the original White Flower Farm barn and garden, now called the Moon Garden, along with extensive display gardens.

White Flower Farm specializes in ornamental perennials, shrubs, bulbs, and houseplants of superior horticultural merit. More than 700 plants are listed in *The Garden Book,* along with seductive descriptions and detailed cultural instructions. Most of the plants are grown in Litchfield, in extensive greenhouses and 25-acre production fields. Spring- and summer-flowering bulbs, imported from Holland, are sold through the fall catalog.

White Flower Farm prides itself on finding and trialing fine new ornamental cultivars in advance of commercial presentation. Its ever-changing plant list includes, in the words of one savvy horticulturist, "old favorites and tantalizing newcomers, sold with much snob appeal, with prices to match." White Flower Farm is big business, and still plays an important role in introducing, to American gardeners, elite garden plants imaginatively suited to the conservatories and flower borders of British manor houses.

The overriding focus of White Flower Farm's *Garden Book* is on ornamental perennials and bulbs. Preeminent among perennials are hybrid tree peonies (including yellow 'High Noon') and a large collection of single and double herbaceous peonies. The perennial list, more wide than deep, includes double bloodroot, black hollyhock, sweet violet, and Japanese candelabra primrose. Somewhat more ample holdings are available in ferns, phlox, and bearded iris (these last include a collection of Dykes medal winners). Perennials are supplemented by large-flowered clematis and small companion shrubs such as caryopteris and clethra. Perennial collections for sun and shade, samplers of daylilies and Oriental poppies, and a "Glory in August" perennial assortment and have been assembled for convenience.

Special fall bulb offerings include a daffodil collection, single and double tulips, fritillaria, trout lilies, stylish ornamental onions (or allium), and a yellow clivia from Japan. The lily collection, long a mainstay of White Flower Farm, includes old-fashioned Turk's-cap, Asiatic, and Oriental lilies, mixtures of butterfly and trumpet lilies, and species lilies for naturalizing. The spring catalog features tuberous begonias, dahlias, and interesting exotics such as lily-of-the-Nile (*Agapanthus* spp.), angel's-trumpet (*Brugmansia* spp.), and a prized yellow lady's slipper orchid *(Cypripedium parviflorum pubescens).*

All plants in White Flower Farm's catalog are sold by mail order. The retail store in Litchfield offers container plants in different sizes, as well as garden tools, books, pots, and gifts. For visiting pilgrims, a self-guided walking tour to extensive display gardens (under renovation, we hear) is outlined in a brochure available at the Visitor Center. An annual open house in July features garden tours, lectures, and tea served with cucumber sandwiches.

Directions: From Route 8, take exit 42, and follow Route 118 west through Litchfield center. White Flower Farm is 3.3 miles south of town on Route 63.

Nearby attractions: Litchfield is famous for its Federal-period mansions; watch for old men playing bocce on the town green. At Laurel Ridge Foundation, a 10-acre field of daffodils planted in 1941 blooms spectacularly in late April; take Route 118 east from Litchfield, turn right on Route 254/Wigwam Road, and the display is a mile on the left. Visitors can picnic at Topsmead State Forest, Buell Road, Litchfield (860-485-0226), a former estate with an authentic Cotswold cottage and English country gardens.

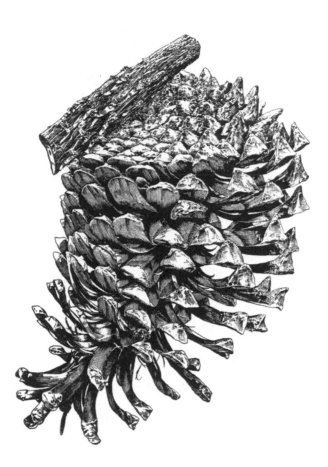

MAINE

MAINE

1. Allen, Sterling & Lothrop
2. Barth Daylilies
3. Eartheart Gardens
4. Everlasting Farm
5. Fedco
6. Fernwood
7. Fieldstone Gardens
8. Fox Hill Nursery
9. Gingerbread Farm Perennials
10. Hedgehog Hill Farm
11. Hidden Gardens
12. Hill Gardens
13. Johnny's Selected Seeds
14. Mainescape Garden Shop
15. North Creek Farm

16. O'Donal's Nurseries
17. Perennials Preferred Nursery
18. Pinetree Garden Seeds
19. Plainview Farm Fine Perennials
20. Plants Unlimited
21. Rock Oak Gardens
22. The Roseraie at Bayfields
23. Snow Brook Gardens

24. Steeplebush Farm Herbs
25. Stone Soup Farm
26. Sunnyside Gardens
27. Valente Gardens
28. Werner's Picket Mountain Farm
29. Wood Prairie Farm
30. York's Hardy Rhododendrons

ALLEN, STERLING & LOTHROP

191 U.S. Route 1, Falmouth, ME 04105-1385
(207) 781-4142; fax (207) 781-4143
Shirley Brannigan and family

Short-season vegetable seed. *Small, family-owned seed store and nursery. Open all year, Monday to Saturday 8–5:30. Seed catalog $1. Mail order. Garden supplies.*

Allen, Sterling & Lothrop is Maine's oldest seed store, founded as a farm supply and seed store on Portland's Exchange Street in 1911. When its property was taken for urban renewal in 1969, the business moved to its current location. Miraculously, despite the disruption, it managed to retain some of the warmth and charm of a turn-of-the-century seed store. Allen, Sterling & Lothrop specializes in selling older, open-pollinated, short-season vegetable seeds, often the improved strains of old favorites adapted to northern gardens. Seed packing is still done the old-fashioned way, by hand, in the back room, using 100-year-old brass seed scoops imported from Germany.

LONDON TREADED SPADE.

Owner Shirley Brannigan is the daughter of Micky Maguire, the alert manager who saved the firm from ruin years ago by acquiring it from founder Harry Lothrop (Allen and Sterling had dropped out in 1914). Brannigan operates the store as a family business engaging four generations. Visitors can purchase the company's 'Sterling Quality' vegetable seed in packets and in bulk; seed is also sold through a small mail-order catalog. Vegetable gardeners confirm that the seed quality is excellent. The company also sells more than 100 varieties of spring bulbs; flower and herb seed; wild bird mixes; grass and clover seed for field and forage; bent grass for golf greens; spring asparagus crowns; wholesale greenhouse supplies; tools and fertilizers; garden pots; dried arrangements and wreaths; and craft supplies for canning and basket-making. Outside its store, much of the company's seed is sold in hardware store seed racks, in old-fashioned packaging that has remained unchanged for decades.

Directions: The seed store is located on coastal Route 1 in Falmouth. From Route I-95, take exit 15B onto Route 1 south, pass 2 lights, and the store is on the left.

BARTH DAYLILIES

71 Nelson Road, Alna, ME 04535-0054
(207) 586-6455
Nick Barth

Daylily hybrids. *Small specialty hybridizer. Free catalog. Mail order. Peak bloom mid-July to mid-August. Visitors welcome; call ahead. Web site: www.tidewater.net/business/Barth.*

Nick Barth, a Maine Yankee, inherited a hybridizer's passion and nearly an acre of daylily seedlings from his father, the late Dr. Joseph Barth, a Unitarian minister and pioneer in the development of tetraploid daylilies. (Tetraploids are plants whose genes have been doubled by treatment with the drug colchicine, giving them brighter color and heavier substance than their diploid cousins.) Nick Barth is a professional conservationist who began breeding daylilies in 1990, continuing his father's work and pursuing his own hybridizing goals. The elder Barth's most celebrated hybrids were introduced through Tranquil Lake Nursery (MA), which still offers an important collection, including some posthumous introductions. Tranquil Lake also introduces Nick Barth's most promising hybrids, such as 'Sheepscot Valley Glow', 'Linda O'Connell', and 'Sheepscot Valley Sun-up'. To support his breeding program, Nick Barth sells his daylilies directly from the growing beds, along with choice older varieties developed by his father and other noted breeders. Barth works his garden (with some paid help) along with his wife, a no-nonsense nurse who once told us she likes weeding because the plants "don't talk back."

Barth breeds daylilies on a hilltop near his small farm in Alna, a lovely town in the Sheepscot Valley, located on the inland reach of a tidal river in mid-coast Maine. The town was named for the alder trees blanketing the countryside. The Barth garden is home to several hundred named daylily varieties, including more than 40 Dr. Barth hybrids and 18 Nick Barth hybrids (and hundreds of unnamed Barth seedlings). Nick Barth's principal interest is in developing large 5-inch tetraploids for mid– to late–season bloom in fiery red, "white" (i.e., cream) and "blue" (i.e., violet). Like Maine Yankees in general, Barth daylilies are hardy to Zone 4 and colder. Although the modern trend in daylilies is toward the round and ruffled, eyed and edged, Barth considers it easier for breeders to produce "a pretty face" than good substance, branching, and high bud count. To pass muster, Barth's own hybrids must achieve a candelabra branching and at least 12 buds per stem; one Dr. Barth hybrid called 'Brick Red Eye' has a bud count of 75. This makes for enduring bloom on the Barth hybrids, a point of merit appreciated by northern gardeners.

Maine

Daylilies are ancient food and medicinal plants native to Asia, first hybridized for ornament in the 1800s. Barth states his endearing faith in "holding onto the old," and believes, perhaps rightly, that many older varieties have refinements that have all but disappeared from modern daylily breeding. Keeping old things that other people throw away is how many New England families came to possess fine antiques, and Barth is no exception. The Barth nursery still offers daylily classics such as Fay's 'Kathleen Elsie Randall', Hardy's 'Paprika Velvet' and many of the Marsh 'Chicago' series, listed in the catalog at bargain prices. The Barth garden also houses a limited collection of species daylilies, the ultimate antiques of the daylily world.

Nick Barth follows the charming convention, common among daylily hybridizers, of naming introductions after his native landscape: Note his iridescent 'Sheepscot Valley Glow' (a radiant vermillion) and the futuristic 'Sheepscot Valley Sunup' (mango with a disappearing cinnamon halo). Other Barth hybrids honor grandchildren and other Barth relatives. Readers can only wonder how deeply plant descriptions reflect on family character. We would love to meet the alluring 'Beth Barth' with her "pink midribs" and "excellent form and substance," as well as the florid 'Susan Elizabeth' ("our largest and most attractive early bloomer"), and the green-throated 'Vanessa Barth' ("attractive and different"). Our tour of the Barth garden revealed 'Outrageous Ramona', a huge, 9-inch, orchid-form, blazing bronze bitone, introduced through Tranquil Lake Nursery (MA) and named after (you guessed it) Mom.

One of the pleasures of a trip to Barth's garden is witnessing a hybridizing effort in process. Visitors can stroll through the growing beds, examine the seedlings produced by a single cross (he calls them "siblings in a line"), and note their favorites. Daylily plants are freshly dug at the nursery or sent by mail order, with bonus plants added to larger orders. The best bargains are divisions of unnamed, discontinued Barth hybrids (not listed in the plant list), which are lifted whole and sold on the spot. Peak daylily bloom here is mid-July to mid-August, the perfect season for visiting mid-coast Maine and the forgotten towns of the Sheepscot Valley.

Directions: From coastal Route 1 in Wiscasset, take Route 218 North (Federal Street). In 8 miles, bear right at the Alna Store (good sandwiches). Go 0.3 mile, turn right onto Nelson Road; the entrance to the growing field is 0.4 mile on your left.

Nearby attractions: At the head of the Sheepscot River, in the town of Alna, is the historic village of Head Tide. This quaint, half-deserted town is the birthplace of the poet Edwin Arlington Robinson, whose eloquent poems of Tilbury Town recount the lives of churchyard ghosts. The fine Old Head Tide Church, open Saturday 2-4, was built in 1838. Swimmers may try the swimming hole located beneath the old milldam, next to a small off-road parking area.

EARTHEART GARDENS

1709 Harpswell Neck Road, Harpswell, ME 04079-3303
(207) 833-6905
Sharon Hayes Whitney

Japanese and Siberian iris. *Open by appointment. Open house days in summer. Catalog $2. Mail order. Display beds. Peak Siberian iris bloom third week of June; Japanese iris third week of July. Plant pickup by appointment. E-mail:eartheart@gwi.net*

Eartheart gardens is a miniature nursery that houses a horticultural treasure: the Japanese and Siberian iris hybrids of Dr. Currier McEwen, Maine's famous breeder. Owner Sharon Hayes Whitney is a friend and neighbor of McEwen, and her garden is the receptacle of all his Japanese and Siberian iris introductions. (Siberian iris introduced by McEwen prior to 1990 are sold by Fieldstone Gardens, ME). Whitney has worked closely with McEwen on hybridizing iris and growing out promising seedlings. Eartheart Gardens also carries many unique Japanese iris bred by McEwen's colleagues at Kamo Nurseries in Shizuoka, Japan.

McEwen's story is a captivating one. As a distinguished rheumatologist and medical dean living outside New York City, his interest in iris was piqued by a Shreiner's catalog that "came to me in 1955," he says, "purely by chance." He began growing and breeding iris and daylilies without any real plan—"just crossed pretty flowers," as he puts it—until a fateful meeting with hybridizer Orville Fay in 1960, when he learned of a process for treating daylilies with the drug colchicine to double their chromosomes and convert them from a diploid to a tetraploid state. Colchicine (a drug derived from autumn crocus) was an old friend of McEwen the rheumatologist, who used it to treat gout; but its effects on plants "was a new discovery, and I was fascinated." McEwen directly undertook an aggressive breeding program applying colchicine to Siberian and Japanese iris, resulting in his introduction of the first fully tetraploid Japanese and Siberian iris in the 1970s. McEwen also takes credit for the first yellow Siberian iris, the award-winning 'Butter and Sugar', achieved through "McEwen luck" by crossing two blue seedlings sent by a hybridizer in England.

Since retiring to Maine in the 1970s, McEwen has devoted himself to breeding iris and writing books on Siberian and Japanese iris. He and his iris hybrids have won numerous prestigious awards. Now in his 90's, McEwen remains widely recognized as the grand old man of iris breeding.

McEwen's hybridizing goals more or less summarize the yearnings of an entire generation of Japanese and Siberian iris breeders: "strong plants with good branching; new colors and true blues, reds, and pinks; attractive pattern;

early, late, and repeat bloomers; and the development of miniatures." Special projects are developing hardy Japanese iris that bloom well in cold climates, and breeding Japanese iris for alkaline soil. The McEwen hybrids sold at Eartheart Gardens embody his attainment of these goals. His Japanese iris introductions include pink, blue, ruffled, veined, branching, and long-blooming varieties, such as 'Variation in Pink', 'Fourfold Pink', light blue 'Midsummer Happiness', and violet 'Enticing Geisha'. McEwen's favorite is the long-blooming 'Southern Son', named for a special son-in-law; "the closest thing to a true blue that we have seen" in a Japanese iris, he says. McEwen's new Siberian iris introduction, 'Pride in Blue', is the first true blue (RHS #100) to emerge from his garden.

For all the hybridizer's talk, our visit to Currier McEwen's garden convinced us that he never really gave up on pretty flowers. The McEwen Japanese iris appear as sumptuous, queenly creatures with fine strapped foliage and clear, gorgeous bloom colors, mingled and smeared in the most bewitching fashion. Though less flamboyant, McEwen's dignified Siberian iris have equal beauty, and perhaps make better team players in the perennial bed. We cannot think of any Siberian iris purer than 'Harpswell Snow', nor one lovelier than 'Soft Blue', which we found reblooming in July. (Our smart Aunt Jean put in her order on the spot.)

Eartheart Gardens sells, through its catalog, some 25 Japanese iris hybrids and 14 Siberian iris hybrids selected by McEwen from his trial beds over the last two decades. Eight more Japanese iris hail from Kamo Nurseries in Japan. Many more McEwen iris are available for sale at the nursery; these can be purchased in pots or ordered and dug for later pickup. Eartheart Gardens holds a few open house days each summer, timed to coincide with a breathtaking bloom display attended by many admirers, including white butterflies. These open houses present a wonderful opportunity to stroll Eartheart Gardens' growing beds, examine its extensive iris holdings, and visit Currier McEwen's intriguing trial and display gardens overlooking a refreshing coastal inlet. Lucky visitors may even meet the spellbinding Dr. McEwen, as we did, and receive personal instruction in the art of iris breeding. He keeps a fascinating stud book.

Directions: Harpswell is on the southern coast near Brunswick. From I-95, take exit 22/Brunswick/Bath, go 2 miles to the big overhead traffic sign, and continue straight onto Main Street. In 0.25 mile, across railroad tracks, turn right. At the gray church, turn left, then right at the light onto Route 123. In 12.4 miles, the nursery is on your left. Be sure to visit on an Open Day or call ahead.

Nearby attractions: Lobster lovers can indulge at Holbrook's Lobster Wharf, open till sunset in Cundy's Harbor (207-725-0708), or at Cook's Lobster House, off Route 123 on Bailey's Island (207-833-2818). The dining room overlooks a marine inlet and what's billed as "the world's only cribstone bridge." Craft studios populate Harpswell Neck.

EVERLASTING FARM

2140 Outer Essex Street, Bangor, ME 04401
(207) 947-8836
Gail and Michael Zuck

Container plants. Annuals, perennials, and herbs. *Small, family-run nursery. Open May 1 to September 15, Monday to Saturday 9–5; Sunday 10-4. No catalog or mail order. Free perennial plant list on premises. Display gardens.*

Everlasting Farm specializes in ornamental container plants and hanging baskets. This aesthetic nursery, located behind Gail and Michael Zuck's Cape house on the outskirts of Bangor, grows many old favorites alongside unusual new varieties that betray the owners' adventurous horticultural taste. The Zucks grow most of their plants in three greenhouses and maintain several small, attractive display gardens where their plant stock can be seen at work. Visitors should not miss Gail Zuck's gorgeous container displays, exhibiting artistry and originality in plant combinations, bloom and foliage contrasts, and choice of planter (we loved the chimney pots). What could be prettier for a wedding than an apple begonia paired with variegated ivy, or a yellow coleus with a salmon diascia from Heronswood (a trendsetting West Coast nursery)?

Although Everlasting Farm is open from May through August, its plant stock is best in May and June; after July 4, stores are depleted and prices reduced. The range of annuals is excellent, even if you just want good petunias (Supertunia and Surfina cultivars), impatiens (including New Guineas and the new yellows), or annual vines (such as scarlet runner bean and Hopi rattle gourd). On our visit, Everlasting Farm had purple hebe, cerulean and white forms of plumbago, three different browallia, blue and pink scaveola, white gomphrena, annual mallow (like a tiny hollyhock), and numerous ivy and scented geraniums, including serene 'Gray Lady Rose' and ruffled, variegated 'Prince Rupert'. Many annuals are available in both pots and hanging baskets. The nursery's ornamental herbs, such as golden oregano and 'African Blue' basil, are also apt for container uses.

Everlasting Farm's perennial stock, while less extensive, includes some very nice plants that Maine gardeners may have trouble finding elsewhere: pink turtlehead, black snakeroot, sea pinks, rose oxalis, variegated filipendula, and chocolate eupatorium. A frilly, lavender–blue lettuce-leaf poppy that had seeded itself in the display beds caused much comment among visitors. We loved the enchanting children's garden enclosed by a wattle fence, featuring easily grown seeds and a nasturtium scarecrow. The garden shop has cute baskets, topiary frames, and bug suits for kids.

Directions: From I-95 in Bangor, take the Broadway exit, and go north on Broadway (Route 15). In about 1 mile, turn right onto Burleigh Road, then left onto Essex Street; the nursery is 2 miles on your left.

Nearby attractions: Windswept Gardens, 1709 Broadway, Bangor, ME 04401 (207-941-9898 and 800-941-9898), open daily, May through September, is a well-known garden center specializing in hardy shrub roses for cold climates. Elaborate display areas include garden rooms, a regulation croquet court, and an interesting trial garden for Weeks hardy roses. Snow & Nealley, 60 Summer Street (off Main Street), Bangor (800-599-0337; www.snowandnealley.com) is opening a retail store for its garden tools, complete with museum-style showroom of Snow & Nealley tools dating to the 19th century. The University of Maine's botanical collections at College Avenue, Orono, ME 04469 (207-581-3112) include an All America Selections trial garden and a greenhouse with tropical and desert plants.

FEDCO

P.O. Box 520, Waterville, ME 04903-0520
(207) 873-7333; fax (207) 872-8317
C.R. Lawn, founder

Seeds. Trees, shrubs, perennials. Bulbs and tubers.
Worker/customer plant cooperative. Office hours from December through April, Monday to Friday, 9:30–5; irregularly the rest of the year. Three catalogs annually, $3. Mail order only. Strict order deadlines. Discounts on bulk orders. Annual spring tree sale. Books. Web site: www.fedcoseeds.com.

Fedco is a Maine-based worker/customer plant cooperative with refreshingly old-fashioned values, bound to warm the heart of the most world-weary cynic. Fedco sells vegetable and flower seeds, bulbs, tubers, trees, and nursery stock at low prices by mail order. It encourages customers to form buying cooperatives to secure even greater bulk discounts. It operates according to a practical rural philosophy, reminiscent of Virgil's *Georgics,* espousing the nobility of farming. Literary quotations and inspiring stories of plant breeders are interspersed with catalog listings. Fedco's newsprint catalogs would seem relics of the 19th century, prices included, if not for the witty advertising copy, hilarious asides, and sight-gag illustrations taken from old garden catalogs. We deeply suspect founder C.R. Lawn, a trained lawyer rejoicing in the occupation of farmer, of indulging a weakness for sick puns during catalog season.

The *Fedco Seeds* catalog is a conflation of several mail-order catagories into a single mailing: Fedco Seeds, Moose Tubers, and Organic Growers Supply. The Fedco Seeds section offers vegetable and flower seeds selected for proven performance in cold-climate gardening (Zone 4). A special focus is on the heirloom seed program, whereby Fedco cooperates with Maine farmers to grow regional seeds such as dried beans and heirloom vegetables rarely offered by commercial growers. All seed is untreated, and absolutely no transgenic cultivars are offered. As to variety, "lettuce" (let us) point to excellent bean cultivars, "amaizing" corn, tomatoes, greens, and other classic garden vegetables—open-pollinated and heirloom, some good for home gardeners, others for truck farmers. The list includes flower seeds for "fancy annuals and perennials," mostly old-fashioned cottage garden plants. We like knowing where to find a 300-year-old sweet pea, heirloom black hollyhocks from Maine, and a neglected double impatiens from the Victorian era. The Moose Tubers section of the catalog offers certified seed potatoes, onion sets, sunchokes, and sweet potatoes, complete with handling instructions and quotations from Shakespeare. The Organic Growers Supply section offers cover crops, organic fertilizers, organic pest controls, books, tools, and garden supplies. Among the last, our favorite is the Flame Weeder, useful for immolating weed seedlings, "burning out webworms, and singeing the tops of meringues and crèmes brûlées."

The *Fedco Trees* catalog is a descendant of its tree catalog, originally for fruit, nut, and shade trees, now expanded to include ornamental trees, flowering shrubs, small fruits, bulbs, medicinal herbs, and perennial plant crowns. Since 1978, Fedco has been an admirable source of inexpensive hardy fruit trees, especially apples, flowering crabs, pears, and stone fruits. Fedco's continuing search for old Maine apple varieties has turned up 15 Maine heirlooms; the most notable, called 'Starkey', was grafted from the last Starkey apple tree in Vassalboro, where the variety was discovered some 200 years ago. All Maine apples are being planted in an orchard in Unity, at the headquarters of the Maine Organic Farmers and Gardeners Association (MOFGA), an organization allied closely with Fedco in origin and philosophy.

Another heirloom available for the first time in decades is the American chestnut, once the most prominent deciduous tree in the eastern United States; Fedco's seedlings are made available through the American Chestnut Foundation, which is working to restore the tree. (The seedlings are blight-susceptible, but, according to Fedco, "will probably thrive if there is no blight infection within a mile.") The *Fedco Trees* catalog also offers cold-tolerant berries, grapes, and hops; roses and lilacs; underutilized fruiting shrubs such as elderberry, Allegheny serviceberry, and cornelian cherry; herbaceous perennials (including Japanese tree peonies); medicinal herbs used in traditional and Chinese medicine; and a few tender summer bulbs such as tuberous begonia and gladiolus. All trees come bare-root; plants may be mail-ordered or picked up at Fedco's annual tree sale in Clinton, Maine, in early May.

Fedco catalogs comprise some of the best reading material available to armchair gardeners with a taste for madcap humor. While *Fedco Trees* is slightly more sober reading than *Fedco Seeds,* both are full of visual puns and amusing literary gags. Among the seed descriptions alone, we noted antic references to *Jurassic Park,* the Russian space program, chess, Marvel Comics, Balkan politics, Johnny Most, and *Alice in Wonderland. Fedco Seeds* almost certainly has the craziest ordering system on earth. The catalog tells customers how to order, how not to order, and the right day of the week to order, depending on where you live. Order deadlines, like edicts from the Red Queen, are at once confusing and strict. Group seed purchasers can use Fedco's "7% solution," which provides individual packaging of component orders for 7 percent of the purchase price. Individual seed orders can be processed on Fedco's Short-Form 1020-EZ, due by mid-March so as not to be mixed up with your federal tax return.

Other than the tree sale, a gardener's only opportunity to meet Fedco's endearing gaggle of eccentrics is to attend MOFGA's Common Ground Fair, held annually in Unity, Maine, in early autumn.

Directions: Fedco is essentially a co-op warehouse staffed by farmers using a temperamental fax machine. Call for directions to the tree sale, held in early May.

FERNWOOD

RR 3, P.O. Box 928, Cross Road, Swanville, ME 04915
(207) 338-4100
Rick and Gail Sawyer

Uncommon perennials for shade and woodland. Native plants. Ferns. Hosta.
Small specialty nursery. Open May and June, daily 9-5; closed Mondays July through September. No catalog or mail order. Display gardens. Group tours by appointment. Quantity discounts. Lectures. E-mail: fernwood@acadia.net

Fernwood is a small collector's nursery just off the northern Maine coast, where owners Rick and Gail Sawyer have developed one of New England's largest collections of unusual perennials and shade-tolerant woodland plants. Rick Sawyer, recently retired as a UPS deliveryman, is actually a talented horticulturist who apprenticed for seven years at Weir Meadow Nursery in Wayland, Massachusetts, an eminent wholesale grower of shade plants.

The Sawyers opened Fernwood in 1991, after transforming a woodland clearing next to their home into a showcase for unusual perennials and wild-flowers. The nursery arrangement is similar to that used by their friend Leo Blanchette (MA): Rows of container-grown plants are set on black plastic, shade-loving plants on one side, sun perennials on the other. Most plants are propagated at the nursery and hardened off by spending the winter outside; if a Fernwood plant cannot survive without being "staked, deadheaded, pruned, or mulched in winter," the Sawyers refuse to grow it.

We were impressed by the sheer lushness of the nursery stock: Using attentive growing practices and chemical-free composted soil, Fernwood produces some of the most luxuriant container plants we have seen in any nursery. Savvy gardeners come from afar to secure them, for the collection is superb and, despite Rick Sawyer's credentials as a UPS driver, no mail order is available. The Sawyers once tried doing mail order, but gave up, they say, due to exhaustion. They now keep the nursery small and quiet "in order to stay sane."

As its name suggests, Fernwood's glory lies in its woodland plant collection, which features many choice shade perennials and native wildflowers that are virtually impossible to find in commercial cultivation. Fernwood has a genius for growing woodland plants with unusual foliage variations, such as mottled wild ginger, fragrant variegated Solomon's seal, and speckled and hairy toad lilies (*Tricyrtis* spp.). Its rich collection of more than 300 hosta varieties includes original hybrids created by Rick Sawyer, who has given them droll names such as 'Margarita' (with salt-edged foliage) and 'Tractor Seat' (its immense, substantial leaves look just like huge tractor seats). The hosta are best appreciated in maturity, where they dominate the display gardens.

Fernwood has also introduced several unique wildflower hybrids, such as the rare double white anemonella 'snowflake' and a choice lily of the valley, solid-gold, called 'Golden Slippers.' For native groundcover, gardeners can choose among twinflower, bunchberry, Oconee-bells, wintergreen, barren strawberry, and uncommon native grasses, rushes, sedges, and ferns. We also found delicate white Bowman's-root, bird-foot violet, yellow lady's slipper, and three rare trilliums, including a stunning double snow trillium (*T. grandiflora* 'Floro Plena'). Other surprising rarities (some not even listed in our 10-pound garden encyclopedia) are a showy rodgersia, some Oriental ligularias, and a plum-colored shooting star (*Dodecatheon* spp.) from eastern Europe. We applaud Fernwood's diverse selection of astilbe and meadow rue (*Thalictrum* spp.), including a western Chinese thalictrum originally botanized by E.H. Wilson for the Arnold Arboretum.

We were so dazzled by Fernwood's woodland plants that we never examined its sun perennials, other than forming a dreamy impression of white asclepias fluttering with monarch butterflies and a backdrop of exotic Japanese grasses. Fernwood's plant collection is not so esoteric that gardeners of all skill levels cannot appreciate its wonders. The nursery easily accommodates novices, connoisseurs, and garden renovators who wish they had come here in the first place. Fernwood is a trendsetter, boasting truthfully of a "new and unusual" plant collection that is ever changing and growing. The Sawyers follow a strict and honorable practice of selling only nursery-propagated native plants; although inevitably more expensive than plants ripped from the wild (according to Fernwood's owner, "anybody selling a trillium for less than seven dollars is not propagating it"), gardeners who buy them will not have to spend time in purgatory for depleting wild plant populations. Fernwood's plant list is unpublished, even though most of its stock is too difficult for commercial growers anyway. Nursery plants are, however, meticulously labeled, as are the sublime shade gardens that thread through Fernwood's quiet woodland setting.

Directions: Swanville is 15 minutes north of Belfast. From coastal Route 1 in Belfast, take Route 141 north. In 5 miles, turn left at the sign, and the nursery is 0.5 mile down a dirt road, on your right.

Nearby attractions: Once redolent of shipping and poultry, Belfast has become an artists' haven with downtown galleries and an excellent organic grocery store. At Young's Lobster Pound, just off Route 1 in East Belfast (207-338-1160), lobsters are "caught, cooked, eaten, and shipped" seven days a week (BYOB). Ducktrap River Fish Farm, Little River Drive, Belfast (207-338-6280; 800-828-3825) sells fresh smoked fish and shellfish, weekdays 8–4:30. The Belfast and Moosehead Railway Company (affectionately known as "The Broken and Mended") runs excursions on vintage locomotives out of an 1870s freight building in Belfast's waterfront rail yard (207-948-5500; 800-392-5500); the train trip to Unity involves a staged holdup by unsavory desperadoes.

FIELDSTONE GARDENS

620 Quaker Lane, Vassalboro, ME 04989-9713
(207) 923-3836 phone and fax
Steven D. Jones

Hardy perennials for sun, shade, and woodland. Nursery stock. *Family-run nursery and tree farm. Open April to mid-November, Tuesday to Sunday 9–5. Catalog $2.50 (free to prior-year purchasers). Mail and phone order. Display gardens and model tree farm. Open house late June. E-mail: info@FieldstoneGardens.com. Web site: www.FieldstoneGardens.com.*

Fieldstone Gardens is a popular perennial plant nursery overlooking an open, rolling, 220-acre family farm that resembles a private estate. Ten miles northeast of Augusta, and arguably the most beautiful nursery in Maine, Fieldstone Gardens is approached by way of a manicured drive flanked with

100-foot fieldstone walls, rich hosta borders, and ancient sugar maples. Farm assets include a magnificent shingled barn, a quaint greenhouse with hand-cut glass, and a blacksmith shop now serving as a garden center.

The resident Jones family is devoted to producing hardy, mature perennials, both field- and container-grown, combining familiar favorites with new and rare varieties. Fieldstone Gardens also operates a tree farm, designated as the 1996 Outstanding Tree Farm in Maine and the Northeast. Among its achievements are a 3-acre woodland pond and a developed sugar bush (maple sugar grove).

Fieldstone Gardens offers more than 1,000 perennials in its mail-order catalog and is unlikely to run out, having 70,000 containers and 10 acres of display and production gardens on hand at the nursery. (The catalog lists plants in high inventory, but more are available at the nursery and on the Web site.) These plants are excellent for cold-climate gardens, grown as they are in Zone 4, not counting the windchill on the hill. An open house is held the last Sunday in June, jokingly considered the end of winter around here.

Fieldstone Gardens offers the full spectrum of garden perennials: handsome shade plants; colorful sun perennials such as campanula, veronica, and poppy; rock garden plants; native woodlanders; and perennial groundcovers such as baneberry, partridgeberry, yellowroot, American cranberry, three kinds of bearberry, and four pachysandras. Many are embellished native plants and updated forms of perennial workhorses, interspersed with some patrician surprises. Fieldstone Gardens has a prodigious hosta collection; extensive peonies and garden phlox; and good assortments of cranesbill geranium, bee balm, daylily, sedum, astilbe, heuchera, lungwort, and (great for fall color) New England and New York asters. Its lily collection includes the prized martagon lilies (with nodding, spotted midsummer flowers) that are often hard to find in nurseries.

Of special interest are the prestigious Siberian iris bred by Maine's Dr. Currier McEwen (see *Eartheart Gardens,* ME) in breakthrough shades of purple, blue, red, white, and yellow. Among the best is McEwen's award-winning 'Butter and Sugar', the first yellow Siberian iris ever propagated. (The nursery also grows some McEwen daylilies hybridized jointly many years ago with Howard Brooks.) Perennial vines include a noninvasive porcelainberry; the beautiful, shade-tolerant Japanese hydrangea vine *(Schizophragma hydrangeoides);* and a number of handsome, well-priced clematis. Fieldstone Gardens grows charming native and Asian woodland plants, such as trillium, tricyrtis, trout lily, cut-leaf violet, five kinds of Solomon's seal, five rodgersias, and, for wet sites, double marsh marigold and bog rosemary. Sold only at the nursery are a handful of specimen trees such as littleleaf lilac standards and yellow magnolias.

The Jones family are intelligent, energetic plantsmen who propagate and grow more than 90 percent of their huge perennial stock. Steve Jones, a University of Maine alumnus, has been in the family business over 15 years, gradually taking the reins in the way of sons on family farms (the man has never had a vacation). He is a horticultural perfectionist who rises at 2 A.M. in winter to stoke the woodstove in the greenhouse, and at dawn in summer to keep the farm's appearance "crisp and prominent."

Most of Fieldstone Gardens' business is mail order, but nursery visitors have greater plant choices and the fun of perusing the farm's production beds and selecting their own field-dug or container plants. (Field-digging provides a rich shovelful of plant material, excellent if you can transplant quickly; mail-order plants are well-priced, 2-year-old perennials packaged and shipped the same day.) Fieldstone Gardens practices good plant citizenship; none of its native woodland plants is dug from the wild. Lush, well-composted display gardens feature exotic perennial borders, verdant shade gardens, wildflower beds, and specimen trees, shrubs, and orchards. Garden tourists will applaud the immense turf-cut signature mowed into the hayfield, JONES TREE FARM, referencing the Jones family's groomed forest of red and white pines, visible at the edge of the fields.

Directions: From I-95 in Augusta, take exit 30/Route 202 east. In 4 miles, at a traffic circle, continue on Route 202 east across the Kennebec River At the second rotary, take Route 201 north. In 10 miles, turn right at the FIELDSTONE GARDENS sign onto Bog Road. In 3 miles, take the second right onto Cross Hill Road. In 1 mile, turn left onto Quaker Lane, and follow straight to the nursery.
From Waterville, take Route 201 south 8 miles to the Waterville/Winslow bridge, turn left at the sign onto Bog Road, and follow the directions above.

FOX HILL NURSERY

347 Lunt Road, Freeport, ME 04032
(207) 729-1511; fax (207) 729-6108
Eric Welzel

Field-grown lilacs. Own-root roses. Shrubs. *Small specialty nursery. Open April 1 to November 15, daily 9–5; call ahead. Catalog $1. Mail order. Peak bloom late May to early June. E-mail: foxhill@javanet.com. Web site: www.lilacs.com.*

Fox Hill is a 28-acre nursery specializing in hardy field-grown lilacs and roses grown on their own roots, a technique that ensures against viral disease and is thought to produce a healthier plant. Owner Eric Welzel began working in nurseries at the age of 14, trained at Weston Nurseries (MA), and opened Fox Hill in 1988 on a tract of fields and woods north of Freeport. After deer decimated his initial plantation of trees and shrubs, he and his family enclosed 10 acres with electric fencing and decided to specialize in deer-resistant lilacs and roses.

Welzel wants to be a "lilac king," and Fox Hill is now the largest lilac retailer in New England. The nursery grows thousands of plants in more than 90 varieties, from heirlooms to modern hybrids; all are trial-tested before being offered to customers. Many of the nursery's lilacs are on the Arnold Arboretum's top-50 list of best cultivars.

Fox Hill occupies the site of an old Quaker farm whose century-old drainage system still keeps the fields loamy and well drained, even in soggy weather. Visitors to the nursery should be sure to climb its Sabbath Hill, a peaceful site with a view over the valley, where local Quakers still assemble at dawn on Easter morning.

We have always found it somewhat shocking that lilacs, those nostalgic guardians of dooryards throughout America, should have originated in Europe, Asia, and the mountains of Persia. Like other American immigrants, lilacs have changed greatly from the simple pair that arrived here three centuries ago. Extensively hybridized, both here and abroad, modern lilacs offer wonderful color range and foliage variation. Fox Hill still grows the original "old farm lilac" and several related antique lilacs, including 'Governor Wentworth', rescued from an abandoned cellar hole in New Hampshire. Many showy 19th- and 20th-century lilac hybrids are also offered: singles, doubles, purples, lavenders, pinks, whites, and bicolors.

We saw some gorgeous white and cream lilacs at Fox Hill (especially 'Avalanche', a pure white bred by a Roman Catholic priest named Father Fiala), and the only pale yellow lilac, ambitiously named 'Primrose'. Among the blue lilacs, we have always loved the classic 'President Lincoln', but Fox Hill also grows a sky blue ('Wonder Blue'), a clear blue ('Blue Danube'), and a Wedgwood blue ('Wedgwood Blue'). Although, thank heavens, no black lilac yet exists, Fox Hill does grow a very dark purple.

Popular varieties are grown alongside others that are little known and hard to find in cultivation. Fox Hill's collection includes French and American hybrids and lesser-known lilacs from Russia, Germany, and Asia. The Russian lilacs turn out to be real knockouts, with huge, fragrant flower panicles. Fox Hill's Preston hybrids (pink lilacs developed by a Miss Preston of Ottawa, Canada) are excellent season extenders, blooming a couple of weeks later than ordinary lilacs. Some unusual lilacs come with hyacinth blossoms, variegated foliage, oval rather than heart-shaped leaves, and red-tipped foliage. Fox Hill even offers heat-tolerant lilacs that can be grown in the South; we once sent 'Excel' to a friend in Washington, D.C., who suffered nostalgia for New England. Fox Hill also grows a Japanese tree lilac, which is really a small tree reaching 25 feet, and our personal favorite, the littleleaf lilac (*Syringa microphylla*, first imported in the 1930s by the Arnold Arboretum in Boston), which has tiny pink panicles and can be sheared into a hedge.

Fox Hill also grows lovely hardy roses that combine romantically with its lilacs. Welzel emphasizes that Fox Hill is "a nursery, not a 'rose company'," and the distinction is a good one, for its roses are all field-grown from cuttings, winter-tested, and utterly fresh. Fox Hill's rose collection includes rugosas, heirlooms, ultra-hardy Morden and Canadian Explorer hybrids, and other tough, decorative roses of great landscape value—more than 30 varieties in all. The nursery also offers a smattering of field-grown azaleas, small-leaf rhododendrons, hydrangeas, and blueberries. Fox Hill sells many of its lilacs as gifts commemorating milestone anniversaries, new babies (pink for a girl, blue for a boy), and of course, weddings. We hear of an old American tradition, dating to pioneer days, of providing newlyweds with a sack of white flour, a spinning wheel, and a lilac bush.

A display garden of unusual lilacs borders the parking area. Interested gardeners should visit the nursery when the lilacs are abloom in late May and early June, not just for the color, but for the perfume.

Directions: Fox Hill is on the edge of Freeport, almost in Brunswick. From I-95, take exit 20; coming from the south, turn right at the ramp, and coming from the north, turn left. Turn right at the YIELD sign onto Route 136. In 0.5 mile, turn right onto Route 125. In 4 miles, turn right at the red general store (decent sandwiches) onto Lunt Road; the nursery is 0.5 mile on your right.

Nearby attractions: Downtown Freeport is New England's fashion outlet mecca, centered on the L.L. Bean outlet (800-341-4341), open 24 hours a day, 365 days a year, for sporting goods and gumboots. Kitschy local tourist traps dating to the 1930s include the 40-foot Big Indian statue (1 mile north of exit 17/Route I-95) and the privately owned Desert of Maine, whose 200 acres of blowing, shifting glacial sands have overwhelmed several large trees and a small Depression-era building just off exit 19/Route I-95. For relief, visit Wolfe's Neck Farm and Gardens, Wolfe Neck Road, Freeport (207-865-3428), an alternative working farm pioneering ecologically sound methods of raising beef and vegetables on 600 acres overlooking Casco Bay.

GINGERBREAD FARM PERENNIALS

RR 1, P.O. Box 3590, 3590 Old Winthrop Road, Wayne, ME 04284
(207) 685-4050
Charles and Anna Cushman

Perennials. Container plants. Daylilies, hostas, and peonies. Roses and lilacs.
Open May 1 to Labor Day, daily 9–6, and September by appointment or chance. Free catalog. No mail order. Open house mid-May. Display gardens. Sculpture gallery. E-mail: gblack1503@aol.com. Web site: http://hometown.aol.com/gblack1503.

Gingerbread Farm, a charming, small-scale nursery just west of Augusta, offers a diverse assortment of hardy perennial plants suitable for Maine gardens. Owner Charles Cushman is a retired English teacher who still enjoys literature as much as gardening; we once saw him reading poetry under a shade tree when we came shopping for plants. Since 1979, Cushman has operated Gingerbread Farm with his wife, Anna, out of a former cornfield next to their 1820 gingerbread Gothic cottage.

The Cushmans are intelligent plant enthusiasts who offer more than 1,000 kinds of perennials, either grown in Gingerbread Farm's fields and greenhouses or brought in from select growers. Thousands of plants are dug each year from the farm's half-acre of growing beds. Besides perennials, Gingerbread Farm carries uncommon herbs and annuals; roses and lilacs; and wonderful moss baskets and English container gardens. Planted cemetery baskets and pillows are available for Memorial Day. Gardeners can use the farm's potting facilities or have pots and containers planted for them; just call ahead and bring your containers along to the farm.

Gingerbread Farm's plant selection reflects the owners' interest in distinctive ornamental plants, often selected for unusual foliage and season-extending habit. The farm has an excellent assembly of hostas, daylilies, peonies, phlox, shade plants, and garden perennials not commonly sold by commercial growers. Its hosta and daylily lists alone take up 16 pages of catalog space, combining new hybrids with known favorites. Peonies include herbaceous peonies, Japanese singles, and one-year tree peonies from Japan. The diverse phlox group offers new, fragrant, and mildew-repellent 'Spring Pearl' hybrids and an excellent blue stoloniferous phlox, the very delight of light shade. There are good blue gentians and some excellent clematis (we like the wilt-resistant, small-flowered varieties and the large-flowered blue ones that need no pruning). Gingerbread Farm's less common shade perennials include variegated brunnera, Chinese rodgersia, double bloodroot, rue anemone, 'Hot Lips' turtlehead, Japanese butterbur, woodland plants such as silver Jacob's ladder and variegated Solomon seal, and lots of good foamflower, lungwort, and astilbe hybrids.

Gingerbread Farm keeps track of European plant awards (why isn't this done more?) and offers a red-stemmed purple euphorbia and a purple pasqueflower that won prizes in Europe. Groundcovers include epimedium and tough little *Mazus reptans,* which can be walked upon. Any number of potted herbs are for sale, along with nice lilacs and ultra-hardy Canadian Explorer shrub roses. All plants are vigorous and reasonably priced. The Gardener's Gallery, located in a wooden shed, offers whimsical tool sculptures, gifts, and pottery by Maine artists.

The Cushmans are our kind of gardeners: They garden for pleasure, take time to enjoy their own yard, and on vacation travel around to visit other people's gardens. For all the huffing and puffing of running a nursery, the Cushmans make it look amusing and fun.

Gingerbread Farm is a bit out of the way, but it welcomes travelers and encourages visitors to feel like guests. Rustic seats and picnic tables, shade gardens under pine trees, herb and cottage beds, pretty container displays, and kooky outdoor sculptures are all provided for public enjoyment. Customers are even urged to spend time in active amusement at Gingerbread Farm: "Pack a lunch, view the gardens, take a walk through the woods to Wilson Pond, play croquet, throw horseshoes, try out Greg's Putting Green, or talk to the cows in the pasture across the road." Artistic souls are encouraged to bring their camera or water-colors, for Gingerbread Farm has the magical look of a Hansel and Gretel cottage, picturesquely surrounded by old sugar maples.

Directions: From Augusta or Lewiston, take Route 202 to Winthrop and pick up Route 133 west. Take the first right after Berry Pond (the only pond on the left after leaving Winthrop) onto Fairbanks Road, then turn right at the cemetery onto Old Winthrop Road. The nursery is on your left.

Nearby attractions: Gardeners who forget to pack a picnic can buy sandwiches at the Wayne General Store (207-685-3818) by the mill pond in Wayne village. Stevenson's Strawberries, located at Berry and Tucker Roads in Wayne (207-685-3532), has pick-your-own berries, peas, and corn in season.

Hedgehog Hill Farm

54 Hedgehog Hill Road, East Sumner, ME 04292
(207) 388-2341
Mark and Terry Silber

Organically grown perennials, annuals, and herbs. Everlastings. Eucalyptus. Small fruits. Vegetable seedlings. *Small organic flower farm and nursery. Open March through December, daily 9–5. Plant catalog $2. No mail order for live plants. Mail order available for dried flowers and herbal products. Display gardens. Herb and everlasting shop. Reference library. Spring Fair in early May. Lectures, tours, and workshops. Fresh-cut flowers by arrangement. E-mail: gardens@hedgehoghillfarm.com Web site: www.hedgehoghillfarm.com.*

Hedgehog Hill Farm is a small, certified organic flower farm and nursery, situated in a pleasantly rural town in south central Maine. The nursery was founded in the 1970s by Mark and Terry Silber, onetime Boston artists (he was born in Warsaw, she is a Maine native) who moved to Hedgehog Hill Farm to become gardeners, writers, and educators. Their transition from city to country, from amateur gardening to professional farming, was recounted in Terry Silber's evocative book, *A Small Farm in Maine.* The Silbers' experience in raising everlasting flowers for use in dried wreaths and arrangements prompted their next book, *The Complete Book of Everlastings*. Growing more than 500 plants from seed each spring led to their latest book, *Growing Herbs and Vegetables from Seed to Harvest.*

During the growing season, farm visitors may purchase organically-grown nursery plants, inspect the herb shop, tour the farm's rich gardens and production fields, attend Sunday lectures and workshops, and take a lovely walk through the surrounding woodland. In spring and summer, able-bodied gardeners are invited to volunteer for Hedgehog Hill's scheduled barter crews, exchanging a day's work for a number of plants. According to the owners, "You'll get unbelievably dirty, possibly a little cold, or perhaps too warm (depending on the weather), and you'll definitely be exhausted at the end of a day ... On the other hand, you'll learn lots about a wide variety of plants ... participate in mixing potting soils, digging and dividing perennials, pruning, potting ... constructing temporary greenhouses, poly tunnels, and cold frames ... and work side by side with long-time members of the staff who will be available to answer gardening questions." Alumni reports are enthusiastic.

Besides functioning as a teaching center and source for dried flower and herb products, Hedgehog Hill Farm is a nursery. Each year the farm produces a colorful assortment of healthy, greenhouse-propagated seedlings and field-grown plants, all raised organically (a rare and difficult achievement in a greenhouse). Plants and flats can be ordered for reserved pickup at the farm in May; all are well priced, and early orders earn a significant discount.

Hedgehog Hill publishes an appealing annual plant catalog (alas, no mail order of live plants). First among its spring offerings are flowering annuals, in which old-fashioned favorites, such as sweet peas and petunias, are mixed with such novelties as tall red ageratum, Japanese thistle, and bronze sunflowers. Perennial gardeners will warm to the farm's inexpensive spring flats of yarrow and columbine, campanula and Shasta daisy, foxglove and delphinium. Nicely potted, field-grown perennials include beguiling collections of daylily, hosta, iris, lily, cranesbill geranium, and native fern. Everlastings (perennials whose flowers are used in dried arrangements) are the farm's stock in trade, and the selection is wonderful: bright-colored statice, cobalt larkspur, red and yellow wheat celosia, rouge chenille love-lies-bleeding, and exotic everlastings with unfamiliar names such as acroclinium (fragrant and daisylike) and ammobium (small winged white flowers on 3-foot stems).

Hedgehog Hill experiments with "fragrant Eucalypts" and offers several to fellow enthusiasts; by following its fumigant perfume to the source, we identified an Australian eucalyptus tree growing outside the shop door. Intriguing field-grown herbs include showy ornamentals such as agastache, society garlic, anise hyssop, and dame's rocket (like a wild phlox); good culinary herbs such as chives, sorrel, and "spicy green Welsh onions"; perfume herbs such as patchouli and sweet grass (used as incense by the American Indians); and useful medicinals such as elecampane and blues-defying St.-John's-wort. We especially liked the nursery's many scented geraniums, rosemaries, thymes, and fruit-scented mints, including a sweet-tart mint called 'Hillary's Sweet Lemon', aptly named for first lady Hillary Clinton.

Hedgehog Hill recommends a number of culinary herbs for the winter windowsill, so useful to snowbound cooks. Vegetable seedlings, selected for home growing in northern gardens, combine the usual suspects with stylish varieties (not easily found in spring flats) such as showy hot Japanese peppers, Italian radicchio, and heirloom Brandywine tomatoes. Also screened for northern garden performance are hardy small fruits such as raspberry, blueberry, grape, elderberry, and highbush cranberry. In response to customer demand, the farm now grows a few "shrubberies" such as winterberry, native buttonbush, weigela, and lilacs.

Hedgehog Hill's nursery plants are found—living or dried—in the farm's twin activity centers, the organic production fields and the herb and everlasting shop. These balanced centers of gravity achieve an almost ideal order and beauty that make the arduous effort of subsistence farming seem like artists' ground: a virtuoso performance seldom achieved on small New England farms.

Outdoors at Hedgehog Hill, thumping fertile soil and thriving production beds testify to the Silbers' skill in organic agriculture. Flowering plants and herbs grow in a long furrowed field extending from the herb house to a distant stone wall and trees, a living example of the lyrical landscape natural to working farms in Maine. Indoors, a Shaker-style herb and everlasting shop, filled to the rafters with air-drying bouquets, offers elegant wreaths and herbal products handcrafted from plants harvested from the farm, also sold by mail order; we especially loved the interesting herb jellies and crates of beautiful dried flowers.

Gardeners of all levels are invited to Hedgehog Hill both to enjoy and educate themselves; a little reference library, reminiscent of the small-town libraries scattered across New England, is open to visitors.

In addition to excellent lectures and workshops aimed at promoting organic growing practices for the home gardener, Hedgehog Hill Farm publishes a delightful newsletter. We clipped the following spring greeting, a well-wishing to gardeners to which we say Amen: "A new season, a new canvas, and the pleasure of setting out thousands of plants begins again. Let's hope that all of our gardens are successful, that the rains come often, gently and mainly during the nighttime. Let's hope for a brief blackfly season, a long growing season, and hours and hours of pleasurable gardening."

Directions: From I-95, take exit 30 in Augusta and follow Route 202 west to Winthrop, Route 133 west to Wayne, and Route 219 west to East Sumner. Follow the signs left onto Bonney Road for 3 miles, then turn left onto Hedgehog Hill Road; the nursery is at the end of the road.
From the Maine Turnpike/Route 495, take exit 12 in Auburn, Route 4 north to Turner, Route 117 south to Buckfield, and follow signs by the bridge and church to the farm.

Nearby attractions: Thrifty gardeners can find spartan but atmospheric accommodation at the international hostel in South Hiram, an 18th-century farmhouse run by a diverting old-timer (207-625-7509), for $12 a night. Those interested in heirloom livestock breeds should visit Kelmscott Farm in Lincolnville (207-763-4088; www.kelmscott.org), a nonprofit foundation with more than 150 farm animals and 30 breeds of rare and endangered livestock, including heirloom poultry, rare ponies, Cotswold sheep, and Gloucestershire Old Spots pigs; open daily except Monday.

Hidden Gardens

96 Seekins Road, Searsport, ME 04974
(207) 548-2864
Carla Brown

Hardy, field-grown perennials. Small organic specialty nursery. Open late April to mid-September, daily 9–5. In September, call ahead. Free plant list and map. No mail order. Display beds. Visitors welcome.

Just off the coast of northern Maine, Hidden Gardens is a treasure trove of field-grown perennial plants suitable for northern gardens. Owner Carla Brown is an accomplished nurserywoman who founded Hidden Gardens in 1979 and now grows more than 1,300 varieties of perennials on nearly an acre of beds adjacent to her country home. The nursery's impressive plant list, always on the increase, includes many unusual perennials of an ornamental standard seldom achieved in cold-climate gardens.

Hidden Gardens refuses to carry marginally hardy plants (such as Russian sage and basket-of-gold) that do not overwinter well in northern New England. All perennials undergo field trials in composted, unmulched, pesticide-free nursery beds, and only if they flourish will the nursery propagate them. This refining process not only produces durable ornamentals hardy to Zone 4, but also deepens Brown's expertise in the culture, habits, and hardiness of each plant offered at the nursery.

Hidden Gardens digs and pots thousands of perennials every year, most sold in gallon containers at very reasonable prices. As a wholesome country bonus, an earthworm resides in every pot, in lieu of chemical fertilizer.

Hidden Gardens is a find for the discerning gardener. The nursery grows more than 30 astilbes, including uncommon bronze-leaved varieties; 28 peonies, both single and double; 10 old-fashioned columbines; 11 unusually hardy delphiniums; 16 Canterbury bells (campanula); six blue gentians; and seven monkshoods. Those with small gardens will relish the many dwarf versions of these plants.

Hidden Gardens has a capacious daylily collection, backed by color photographs and a complete daylily list for reference at the nursery. Also growing here are many classic hostas, Siberian iris, Oriental poppies, Asiatic lilies, ornamental onions, sedums, veronicas, cranesbill, and phlox. Rarities include a greenish-yellow Japanese poppy; red-eyed white violet; pink lily of the valley; yellow monkshood; and a pure white violet that blooms all summer.

Hidden Gardens is one of those magical, green-fingered nurseries where new cultivars appear as unannounced sports (offshoots with unusual traits) of established plants. Here gardeners savoring novelty can find a new, variegated sedum (a sport of 'Autumn Joy'), a new, reddish lungwort (pulmonaria), and an old, tough delphinium grown by Carla Brown's grandfather, a potato farmer in Caribou. Available nowhere else, this long-lived cobalt blue delphinium is both damp-proof and mildew-resistant. Hidden Gardens' unusual foliage plants include variegated rock cress, a superior lady's mantle called 'Thriller', and a dwarf alpine potentilla with silver foliage.

For those who enjoy horticultural puns, Hidden Gardens grows a number of uncommon perennials that resemble beloved garden plants: pink, primrose-like *Cortusa mattheoli;* pink, hollyhock-like sidalcea; pale yellow, scabiosa-like *Cephalaria leucantha;* blue, asterlike erigeron 'Blue Beauty'; and lavender, bell-like *Codonopsis cardiophylla.* Our Aunt Jean, an accomplished gardener with a good eye, zeroed in on Hidden Gardens' interesting alpine and rock garden collection, and promptly bought a fragrant pink alpine silene that has since colonized her gravel driveway.

Although most of Hidden Gardens' selection is of garden perennials, it also carries hardy woodland plants such as meadow geranium, wild lupine, wild columbine, and white wood anemone; some interesting shrubs, such as flowering raspberry; and a few roses and lilacs.

While not far from Route 1, the aptly named Hidden Gardens would be tricky to find without its helpful yellow directional signs, until recently banned by bureaucrats in the state highway department. Do not be deterred from seeking out this secluded treasure for cold-climate gardeners. The nursery's field-grown plants give excellent value and grow reliably in the garden. Visitors are welcome to stroll Hidden Gardens' colorful growing beds, small rustic lily pond, and raised alpine garden, surrounded by open fields grazed by sheep and other pet farm animals. Off-season, Brown and her husband are ballroom dancers who teach the waltz, jitterbug, fox-trot, rumba, two-step, lindy, and tango in Belfast; gardeners with rhythm are welcome to join them during the winter months.

Directions: Searsport is on the northern Maine coast at the mouth of the Penobscot River. From Route 1 in downtown Searsport, drive west on Mt. Ephraim Road. In 3.8 miles, turn right onto Bog Hill Road, which becomes Seekins Road, and the nursery driveway is signposted on your right.

Nearby attractions: From mid-April through October, frugal gardeners can stay overnight for $18 at the Penobscot Bay International Hostel (207-548-2506), in the Captain Butman Homestead on Route 1. The Penobscot Marine Museum in Searsport (207-548-2529) has a fine collection of marine paintings, China trade table- and lacquer-ware, and rare photographs of a Portland bark's voyage to Argentina in 1902.

HILL GARDENS

P.O. Box 39, 107 Route 3, Palermo, ME 04354
(207) 993-2956; fax (207) 993-2246
Fred Davis

Hostas and daylilies. Small specialty nursery. Display gardens. Clinics and demonstrations. Fresh compost. Garden book and disk. E-mail: hillgdns@lack.net. Web site: www.hillgardens.com. [Retail operations discontinued in 2001.]

Founded in 1987, Hill Gardens is a small organic nursery intent on facing down the odds, if any, of growing hostas and daylilies hardy to Zone 4 in rural Maine. These ubiquitous garden plants, native to Asia, have been extensively hybridized and improved in recent years, and have caught the attention of many New England gardeners. Hill Gardens is owned and operated, in the words of the owner, by "Nurseryman/Author Fred Davis and his long-suffering and infinitely patient wife Linda." Fred Davis, who opened his first Hill Gardens Nursery as a teenager in California, received a degree in ornamental horticulture from Cal Tech Poly and, as he puts it, "wasted 20 years in the Navy" before opening the present Hill Gardens Nursery.

Armed with only a garden fork, lime, and a powerful heap of compost, Davis grows all his own nursery stock in a woodland garden wrested from the roadside brush in central Maine, 17 miles east of Augusta. An accomplished organic gardener and passionate opponent of horticultural chemicals, Davis is leading the charge against the chemical industry, and writes an instructive gardening column for several Maine newspapers. His published book, *Ten Steps Through the Garden Gate,* presents "plain talk about gardening" designed to blow the socks off any benighted gardener who even thinks of reaching for Roundup or Miracle-Gro. Readers should prepare themselves for what Davis calls "a hard-hitting, straight talking and revealing look into what it *really* takes to be successful in the flower and vegetable garden," undiluted by "unjustified 'fluff' and sleepy-time entertainment."

Visitors to Hill Gardens Nursery can see for themselves the results of Davis's zeal. The nursery's propagation beds have the rich, fudgy look of exceptional garden soil, and the thriving assemblages of hosta and daylily have excellent substance and seem almost edible, like vegetables. (We assume the garden is wired against deer.) The plants are tough, too; the nursery stock spends one full winter outside, without mulch or cover, before being offered to customers.

Hill Gardens grows some 300 kinds of daylily and 170 hostas, including some of the best new hybrids. The hosta flock, which seems to be gaining on the daylilies, has all the waffled, wavy, crinkled, corrugated, blue, gold, creamy, smeared, streaked, and edged varieties a person could wish for. Hill Gardens' own 1996 introduction, a large, satiny, forest green hosta called 'Shimmering Silk', holds its own against big-name stalwarts such as 'Abba Dabba Do', 'Abiqua Drinking Gourd', 'Spilt Milk', and the 1999 Hosta of the Year, 'Paul's Glory'. (We still love *Hosta sieboldiana* 'Elegans', a lovely blue-green classic offered here for a modest price.) The daylilies are equally diverse, spanning the color wheel and offering some fine choices, old and new. To help off-season selection, a looseleaf photo album shows each named daylily hybrid in bloom.

Daylilies and hostas can be ordered by mail from Hill Gardens' catalog, or purchased, freshly dug, at the nursery. Hill Gardens also grows a smattering of complementary perennials for northern gardens, augmented, in early spring, with annuals, vegetables, baskets, and planters.

Hill Gardens' 2-acre grounds comprise a series of "walkabout idea gardens" in a parklike setting under a canopy of native trees. These display gardens are a work in progress: They begin with propagation beds and a small pond, but are intended to include a much grander pond and a linked rockery/waterfall/stream (under construction). Davis is nearly always on hand to provide horticultural advice, and offers periodic classes on his favorite subjects: hostas, daylilies, and 21-Day No-Turn Composting. In back of the gardens, Mr. Davis (a fully credentialed Master Composter) keeps a mountain of "black gold," a clean, wood-based compost fresh from a stud mill in northern Maine. This excellent stuff can be purchased by the yard, the 30-gallon trash bag, or the 5-gallon pail. (Bring your own container; the nursery provides shovels.) We once put a pail of this compost into our urban window box and, feeling like a character in *Jack and the Beanstalk,* watched the purple runner bean soar to heaven.

[Although Hill Gardens closed its retail operations in 2001, Davis continues to offer interesting hands-on horticultural advice through his web site.]

Directions: From Augusta, take Route 3 east (toward the coast) for 17 miles. The nursery is on your right (signposted), 1 mile past Tobey's General Store and halfway up a hill. Alternatively, from Belfast, take Route 3 west for 27 miles. The nursery is on your left, 0.8 mile past the Palermo Consolidated School.

Nearby attractions: The 224-acre nonprofit Pine Tree State Arboretum, 15 Hospital Street/Route 9, Augusta, ME 04333 (207-623-2371; www.wtvl.net/arbor/), has 5 miles of hiking trails and a fascinating series of "outdoor classrooms" on Maine forests.

Johnny's Selected Seeds

RR 1, P.O. Box 2580, Foss Hill Road, Albion, ME 04910-9731
(207) 437-4301; fax (800) 437-4290
Rob Johnston Jr.

Seeds for vegetables, flowers, herbs, and farm gardens. Spring vegetable flats.
Independent seed house, certified organic. Business hours January to May, Monday to
Friday 8–7, Saturday 8–5; June through December, Monday to Friday 8:30–5. Fax
24 hours. Free catalog. Fax, internet, and mail order. Retail store open year round,
Monday to Saturday 8:30–5. Visitors welcome. AAS trial and display gardens.
Workshops and farm tours. Vegetable flats in May. E-mail:
homegarden@johnnyseeds.com. Web site: www.johnnyseeds.com.

Like anything grown from seed, Johnny's Selected Seeds, according to its
owner, "had the smallest of beginnings." An independent Maine seed house
that functions as the L.L. Bean of vegetable gardening, Johnny's Selected
Seeds, named for Johnny Appleseed, was started from scratch in 1973 by Rob
Johnston Jr., a native of suburban Massachusetts whose grandfather liked to
take him out on summer nights to, as he puts it, "listen to the corn grow." In
college, Johnston helped found a successful counterculture food cooperative
in Amherst, Massachusetts, and engaged in communal truck farming in New
Hampshire before starting a small import operation to
secure hard-to-find Oriental vegetable seed. Johnny's
Selected Seeds has since prospered into an excellent
organic source for more than 4,000 varieties of field-
tested vegetable, herb, flower, and farm seeds.

   Johnny's operates out of a 25-acre farm in Albion,
a central Maine agricultural community east of
Waterville (population: 1,500), where it does just
about everything that can be done with seed for 100,000 customers:
researching, testing, importing, producing, storing, packaging, selling, and, in
some cases, giving it away. The seed is guaranteed to be of high quality, and,
as far as possible, organically grown and chemical-free. Johnny's is not only a
seed purveyor, but also a certified 40-acre organic farm that, in an almost-
unheard-of throwback to 19th-century agricultural practice, actually
produces some of its own seed (especially beans, melons, corn, cucumbers,
peppers, tomatoes, squash, beets, and rutabagas). Founder Johnston continues
to function as plant breeder, director of research and production, and
chairman of the board, in addition to such outside titles as president of the
Maine Organic Farming and Gardening Association (MOFGA), listed
member of the Seed Savers Exchange, and, since 1982, official Vegetable

Judge for All-America Selections (AAS), which determines the year's best new seed varieties.

Doing descriptive justice to Johnny's vast seed list would be an exhausting undertaking; instead, we recommend readers to seek out Johnny's free, illustrated, no-nonsense catalog, which doubles as a sourcebook for gardeners and an energizing tonic against the winter blahs. Notable among its vegetable seeds are Johnston's top-10 favorites, which include frost-tolerant red romaine lettuce, 'All Yellow' Swiss chard, bicolor summer squash, 'Tendersweet' cabbage, and, for Tex-Mex freaks, an Anaheim-style chili adapted to northern gardens. Johnston's own hybridizing efforts have attracted AAS awards for 'Baby Bear' pumpkin, 'Juliet' plum cluster tomato, and 'Bright Lights' Swiss chard (a brilliant, multicolored vegetable that easily works as an ornamental annual). Johnston's strong interest in superior heirloom seeds is reflected in wonderful old-fashioned vegetables for short-season gardens, including vintage tomatoes, trout beans from Maine's Passamaquoddy tribe, and an antique Scottish kidney bean obtained from an elderly gentleman on North Haven Island. We hear rave reviews for the wild arugula and the tiny, intense raisin tomatoes derived from the original wild tomatoes of eastern Mexico. Vegetable seeds also include cool-weather varieties that can be planted late and harvested in fall and winter, such as Brussels sprouts, corn salad, kale, and collards.

Among the flower seeds are sunflowers, salvias, and sweet peas; many-colored salpiglossis; creamy angel's-trumpet; plumed celosia, and red-hot poker. We could go on about the decorative annuals, vines, and grasses; the everlastings and wildflowers; the medicinal and culinary herbs; not to mention the grains, green manures, salad sprouts, potato tubers ... but that would take the fun out of it. Peruse the catalog, make your lists, and plan your own garden, real or imagined. For literary gardeners, Johnny's offers a good selection of garden books. For practical souls, there are good supplies for home and market gardens, including sound gardening tools and an effective cold frame designed by Maine author/educator Eliot Coleman.

Visitors are welcome at Johnny's organic farm, whose barns (now administrative offices) and large building (housing the retail store, packing department, and seed lab) are surrounded by fascinating AAS trial gardens for more than 3,500 vegetables and flowers. The Albion farm is set amid a rolling landscape of spare antique farms with peeling paint; above a blue distance, clouds accumulate like sheep on summer afternoons. Johnston is in contact with dozens of breeders in different countries, who send flower and vegetable seed for the trial and breeding gardens; here one can glimpse the future of American vegetable and flower beds. (Occasionally, home gardeners are given a chance to participate in Johnny's experimental seed and taste trials.)

The beautiful herb gardens are overseen by Janicka Eckert, now Mrs. Johnston. Johnny's greenhouses are loaded with seedlings for sale in May, attracting vegetable lovers far and wide; later visitors may attend tours and workshops.

For all its rural roots, Johnny's is a sophisticated independent seed house, employing nearly 100 staff at the height of the season. Demonstrating its far-flung connections are wooden directional signs posted outside the seed store, droll indicators of the number of miles to seed suppliers: Burpee, 509; Gurney, 1,804; Shepherd's, 3,372; Tozer (London), 3,345; Starke-Ayers (Cape Town), 8,104; East West (Bangkok), 11,008; and Johnny's, 0.

Directions: From Augusta, follow Route 202/9 east to Albion, and turn left in town at the L+M Market onto the Albion-Winslow Road. After 3.25 miles, turn left onto Foss Hill Road (signposted), and Johnny's is 0.5 miles on your right.
From I-95, take exit 33/Waterville and follow Route 137 across the Kennebec River. Turn right at the first set of lights (still Route 137), and turn left at the second set of lights (still Route 137). In 0.25 mile, up the hill, turn left after the bank onto Garland Road. In 3.5 miles, turn right onto the Albion-Winslow Road. Drive 4.5 miles and turn right onto Foss Hill Road; Johnny's is 0.5 mile on your right.

Nearby attractions: The Heirloom Seed Project, P.O. Box 300, Waldoboro, ME 04572 (207-832-5389 school; 207-832-6321 greenhouse), is a seed-savers program run by biology students at Medomak High School; they research and grow each heirloom, save the seed, and distribute it through a free catalog. Donations accepted.

MAINESCAPE GARDEN SHOP

P.O. Box 356, South Street, Blue Hill, ME 04614
Route 3, Bar Harbor, ME 04609
(207) 374-2833; (800) 244-2833; fax (207) 374-8832
Donald C. Paine

General nursery stock. *Small retail garden center. Open May to December, Monday to Saturday 8–5, Sunday 10–4, shorter hours in winter. No catalog or mail order. Display gardens. Landscape design and installation. Holiday shop. Web site: www.mainescape.com.*

Mainescape Garden Shop is a delightful retail garden center located on the coast of northern Maine, set on 5 acres in Blue Hill, with a smaller outpost in Bar Harbor. The Blue Hill site has artful display gardens showcasing the talents of its owner, landscape architect Donald Paine. Mainescape offers well-selected annuals, hardy field-grown perennials, ornamental trees, and woody shrubs, all bought in from regional growers, mainly in Maine and New Hampshire. Responsibly sourced native plants include fern and lowbush blueberry sods rescued from development sites. Container plants are attractively interspersed with naturalistic display areas to demonstrate imaginative garden uses.

Mainescape is a destination nursery for garden tourists, due partly to its atmospheric display gardens, with their view of Blue Hill Mountain, and partly to its location in the town of Blue Hill, a refreshingly lovely summer community not far from Deer Isle artisans and Acadia National Park.

Although Mainescape has no catalog or mail order, visitors can count on well-chosen ornamental perennials, shrubs, and trees throughout the season. Many perennials are enhanced varieties of cottage-garden classics such as campanula, veronica, delphinium, and cranesbill geranium, screened for durability and useful in both year-round and summer gardens. Mainescape carries pretty roses; charming rock garden plants such as draba (a small tufted alpine with yellow flowers) and dragonhead (a spiked blue perennial from Siberia); and interesting native plants such as Culver's root, meadow rue, and blue-leaved St.-John's-wort. Gardeners with moist sites can choose red or blue cardinal flower and Japanese butterbur, a striking bog plant with enormous leaves. Paine's direct involvement  in woody shrub selection is apparent in handsome architectural varieties of willow, viburnum, barbary hedge, twig dogwood, boxwood, and bottlebrush buckeye. Colorful fluttering annuals are sold in spring, along with vegetable flats, grapes, and highbush blueberries. A holiday shop sells lovely wreaths in winter months.

Directions: From coastal Route 1 in Bucksport, take Route 15 South through Blue Hill, 2 miles past town go left on Route 172/176, and Mainescape is 0.2 miles on the left.

Nearby attractions: Surry Gardens, Route 172, P.O. Box 145, Surry, ME 04684 (207-667-4493; fax 207-667-5532), is a popular nursery/garden center with an extensive mail-order catalog of excellent perennials, alpines, and houseplants. In Stonington, in 1932, someone threw three stone-anchored water lily roots into Ames Pond, where they have spread naturally and now produce thousands of blooms (red, pink, white, and native yellow) from June 15 to September 15, daily 9:30–2:30 (unless it's cloudy). A stream was dammed to create Ames Pond in the 19th century in order to produce ice blocks, packed in hay, for shipment to the West Indies. Hushed visitors are welcome at this contemplative site, located on private property and now quietly abuzz with dragonflies when the lilies open. On Route 15 in Stonington, turn east at St. Mary-of-the-Sea Catholic Church. Go 1 mile; Ames Pond is on the left.

NORTH CREEK FARM

24 Sebasco Road (Route 217), Phippsburg, ME 04565
(207) 389-1341 phone and fax
Suzy Verrier

Unusual hardy roses. Perennials. Choice annuals. Small specialty nursery and organic farm. Open May through October, daily 9–5, and by chance or appointment year-round. Rose and plant lists $1. Mail order. Plants reserved by arrangement. Expert advice and planting instructions. Display gardens. Cut flowers and fresh vegetables. E-mail: northcreek@clinic.net.

Suzy Verrier is an accomplished rose expert and garden stylist who deserves much credit for promoting the current fascination with hardy roses. Her credentials include authorship of two distinguished books, *Rosa Rugosa* and *Rosa Gallica,* containing beautiful photographs and definitive descriptions of hardy heirloom roses. Verrier was the genius behind Forever Green Farm, a now vanished Portland-area nursery renowned for its hardy roses.

In her current renaissance, Verrier has returned to her rugosa roots. With considerable flair, she has established a stylish nursery and market garden on a mid-1800s saltwater farm in Phippsburg, on what has been called Maine's prettiest peninsula. There, alongside her partner, Kai Jacob, she propagates over some 250 uncommon perennials and, in her words, "noteworthy and out-of-the-ordinary roses." Choice annuals, tender perennials, and summer-flowering bulbs appear in spring, including the best tender salvias and some wonderful, unusual lilies and sunflowers. (Ask Suzy Verrier for her favorites.) All crops and gardens are organically grown, using intensive and innovative methods.

Verrier lives in the antique farmhouse at the nursery, where visitors may view her display gardens and organic vegetable beds, both the very embodiment of country style.

Unusual hardy roses are the specialty of the house at North Creek Farm. The farm's rose list offers uncommon spinoisissima ("very spiny") roses, including a double white Scotch brier and a double pink Siberian; tough little polyanthas, which bloom in clusters; and romantic old Gallicas, including the fragrant, peppermint-striped *Rosa mundi* from the 16th century (supposedly named for the beautiful Rosamund, mistress to King Henry II, whom Queen Eleanor of Aquitaine had murdered, and whose grave was annually covered, to the queen's intense chagrin, by order of the king, with an immense pile of *Rosa mundi* blossoms). North Creek Farm's old garden rose collection embraces many wonderful rugosa roses, termed "a special specialty with specialists." These superb plants are beautiful, colorful, fragrant, hard as nails (Zone 3), and perfect for nearly any garden use. They range from wild rugosas (the original vivid pink and its white double form), to blushed and tinted old garden hybrids (gardeners still sigh about 'Blanc Double de Couvert', a snow white companion to perennials), and the best new ultra-hardy landscape roses, including the unkillable Canadian Explorer hybrids.

Along with a select miscellany of modern shrub roses (we share Verrier's love for Graham Thomas' warm, glowing pink 'Country Dancer', which we first saw at North Creek), the farm offers David Austin English roses and a diverse collection of ramblers and climbers, called "scramblers, and clamberers." One unforgettable example, which stopped us in our tracks on the California coast one June, is a popular old rambler called 'Seven Sisters', which produces a single stupendous bloom display in seven simultaneous shades, from deep pink to ivory. Aficionados of yellow roses may prefer 'Alchemist', another multihued rambler from the 1950s displaying yolk yellow, apricot, orange, and pink all at once.

North Creek Farm is the only place we know that has successfully combined serious organic farming practices with authentic garden chic. Visitors are welcome to view its vibrant organic vegetable garden, raised herb and cut-flower beds, and imaginative rose and perennial borders garnished with wattle fencing, driftwood sculptures, and live ornamental fowl. Behind the vegetable beds, a path leads through the meadow to a waterfall. Fresh farm-raised vegetables, herbs, cut flowers, eggs, and goat cheese are sold inside the front porch, alongside sophisticated garden supplies, nurseryman's tools, unusual spring bulbs, and organic seaweed fertilizers. For literary gardeners, the shop offers copies of Suzy Verrier's rose books ("gladly autographed," she says) and a comfortable wicker chair in which to examine them. The farm fields, gardens, and rose beds, dashingly twigged and trellised, have an insouciant charm that comports gaily with the peninsula's wild beach roses, coastal flora, and fresh salt air.

Directions: North Creek Farm is a scenic 12-mile drive south of Bath. From I-95, take Route 1 east to Bath and turn onto Route 209 south. In 12 miles, turn right onto Route 217; the farm is 400 feet on the left (signposted).

Nearby attractions: Note the 104-foot European linden tree (Maine's largest) next to the Phippsburg Congregational Church. Popham Beach State Park, with miles of pristine beach and good bird-watching, is minutes away. Phippsburg boasts the first attempted British settlement in America, founded in 1601, some years before Jamestown and Plymouth. The peninsula's winding roads were once Indian trails; immediately south of Bath on Route 209 (just over the causeway leading to Phippsburg) is Winnegance, an ancient Indian camp, later the site of 10 tidewater mills. Two peninsulas eastward, below Bar Harbor in Southport, Maine Millstones (207-633-6091) sells newly hand-furrowed granite millstones for gristmill restorations and landscape use.

O'DONAL'S NURSERIES

6 County Road, RFD 4 (Routes 114 and 22), Gorham, ME 04038
(207) 839-4262, fax (207) 839-2290
Royce and Jeffrey O'Donal

Northern-grown trees and shrubs. Specimens. Perennials. Retail and wholesale nursery and garden center. Open daily 8–6, Thursday 8–8, Sunday 9–5. Closed major holidays. Extended evening hours in May and June, shorter hours in winter. Free tree and shrub catalogs in spring and fall. Separate perennial catalog in spring. Display gardens. Information services. Lectures. Newsletter. E-mail: onurser1@maine.rr.com. Web site: www.odonalsnurseries.com.

O'Donal's Nurseries has been voted the most popular garden center in Maine, and it is one of the finest. Located 8 miles from Portland, O'Donal's is a vibrant nursery/garden center featuring an impressive list of hardy northern-grown trees and shrubs, including many large specimen plants. O'Donal's was founded in the 1950s as a tree service company, and became a nursery in 1960 upon moving to its present location, which had been operated as a nursery since 1850. Owner Royce O'Donal, now retired, is an arborist, founding member of the Maine Landscape and Nursery Association, and past governor of the American Nursery and Landscape Association. His son Jeffrey O'Donal, a respected educator and tree expert with equivalent credentials, is now in charge of the nursery. (Still vital, the senior O'Donal is renowned among the staff as a "crazy man for pruning.")

Unlike most nurseries, O'Donal's actually propagates many of its own trees and shrubs, and grows others from seedlings on nearby acreage. Field-grown trees include birch, yellowwood, linden, katsura, native red maple, and sugar maple. Most of the remaining trees are bought in from upper New York State. This ensures that O'Donal's tree stock is exceptionally cold-adapted and root heavy, characteristics that greatly improve survival rates in New England. O'Donal's also grows many of its own rhododendrons, which do surprisingly well in Maine, and hardens off other ornamental shrubs. The nursery's propagating fields, among the northernmost of their kind, occupy 80 acres in the vicinity and are overseen by Jeffrey O'Donal. Despite his achievements as a tree expert, we hear that he struggles like the rest of us to find a peach tree that will grow reliably in the North.

Although spring and fall are best for tree and shrub buying, even in high summer O'Donal's offers many choice trees such as fringe tree, Magyar ginkgo, weeping Rivers beech, Kentucky coffee tree, 'Dr. Merrill' magnolia, and other worthy ornamentals, some little known and underutilized. We were swept away by a beautiful green Korean maple, as lovely as her Japanese maple cousin, but hardy to Zone 3. O'Donal's tree yard includes native woodland trees such as shellbark hickory, black walnut, and columnar white ash, as well as hardy fruit trees for home orchards. Its well-stocked collection of ornamental conifers (also partly field-grown here) includes weeping coastal white cedar, dwarf Norway spruce, white-tipped Canadian hemlock, yellow chamaecyparis, weeping larch, and a sparkling dwarf blue juniper called 'Blue Star'. We especially loved the dwarf form of our beautiful Eastern white pine *(Pinus strobus),* perfect for small naturalistic gardens. The shrub yard holds handsome varieties of hardy rhododendron, viburnum, holly, and clethra; an especially hardy boxwood called 'Green Mountain'; some beautiful mountain laurel; and all the latest Carey Award shrubs, chosen by the Worcester County Horticultural Society for their superior, multiseason performance in northern gardens.

O'Donal's knowledgeable staff diligently tends the nursery's tree and shrub stock, succeeding with even the more difficult large specimens. Most trees are balled and burlapped with good bulky root systems; some small trees come in pots. Considering the trouble taken to grow them for New England conditions, the trees and shrubs at O'Donal's Nurseries are reasonably priced. All come with a one-year replacement guarantee and volume discounts. Gardeners seeking a particular tree or shrub can place an order in advance or on reserve, a useful service when looking for unusual specimens. A mark of quality is found in the nursery's pitiless discard practices: Woody plants that are outgrowing their pots are swiftly relegated to a back area—"the Orphanage"—where they are sold at lowball prices without any guarantee of survival.

As an adjunct to its signature trees and shrubs, O'Donal's offers an excellent selection of ornamental perennials, herbs, and water garden plants under a large pergola behind the garden center. These include labeled plants from Blooms of Bressingham, heirloom hostas and irises, and showy native woodlanders such as yellow lady's slipper and trillium (reliably sourced). Selection is best in May and June, but as with everything else, O'Donal's has good plants throughout the season, including some oversized specimens in 3-gallon pots. We ourselves, perhaps irresponsibly, bought a delicious-looking blackberry lily here one summer's end.

Besides live plants, O'Donal's generously offers its customers an information service, free lectures, two catalogs, a biannual newsletter, landscape services, a shop with quality garden wares, Christmas greens in season, and several small display gardens featuring aquatic plants, trees, shrubs, and "wildlife welcome" plants.

Directions: From 1-95, take exit 6 and turn left at the light onto Route 9. Turn left at the second light onto Route 114 north and left again onto Route 22; the nursery is on your left.

From Route 295 in Portland, take exit 5B/Congress Street west, follow Congress Street (Route 22) for 8 miles, and shortly after bypassing Route 114, the nursery is on your left.
From Route 302, at the Windham rotary take Route 202 west to Gorham, turn left onto Route 114, left again onto Route 22, and the nursery is on your right.
From Route 1 south of Portland, turn west onto Route 114. In 6 miles, turn left onto Route 22, and the nursery is on the left.

Nearby attractions: A mile east on County Road from O'Donal's is Smiling Hill Farm (207-775-4818), a 450-acre working dairy farm notable for its fresh ice cream and its Holstein milk and buttermilk in old-fashioned glass bottles.

PERENNIALS PREFERRED NURSERY

P.O. Box 17, 906 Feylers Corner Road, Waldoboro, ME 04572
(207) 832-5282
Jean Moss

Ultra-hardy perennials. Verbascum, nepeta, primula, pulmonaria, and cranesbill geranium. *Open Mid-May through August, Tuesday to Saturday 10–4 and by appointment. No catalog or mail order. Display garden.*

Perennials Preferred Nursery is located in what at first may look like a weedy meadow surrounding a failed farmstead. Despite the garden's mischievous, slightly disreputable air, Perennials Preferred houses as sophisticated a population of perennial plants as can be found in New England. The nursery's greatest disadvantage—its harsh microclimate—has been cleverly turned to advantage by its owner, adept plantswoman Jean Moss. The farm's marshy bottomland has had frost every month of the year, a climatic insult that virtually guarantees any plant grown here to be ultra-hardy and tough, a real survivor. What is remarkable is just how elaborate a brocade of choice plants has been woven in such an unlikely garden.

Perennials Preferred Nursery cannot be fully appreciated without a tour by its owner. Unannounced visitors are met by the nursery's Official Greeter, a resident dog named Posy. Jean Moss herself may then appear, as she did for us, in a whimsical brimmed straw hat and leather tool belt, her hands covered in fresh earth. As both owner and keeper of the garden, Moss can recount the common name, Latin name, growth habits, history, and origin of each plant in her distinguished collection.

If she is preoccupied, you may wander through the sunny borders and shady glades surrounding the farmhouse, seeing what plants you can identify on your own, and making note of those that interest you. Plants are labeled, but the system is eccentric and not consistently enforced. This is a nursery where it pays to take along a notebook, for the plant selection is diverse, many cultivars are rare or noteworthy, and no plant list or catalog is available to guide you. Seats and arbors are situated here and there where visitors can rest, gaze, and scribble away at their own pace.

The Perennials Preferred display gardens double as growing beds for its fascinating assortment of perennial and rock garden plants. Because the owner works alone without help, the displays are un-manicured, exhibiting the carefree fecundity of a connoisseur's perennial yard allowed to behave as a wildflower garden. The displays are divided into sunny perennial borders, raised beds, a dry rock garden, a rosarium, and shade gardens winding through a wet woodland. Although the nursery's specialty is ultra-hardy choice perennials, its unique collections of verbascum, nepeta, primula, pulmonaria, and cranesbill geranium are noteworthy. One August, we saw giant sea kale (favored by Gertrude Jekyll), pale lavender jewelweed, wild cucumber vine, orchid primroses, a blue-flowered corydalis with purple foliage, and an endangered native Allegheny vine (permissibly grown from seed). We noticed a consistent playfulness in Moss's arrangements, witty horticultural puns and related plants mimicking each other, like the shade-loving cousins *Corydalis ochroleuca* and *Dicentra eximia* sighing together, each with a sleeve full of white bleeding hearts.

Perennials Preferred is a garden that gets better the more you look at it; even the weeds are captivating. Indeed, ornamental weeds are one of Moss's specialties, beginning with the unusual silverrod *(Solidago bicolor)* growing in the wasted meadow among wild goldenrod and ending with the mullein family inter-marrying promiscuously in the rock garden. Our own Aunt Jean bought a wonderful English foliage plant, augustly named *Rumex sanguineus,* which turned out to be a red-leaved form of dock, a native weed often found growing in abandoned driveways. Perhaps this tolerance for wildness accounts for the numerous butterflies at this nursery, in more colors than we have seen anywhere else.

Plants sold at Perennials Preferred are not potted and set out in rows as in most nurseries, but instead are growing in garden nooks where their clumps expand or self-sow freely. Any plant you buy will be freshly dug on-site, and put in a box or bag along with a handwritten (in Latin) wooden label. Often the dug soil of one plant will contain a "dividend" of some other plant, a tiny neighboring seedling that hitchhiked along for the ride; and Moss will label that one for you, too.

Directions: Travel the coast on Route 1 to Waldoboro. From Moody's Diner on Route 1, take Route 220 north. In 2.5 miles, take your first right onto Feylers Corner Road and proceed 1.5 miles to the nursery. Call first if coming from a distance.

Nearby attractions: For food lovers traveling Route 1, a chrome yellow building diagonally across from Moody's Diner (207-832-7468) houses a scrumptious bakery called Borealis Breads, the self styled "Van Gogh of Dough" (888-595-8100; e-mail Jim@borealisbreads.com).

PINETREE GARDEN SEEDS

Box 300, Old Lewiston Road, New Gloucester, ME 04260
(207) 926-3400; fax (888) 52-SEEDS (527-3337) and (207) 926-3886
Dick Meiners

Seed for vegetables, annuals, perennials. Bulbs and tubers. *Phone orders Monday to Friday 10–4. Free mail-order catalog. Small trial garden. E-mail: superseeds@worldnet.att.net. Web site: www.superseeds.com.*

Pinetree Garden Seeds was founded in 1979 with a one-page flyer offering vegetable seed in small quantities to home gardeners. Its aim remains the same, but its seed list has expanded exponentially to include all manner of seeds suited to home garden use—vegetables, herbs, annuals, and perennials—more than 800 in all. Pinetree Garden Seeds carries good seed with high germination rates, mostly untreated with chemicals; like other commercial seed houses, though, it buys in all its seed. What sets Pinetree apart is its practice of selling small packets with plenty of seed for a home garden, beginning at 35 cents a pack. Acquiring small allotments of fresh seed each spring can be a valuable advantage, if only in reducing the number of mason jars storing leftover seed in your refrigerator.

Pinetree subjects a third of its vegetable seed to field trials each year to ensure flavor and distinction, taking care to reject bland, long-keeping varieties developed for the supermarket trade. Although it is principally a mail-order seed house, gardeners can visit Pinetree's headquarters in New Gloucester to inspect its modest trial gardens and, from May 1 to June 15, buy field-grown perennials in 4-inch pots. (A small store that is "usually open" was, alas, closed when we came by.)

The 168-page *Pinetree Garden Seeds* newsprint catalog is an instructive guide for gardeners, and vegetable seed is its primary focus. Any reader with a bit of ground will be inspired to put it in vegetables, so lush are the choices and so tempting the prospect of turning a pennyworth of seed into a pound of vegetables. Uncommon seeds include pink popcorn, golden tomato, 'Eight Ball' summer squash, and an heirloom yellow cucumber from Maine called 'Boothbay Blonde'. A section called "Vegetables from Around the World" lists seed for vegetables used in French, Italian, Oriental, American Indian, and Latin cooking. Gardeners will find some wonderful stuff here, such as purslane, perilla, epazote, red Russian kale, heirloom corn, and (our favorite) rattail radish with edible pods. The company also carries seed for culinary herbs, edible sprouts, and green-manure cover crops. Besides seed, Pinetree Garden Seeds is a source for strawberry seedlings, raspberry canes, onion and garlic sets, seed potatoes, horseradish, asparagus, rhubarb roots, and, for those with a moist basement, boxed mushroom spore farms.

Although vegetable seed is its specialty, Pinetree's flower seed list expands yearly, and now includes a respectable range of annuals, perennials, vines, wildflowers, everlastings, and ornamental grasses and grains. Among the annual vines are white-flowered hyacinth bean and pretty sweet peas. A section called "Expensive Bedding Plants That You Might Be Able to Grow at Home" offers seed that a home gardener hardly ever sees, for such staples as petunias, begonias, geraniums, and impatiens. Where else can a gardener get cactus seed, banana tree seed, and seed for begonia 'Pin-Up Flame' (an AAS award winner, and the only begonia that can be grown from seed)? Flower seed is supplemented with ornamental bulbs, from tulips to dahlias.

Ornamental bulbs, organic gardening supplies, tools, bat products, hummingbird feeders, bee and butterfly attractants, soap-making aids, and discounted gardening books are listed in back of the catalog, which makes fun winter reading.

Directions: New Gloucester is north of Portland on Route 202. Follow Route 202 to Gray, where it merges with Route 100 (Old Lewiston Road). Continue on Route 202/100; Pinetree is about 6 miles on your left.

PHILADELPHIA EARLY TURNIP.

PLAINVIEW FARM FINE PERENNIALS

529 Mountfort Road, North Yarmouth, ME 04097
(207) 829-5004; (800) 396-1705
Steven and Donna Palmer

Garden perennials. Large, owner-operated nursery. Open daily 9–5. Catalog $3. Shrub list on request. Mail order. Christmas greens. Visitors and tour groups welcome. Display gardens. Lectures and seminars. Garden design. Landscaping services. E-mail: dpalmer@gwi.com. Web site: www.plainviewfarm.com.

Plainview Farm Fine Perennials is a large, popular nursery just 15 miles north of Portland. Owners Donna and Steven Palmer are savvy horticulturists and landscapers who established Plainview Farm in 1988 as a destination nursery aimed at elevating the skills and buying habits of home gardeners. (Steve Palmer, the nursery's prime mover, is a plant-crazed former school principal who earned money as a teenager by operating a nursery in his parents' backyard.) Plainview Farm specializes in its namesake perennials, with emphasis on new, unusual, and underutilized plants.

Sited on 17 acres, the nursery operates out of a bespoke pink neo-Victorian cottage encircled by wooden porches and white picket fences; potted perennials adorn its gravel pathways. The Palmers built Plainview Farm as an attractive nursery stage set in which container-grown perennials are displayed (alphabetically) against a backdrop of the American Dream. The nursery's commercial allure is enhanced by an extensive plant selection, a well-stocked gift and garden shop, a trained horticultural staff, manicured display gardens, free lectures and seminars, professional instruction, a spring bulb festival, a user-friendly catalog, a free newsletter, a Web site, personalized garden design, and mail-order services. We suppose it must be a bit like fantasy baseball: If you build it, they will come. Plainview Farm is popular with both hands-on gardeners and garden tourists, successfully accommo-dating spring and summer shopping crowds and all-season tours, sometimes by the busload.

Plainview Farm's fine collection of 1,500 perennials and companion plants spans the range available in the market today. Priding itself on growing "the newest, the trendiest, the hottest, the plants of the future," according to the catalog, the nursery sells patented perennials from Etera, Sunny Border Gold and its own private label collection, The Pride of Plainview. Designer labels or not, what we like best here is the combined dazzle and depth of perennial plant offerings. Orange campion, apricot basket-of-gold, unusual violets, hardy hibiscus, and colorful "steppable" thymes are all examples of Plainview Farm's energetic plant sourcing efforts. We counted six different kinds of joe-pye weed,

11 monkshoods, 10 bee balms, and a dozen foamflowers, including the must-have new hybrids.

Besides perennials, Plainview Farm offers companion shrubs, grasses, ground covers, and annuals selected from what is called the "magic and exotic new universe of summer-season plants." Plainview Farm's printed catalog adds to the fun by offering useful plant descriptions, cultivation advice, garden "friendliness ratings," procurement lists, a soil recipe, directions for building a woodland garden, and garden-related quips and quotes ("The most serious charge that can be brought against New England is not Puritanism, but February").

Floriferous display beds and stunning ornamental woodlands showcase the plants that can be bought at Plainview Farm, including prodigious amounts of hosta and astilbe. From April through June, the nursery blooms with thousand of flowering bulbs that can be ordered for fall delivery. Christmas wreaths, kissing balls, and "lobster lites" (lobster-shaped red Christmas-tree lights) arrive at Thanksgiving. Plainview Farm offers gardeners and tourists a rich promotional smorgasbord, of both plants and horticultural products. Eat, eat.

Directions: From I-95, take exit 17/Yarmouth. From the north, go straight on Route 1; from the south, turn left onto Route 1. Then take the first right. At the top of the rise, turn right onto East Main Street, then immediately left onto North Road. In 5 miles, at a flashing red light, turn right onto Route 9. In 0.6 mile, go right onto Mountfort Road; the nursery is on your left.

Nearby attractions: In Yarmouth, tree worshipers can visit Big Herbie, the largest American elm in Maine, 93 feet tall, with a crown circumference of 110 feet and a trunk diameter of 229 inches. To get there, take Route 115 in Yarmouth toward the water, bear left at the marina, and just before Estabrook's Nursery, 337 Main Street (207-846-4398) Big Herbie is on your left, wearing an engraved plaque.

PLANTS UNLIMITED

U.S. Route 1, Rockport, ME 04856
(207) 594-7754 and (800) 830-7754; fax (207) 594-8510
Hammon Buck

Perennials. Annuals, shrubs, and trees. *Nursery and garden center. Open daily 8:30–5, March through Thanksgiving. Free perennial catalog and rose list. No mail order. Spring perennial sale. November shop sale. E-mail: info@plantsunltd.com. Web site: www.plantsunltd.com.*

Located on busy Route 1 in mid-coast Rockport, Plants Unlimited is a popular nursery and garden center much frequented by Maine landscapers, designers, and gardeners for its selection of more than 1,000 quality garden plants. Plants Unlimited was founded in 1978 by owner Hammon Buck, a Long Island–born nurseryman and former president of the Maine Landscape and Nursery Association, whose whole family was in the plant business; years ago, his parents operated a nursery in Searsport. Plants Unlimited fills a 26-acre site, formerly home to the Rockport Drive-In; material from the demolished movie screen was salvaged for the present arbor, and the old concession stand was converted to offices and a garden shop.

Although Plants Unlimited boasts of being a "one-stop resource for Maine gardeners," it is, first and foremost, a terrific source of garden perennials: border perennials, shade perennials, foliage plants, native plants, alpines, groundcovers, and ornamental vines. Classic hardy perennials (including many awardwinners) are augmented by unusual varieties not often found in commercial settings, such as double marsh marigold, double lily of the valley, Chinese gentian, and species lilies. The nursery is particularly appreciated for its assortments of phlox, primula, allium, and violet. The nursery's 10 greenhouses produce pot-grown perennials that are healthy and well priced. Every spring, a discount sale of perennials in 4-inch pots is popular with every gardener within driving distance.

Besides perennials, Plants Unlimited carries spring annuals, hanging baskets, and flats of vegetables sprouted from Johnny's Selected Seeds (ME). Plants Unlimited also carries a good stock of ornamental shrubs and trees, and its hardy rose selection is judged one of the best in Maine. A perennial catalog and rose list are distributed free of charge; no mail order is offered, but plants can be ordered ahead and delivered locally or held for pickup. Hammon Buck and his staff are dedicated and knowledgeable, and Ace, the dog, is a frequent greeter at this user-friendly nursery. An end-of-season shop sale produces great November bargains for early Christmas shoppers.

Directions: From points south, take I-95 north up the Maine coast, then take exit 22 onto Route 1 east. Proceed through Rockport, and the nursery is directly on Route 1, on your left.

Nearby attractions: Immediately north on Route 1, the State of Maine Cheese Company (800-762-8895) has an outlet store selling farmstead cheddar and Monterey jack made of natural cow's milk. In Camden, the Camden Library's restored amphitheater garden was designed by noted landscape architect Fletcher Steele. Merryspring Horticultural Nature park, Conway Road, P.O. Box 893, Camden, ME 04843 (207-236-2239) open down to dusk, is a 10-acre arboretum with connecting trails and display gardens. The Camden Farmer's Market takes place from May through October, Saturday 9–noon and Wednesday 4:30–6:30, rain or shine, on Concord Avenue between Limerock and Union Streets (207-785-3521). ABCDef Books in Camden (207-236-3903; 888-236-3903) is noted among bibliophiles for used and rare books.

ROCK OAK GARDENS

197 Portland Road, Gray, ME 04039
(207) 657-4655
Don Celler

Maine-grown daylilies. Small specialty nursery. Open July 1 to August 15, Thursday to Sunday 8:30–5, and by appointment; call ahead. catalog $1. Mail order. Display garden. Peak bloom July 20 to August 10. Visitors welcome.

Don Celler is one of the "new" breed of daylily hybridizers: Using the latest hybrids, he creates cold-hardy plants with showy, prizewinning characteristics; he has also pioneered the development of evergreen daylilies that will flourish in the North. Rock Oak Gardens is a specialty grower of more than 1,200 named daylily hybrids and several thousand of Celler's own seedlings. The nursery contains an acre of daylilies grown on bottomland next to Celler's home in Gray, just north of Portland.

Celler is an electronics technician who began doing a bit of landscaping before he became obsessed with daylily breeding. Now, he says, his "biggest struggle is keeping ahead of the weeds." His field-grown plants are sold mainly by mail order, but visitors to Rock Oak Gardens can have the fun of inspecting well-labeled trial and growing beds containing thousands of blooming seedlings from Celler's breeding program. This is like visiting the artist while he is still in the studio; we never met a breeder who was not interested in reactions in the trial beds. Rock Oak's growing fields are pleasantly located behind Celler's antique brick Cape home, past an avenue of old sugar maples and down a footpath leading to an old hayfield.

Don Celler's breeding goals are to produce problem-free "unfussy" daylilies that are adventurously ornamental for this part of the country. His technique is to cross the best plants, including his own seedlings and parent stock from other breeders, in search of high bud count, branching habit, evergreen foliage, cold-hardiness, and, of course, overall good looks. Rock Oak Gardens' first introduction, 'Boothbay Harbor Gold', is a gold-flowered rebloomer generating 50 buds per scape (flower stalk)—considerable bloom power for a northern daylily. Rock Oak also carries huge, ruffled, picotee-edged, and ornamentally eyed daylilies from well-known breeders; some come in amazing new colors such as strawberry, coral, raisin, and lime. A serious New Hampshire collector we know buys many of her daylilies from Rock Oak Gardens on the grounds that it has "great plants, great prices, and great quality." Our favorites include the award-winning 'Wedding Band' (a charming gift for brides), Stamile's 'Strawberry Candy' (pure fructose), and one of the nursery's few tetraploid daylilies, 'Tet Lullaby Baby' (little but tough).

Rock Oak Gardens sells daylilies in freshly dug double fans or divisions; bonus plants are sent with each order. Being a small nursery, Rock Oak has a limited supply of each variety. All plants are field grown and have survived at least one Maine winter. A dig-your-own seedling sale takes place in mid-July and includes many of Celler's numbered seedlings. Such hybridizer's sales can produce some enchanting bargains, for the passed-over seedlings of a talented breeder are often uniquely showy plants with expensive parents, costing far less than named hybrids.

Peak daylily bloom at the nursery extends from late July to early August, the very height of summertime in southern Maine.

Directions: From Route 495/Maine Turnpike, take exit 11/Gray. Turn right onto Route 115, and right again at the light onto Route 100/26 south; the nursery is 2 miles on your left, at an antique-brick Cape just after Long Hill Road.

THE ROSERAIE AT BAYFIELDS

P.O. Box R, Waldoboro, ME 04572-0919
(207) 832-6330; fax (800) 933-4508
Lloyd Brace

Hardy landscape and garden roses. *Small specialty nursery. Open late April to October, Monday to Saturday 10–5, Sunday 8:30–noon. Closed Sunday in August, Sunday and Monday after August. Free catalog by mail or Web site. Spring and fall nursery lists for a first-class stamp, or by fax or Web site. Video catalog supplement $6. Rose books and lectures. Admiration Day in late June. E-mail: roses@midcoast.com. Web site: www.roseraie.com.*

Once an apprentice of rose expert Suzy Verrier (see *North Creek Farm*, ME), Lloyd Brace is the proprietor of The Roseraie at Bayfields, a delightful little nursery focused exclusively on growing old garden roses in mid-coast Maine. The Roseraie is picturesquely situated on Bayfields Farm, an antique farmstead overlooking the tidal Medomac River, on the grounds of an old apple orchard (apples, too, are members of the rose family). According to the catalog, the nursery specializes in "practical roses for hard places," and carries more than 300 varieties of hardy, nursery-grown roses adapted to Maine's coastal climate (Zone 5B or colder).

Because of their toughness, beauty, and historical interest, more than half the roses offered here are species, heirlooms, and rugosas. Also available are David Austin's new English hybrids (a bit more tender than the old-timers), which blend the old rose style with modern repeat bloom. The Roseraie's specialty is its collection of hardy roses that grow well in landscape conditions. While a good deal of the nursery stock looks as though it already *has* survived landscape conditions, we hear that The Roseraie's plants perform well in the ground. Roses are propagated and grown on-site, free of chemical sprays, and sold as grade-1, two-year plants. Propagation is either by grafting (pink tag) or own-root method (beige tag)—customers may specify which. (Own-root roses are slow-growing and hard to produce, but are tougher and much longer-lived.)

The Roseraie's dense newsprint catalog, best read with a magnifying glass, provides information on the origin, parentage, dimensions, and bloom of each rose in the collection. Even the most visually imaginative reader will appreciate an illustrated companion to make full sense of The Rosearie's catalog. Brace provides a 60-minute narrated Video Catalog Supplement (for only $6) with color slides of his best roses; his lecture schedule is published on the Web site. Roses ordered by mail are shipped bare-root, while those purchased at the nursery come either potted or bare-root. Spring and fall nursery lists (separate from the catalog) offer potted roses wintered over from the previous season.

The Roseraie's display beds at Bayfields Farm, set parallel to the distant shoreline, are arranged alphabetically as a "catalog in the ground," a kind of arboretum of roses. Scrutinizing mature roses gives gardeners an invaluable sense of each plant's characteristics—its hips, its leaf color, its shape as a shrub—that cannot be had from photographs. Okay, we confess to having a weakness for old garden roses. Still, our gardener's heart was unprepared for the sheer beauty of these roses: the blue foliage of *Rosa glauca,* delicately suffused with rouge; the winged thorns of *Rosa primula,* set off against ferny leaves; and the shining black hips of the Scotch rose *(Rosa spinosissima),* gleaming on the bush like tiny plums. These and other lovely old roses can be seen in high bloom at The Roseraie from late June to early July, although the garden remains interesting throughout the growing season.

A little wooden outbuilding carries the nursery's small supply of books, fertilizer, and cultural materials for roses. On-site amenities include a pair of wooden chairs under an apple tree, facing the sea, where with permission you may eat your picnic lunch.

Directions: The Roseraie is 61 miles northeast of Portland (90 minutes). From I-95, take Route 1 north over the Bath and Wiscasset Bridges (traffic can be very slow) to the only light in Waldoboro, and turn right onto Route 32/Bremen Road. In 1.7 miles, you'll see the nursery's sign, on your left.

Nearby attractions: The town of Waldoboro issues more clam licenses than any other town in Maine. Moody's Diner, Route 1, Waldoboro (207-832-7468), a legendary diner classic complete with Formica counter and wooden phone booth, is said to serve the finest fish chowder in the state.

SNOW BROOK GARDENS

315 Bridge Road, Parkman, ME 04443
(207) 876-3220
Mary S. Betts

Ultra-hardy field-grown perennials. Iris hybrids. Small specialty nursery. Open May and June, Wednesday to Sunday 10–5, and summer hours by chance or appointment (weekdays best). No catalog or mail order. Display gardens. Garden design and consultation.

Snow Brook Gardens is located in Parkman, 30 miles northwest of Bangor, in one of the last settled towns in northern Maine before the state highway system gives way to private logging roads. The nursery specializes in hardy perennials of iron constitution, field-grown in cold Zone 3 conditions. Proprietor Mary Betts is a self-trained horticulturist with 25 years of experience working a perennial garden that stays frozen until Memorial Day. Her perennial cultivars are the survivors, planted in 80 raised display beds that include veronicas, daylilies, sedum, ornamental onions, herbs, and an assortment of groundcovers. Snow Brook Gardens' reasonably priced plants come field-dug or in gallon containers. We prefer the field-dug plants, provided they can be transplanted fairly promptly. Cut flowers, dried flowers, and seeds are also sold at this valiant little nursery.

Perhaps the most astonishing thing about Snow Brook Gardens is its assembly of hardy iris cultivars and species. The nursery grows numerous Japanese, Siberian, and species iris, many of which normally require much balmier growing conditions, with or without snow cover. Betts has gathered an especially good collection of *Iris versicolor,* our native blue flag. In an almost unbelievable stroke of chance, Snow Brook Gardens was the site of a fluke cross between a native blue flag and a showy Siberian iris hybrid, named 'Orville Fay' by its breeder, Dr. Currier McEwen (see *Eartheart Gardens, ME*). Frustrated scientists have been trying to breed these genetically incompatible iris species for decades. At Snow Brook Gardens, it seems, the bees did the job on their own, without human intervention. This serendipitous cross opened the brave new world of iris breeding to Mary Betts, who declines to speculate on her good fortune, other than to observe that "everybody's got their own opinions, being gardeners." Peak bloom in the Snow Brook Garden iris beds is late June to mid-July, not to be missed by gardeners venturing north to Moosehead Lake in early summer.

Directions: From I-95, take exit 39/Newport, and proceed north on Routes 11/7 into Dexter. Turn left onto Route 23. In 2 miles, take the second left, and drive 4 to 5 miles, then turn right after a red-roofed barn onto a gravel road (signposted).

Nearby attractions: From mid-May to mid-June, this area of Maine celebrates Moosemainea (207-695-2702), an annual event featuring a Moose River canoe race, a Tour de Moose bike race, and Family Fun Day with Moose Tales and moose d'oeuvres. Spring visitors should brake for live moose on the highway; they're licking up the leftover road salt.

STEEPLEBUSH FARM HERBS

Box 1572, 102 Staples Road, Limington, ME 04049
(207) 637-2776
Lauriejane Kelley

Annual and perennial herbs. Holiday herbs. *Small specialty nursery. Open from May to Christmas, Wednesday to Saturday 10–4, Sunday noon–4; closed Wednesday from November to Christmas. Plant catalog on request. No mail order of plants. Herbal display beds. Holiday open house third weekend in November. Herb products by mail order. Classes.*

Steeplebush Farm Herbs is located in rural Limington, a small town in apple country, 30 miles west of Portland. Owner Lauriejane Kelley, a graphic artist turned plantswoman, operates Steeplebush Farm out of a saltbox-style herb shop next door to her family's 1860 Cape house and barn. Over 15 years, she has transformed a pounded-dirt farmscape into a picturesque working herb garden, complete with dogs, cats, ornamental Pekin ducks (to consume slugs), and llamas (to repel coyotes). Kelley propagates and sells more than 350 varieties of herbs, as well as fragrant perennials and ever-lastings. A selection of hardy heather bought in from Rock Spray Nursery (MA) is also available. Attractive display gardens surrounding the house demonstrate how cleverly herb gardens can enhance the vernacular architecture of New England.

Steeplebush Farm specializes in annual and perennial herbs for ornamental, medicinal, and culinary use. Kelley grows perennial herbs in great variety, including uncommon specimens such as mountain mint, teasel, balm of Gilead, and dittany of Crete. Many of her plants are old or heirloom varieties that gardeners find hard to locate. A particular interest in unusual foliage herbs is in evidence: Note the variegated forms of germander, marjoram, mint, scented geranium, sedum, Solomon's seal, and milk thistle. Distinctive ornamental herbs include sweet violet, apricot tufted violet, silver sage *(Salvia argentea),* "greasewood" white sage, pink Culver's physic, and old-fashioned single hollyhocks. To complement a mother-of-thyme border on a city sidewalk, we acquired rupturewort, a flat creeper useful in walkways and effective for bladder disorders.

Kelley jokingly wonders if (due to her collection of medicinal herbs) some of her neighbors may think she is a witch. Local rumor aside, Steeplebush Farm is a reputable source of traditional healing herbs, called simples, many with valid medicinal applications. Healing herbs are plants once officially used in medicine (indicated by *officionalis* in the Latin name) or effective as folk cures, such as St.-John's-wort, goldenseal, coltsfoot, and gotu kola (a tropical Asian salad herb believed to stimulate brain function). Culinary herbs include caraway, true licorice, salad burnet, cardoon, and such tender perennials as caper bush and sweet bay, which must be wintered indoors. Steeplebush Farm also carries dyer's herbs such as madder and broom, and unusual ornamentals including black heliotrope and fernleaf lavender, which bloom all season.

Most herb plants are grown and sold by the nursery in 4-inch pots. Steeplebush Farm's plant catalog contains useful information about each herb's hardiness, habits, and traditional uses, and also lists unusual seeds and annual everlastings.

A visit to Steeplebush Farm necessarily includes a few moments in its small, aromatic herb shop, whose lintel ornament echoes the universal gardener's lament, THERE IS NEVER ENOUGH THYME. Under eaves lavishly hung with dried flowers, visitors are offered fragrant potpourris, herbal salves, tinctures, lotions, and other scented herb products of Steeplebush Farm, alongside twig and rush skeps, birdhouses, organic fertilizers, plant markers, and saffron crocus bulbs. Kelley makes her own freshly dried herb teas with names such as Winter's Tale and Northern Nap. For homemade herb infusions, visitors can buy dried herbs and little muslin bags with drawstrings. Herbal products (but not, alas, plants) can be ordered by mail.

Classes on herbs and gardening subjects are occasionally conducted on the premises. A holiday open house, held in November, is a perfect source for delightful dried wreaths and other fragrant and edible Christmas presents.

Directions: Limington is 30 miles west of Portland. From Portland, take Route 25 west to East Limington, then left onto Route 11 south. In 3.5 miles, turn right at the sign onto Staples Hill Road; the herb farm is on your right.

Nearby attractions: Brackett Apple Orchards, 1 mile north on Route 11, is a family farm selling field-grown pumpkins and apples in autumn.

STONE SOUP FARM

RFD 1, Box 2760, Red Barn Road, Monroe, ME 04951
(207) 525-4463
Kate NaDeau

Herbs, perennials, and everlastings. Lilies and daylilies. Small organic speciality nursery. Open May to August, daily 9-5; fall hours by appointment. Open for Thanksgiving weekend and Yuletide Fair in early December. No catalog or mail order of plants. Workshops. Display gardens. Garden consultation and design. Group tours and teas by arrangement. Seasonal events. Mail order Yule wreaths.

Every one knows the folk tale about the traveler who comes to the door claiming he can make soup from a stone, and the grudging housewife who agrees to let him try. He boils the stone, tastes the soup, and proclaims it delicious; but just as he is about to serve it, he cocks his head and remarks, of course, this soup would be even better with a bit of butter ... of leeks ... of potatoes ... of herbs ... and in the end, after all the additions, the amused housewife agrees that stone soup is simply wonderful.

Kate NaDeau of Stone Soup Farm has her own magical story about making something wonderful out of nothing. Over many years, through her own wit and knowledge, assisted by neighbors and friends, NaDeau has created a beguiling nursery on a stony, unpromising site in northeastern Maine. A California native and follower of Helen and Scott Nearing's back-to-the-land philosophy, NaDeau is the sole proprietor of Stone Soup Farm, a 26-acre organic farm/nursery producing hundreds of hardy perennials, herbs, and everlastings in an ever-changing array. NaDeau lives in a hand-built stone house on the farm, around which she has woven organic multi-seasonal display gardens. As a nurserywoman who is at heart a teacher, NaDeau offers craft seminars and gives inspiration to a devoted following of customers on the delightful garden sanctuaries that can be created on stony northern soil; though, of course, they would be even better with a bit of herbs...of lilies...of lilacs...

Stone Soup Farm offers its stock of potted herbs, lilies, lilacs, and garden-worthy perennials near a pretty wooden herb shop. No plant list or catalog is available, and the stock changes with the seasons. Although the selection contains attractive classics and an astonishing number of plants that survive to 25 degrees below zero, NaDeau's particular loves are the hardy lilies (including Asiatic, Oriental, and American lilies) and daylilies in pastel colors. We noticed lovely scented geraniums and potted herbs; these and NaDeau's craft skills inspired us to request a living wreath made of herbs. Much of the plant stock can be seen in beautifully kept gardens containing colorful drifts of thyme, heath, heather, alpines, and uncommon hardy perennials (we spied a lovely, pale lavender Veldt daisy). Hillside scree gardens and perennial borders are punctuated by old iron farm tools, rustic pergolas, and hand-bent wattle fencing. Visitors are offered painted Chinese parasols for protection against sun and rain. A moon garden glows in the evening, overlooking a view of distant hills. In autumn, the gardens are left to self-sow and provide food for wildlife. NaDeau offers advice on plant selection and is available for consultation on garden creation and design.

Inside the wooden herb shop, Stone Soup Farm sells herb vinegars, baskets, books, and pretty herbal gifts. The farm stays open Thanksgiving weekend, and in December hosts a Yuletide Fair where gardeners can purchase wreaths, potpourri, holiday gifts, teas, and sweets. Fragrant herb and balsam wreaths are sold by mail order at the holidays. If possible, visitors should visit Stone Soup Farm for one of its celebrated workshops on crafting twig trellises, wild nests, children's fairy garlands, and winter wreaths for birds. Kate NaDeau is an artist who weaves gracefully, with the seasonal materials of her garden, a spirit of natural delight that has few equals in stony New England. Her fey genius makes the hard life on a Maine subsistence farm seem like a page from a folk tale.

Directions: Monroe is 15 miles north of Belfast. From Route 1 in Belfast, take Route 141 north to Monroe, turn right onto Route 139, after the Monroe General Store turn left onto Monroe Road for 0.7 miles to the nursery on the left. From Route 1A in Hamden (south of Bangor), pass Route 9/202, go left onto Kennebec Road for 4 miles to the Four Seasons store, and left on Monroe Road for 10 miles to the nursery on the right.

Nearby attractions: The largest Eastern white pine in Maine (132 feet high) is located on Route 131, just south of Morrill on the right. Dedicated to preserving New England's film heritage, Northeast Historic Film in Bucksport (207-469-0924; Web site: www. acadia.net/pmmuseum/) shows old films by and about New Englanders in Bucksport's old Alamo Theater.

SUNNYSIDE GARDENS
Route 2, Box 1584, Turner, ME 04282
(207) 225-3998 phone and fax
Edith E. Ellis

Ornamental perennials. *Daylilies. Spring annuals. Small specialty nursery. Open Mothers Day to September 1, Tuesday to Sunday noon-6, and by appointment. No catalog or mail order. AHS daylily display garden. Open house Mother's Day weekend. Group teas and tours by arrangement. Design services.*

Sunnyside Gardens is a small country nursery specializing in perennials of superior ornamental value. Tucked away inland in southern Maine, its 1820 farmhouse is surrounded by cottage gardens. Owner Edith Ellis is a certified horticulturist and garden designer (also president of the Maine Landscape and Nursery Association and codirector of the Portland Flower Show) who exercises the kind of discretion most appreciated by experienced gardeners: She separates the sheep from the goats. Established in 1989, Sunnyside Gardens offers a well-screened assortment of more than 900 perennials, chosen for good looks and garden performance. The nursery's governing aesthetic is inspired by the English perennial border, with farm animals such as hens and goats lending an air of chic rusticity. On our visit, a memorably pretty entry garden was composed entirely of pink flowers, its sweet tone counterbalanced by the curmudgeonly attitude of a nearby sign: UNATTENDED CHILDREN WILL BE CAUGHT AND SOLD AS SLAVES.

Sunnyside Gardens offers hardy perennials, herbs, and complementary shrubs, natively grown and wintered at the nursery. The emphasis is on improved garden performers, keenly appreciated by neophytes as well as seasoned gardeners seeking to refresh outmoded perennial beds. Sunnyside Gardens is an official American Hemerocallis Society display garden. Its daylily collection includes new hybrids in intriguing colors such as 'Blue Sheen' and 'Grape Velvet'. Our visit also revealed unusual primroses and veronicas, appealing cranesbills, new 'Spring Pearl' phloxes, hostas, ornamental onions, and yarrows in stylish shades. Colorful variations on native woodland plants include pink rodgersia and 'Red Wing' shooting star (dodecatheon). We admired Sunnyside's black centaurea, red honeysuckle, double rose hollyhock, 'Lemon Silver' sundrops, and a small, lacquered coral lily from Siberia *(Lilium pumilum)*, imported from the St. Petersburg botanic garden 150 years ago.

Scree gardeners will delight in the assortment of saxifrages and thrifts, and those with ponds will probably want the variegated *Iris pseudacorus*. For groundcover, we liked two attractive rock cresses, one variegated and the other with especially tiny leaves. Among the ornamental herbs were giant angelica and excellent catmints and thymes. Complementary shrubs, located beside the barn, offer a choice of roses, lilacs, and viburnums, the bird-friendly double-file viburnum being Ellis's favorite shrub. Some unusual annuals and container plants are brought in for the spring.

Most herbaceous plants at Sunnyside Gardens are grown in large pots at good value. There is no mail order. All plant sales take place at the nursery, attended by educational advice from Ellis, nearly always on the premises in the company of her little granddaughter, Daphne, who has not yet been sold as a slave. A wee garden shed offers rush cloches, pot feet, teapots, and a few books.

Directions: From Route 495, take exit 12, and proceed on Route 202 north to Auburn. Bear left onto Route 4 north, then turn right onto Route 117 north. Go through Turner Center; the nursery is 2.3 miles on your left. From I-95, take exit 30 in Augusta, Route 17 west, Route 202 south, then Route 106 to Leeds, and follow signs to Turner Center. Take Route 117 north; the nursery will be 2.3 miles on your left.

Nearby attractions: Nezinscot Farm's natural food store, Route 117, Turner (207-225-3231), sells organically raised milk, cheese, vegetables, natural foods, wool yarns, and knitted items. The McLaughlin Foundation, Route 117, South Paris (207-743-8820; www.dma.net/garden/), maintains one of inland Maine's most beloved perennial gardens, a 2-acre sanctuary located directly on Main Street, first cultivated by the late Bernard McLaughlin in 1936. A tearoom in the barn serves lunch and afternoon tea.

VALENTE GARDENS

123 Dillingham Road, North Berwick, ME 03906
(207) 457-2076
Ron and Cindy Valente

Daylilies; hostas. *Hybridizer's nursery. Open in May and June, weekends 10–4, and July and August, Wednesday to Sunday 10–4. Mail-order catalog $1. AHS daylily display garden. Peak bloom mid-July. Group tours available.*

Daylily hybridizer Ron Valente grows more than 1,600 cultivars at Valente Gardens, his home nursery in southern Maine. Valente is a mad scientist and genetic adventurer who supports an aggressive daylily breeding program by teaching high school biology to mesmerized teenagers. He has an intelligent eye, a puckish smile, and often wears a Red Hook Ale T-shirt while working in the garden. His aim is to breed the best hardy daylilies in the country. To do this, he makes 2,500 crosses per year, subjects them to the worst winter conditions possible, and selects the 10 best survivors. He applauds what he calls Maine's "deliciously awful" winters for weeding out vulnerable seedlings, on the premise that "the weak were never meant to live in the North." When asked what impels him to push the edge of daylily breeding in New England, he responded, in the true spirit of adventure, "I just want to *know*."

Valente strives to produce advanced daylily hybrids like those cultivated by southern breeders, but fully hardy in the North. The sought-after southerners are highly floriferous evergreen daylilies bearing large, richly colored blossoms, ornamented with baroque ruffles, edges, and eyezones. A measure of Valente's success in breeding competitive daylilies for northern gardens is 'Cape Porpoise', his award-winning ruffled pink daylily with gold wire edges and yellow-green throat, bearing more than 30 large blossoms per scape, bone-hardy to New England. Similarly imposing are his deep black-purple 'Storm Watch' (30 to 35 blooms per scape) and rose-purple 'Down East Royal' (25 blooms per scape), useful for both gardening and breeding and tough as nails. Our favorite Valente hybrid is 'Moon Over Ogunquit', a luminous near-white tetraploid subtly tinged with green and gold.

Valente Gardens' catalog offers more than 450 daylilies by mail order, listing the breeder, introduction year, and bloom habit of each plant. The list includes the Valente introductions and hardy hybrids produced by other breeders, including many unusual pink, peach, lavender, and black daylilies. Valente is a particular fan of Ray Moldovan, a noted midwestern hybridizer whose black–purple 'Salem Witch' is much used by breeders. Although new hybrids can cost $100, Valente Gardens offers wonderful plants at $6, and landscape collections for even less. Valente Gardens also carries hundreds of daylilies not listed in the catalog, available by special order. Daylilies are shipped freshly dug and bloom-size, with double divisions when possible.

Valente Gardens is an American Hemerocallis Society display garden, and visitors are welcome to stroll the garden, whose peak bloom occurs in mid-July. The Valentes encourage guests to tour the seedling beds and help flag the best new hybrids, a fascinating exercise for any gardener. We admired EX-T-97-67, a beautiful rosy daylily with a white edge and 40 buds per scape, hoping it makes the grade. Original Valente hybrids intended for discard can be acquired at the nursery for $10 a clump—considering the cost of their parents, one of the great bargains of the daylily world. Visitors to the nursery can also purchase 200 varieties of hosta, container-grown by Cindy Valente.

Directions: North Berwick is in southern Maine, across the river from New Hampshire. From I-95 North, take exit 2/Wells. Turn onto Route 109 west. In 0.5 mile, turn left onto Route 9 south. Follow for 6.6 miles to North Berwick, and turn right at the light onto Route 4 south. In 0.2 mile, turn left onto Lebanon Road, then left at Five Corners (continuing on Lebanon Road). In 5.6 miles, turn right onto Dillingham Road, to the second house on the left.
Alternately, from I-95 south, take exit 4/Freeport, and turn right onto Route 111 west. Merge with Route 202 in Alfred and follow Route 202 south into Sanford. Go straight at the light, continue on Route 202 to East Lebanon, and turn left at the light onto Little River Road. In 3 miles, turn left at the fork, and then take the first left onto Dillingham Road.

Nearby attractions: A local tradition, Fogarty's Restaurant and Bakery, Main Street, South Berwick (207-384-8361), specializes in good Yankee food such as New England boiled dinner and an apricot cheesecake said to be "worth a year off your life." Hamilton House in South Berwick (207-384-5269) is an elegant 18th-century mansion with formal gardens now owned by the Society for the Preservation of New England Antiquities (SPNEA); Sarah Orne Jewett used the setting in one of her romantic novels, The Tory Lover. *Snug Harbor Farm, Route 9, Kennebunk (207-967-2414), is a small, beautifully kept horticultural farm run by landscape designer Anthony Elliott, growing uncommon annuals, perennials, and "plants for connoisseurs"; ponies, ducks, and exotic pigeons enliven its chic barnyard atmosphere. Ron Valente recommends fellow beer lovers to the Red Hook Ale Brewery in Portsmouth, New Hampshire (603-430-8600), for brewery tours, free samples, an outdoor beer garden, and a pub offering "fresh beer made right upstairs"; take exit 1 on Route 16/Spaulding Turnpike, turn left at the ramp, and then left at the second light; the brewery is on your left.*

WERNER'S PICKET MOUNTAIN FARM

P.O. Box 41, Bridge Street, Newfield, ME 04056
(207) 793-8360
Werner and Pam Kabitzke

Houseplants and hanging baskets. Seasonal plants. Orchids. Family-run greenhouses. Open daily all year, Monday to Friday 8–5, Saturday and Sunday 8–noon; in May and June 8–6 daily. Fall and Spring Open House. E-mail: werner's@cybertours.com.
Werner's Picket Mountain Farm consists of an impressive lineup of well-built greenhouses on a rural mountain road in Newfield, 35 miles west of Portland, near the New Hampshire border. Proprietor Werner Kabitzke is the son of the original Werner, a German native who established this family-run greenhouse operation in 1974. Werner's is a wholesaler selling tropical houseplants, hanging baskets, and seasonal plants to the trade, but is open daily to anyone willing to travel for lush plants at wholesale prices. On our visit a luxuriant 8-inch hanging basket of ivy geraniums was only $12.50. Visitors wandering through the greenhouses will notice huge tropical specimen orange trees, tropical aralias, bird-of-paradise plants, and tree yuccas.

Werner's greenhouses are clean and well run, and the tender and tropical plant stock beautifully grown. All plants are propagated in large quantity by cuttings and some tissue culture. We saw numerous varieties of gloxinia, spathiphyllum, wandering Jew, ficus, hoya, dwarf cactus, African violet, and colorful vines such as bougainvillea and mandevilla. Hanging baskets are filled with European varieties of ivy geranium (our favorites are 'Bluebeard' and 'White Blizzard'), as well as fuchsia, tuberous begonia, English and Swedish ivy, pencil cactus, bidens, helichrysum, and so on. Among the seasonal plants are spring primroses, fall mums, and Christmas poinsettias in striped, speckled, and salmon-colored varieties. The senior Kabitzke will occasionally sell orchids from his own collection, and observant visitors might see one or two banana or hibiscus plants for sale.

Werner's philosophy is to beat commercial suppliers by offering better plants earlier and at reasonable prices. Nothing here is rare or extraordinary, but gardeners needing a lift can come for primroses when they really need them, in February, or join the crowd for hanging baskets just before Mother's Day.

Directions: From Portland, take Route 25 west, then Route 11 south into Newfield. In 1 mile after the elementary school, turn left onto Bridge Street; Werner's is 0.25 mile on your left. Alternatively, from New Hampshire Route 16/Spaulding Turnpike, take Route 110 east through West Newfield. In a few miles, turn right onto Bridge Street. In 0.25 mile, Werner's is on your left.

WOOD PRAIRIE FARM

49 Kinney Road, Bridgewater, ME 04735
(800) 829-9765; fax (800) 300-6494; farm (207) 429-9765
Jim and Megan Gerritsen

Certified organic seed potatoes. Family-run organic seed potato farm. Open for phone or fax orders Monday to Friday 7 A.M. to 9 P.M., Saturday 9-4, Sunday 12-6. Free catalog. Potato growing supplies. Mail order fresh vegetables and gourmet potatoes. Open farm day in late July. E-mail: jim@woodprairie.com. Web site: www.woodprairie.com.

The humble potato, developed as a food crop by the Incas 12,000 years ago, is now a gourmet vegetable with more varieties and colors than anyone could guess by visiting a modern supermarket. Wood Prairie Farm, a certified organic potato farm in Aroostook County, offers vegetable gardeners 16 varieties of certified organic seed potatoes through *The Maine Potato Catalog*. Run by the Gerritsen family and their neighbors, Wood Prairie Farm aims to satisfy the "true potato lover," the one "left chronically disappointed by the common unnamed supermarket potatoes" that favor yield over taste. All seed potatoes have been test-grown for culinary quality and compatibility with organic cultural methods. Potato-grower supplies like sacks, needles, and string are available, along with cedar potato barrels and sturdy gathering baskets woven by the Micmac tribe.

The Maine Potato Catalog sells seed potatoes for early, mid-season, and late-maturing varieties; for moist potatoes, mid-dry, and dry potatoes; for creamy and waxy potatoes; for red and blue potatoes; and for fingerlings. The characteristics of each seed potato are listed on a chart indicating skin color (purple, red, gold, and white), flesh color (gold, red, and white), tuber shape (round or oblong), flower color (pink and purple), plus texture, yield, disease resistance, and best kitchen use. Some potatoes, such as 'Russian Banana' and 'Rose Finn Apple' fingerlings, are heirloom varieties. Others can be grown for color novelty alone, such as 'Cranberry Red' (rose-red both inside and out) and 'All-Blue' (ditto in purple-blue). The 'Prince Hairy' potato, developed by agriculturists at Cornell University, is the first in a new Hairy Line of Royal Potatoes whose hirsute foliage repels potato pests naturally, without chemicals, by tickling their feet. All seed potato orders are accompanied by potato postcards and organic growing instructions. Lazy gardeners can skip the growing process entirely and order fresh organic tablestock potatoes, organic vegetables and organic dried fruit by mail order from Wood Prairie. Farm visitors can also buy milling grain and hay. Tours of the farm's organic crop and livestock systems are held on Open Farm Day in late July.

The Maine Potato Catalog takes its tone from nostalgic ads in old garden catalogs. An 1892 catalog quotation from Caribou, Maine, asserts proof positive that Maine's latitude improves seed potato yield: "At harvest time the total yield was four and four-fifths times greater from the Maine seed than from that grown in Pennsylvania." Although 1892 latitude research is not exactly fresh, customer testimonials do confirm that Wood Prairie seed potatoes perform well in cold-climate gardens.

Directions: Take I-95 through Bangor to Houlton, on the New Brunswick border. Exit onto Route 1 north, and proceed to Bridgewater (south of Presque Isle). Take West Road (by the Bridgewater Grammar School) 3 miles to its end, then turn left onto Kinney Road. The farm is 0.3 miles on your right.

Nearby attractions: Aroostook County, Maine's potato-growing capital, is farther north than parts of Canada. Visiting gardeners may be interested to know that a single gram of soil from Aroostook County's rich farmland is estimated to contain 30,000 protozoa, 50,000 algae, 400,000 fungi, and (almost unbelievably) 2.5 billion bacteria. The Maine Potato Blossom Festival, Aroostook County's premier event, held in Fort Fairfield each July (207-472-3802), features a mashed potato wrestling contest that must be seen to be believed.

YORK'S HARDY RHODODENDRONS

77 Ridge Road, Bath, ME 04530
(207) 443-5865 phone and fax
Tom York

Hardy rhododendrons and azaleas. Mountain laurel, magnolia. *Small specialty nursery. Open April 15 to July 1, daily except Tuesday 9–5; July 2 to November 1, Thursday to Tuesday 9–5; and by appointment. Call ahead if traveling a distance. Free catalog. Mail order. Display gardens. Gift certificates. E-mail: york-rhodies@loa.com.*

York's Hardy Rhododendrons is a small specialty nursery bent on persuading cold-climate gardeners to grow rhododendrons that are not normally cultivated in northern New England. Only a few kinds of rhododendron are generally grown in Maine, but hundreds more could be, for they love a cool, moist climate and the acid soil so abundant in the region. Owner Tom York is a lifelong gardener who began growing rhododendrons as a hobby in 1987; he opened his nursery as a "new adventure" 10 years later, after leaving his job as a facilities engineer at Bath Iron Works. York's Hardy Rhododendrons, located in a cold pocket next to York's home in Bath, affords his rhododendron collection an excellent proving ground for plant hardiness. The nursery specializes in growing cold-adapted rhododendrons and azaleas (botanically classified as rhododendrons), as well as some mountain laurels and magnolias, all proven hardy to coastal Maine.

York's Hardy Rhododendrons offers more than 200 varieties of hardy rhododendrons: deciduous and evergreen, broad-leaved and small-leaved, cultivated and species, dwarf and giant. These include several old favorites traditionally grown in Maine; showy American cultivars; ultra-hardy rhododendrons from Finland; species from China; and some popular "yak" hybrids *(Rhododendron yakusimanum),* including the gorgeous, apple blossom pink 'Ken Janeck'. Many York rhododendrons have uncommonly beautiful foliage and multiseasonal interest. We were entranced by the effects of tomentum and indumentum, a silvery fuzz on the top and underside of leaves that assumes salmon and golden hues on some plants. The small-leaved rhododendrons were also captivating, especially 'Pioneer Silvery Pink', which York recommends as a good alternative to the ubiquitous 'PJM'. The bloom color on these plants is wonderful. We spied a tiny blue-flowered rhododendron in the greenhouse (pray it proves hardy), and were thrilled to find an early, fuchsia-flowered rhododendron *(R. mucronulatum),* which we knew as a child in our grandparents' garden, scented deliciously of grape juice.

York's Hardy Rhododendrons is an excellent source of native rhododendrons and azaleas for woodland gardens. These include ultra-hardy rhodora and rosebay rhododendrons; Carolina rhododendrons from the Appalachian Mountains; Cumberland azaleas from the Great Smoky Mountains; showy flame azaleas; fragrant swamp azaleas (scented of cloves); roseshell and pinxterbloom azaleas from New England; and plum leaf, pink shell, and sweet azaleas from farther south. The new, ultra-hardy 'Northern Lights' azalea hybrids from Minnesota (developed by crossing the native roseshell azalea with Chinese hybrids) are also offered. Tom York knows and loves his plants, and will cheerfully provide planting advice and even "home visits" to ensure the suitability of his rhododendrons in a customer's garden.

Rhododendrons are sold as vigorous, nursery-grown plants in 1- to 5-gallon containers, which can be either shipped or picked up at the nursery. We recommend nursery retrieval, so gardeners can stroll the attractive display gardens, inspect York's unusual plant collection, and talk about rhododendrons with the engaging owner. Bloom season extends from May through July, peaking from late May to mid-June, but the foliage remains interesting all season. For connoisseurs, York grows many rhododendrons and azaleas not listed in his catalog. Some pretty mountain laurel hybrids and hardy magnolias (including yellow 'Butterflies') are also offered. Nursery visitors may notice the mature magnolia tree next door, which York planted in his parents' garden as a Mother's Day gift 45 years ago.

Directions: From coastal Route 1, take the Bath exit, and turn right onto New Meadows Road. In 0.8 mile, cross the irregular four corners at the stop sign, and continue 0.4 mile on Ridge Road to the white Cape on the right (Box 237).

MASSACHUSETTS

MASSACHUSETTS

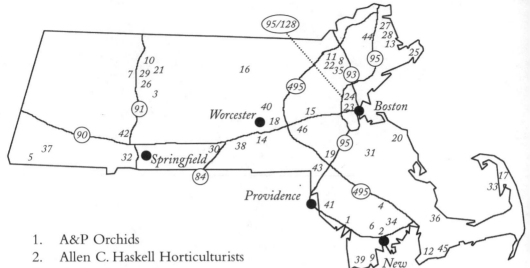

1. A&P Orchids
2. Allen C. Haskell Horticulturists
3. Andrew's Greenhouse
4. Around the Bend Nursery
5. Ashley Falls Nursery
6. Avant Gardens
7. Bay State Perennial Farm
8. Blanchette Gardens
9. Blisscapes Nursery
   and Wildlife Sanctuary
10. Blue Meadow Farm
11. Burt Associates Bamboo
12. Cape Cod Violetry
13. Completely Clematis Specialty
    Nursery
14. The Farmer's Daughter
    at Hillcrest Farm
15. Garden in the Woods Nursery
16. Garden Vision
17. Gaskell's Garden Shop
    and Nursery
18. Hardwicke Gardens
19. Hermit Medlars Walk
20. HillBilly Acres
21. Hunting Hills Farm
22. Joe Pye Weed's Garden
23. Lyman Estate Greenhouses
24. Mahoney's Garden Centers

25. New England Bamboo
    Company
26. New England Wetland Plants
27. Newbury Perennial Gardens
28. Nor'East Miniature Roses
29. Nourse Farms
30. Old Sturbridge Village
31. Paradise Water Gardens
32. Pleasant Valley Glads
    and Dahlias
33. Rock Spray Nursery
34. Roseland Nursery
35. R. Seawright
36. F.W. Schumacher Co.
37. Shady Gate Gardens
38. Stonehedge Gardens
39. Sylvan Nursery
40. Tower Hill Botanic Garden
41. Tranquil Lake Nursery
42. Tripple Brook Farm
43. Underwood Shade Nursery
44. Walter K. Morss & Son
45. Waquoit Heather Nursery
46. Weston Nurseries

A&P Orchids

110 Peters Road, Swansea, MA 02777
(508) 675-1717; fax (508) 675-0713
Dr. Azhar Mustafa

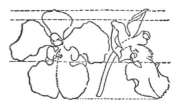

Tropical orchid hybrids. Large wholesale and retail grower. Open all year, Friday and Saturday 10–4, and by appointment. No catalog. Mail and phone orders. Visitors welcome. E-mail: aporchids@aandporchids.com. Web site: www.aandporchids.com.

Orchid, **perspective views**

A&P Orchids, one of the largest orchid propagators in the world, occupies an acre of greenhouses in southeastern Massachusetts. Founded in 1987 by Dr. Azhar Q. Mustafa, an ENT physician in New Bedford, A&P Orchids is the only regional nursery we know that claims to stock over a million plants. A&P, named for Mustafa and his wife Penny, specializes in phalaenopsis orchids (called moth orchids, or "phals"), and paphiopedilums (known as lady-slipper orchids, or "paphs"). These are mass-market tropical orchids of great beauty, popular with hobbyists because they tolerate low light and flower readily in home conditions.

A&P Orchids grows spectacular orchid hybrids, including many of its own creation; at least 100 of A&P's hybrids have effortlessly won American Orchid Society awards. All plants are greenhouse-propagated and sold as seedlings or mature plants.

Although no catalog is published, some plants are listed on the Web site. A&P lures collectors and connoisseurs from all over America, and even from Europe and Japan, for as Mustafa once told us, "Sane people don't grow orchids."

Gardeners wishing to purchase plants must go to the A&P Orchids greenhouses, where the choice of hybrids is extremely broad. Greenhouse tours are surprisingly interesting. We expected an assembly line of seedlings, but instead found a brilliant sea of A&P orchid experiments, interspersed with known hybrids abloom in bright, splashy colors. A brief look at the tissue-culture lab revealed five employees engrossed in transplanting minute seedlings with tweezers.

Visitors should bring a notebook to organize their choices, for greenhouse upon greenhouse brims with bewildering, many-hued hybrids, each one uniquely ribbed, ruffled, winged, striped, splotched, mottled, variegated, or fragrant. The complexity of form and bloom color is indescribable. An A&P moth orchid called 'Melon Delight', for example, is a gooey swirl of creamy, peachy, melony apricot; 'Sweet Revenge' is a strange blend of yellow, lavender, and tangerine, resembling a bruise with an orange tongue sticking out; and A&P's award-winning 'Julius' is a bird-of-prey orchid tinted livid brown and chartreuse, curiously art deco in style. We actually recoiled from one sinister, liverish orchid that, like a venomous insect, had fledged a pair of yellow-spotted wings.

A&P's collection is rich in moth and lady-slipper orchids, but covers all the major orchid alliances, including oncidium, dendrobium, cymbidium, vanda, and masdevallia. The orchid we most coveted, an astonishingly pretty strawberry-colored pansy orchid (of the meltonia tribe), was a brand-new hybrid, and decidedly *not* for sale; we nearly had our hand slapped for even thinking about it. The orchid world is strangely covetous; and after all, orchid prizes go to the plant, not the hybridizer. (The vast majority of A&P plants are, of course, readily for sale to customers.)

A&P Orchids may not deal in wild tropical orchids pirated from the jungle and smuggled abroad (it's illegal, anyway), but there is still plenty of drama in orchid breeding. Azhar Mustafa, himself a confessed orchid maniac, described orchid collecting as "a very complicated nonsense" that attracts "obsessives and paranoids." He then remarked, rather darkly, "This is not like buying geraniums."

Directions: From Route 195, take exit 3/Swansea/Rehoboth and turn onto Route 6 west. Pass the traffic light at Maple Avenue, and after 1 mile turn right onto Colletti Lane (across from the Columbus Oil station). Turn left at the end onto Stephen French Road. In 0.25 mile, turn right onto Peters Road; the greenhouses are 0.5 mile on your left.

Nearby attractions: Edna and Wil Dufresne of Sunburst Show Gardens, 357 Winthrop Street/Route 44, Rehoboth (508-252-3259), are award-winning gladiolus hybridizers who sell gladiolus and dahlia bulbs and cut flowers from their home-based garden. July is high season; call ahead to be sure they are home.

ALLEN C. HASKELL HORTICULTURISTS

787 Shawmut Avenue, New Bedford, MA 02746
(508) 993-9047
Allen C. Haskell

Choice ornamental garden plants. *Specialty nursery. Open all year, daily 8–5, except major holidays. No catalog or mail order. Ornamental display garden. Visitors welcome. Garden pots and statuary. Christmas wreaths.*

Horticulturist Allen Haskell, the region's reigning plant genius, maintains an eponymous nursery in southeastern Massachusetts that is deservedly celebrated as an exceptional source of stylish and rare ornamental plants. Haskell, who has the equivalent of a black belt in horticulture, is an award-winning garden designer who has pioneered many important plant introductions and gardening trends. As with leading purveyors everywhere, plant selection changes every year, but contains both novelties and classics.

Most of Haskell's plants are freshly propagated on nearby acreage and in the nursery's greenhouses; none is the product of the mass-market horticulture industry. Allen C. Haskell Horticulturists has a knack for producing the plants that sophisticated gardeners want each year, or would if they knew what to look for. Without exception his nursery seems to carry the choicest plants, the "holy grail" varieties that cannot be found elsewhere, certainly not all in one place.

Haskell and his staff spend much time tending plant material, and the selection is diverse. The nursery has wonderful annuals, lovely perennials and vines, unusual ivies, numerous Japanese maples, good bamboos and roses, and exotic trees and shrubs. Haskell is known for his unusual crinum lilies and clivias (including the coveted yellow), rare conifers, and cascading chrysanthemums. He was an important early promoter of hostas, and maintains a rich collection of more than 100 unusual hosta varieties. He is a major regional supplier of topiary, and offers spiral and mop-head evergreens, bird's-nest spruces, rosemary globes, and charming flower standards clipped into classic lollipops. (Coleus standards are excellent poinsettia substitutes).

Although May is when the best plants are available, wonderful things can be had well into autumn. As Haskell has rightly observed, "Anyone can have a spring garden." One stifling August day, we found a thriving population of dwarf conifers, rose-leaved hydrangea, white lilies, hallucinogenic double purple datura, and interesting little containers crammed with tiny sedum gleaming like cabochon emeralds.

Glamorous display borders surround the nursery stock in this oasis for serious gardeners. Novices should bring their notebooks to record the elegant effects achieved by Haskell's plant combinations. We noticed white panicles of Japanese climbing hydrangea blooming high in a shade tree, underplanted with Labrador violets; a row of peach canna lilies offset by a boldly funereal, purple-leaved border; an "echo" garden of diverse white-flowering perennials and lilies; and a turquoise-berried partridge vine twirling prettily in a trellis beside the garden shed. Visitors should remember to respect privacy; Haskell lives on the nursery property, and this is his garden. As you walk around, stay alert for abrupt encounters with the fractious camel, noisy African guinea fowl, cross-tempered white peacocks (not always in their cages), and other exotic creatures favored by the owner.

A New Bedford native who once sought to be a veterinarian, Haskell has a national reputation as New England's foremost plantsman. He has won countless gold medals at major flower shows, made his contribution to the

White House gardens, and appeared on Martha Stewart's television show. Garden wags may refer to "Allen Hassle," but if Haskell enjoys the privileges of a prima donna, he is also a tireless workhorse who is not afraid to get his blue jeans dirty. His staff is knowledgeable and engaging. This is fortunate, for there is no plant list to steer you around, few price tags, and plants are not always labeled. Nursery visitors may find it hard to shop without some guidance. If Haskell is preoccupied, try for smart, sassy Eugene, the nursery manager, distinguishable by his stud earring and Barbary pirate's tan. Original garden design services are available from Haskell.

Some handsome Italian terra-cotta pots and a few eerie antiques can be found in an outbuilding. Do not miss this exceptional nursery and its marvelous, healthy plants, improbably located on a modest residential side street in New Bedford.

Directions: From Route 195, take Route 140 north. From Route 24, take Route 140 South. Either way, exit Route 140 at Hathaway Road, proceed north about a mile, and turn right at the light onto Shawmut Avenue. The nursery (not well marked) is one block on the right, behind a stone wall.

Nearby attractions: The Shawmut Diner, a block away at the corner of Hathaway Road, is a diner classic with economically priced food. A few streets away in New Bedford, Sid Wainer & Co. (508-999-6408) is a terrific gourmet food outlet frequented by professional chefs. The Rotch-Jones-Duff House and Garden Museum, 396 County Street, New Bedford (508-997-1401), has showcase gardens complementing a fine 1834 Greek Revival house; noted rosarian Steven Scaniello updated the rose garden. Bored children can be dispatched to the New Bedford Whaling Museum (508-997-0046) or, in summer, to lovely public beaches in South Dartmouth and Westport.

ANDREW'S GREENHOUSE

1178 South East Street, Amherst, MA 01002
(413) 253-2937
Andy and Jacqui Cowles

Perennials; annuals; heirloom pansies. *Family-run horticultural farm. Open mid-April to July 4, daily 8–6, July and August, daily 9–5. Catalog $3. No mail order. Display garden. Pick-your-own cut flowers.*

New England's farms may be in general decline, but innovative horticultural enterprises have sprung up among some of the old farming families, who are bent on finding ways to retain and use their rural heritage. Andrew's Greenhouse, a horticultural farm in Amherst, is one of our favorite resources for sophisticated flowering plants in spring and early summer. Owners Andy and Jacqui Cowles operate the greenhouses on a picturesque farmstead that has been in the Cowles family for a century. The owners specialize in fine ornamental annuals and perennials, propagated or pot-grown in the farm's greenhouses and outdoor growing beds. The herbaceous plant stock is ample, ranging from well-known garden plants to exotics lacking common names. The result approaches an ideal much sought by gardeners: superior and unusual plants that are healthy, well labeled, and reasonably priced.

Andrew's Greenhouse grows its own ornamental annuals and tender perennials, in varieties both familiar and novel. Traditional choices include charming fuchsias, ivy geraniums, lantanas, double impatiens, and begonias—supplemented by sweet peas, mignonettes, four-o'-clocks, and night-scented phlox. Among the less common annuals are Japanese thistle, wheat celiosa, various annual salvias, and something called Chinese houses. An exceptional offering is wildflowers from Germany (*Glechoma* spp.), New Zealand (*Hebe* spp.), and Australia (*Isotoma* spp.). Andrew's also manages to stock cute little bunny tails (an annual grass) and colorful climbers such as canary bird vine, cardinal climber, hyacinth bean, and cup-and-saucer vine. Unique to Andrew's are a small, pale pink *Petunia integrifolia* found as a natural variation in its greenhouse and a collection of field-grown heirloom pansies, inherited from a neighboring farmer and dating to the 19th century.

For container gardeners, the greenhouse supplies unusual foliage plants such as beupleurum (green-gold) and *Alternanthera purpurea,* a striking accent plant with purple leaves. We used Andrew's *Agastache* 'Licorice Blue' to ornament a pot of kitchen herbs, and took compliments throughout its long bloom season. Spring visitors find thriving flats of herbs and vegetables in the greenhouse; we always buy a flat of cobalt-blue *Salvia guaranitica* for an outdoor container garden.

Andrew's excellent perennial collection is necessarily more mainstream, but contains many distinctive cultivars and native woodland plants. We saw good choices of catmint, bellflower, veronica, and cimicifuga, as well as handsome hostas, cranesbill geraniums, clematis vines, and ornamental grasses. The greenhouse grows the interesting new intergeneic hybrids of aster–goldenrod (x *Solidaster*) and tiarella–heuchera (x *Heucherella*)—as well as Japanese asters, Asian woodland plants, and a rare creeper from Spain called sea heath (*Frankenia* spp.). The "many species" mixes of sedum and sempervivum will stock an instant succulent garden; we used it once to fill a window box.

Besides perennials, Andrew's Greenhouse offers hardy vines, rock-garden plants, and garden roses. Customers unable to find a particular plant can ask the Cowleses to order or grow it for them.

Our warm feeling for Andrew's Greenhouse extends to its 90-page catalog, which provides intelligent and sensible information about each cultivar grown at the farm. Some catalogs make stiff and dry reading, but this one sounds like a farm lady with a degree in horticulture. Because mail order is not available, advance consultation of Andrew's catalog not only streamlines plant selection, but also leaves time to hunt for new items, examine the perennial beds, admire the view, and cull fresh cut flowers from the pick-your-own garden near the field.

Directions: From I-91, take exit 19 onto Route 9 east. In Amherst center, turn right onto Route 116 south and turn left onto Shays Street. At a small triangular green, take the far right turn onto South East Street; the nursery will be on your left.

Nearby attractions: Amherst is a gracious college town with many good cafes and bistros. The home and birthplace of the poet Emily Dickinson, 280 Main Street, Amherst (413-542-8161), is open for tours seasonally, by appointment. The Hadley Garden Center, Route 9, Hadley (413-584-1423) is a superior, well-stocked garden center with a knowledgeable staff and helpful newsletter.

AROUND THE BEND NURSERY

290 Bedford Street (Route 18), Lakeville, MA 02347
(508) 946-0302
Peter Sadeck

Topiary; special seasonal plants. *Small specialty greenhouses. Florist. Landscaping services.* [Retail nursery discontinued in 2001.]

PALMETTE IN SECOND YEAR

Around the Bend is a small nursery specializing in topiary plants grown in three greenhouses on a back road in Lakeville. Proprietor Peter Sadeck is a longtime topiary expert, having apprenticed for many years at Allen C. Haskell Horticulturists (MA), where topiary is a specialty. Sadeck also does landscaping for discriminating clients, having to his credit the award-winning gardens at the Chestnut Hill Mall outside Boston. The nursery offers exceptional perennials not needed for landscaping, and lovely cut flowers and seasonal plants.

Around the Bend's greenhouses produce topiary fashioned of myrtle, ivy, rose, lavender, scented geranium, Marguerite daisy, and tender species shrubs such as *Westringia* and *Teucrium*. Topiary plants are trained and pruned into cones, standards (tree-form), and single, double, and triple balls; considering the effort involved, they are moderately priced. The nursery will baby-sit topiary for regular clients during winter months, an invaluable service for absentee gardeners or those lacking a conservatory. Peek inside the storage greenhouse to admire Sadeck's amazing specimens of mature show topiary (not for sale), as grand as those in the gardens of Versailles.

Besides creating topiary, Around the Bend operates a florist and seasonal plant nursery. Ornamental annuals and perennials used in Sadeck's landscaping projects are for sale in the warm months, including unusual herbs and rare cascading mums (possibly unused extras from the famous Chestnut Hill Mall waterfall display; such cascades are extraordinarily demanding to grow, and all but unobtainable). Boxwood wreaths, kissing balls, Christmas trees, and elegant poinsettia are sold at the holidays. The nursery yard has a collection of handsome copper-roofed birdhouses handcrafted by a local artisan. Be sure to see Sadeck's ornamental Black Rose Comb chickens and Indian Fantail pigeons, roosting nervously in the poultry shed; apparently Wile E. Coyote eliminated their companions, the ornamental turkey. [Nursery closed in 2001.]

Directions: From Route 495 south, take exit 5 and turn right onto Route 18/Bedford Street; the nursery is 3 miles on your left.

Nearby attractions: Dave's Diner on Route 28 in Middleboro (508-923-4755) is open daily to 5:30 P.M. In Marion, Great Hill Dairy (508-748-2208; toll-free 888-748-2208) produces an excellent gourmet cow cheese called Great Hill Blue.

ASHLEY FALLS NURSERY
159 Ashley Falls Road (Route 7A), Ashley Falls, MA 01222
(413) 229-3153
Jeff Steele

Unusual hardy perennials, shrubs, vines, and trees. *Open May through October, Thursday to Saturday 9–5 and by appointment. Plant list for SASE. No mail order. Display gardens. Bulk orders. Garden design.*

Jeff Steele is a double-degree horticulturist and landscape designer—and former director of the Berkshire Botanical Garden—who has managed botanical gardens in Atlanta, Tennessee, and Rhode Island. A few years ago he bought an antique Greek Revival house in the southern Berkshires with a friend, and in 1997 he opened Ashley Falls Nursery. Now he claims to have "four full-time jobs": restoring the house, creating its formal gardens, developing a small specialty nursery, and performing landscape design services for clients. Everything Steele puts his hand to seems compact and of the highest quality.

Ashley Falls Nursery is a one-man operation specializing in rare and unusual garden plants that are hardy to the area and pass the owner's rigorous aesthetic standards. As a landscape designer, Steele favors formal garden rooms, and his nursery selections are designed to enhance compact, elegant spaces. Steele's passion for variegated foliage is much in evidence: Note the excellent specimens of variegated boxwood, cotoneaster, physostegia, columbine, porcelainberry, Solomon's seal, and maple. The controlling design sensibility here is quintessentially English. We suspected Steele of British royalty worship (a not uncommon failing of Eastern gardeners) after spying a sedum called 'Highgrove' (named for the Prince of Wales's private garden), but we discovered that he came by it honestly, after being invited by his friend Rosemary Verey for a consultation at Highgrove itself.

Ashley Falls Nursery offers horticulturally interesting perennials, shrubs, vines, and trees, but no annuals or tropical plants. Steele grows an heirloom daylily that went west with the wagon trains. A plant list is forthcoming, but no mail order. This being a developing nursery, visitors should come with their minds open to exotic possibilities, but without any assurance that particular plants will be in stock. (Customers with particular needs can readily arrange for special or bulk orders through the nursery.)

Steele's charming display gardens include an allée of white rose-of-Sharon 'Diana', an alpine-clad stone walk, an iris and bulb border, three hosta gardens, a perennial border running the length of a picket fence, a boxwood-lined knot garden reminiscent of those in Steele's native Atlanta, and other delightful gardens that are still ideas in his mind.

Directions: From I-90/Mass. Pike, take exit 2/Lee onto Route 102 west. Turn left onto Route 7 south and follow into Sheffield. Turn right onto Route 7A, and the nursery is beside the second house on the left.
From northwest Connecticut, take Route 7 north into Sheffield, Massachusetts. Turn left onto Route 7A; the nursery is beside the second house on your left.

Nearby attractions: Bartholomew's Cobble, Cooper Hill Road (off Route 7A), Sheffield, is a 277-acre nature preserve whose picturesque limestone outcroppings support rich populations of ferns and wildflowers and give sanctuary to 240 bird species; its yellow poplars and giant cottonwoods are rarely found elsewhere in the region. Open from May through July, Rick Curtiss Perennial Ranch, Konkapot Road, Sheffield (413-229-8686), is a small nursery run by the caretaker of a country estate, assisted by his kids, whose unique homey style endears him to local gardeners; the Ranch carries mainstays such as coreopsis 'Moonbeam' and unlabeled iris varieties in large pots, all at extremely reasonable prices.

AVANT GARDENS

710 High Hill Road, North Dartmouth, MA 02747
(508) 998-8819; fax (866) 442-8268
Chris and Kathy Tracey

Annuals and tropicals. Uncommon perennials. Alpines. Container garden plants. Ornamental trees and shrubs. Specialty nursery. Open May to October. Hours from May through June, Tuesday to Saturday 9:30–4:30; call for summer/fall hours. Catalog $3. Mail order. Shipping orders begin mid-March. Will-call orders and special orders accepted. Trial and display gardens. Visitors welcome during business hours. Group tours by arrangement. Lectures and workshops. E-mail: plants@avantgardensne.com. Web site: www.avantgardensne.com.

Creative gardeners have a way of seeing plants with new eyes, appreciating their essential strangeness—their dynamic forms, curious seeds, and odd habits—in a way that refreshes the relationship between plants and gardens. A cutting-edge nursery in southeastern Massachusetts, Avant Gardens is owned and run by horticulturists Chris and Kathy Tracey, trained artists who bring a radical aesthetic vision to the operation of their nursery.

Avant Gardens operates out of greenhouses behind the Tracys' 18th-century farmhouse and gardens. Avant Gardens claims to be a "specialty nursery devoted to serious gardeners and collectors of fine plant material"—it has been called "a little gem." It focuses on growing a varied range of uncommon plants spanning many categories; a recent emphasis is on some unusual annuals and tropicals that have attracted so much attention in recent years. Avant Gardens also grows excellent structural plant material: perennials, rock-garden plants, woody shrubs, and trees. All these are well described in the nursery's mail-order catalog, one of the few catalogs we really pore over in spring.

Avant Gardens built its reputation growing perennials that are hard to find in the horticulture trade, and remains a superior source of these plants. The nursery has unusual holdings of aquilegia, or columbine, "a flower that could entice fairies to your garden"; of cranesbill geranium, that "most rewarding" of ground covers (25 kinds); of New England asters in vibrant shades of purple, pink, and blue; and of extra-hardy fall mums (*Dendranthema* spp.) in unusually clear colors. Special collections have been assembled for hellebores, primulas, epimediums, euphorbias, thalictrums, bleeding hearts, and foxgloves (including a chocolate foxglove, and wild Grecian and Spanish varieties). Decorative herbs such as nepeta, salvia, and ornamental oregano represent stylish plants that have leaped "from the herb garden to the sunny border." A fine group of hosta includes the classics and some Japanese hybrids.

Avant Gardens was the first nursery we knew that grew golden hops and

European sweet violets. Garden mavens now champion *Veronicastrum sibericum,* a long-flowering relative of Culver's root resembling lavender-blue gooseneck loosestrife; Avant Gardens had it all along. Charming miniature alpines and rock garden plants, and the custom-cast hypertufa containers in which to grow them, offer a special lure to trough gardeners. Grasses and sedges form another fine resource, as do the companion shrubs and trees.

Wonderful as its perennial stock may be, in recent years Avant Gardens has really excelled in its selection of greenhouse-grown annuals and tender perennials. These are plants of superior flower-power that often begin blooming in spring or early summer and do not quit until fall or frost; smart gardeners have learned to welcome them into their borders and container gardens. Avant Gardens grows scads of flowering maple (*Abutilon* spp.), angelonia, diascia, nicotiana, canna lily, passionflower, and variegated ivy. It has yards of coleus, in all forms and colors; an amazing array of annual salvias; and many bushy, trainable fuchsias, some with variegated foliage—not to mention geraniums, or pelargoniums ("you know, the window box kind"), especially those with bronze or black foliage.

Many other extraordinary plants, still little known among gardeners, appear on Avant Gardens' plant list. We once found lavender African snapdragon here, and a white cup-and-saucer vine. Avant Gardens is a marvelous place for experimental purchases, for the Tracys themselves are horticultural adventurers who have trialed the plants in their catalog, thus reducing the risks, but none of the fun, of trying out some of their novelties.

Avant Gardens is a small nursery by industry standards, but its intimacy with the plant stock permits it to maintain consistently high standards of quality and care. Mail-order plants come in small pots, nursery purchases in larger sizes. Lectures and workshops are offered to the experienced and novice gardener on such subjects as uncommon perennials, hypertufa troughs, and drystone wall construction. Display gardens (which are the Tracys' private gardens, and also their trial gardens) offer a delightful opportunity to view the nursery stock in action. These include shady woodland beds, mixed borders, container gardens, a pergola, and a bluestone patio surrounded by sculpted alpine gardens. A catalog-based Web site offers plant list updates to garden futurists who cannot wait for the next new thing.

Directions: From Route 195, take exit 12B/Faunce Corner and follow Faunce Corner Road north to the very end. Turn left onto High Hill Road; the nursery is 1.5 miles on your right.
From Route 140, take the Mt. Pleasant exit, bear right off the ramp, and follow around the airport (becomes New Plainville Road). Take your first right onto Shawmut Avenue and pass the Dartmouth town line (becomes High Hill Road); the nursery is at #710 on your right.

From Route 24, take exit 10 and go east off the ramp on North Main Street. In Freetown, turn left onto Route 79 north and take the first right onto Elm Street. In about 8 miles (becomes High Hill Road), the nursery is at #710 on your left.

Nearby attractions: Sandwiched between areas of suburban sprawl, the landscape retains patches of rolling farmland interspersed with river views. Observe in passing the old Faunce family graveyard on the east side of Faunce Corner Road; the Faunces were original settlers from Plymouth, and their cemetery is still tended by a descendant. The Berkeley Bridge, a one-lane iron suspension bridge built in 1888 between Berkeley and Dighton, is arguably the prettiest bridge in the state, affording rustic views of the Taunton River and a streamside dairy farm. Dighton Rock State Park, Bay View Road, Berkeley, open daily 9–6, has a riverside picnic grove and a museum housing Dighton Rock, whose prehistoric petroglyphs are variously attributed to Algonquin tribes, visiting Norsemen, Portuguese fishermen, Phoenician traders, and Irish monks.

BAY STATE PERENNIAL FARM

36 State Road (Routes 5 and 10), Whately, MA 01373
(413) 665-3525
Peter Flynn

Perennials. Hosta. Woodland plants. Roses. General nursery stock. *Nursery and garden center. Open mid-April through September, daily 9–6. Closed Monday from July through September. Catalog $3. No mail order. Free gardening workshops.*

Bay State Perennial Farm is a popular roadside nursery/garden center in the Pioneer Valley that boasts of being a "gardener's destination in western New England." It specializes in superior perennials of the kind that flourish in northern gardens. Bay State undertakes what it terms a "potting frenzy" every spring to ensure that its pot-grown perennials are healthy specimens in time for the busy season. This is an energetic plant source that keeps in vogue with the best plant introductions, carrying such stylish newcomers as metallic glazed heucheras, 'Hillside Black Beauty' snakeroot, and Asian corydalis 'Blue Panda' (a dicentra relative with electric blue hearts).

While not exactly a farm, Bay State Perennial Farm exceeds the norms of most garden centers by advancing ornamental plants that are both intriguing and satisfying: geums and hellebores, poppies and peonies, lilies and daylilies, asters and grasses. Area gardeners rarely encounter such distinctive perennials as candylily *(Pardancanda* x *norisii),* horned poppy *(Glaucium* spp.), candelabra primrose *(Primula japonica),* crosswort *(Phluopsis stylosa),* and ornamental rhubarb. Bay State's impressive hosta collection, a special love of owner Peter Flynn, grows in stature and girth every year; Mr. Flynn's current favorite, the much admired 'Olive Bailey Langdon', is described as "a huge, lovely, layered masterpiece" with blue seersucker leaves edged in gold. Bay State carries good sedums, including some with variegated and ruby foliage, and encourages gardeners to "think of a forest of sedum," something like an ornamental broccoli forest. A welcome addition is Bay State's new collection of woodland perennials, featuring trillium, fringed gentian, bird's-foot violet, and hardy ferns. The dramatic Japanese jack-in-the-pulpit *(Arisaema sikokianum)* is still sufficiently rare in mainstream nurseries to draw raves from passing visitors.

The perennials at Bay State are set out alphabetically on long tables around a rustic shed; shade plants are out back under tobacco awning. One large section is devoted to ornamental trees, shrubs, and an ever-expanding collection of romantic hardy roses: albas, Bourbons, centifolias, damasks, Gallicas, hybrid perpetuals, musks, polyanthas, English roses, wild species roses, climbers, and, of course, shrub and landscape roses. For gardeners, cooks, and homeopaths, the herb list has both interest and depth. Customer demand has pressed Bay State into experimenting with ornamental annuals in the cutting garden, and it has more than met the challenge: Initial offerings include pretty annual vines, spring container plants, and a moon garden collection.

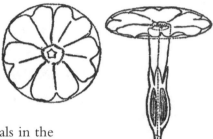

Well patronized by area gardeners, this pleasant nursery/garden center also offers excellent educational workshops, and is conveniently located just off I-91, north of Springfield.

Directions: Whately is north of Springfield. From I-91 north, take exit 22 and turn right onto Routes 5/10 north; Bay State is about 1 mile on your right, after two big tobacco barns. From I-91 south, take exit 23 and turn left onto Routes 5/10 south; Bay State is 0.8 mile on your left.

Nearby attractions: The Smith College Botanic Garden, Northampton, MA 01063 (413-585-2740), embraces the entire college campus, designed by Frederick Law Olmsted a century ago; the Lyman Conservatory, open 8:30–4 daily, houses tropical plant collections and an annual fall display of cascading chrysanthemums, grown with difficulty in the original Japanese manner. Weeds Garden & Home, 7 Old South Street, Northampton (413-584-0375) offers delightful garden supplies and gifts. Hadley Garden Center, 285 Russell Street, Hadley (413-584-1423) is an excellent local supplier of plants and horticultural advice. Annie's Garden and Gift Store, 515 Sutherland Road, Amherst (413-549-6359) carries plants and wonderful garden pots.

BLANCHETTE GARDENS

223 Rutland Street, Carlisle, MA 01741
(978) 369-2962
Leo Blanchette

Shade perennials; astilbe and hosta. Specialty nursery. Open late April through August, weekdays except Wednesday, 10–4, weekends 9–5. Open in September, weekends 10–4. Closed during thunderstorms. Catalog $3. Mail order of astilbe only. Seminars. Web site: www.blanchettegardens.com.

Situated in the pleasant town of Carlisle, just north of Concord, Blanchette Gardens is a specialty nursery renowned for its collection of hardy shade perennials. Owner Leo Blanchette and his wife, Pam, opened the nursery in 1981 on land contiguous to their ranch-style home. Blanchette Gardens is a major grower of astilbe and hosta, and attracts collectors and connoisseurs with its many new and rare plant varieties. The nursery's plant stock is imaginatively selected and propagated in pots on-site. For shade gardeners, Blanchette Gardens is considered to be one of the finest plant sources in the Northeast.

The shade perennials at Blanchette Gardens expand one's consciousness about what can be grown in New England. On a spring visit we saw large collections of primrose and fern, two rows of perennial phlox, and eight different lady's mantles, each cradling mercurial beads of dew. We admired a gold-leaved lamium, bronze-leaved snakeroot, variegated brunnera, and a gold-edged lily of the valley from Fernwood (ME). Collectors of rare shade perennials will appreciate treasures such as *Glaucidium palmatum,* with its large, palmate leaf; Japanese giant butterbur *(Petasites japonicus),* with huge, variegated foliage; and an exotic skunk cabbage whose fragrance is, thankfully, according to Blanchette, "not at all like the East Coast native." We once bought a pink corydalis and an ever-blooming strawberry here for a friend. Also on display are huge arrays of hosta (240 cultivars) and astilbe (160 cultivars)—about one third of Blanchette's vast private collection.

It is something of a marvel that this large, organized nursery lot, carpeted in black plastic and filled with container plants, could be the work of just two people. The Blanchettes produce 250,000 plants a year, all propagated by division, cuttings, and seed; each cultivar is tagged with its correct Latin name. Plants are small and come in a potting mix containing two beneficial nematodes—kindly parasites that feed on unwanted fungus gnats and beetle grubs. Because of the nursery's shallow well, chemical pesticides are strictly avoided.

People this busy cannot be expected to provide mail order, and they do not. The Blanchettes do, however, employ an innovative plant identification system that simplifies self-service at the nursery. Plants are divided by sun and shade and organized alphabetically by genus, beginning with *Acaena* (New Zealand burr). The catalog assigns each plant cultivar a row number, which means that if you want Leo Blanchette's favorite astilbe, the white 'Queen of Holland', you find it listed in the catalog at "25M" (the middle of the 25th row). Identification tags describing the plants are suspended on a taut, waist-high rope dividing each row.

Leo Blanchette is a trained biologist, popular lecturer, and accomplished plantsman who was apparently born to the job, for as a boy he worked on his grandfather's farm in Concord and, as he says, "learned to pull weeds early." His plant propagation workshop is consistently sold out. Time permitting, Blanchette tries his hand at hybridizing, and the fruits of his labor can be found at the nursery. His introductions include *Astilbe* 'Becky Lynn' and *Phlox stolonifera* 'Pamela', both named after female relatives. (*Allium cernuum* 'Leo' was named for Blanchette by a hybridizing friend.) The Blanchettes' son Jimmy, a plant biologist, has joined Blanchette Gardens, which frees his father for more hybridizing. Watch for new astilbe introductions in upcoming years.

Directions: From Route 95/128, take Route 4/225 west through Bedford center. When Route 4 and 225 diverge, stay on Route 225 west. In Carlisle center, turn right onto East Street and bear left at the fork onto Rutland Street; the nursery is 0.5 mile on your left.
From Route 495, take Route 3 south and exit onto Treble Cove Road. Turn right off the ramp and right again at the second stop sign onto Rutland Street; the nursery is 0.5 mile on your left.

Nearby attractions: A short way down Route 225 east is Kimball's Ice Cream, an old-fashioned soda stand with freshly made ice cream. Cold drinks are sold at Daisy Market at the Carlisle center rotary, and can be enjoyed in the antique cemetery across the street. The Concord Museum (978-369-9763) hosts an annual tour of local gardens in early June.

BLISSCAPES NURSERY AND WILDLIFE SANCTUARY

751 Potomska Road, South Dartmouth, MA 02748-1330
(508) 636-6535
William R. Gil

Native and woodland plants. Ground covers. Wildlife support plants.
Small specialty nursery. Visitors welcome. Open by appointment. No catalog or mail order. Display gardens. Lectures. Landscape design and construction. Environmental restorations. Web site: www.channel1.com/hb/bliss/html.

Have you ever wondered what kind of garden a bird finds most attractive? Blisscapes is a 12-acre nursery specializing in plants, mostly shrubs and trees native to the woodlands of Asia and North America, that give sanctuary to birds and other wildlife. Owner William Gil, a landscape designer and ardent birder, has managed to landscape the area around his home in South Dartmouth with an extraordinary eye, the eye of a wild bird. The result is not an ornamental garden but instead a naturalized environment that integrates wildness into an orderly whole. The key to successful bird gardening is re-creating natural places of sanctuary, using ornamental plants to emulate the growth patterns of native plant communities and invite the return of birds to our backyards. The aim of such a garden is to use ornamental plants to create soothing, enticing prospects, not for our eyes, but for the birds'.

Gil is a lifelong bird-watcher, and has a sophisticated understanding of wildlife possessed by few landscape designers in our day. His ability to assess a plant's bird attractions, and to combine it with other plants into a natural ecosystem, is the essence of his work as a landscape designer. Gil's are not gardens in the ordinary sense, and they can seem disorderly until one's eyes adjust to their purpose. Blisscapes Nursery grows woodland plants to provide food, cover, and a home to wildlife through the seasons.

As food sources, for example, Blisscapes grows alternate-leaf dogwood for great-crested flycatchers and yellow-shafted flickers; Washington hawthorn for the cedar waxwings and finches (shrikes will also impale food on its thorns); bayberries for yellow warblers; and white spruce for siskins and crossbills. We were charmed to learn that chickadees use the live cones of Eastern white cedar to store dead spiders for breakfast on cold days, though deer may devour the lower branches.(We have yet to hear of a wildlife garden deliberately made hospitable to deer.) Birds also love Blisscapes' native holly and hackberry for winter fruit; Japanese red pine for nutritious cones and sap; and Eastern red cedar, which Gil considers "the foremost bird attractant in the Northeast," for both food and shelter.

Blisscapes specializes in growing many innovative, ecologically valuable shrubs and trees in small quantities. Some plants are grown in containers by the barn, and larger specimens in an overgrown meadow near the nursery. None is priced or tagged, making it necessary for gardeners to call ahead for specimen availability or to arrange a nursery tour with the owner. Unusual woodland plants grown at Blisscapes include American fringe tree, dwarf cherry laurel, drooping leucothoe, bottlebrush buckeye, ground-cherry, highbush cranberry, and Mayflower viburnum. Native forms of dogwood, holly, and rhododendron are also available. Specimen trees include American hop hornbeam, red mulberry, sweet gum, sugarberry, and hybrid chestnut. For ground cover, Blisscapes grows choice native Oconee-bells *(Shortia galacifolia)*, ferns, variegated partridgeberry, and bearberry. Its conifers include Canaan fir, Korean fir, Brewer spruce, Sitka spruce, adelgid-resistant Western hemlock, and weeping Alaskan cedar (an arborvitae substitute disliked by deer). Blisscapes carries a variegated, salt-tolerant form of white pine, the region's great native conifer. Soon Gil promises to grow bristlecone pine, our longest-living native American conifer, routinely used by western archaeologists to date ancient sites.

Oriental woodland plants incorporate well into naturalistic gardens and add an exotic flavor to Blisscapes' wild garden. Gil once designed an award-winning Japanese tea garden for the Boston Flower Show, and Japanese trees and shrubs remain one of his major interests. Prize plants include Japanese snowbell and Asiatic long-stalk holly, which he considers one of the top 20 trees for wildlife gardens. Other unusual Asian plants grown at Blisscapes are the Japanese beautyberry, red-berried Japanese skimmia, Nanking cherry, full-moon maple, and the better kousa dogwoods. Gil also experiments with interesting half-hardy trees to see if they can be enticed to live in Zone 6 conditions.

TYPHA LATIFOLIA.

Gil's landscape philosophy is an ecological one that helps gardeners see the woods as a wildlife garden. Visitors are welcome to walk in the woodland next to the nursery, where Gil has created a bird sanctuary on land donated for conservation. Fortunate visitors may accompany Gil on a woodland walk, where they may see suet feeders, broken-open pumpkins, and seed offerings for wildlife. Blow-downs and dead trees are left for shelter, and naturalistic birdbaths reflect the sky. Weeds are let to grow: wild thistles for the finch, pokeweed for the hermit thrush. On snapped-off pines, nesting boxes are provided for piliated wood-peckers. The woods house a gray fox den, a hawk family, flying squirrels, bats, bluebirds, kestrels, and tiny golden crown kinglets that swarm around white spruce. As the measure and reward of his labors, Gil takes his Christmas bird count here each year on the winter solstice.

Directions: South Dartmouth is on the coast of southeastern Massachusetts. From Boston, take Route 95/128 to Route 24 south. In Fall River, exit onto Route 195 west and take exit 12A. Turn south onto Faunce Corner Road, passing over Route 6, where it becomes Chase Road. In 4 miles, turn right at the T-junction onto Russell's Mills Road. In Russell's Mills village (just before Davoll's yellow store), turn left onto Rock O' Dundee Road. Turn right onto Potomska Road; Blisscapes is on your left. Call ahead for an appointment.
From Providence, take Route 195 east and follow directions above.

Nearby attractions: Village Gardens, 27 Slades Corner Road, South Dartmouth, MA 02738 (508-636-8260), is a small grower of pretty hanging baskets, flowering annuals, perennials, and vines; children's gardens are a specialty.

BLUE MEADOW FARM

184 Meadow Road, Montague, MA 01351
(413) 367–2394
Alice and Brian McGowan

Unusual annuals and container plants. Perennials. *Small specialty nursery. Open April 15 to August 31, daily 9–5. Closed July 4. Catalog $3. Mail order. Display garden. Daylily Viewing Day in July. Open Garden Day in August. Slide lectures and group tours by arrangement.*

Blue Meadow Farm is a premier resource in New England for annuals, tropicals, and tender perennials that function as annuals in our raw climate. This small, family-run greenhouse nursery is sited behind an old farmstead on a country road in western Massachusetts, two hours from Boston. A cutting-edge nursery continually on the hunt for new plants, Blue Meadow specializes in flower and foliage plants that are not always available in the nursery trade. Pick a sunny morning and make it a day trip; the nursery is sited in the rich soil and rolling fields of the Connecticut River Valley, where the air is tonic and the sky seems larger than usual. Blue Meadow is a favorite destination of gardeners and connoisseurs seeking uncommon plants and annual color in the garden.

Because of variations in plant readiness dates, repeat visits to Blue Meadow during spring and early summer can be rewarding. In April, Blue Meadow's greenhouse is the scene of a color riot in the viola family. By mid-May, when the selection of annuals is at its peak, the greenhouse offers remarkable collections of annual salvia (45 varieties), nicotiana (10 kinds, including a variegated *N. langsdorfii*), verbena (13 varieties), and several unusual lewisia and clarkia (named for the American explorers Lewis and Clark). The nursery's coleus collection, embracing more than 50 varieties, is the largest in the East and features amazing, multicolored hybrids such as 'Japanese Giant' and 'Crazy Quilt'. We were wowed by the many choices of fuchsia, diascia, and cosmos (including white, sulfur and chocolate cosmos). Blue Meadow has a large collection of tender and scented geraniums (actually pelargoniums); one Victorian-era pelargonium called 'Vancouver Sentinal' has multicolored leaves shaped like the Japanese maple. Some choice annuals, such as the white California poppy, have won quality awards. Much greenhouse space is devoted to unusual foliage plants, often with heat- and drought-tolerance capabilities that guarantee them a prime place in container gardens.

Many plants at Blue Meadow Farm are little known and lack common names, including interesting natives of South Africa, South America, and

India well suited to specimen planting. Each year brings exciting introductions: perhaps a rare native baptisia from Georgia (hardy to Zone 5), or a clump-forming red rice called 'Red Dragon', used as a row marker in Philippine rice fields. We know nowhere else to find Japanese morning glories. Blue Meadow's variegated cobaea vine is an original sport (a shoot differing from the parent plant) found at the farm. Gardeners with children may choose African peanut butter plant *(Melianthus major)* for its fragrance, and cinnamon vine *(Dioscorea batatas)* on account of its tuberous fruit, which "make great dollhouse potatoes." Deft gardeners may secure the legendary Himalayan blue poppy *(Meconopsis betonicifolia)* before it is snapped up by collectors.

Outside the greenhouse, Blue Meadow Farm offers its collection of hardy perennials, alpines, ornamental herbs, and a few woody shrubs and grasses, all arranged in well-labeled rows. The perennials include more than 50 daylilies, 50 hostas, colorful succulents, numerous ornamental grasses, and some lovely, old-fashioned campanulas and cranesbills. The nursery also carries intriguing items such as variegated horseradish, ivory monkshood, and a fragrant vernal grass grown by Thomas Jefferson at Monticello. We admired the unusual thymes, including one with salmon flowers and another scented, gold-tipped variety that looks permanently in bloom.

Select woody plants are offered in gallon pots, such as shrub willow, miniature cotoneaster, native *Conradina canescens* from coastal pinelands, and a lilac relative, the American fringe tree *(Chionanthus virginicus),* which British authorities think should be our national shrub. Gardeners may notice a fey quality at this nursery, affording ineffable moments of delight to the visitor. We saw an iridescent ruby-throated hummingbird sipping the red salvias in the greenhouse. A little wooden table outdoors once bore a sign that declared, in a child's writing, MUD PIES, 10 CENTS.

Since its founding in 1987, Blue Meadow Farm has benefited from its owners' expertise and good contacts with prominent horticulturists. This winning combination produces constant innovation and an intriguing catalog deserving special scrutiny. Blue Meadow propagates its plant stock from seed or cuttings, and sells well-labeled plants in small pots with substantial roots. Beneficial insects are used for pest control in lieu of chemicals. We once battled surface weeds in the soil of some Blue Meadow succulents we bought for a window box (we had to remove them with chopsticks), but such lapses are rare. Blue Meadow is for early birds: The nursery cannot hold plants, and sometimes runs out of its best horticultural treasures. Visitors who do not know a plant or its habits should converse with the McGowans about their fascinating collection. Mail order is available, but we still prefer coming in person with the station wagon.

Directions: Montague is near Greenfield. Take Route 2 west to Turners Falls and turn left (south) onto Greenfield Road. In 2.4 miles, turn right onto Meadow Road; the nursery is 1 mile on your left.
From Route 91 south, take exit 27/Route 2A to Turners Falls, and follow directions above. From Route 91 north, take exit 24 onto Route 116 south, go over the bridge, and turn left at the lights onto Route 47 north. In 1 mile, take the first left onto Falls Road; the nursery is 3 miles on your right.

Nearby attractions: Bibliophiles can lunch, browse for used books, and admire the waterfall at the Book Mill Café in Montague (413-367-9206). The Bridge of Flowers in Shelburne Falls is a charming perennial garden sited on a disused suspension bridge span-ning the Connecticut River; some odd natural blowholes are located nearby. Gould's Sugar House on the old Mohawk Trail (Route 2), Shelburne Falls (413-625-6170), sells maple ice-cream cones for 25 cents. The Agway in Greenfield (413-773-9639) carries Turface, a hard-to-find soil aeration material used on athletic fields (and great for container gardens). The Blue Meadow catalog lists attractive hikes and drives in this scenic region.

BURT ASSOCIATES BAMBOO

P.O. Box 719, 3 Landmark Road, Westford, MA 01886
(978) 692-3240; fax (978) 692-3222
Albert Adelman

Bamboo. *Small specialty nursery. Open early May to early October, Wednesday to Sunday 10–5. Free price list. Bamboo guide $2. Mail order. Display garden. Visitors welcome. Web site: www.bamboos.com.*

Burt Associates Bamboo specializes in container-grown exotic bamboos, ranging from 6-inch houseplants to 40-foot giants. Owner Albert Adelman grows bamboo at his home in Westford, 30 minutes west of Boston. As remark-able "tree grasses" of legendary interest, bamboos are prized by gardeners as outdoor specimens, screens, houseplants, container subjects, and bonsai. Bamboo produces lovely creaking and rustling sounds in the garden, and is the subject of much poetry from Asian cultures, where it is a constant backdrop.

Burt Associates Bamboo has a good collection of bamboos in "tall" and "low" sizes. The catalog lists 30 varieties, but more are available in limited quantities. Tall bamboos are landscape specimens that grow from 10 to 60 feet, depending on conditions. These include 'Yellow Groove' with striped culms (or stems), ebony-stemmed black bamboo, and the amazing 'David Bisset' bamboo, which can grow a foot a day in hot, wet weather. Low bamboos are useful as ground cover in Oriental-style gardens. They include 'Tsuboi', with jazzy white stripes; 'If-If-If', with cream variegation; and 'Silver-Edge' bamboo, popular in Japan. Our favorite are the hardy fargesia bamboos *(Fargesia nitida and F. murielae),* native to the mountains of China, where they form fine-leaved clumps that bloom every 100 years and are fodder for panda bears. A collector's list printed in the catalog offers giant timber bamboo, marbled bamboo, and some unusual Himalayan and South American varieties.

Burt Associates sells 1- to 3-foot bamboo plants in gallon pots, mostly to mail-order customers from Texas to Canada. Landscape-size specimens can be bought at the nursery. Gardeners are welcome to select their own plants and survey the bamboo display gardens surrounding Adelman's suburban home. Adelman, a retired physical chemist who once studied the impact of light on physical processes (such as photosynthesis), took up growing bamboo in retirement. He can tell you how to keep bamboo from taking over the garden. Those who cannot come to Adelman's garden can visit his Web site for photo images of bamboo as container and bonsai subjects.

Directions: Westford is 30 minutes northwest of Boston. From Route 95/128, exit onto Route 225 Bedford/Carlisle and follow Route 225 past the rotary in Carlisle. In 2.5 miles, turn right onto Landmark Road; the nursery is up the first driveway on your right. From Route 495, take exit 31 and turn left at the light onto Route 110. When Route 110 joins Route 225, continue on Route 225 east and turn left onto Landmark Road; the nursery is up the first driveway on your right.

Nearby attractions: The Butterfly Place, 120 Tyngsboro Road, Westford (978-392-0955), open from April 15 to Columbus Day, is a "living butterfly environment" comprising a 3,100-square-foot glass atrium planted with colorful flowers providing nectar to 40 species of live butterflies. The shop sells plants suitable for butterfly gardens. The grounds outside are planted to support local butterflies; nesting and breeding areas can be observed along the pathways. Picnicking is allowed.

CAPE COD VIOLETRY

28 Minot Street, Falmouth, MA 02540
(508) 548-2798; fax (508) 540-5427
John and Barbara Cook

African violets. *Small specialty grower. Hours by appointment only. Catalog $2. Mail order. Send SASE with horticultural questions. Plant food and greenhouse accessories. E-mail: violets@cape.com.*

Cape Cod Violetry is a small nursery specializing in African violets, the most popular houseplant in America, sold to hobbyists and collectors all over the country. African violets are not violets at all, of course, but well-loved members of the *Saintpaulia* family, tropical plants from Africa (where they are called *usambara*) related to gloxinia and other gesneriads. Devoted followers consider them the perfect houseplant, being simple to grow, inexpensive, and practically always in bloom.

At Cape Cod Violetry, owners John and Barbara Cook have assembled an amazing collection of almost 400 varieties of African violet suited to home gardeners. The nursery sells starter plants in 2 1/2-inch pots and leaf cuttings by the dozen (used for easy propagation), at modest prices. Cape Cod Violetry grows its stock under fluorescent lights in the Cooks' basement, and operates almost entirely by mail order.

Cape Cod Violetry puts out a dense plant list briefly describing its collection of African violets: species plants, show plants, award winners, selections from noted hybridizers, and many unusual and oddball plants chosen for sheer visual fascination. The variety is mind-boggling. We have not fully decoded the connoisseur's language, but for the benefit of catalog readers, a "fantasy" African violet has one bloom color splashed with another; "chimeras" have striped or white-edged blossoms; "dates" are bustle-leaved (that is, one leaf growing atop another); and "clackamas rattlers" (we love this name) have long, veined, "watermelon" foliage. Original hybrids bred by Cape Cod Violetry include its award-winning 'Jennifer Christine' (frilly white blossoms with red centers), 'Amanda Ruth' (bright pink doubles), and 'Brian's Girl' (large pink blooms with bold blue splashes). Gardeners who are disoriented by the choices can order a special collection selected by the Cooks. African violet food and greenhouse supplies are included in the back of the catalog.

Cape Cod's plant selection wildly exceeds anything one might have seen in the flower section of the supermarket. Examples are African violets with bicolor pink/blue flowers and plum foliage with green tips; white blooms marked with purple thumb prints; silver blooms with a veined overlay and variegated leaves; and purple flowers with veined watermelon foliage. The most popular African violets are double-flowered varieties that generally last longer and do not drop their petals. Interesting novelty plants include green-flowered hybrids; rare yellow- and ivory-flowered hybrids; chimeras with striped blossoms; and trailing plants (including one from Japan). We can see why gardeners might give a sporting chance to 'Suncoast Circus Lady', with her heavily ruffled pink blooms piped in chartreuse (wearing sunglasses, we hope), and 'Vampire's Kiss' with its blood-red blooms stained with black. 'Saint Paul' himself (*Saintpaulia ionantha* 'Saint Paul'), enrobed in wine-red velvet, has an orchid-fuchsia halo on his lower lobes.

Directions: The nursery is open only by appointment. Call for directions.

COMPLETELY CLEMATIS SPECIALTY NURSERY

217 Argilla Road, Ipswich, MA 01938-2617
(978) 356-3197 phone and fax
Susan G. Austin

Rare and unusual clematis. Small specialty nursery. Open to visitors May 15 to September 30, Monday through Friday 8–3. Catalog $3. Mail order, phone order, or pickup. Books on clematis. Slide lectures. Clematis newsletter by subscription. Web site: www.clematisnursery.com.

Completely Clematis Specialty Nursery is exactly that—a nursery specializing exclusively in clematis. Cultivated in America since 1726, and long a passion of British gardeners, clematis is a woody, flowering vine whose function in American gardens until recently has been limited to covering lampposts and draping over mailboxes. In recent years, savvy gardeners have begun to appreciate the versatility of clematis as an ideal companion for roses, shrubs, and other vines. Light-footed and hardy to Zone 5, clematis interweaves romantically among companion plants, making them appear to flower after their own bloom is spent. Companion planting and trellis gardening are causing a quiet revolution in clematis use. Banish the vulgar purple *Clematis x jackmanii* and toothpaste-pink *C. lanuginosa* 'Nelly Moser'. American gardeners now have their choice of the fine rare clematis and excellent hybrids long trumpeted by the plant's august champion, the British Clematis Society.

Established in coastal Ipswich in 1993, Completely Clematis Specialty Nursery is one of the best sources of clematis this side of the Atlantic. The nursery's objective is to stock clematis varieties not normally available in garden centers. That the nursery is operated by a clematis fanatic is apparent from its large assembly of remarkable plants: More than 200 available varieties of small- and large-flowered clematis are listed in the catalog, and a collector's list adds uncommon species clematis that have been house-propagated from seed. Owner Susan Austin has a special interest in rare small-flowered and species clematis, including some North American natives. Because many clematis hybrids are little known, a careful study of catalog descriptions is recommended.

The nursery's offerings are evenly divided between large- and small-flowered clematis. In general, small-flowered clematis look delicate, act tough, and are immune to wilt. Though lesser known to gardeners, small-flowered clematis are championed by Austin for their superior performance during our hot, short New England summers. Of the many tribes of small-flowered clematis, the nursery's dainty *Clematis alpina* hybrids (including award-winning 'Frances Rivis') produce early, blue, lanternlike flowers. The *C. montana* hybrids are fragrant, rampant, pink- and white-flowered vines, useful for running up trees and pergolas. The heat-loving *C. texensis* hybrids (originating, of course, in Texas) sport tiny, red-plum flowers. The *C. macropetala* hybrids bear small double flowers in pink, lavender, indigo, and white; the southern European *C. viticella* group has delicate pastel flowers. We applaud the collector's spirit that secured a wild Mediterranean clematis; a green-flowered Tibetan species with fine foliage; yellow "orange-peel" Oriental hybrids; and a vexing native woodbine (popularly known as Devil's-darning-needle) from the American South.

Better known and more common in garden centers, the large-flowered clematis produce huge satin and velvet blooms in rich colors. Completely Clematis carries all the most gorgeous varieties, along with products to deal with their only drawback, clematis wilt. The catalog notes the large-flowered hybrids that have achieved the nursery's Top Ten list or won British Clematis Society awards. Two of the best are the show-stopping white 'Marie Boisselot' and the indiscreet mauve 'Comtesse de Bouchaud'. We had to order a season ahead to acquire 'Perle d'Azur' (a large, blue-flowered classic recommended by British gardener Christopher Lloyd) and 'Silver Moon' (a mother-of-pearl prize, so shade tolerant that it will, reportedly, "bloom in a closet"). The nursery's sky blue 'Fuji-musume' hybrid is one of several excellent introductions from Japan. Wedgwood blue 'H. F. Young' makes a good container plant; Roman Catholics may take special interest in 'Jan Pawel II', a white clematis hybrid produced by a Polish monk in honor of Pope John Paul II.

In keeping with the collector's spirit, Completely Clematis Specialty Nursery is, according to its catalog, "open to buy, barter, or trade interesting varieties" of clematis. Because clematis acquisition can be a competitive sport, we recommend early ordering to gardeners intent on rare plants. In addition to regular nursery stock, six-year, landscape-size clematis are available to gardeners seeking immediate splendor. Printed in the catalog are vital instructions for clematis planting and pruning, the bane of home gardeners. Although Completely Clematis operates mainly by mail order, customers over the age of 14 are welcome to visit during open hours, pick up plants, and get wet-nosed by Grendel and Willard, the two gregarious resident dogs.

Directions: Ipswich is 45 minutes north of Boston. From Route 95/128 north, exit onto Route 1A/133 north. In Ipswich center, turn right at the flashing light onto Argilla Road (toward Crane's Beach); the nursery is 1.5 miles on your right.

Nearby attractions: The Ipswich River Wildlife Sanctuary (978-887-9264) is an Audubon Society refuge, located on a former private estate with a spectacular rockery. On Argilla Road, Goodale Orchards (978-356-5366) is a 125-acre working farm selling fresh fruit, hard cider, and pick-your-own apples. Seafood lovers can stop at The White Cap, 141 High Street, Ipswich (978-356-5276), or The Clam Bar, 206 High Street, Ipswich (978-356-9707).

THE FARMER'S DAUGHTER AT HILLCREST FARM

153 Millbury Street, Auburn, MA 01501
(508) 832-2995
Donald, Sylvia, and Cindy Post

Perennial plants. Commercial farm nursery. Open daily 9–6, closed Tuesday. Free plant list. No mail order. Mailing list and free seminars. Christmas greens. E-mail: cindybertrand@charter.net. Web site: www.thefarmersdaughtergc.com.

The Farmer's Daughter is a retail nursery located on Hillcrest Farm, a former dairy farm owned by the Post family in Auburn, just south of Worcester. Mrs. Post, the original farmer's daughter, inherited the operation from her parents; her daughter Cindy is the second generation of daughters involved in the business. If you can get past the kitschy festival atmosphere, the raffles and hayrides, and the gift shop crammed with candies and collectibles, you will find a reputable source of farm-bred perennial plants and herbs, attractive vines, antique roses, specimen trees and shrubs, grapes, and strawberries.

Set on an attractive hay-clad hillside down the street from the Auburn Mall, the Farmer's Daughter propagates and grows 80 percent of its perennials and about half its trees and shrubs, with the rest bought in from New England growers. We have always been suckers for family farms—even kitschy ones—that retain their land in the face of encroaching suburban development. The Farmer's Daughter may pay the bills by selling scented candles and garden gags, but it also grows its own violets, primroses, and sweet peas.

The Farmer's Daughter arranges its perennials on outside tables, with large informative placards giving the name and characteristics of each plant. The best selection and freshest plants are, of course, in spring and early summer, but good stock is offered throughout the season. (Pots do get jostled, so check the plant against the placard to ensure that it is correctly identified.) The farm's perennials are cottage-garden favorites, interspersed with some less common ornamentals; we noticed Japanese anemone, bloodroot, donkeytail euphorbia, and a pale purple penstemon called 'Sour Grapes'.

The British Blooms of Bressingham plants are well represented here. The vine selection is also well stocked, although some "Easy to Grow" vines, touted as ornamental, can become invasive pests if not properly curbed. (We hope no gardener is going out of her way to grow Japanese honeysuckle or bittersweet, when they are already out there, choking the landscape.) On the other hand, we found it heartening to find native American ginger, pachysandra, and ferns alongside the European ginger in the ground cover section. The shrubs included such low-growing natives as bearberry, winterberry, and prostrate witch hazel.

Gardeners seeking plants should approach the Farmer's Daughter with a persevering attitude. Just when we think to write this nursery off as too Disneyfied, we find a well-grown plant in a charming new variety, talk to an experienced gardener who thinks there is something for everyone here, or consider what will happen to the land if it is not used for farming. Visitors should nevertheless brace themselves for a stagy surprise such as a pen of donkeys braying among the ornamental evergreens, or a farmer sitting outside the gift shop on a hay bale, in ironed overalls. Apples and pumpkins (including spooky white pumpkins) are sold in quantity in the fall. Reservations for seven varieties of fresh-cut Christmas trees (and related greens and poinsettias) can be made during the holiday season, which begins here just after Halloween.

Directions: From Worcester, take Route 290 south, exit at Auburn Street/Auburn, and turn left off the ramp onto Millbury Street. Go straight past Route 12, straight over the railroad tracks, under the turnpike, and past Route 20; the entry drive (signposted) is on your right.

GARDEN IN THE WOODS NURSERY

180 Hemenway Road, Framingham, MA 01701
(508) 877-7630; fax (508) 877-3658; directions (508) 877-6574
The New England Wildflower Society

Native plants. Bog plants. Perennials. Shrubs and trees. *Nonprofit native plant nursery. Open mid-April through October, Tuesday to Sunday 9–5; daily in May 9–7; last admission one hour before closing. Plant catalog $3. No mail order. Seed catalog $2.50. Garden shop open in season; also November to Christmas. Annual plant sale. Display gardens. Walking trails. Courses, lectures, and field trips. Books and publications. Wildflower conservation. Volunteer corps. Entry fee; free to members. E-mail: news@newfs.org. Web site: www.newfs.org.*

The Garden in the Woods is a unique, 45-acre botanical preserve showcasing New England's largest landscaped collection of native plants. The garden itself dates to 1932, when landscape designer Will Curtis bought an undeveloped parcel on Framingham's Hemenway Road, built a cottage in the forest, and groomed the native woodland to demonstrate his design skills. Over the next 30 years, Curtis and his partner, Richard Stiles, created a wild-flower sanctuary that blends native and cultivated plants into a lyrical, naturalistic whole, described as an "ever-changing living museum" of indigenous plants. Unusual in its day, their garden anticipated the modern trend toward ecological gardening and the appreciation of native plants. In 1965, with suburban development encroaching on all sides, Curtis donated the garden to the New England Wildflower Society (founded in 1900, but then lacking a headquarters).

The New England Wild Flower Society is the region's leading nonprofit conservation organization dedicated to the preservation of native flora from the temperate woodlands of North America. According to the society, "Few people realize that wild plants are in crisis worldwide—even here in our own regional 'backyard.' In New England, nearly 350 of 2,000 indigenous plant species are at risk, and some have already vanished from historic locations." To address the problem, the society operates a conservation program for the recovery of endangered flora; educational programs; a slide library; a code of ethics and source lists for native plants; and a plant nursery to meet the need for ethically propagated native flora as a substitute for wild collecting.

The society's nursery, first started in 1977, is now the region's largest source of native plants. The best introduction to its holdings is the Garden in the Woods itself, where more than 1,600 native flora grow in woodland groves, lily ponds, sunny bogs, pine barrens, rock gardens, and meadows; a special garden is devoted to rare and endangered species. Using this superb resource, the nursery propagates and sells more than 10,000 individual plants per year. An annual catalog lists nearly 400 varieties of native plants, including wildflowers, woodland plants, shrubs, trees, bog plants, and garden perennials. Expansion of nursery operations is a continuing priority for the society.

This nursery's clear purpose is to offer gardeners an appealing alternative to ripping desired plants from the wild, or to supporting nurseries that do. The nursery grows many lovely spring ephemerals threatened by wild collection, such as double bloodroot, merrybells (*Uvularia* spp.), white toothwort *(Dentaria diphylla),* and showy trillium. Unlike commercial growers, the garden's propagators know how to work with threatened and difficult native plants, making it a unique source for some species. This is the gardener's sole source for the endangered Plymouth gentian *(Sabatia kennedyana)* and box huckleberry *(Gaylussacia brachysera).* The same is true for rare Appalachian Jacob's ladder *(Polemonium van-bruntiae)* and two slow-growing lily relatives, turkeybeard *(Xerophyllum asphodeloides)* and swamp pink *(Helonias bullata).* Here Massachusetts gardeners can reputably acquire the state flower, the mayflower or trailing arbutus *(Epigaea repens).*

The nursery is a special trove of woodland plants native to New England. Many of these make excellent ground cover, such as partridgeberry, wintergreen, wild ginger, lowbush blueberry, and three-toothed cinquefoil. Perhaps most beautiful of all is bunchberry *(Cornus canadensis),* a ground cover dogwood from the northern woods. Woodland shrubs include native hollies, azaleas, and witch hazels. Among the woodland wildflowers are indigenous Oconee-bells *(Shortia galactifolia)* and yellow fairy bells (*Disporum* spp.) from

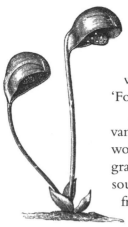

Asia. The jack-in-the-pulpits include a stunning black-striped Asian variety *(Arisaema sikokianum)* and a rare native species called green dragon *(A. dracontium)*. Graduates of the cold war may wish to plant Virginia bluebells next to the nursery's 'Former Soviet' bluebells *(Mertensia siberica)*.

Many nursery-grown plants may be familiar to observant hikers. The nursery carries wood anemone, blue wood aster, wild leek, goldenrod, dwarf crested iris, native grass, sedge, and a rich array of ferns. It is a responsible source for goldenseal, a wild herb under much pressure from collectors. It has assemblies of native violet, gentian, meadow rue, phlox, foamflower, and coneflower.

Native bog plants include marsh marigold and marsh mallow (a native hibiscus). Among its woody flora are speckled alder, white fringe tree, species viburnums, and wild lilac *(Ceanothus ovatus),* which is not really a lilac at all but, rather, a compact shrub said by society propagators to be "abuzz with every sort of pollinator" when in bloom.

The Garden in the Woods puts on the region's largest plant sale in mid-June. A major resource for native plant collectors, the sale is madly popular, often attracting 3,000 attendees, even in pouring rain. (Aggressive tailgaters arrive at dawn with folding chairs and take-out coffee.) Although the sale is salted with rarities, laid-back gardeners can buy many plants through the nursery before and after the sale. (Some prizes do sell out, however.) The nursery's dedicated staff provides expert advice on the selection, planting, and care of natives. Wildflower seed, fern spores, and books are sold in spring through a separate mail-order catalog.

The history of wild collecting holds painful memories for New England. Robbins' cinquefoil, a tiny member of the rose family indigenous to the White Mountains, was culled wild at the turn of the century and sold in Boston by the thousands for 10 cents apiece. By the 1980s, the plant, which resembles little buttercups, had nearly vanished. Conscientious gardeners seeking to repair such predations can volunteer for conservation work through the society's chapters in Massachusetts, Connecticut, Maine, and New Hampshire. In recent years, volunteers have helped replant rare and endangered native species around the Pinkham Notch Visitors Center in the White Mountains—including robbins' cinquefoil, which is now making a comeback. Despite such small successes, however, the native tundra of the White Mountains—postglacial alpine plants that have survived for 12,000 years in what has been called "a thin zone of life between rock and sky"—are still being wiped out by mountain bikes and hiker's boots. Some 55 alpine species that were once known to exist in the northern Appalachians, many as late as the 1970s, can no longer be found.

Directions: From I-95/128, take Route 20 west. In 8 miles, turn left in Sudbury center onto Raymond Road. In 1.3 miles, turn right onto Hemenway Road and follow signs to the Garden in the Woods.
From I-90/Mass. Pike, take exit 12/Framingham and bear right onto Route 9 east. In 2.4 miles, take the Edgell Road exit, and at the top of the ramp turn left onto Edgell Road. In 2.1 miles, turn right onto Water Street, then left onto Hemenway Road, and follow signs to the Garden in the Woods.

Nearby attractions: Russell's Garden Center, 397 Boston Post Road/Route 20, Wayland (508-358-2283 and 508-358-5183) is an excellent one-stop garden center that indirectly inspired this book; the Saturday afternoon traffic crush on Route 20 got us to wondering how far we could go for plants in the same commuting time.

GARDEN VISION

63 Williamsville Road, Hubbardston, MA 01452-1315
(978) 928-4808 phone and fax
Darrell R. Probst

Rare epimedium. *Small specialty nursery. Free catalog. Mail order only. No visiting hours except weekends in bloom season. Small group tours by arrangement. Call ahead. E-mail: darrellpro@earthlink.net.*

Horticulturist Darrell Probst has a boyish charm that might fool you into thinking he is new to professional horticulture. In fact, he is a distinguished plant collector, explorer, lecturer, garden designer, hybridizer, and general botanomaniac. Probst has designed several displays for botanical gardens in Massachusetts, but in recent years he has focused on collecting, cataloging, and hybridizing rare plants. As someone observed of a plant collector more than 200 years ago, "the mere suspicion of a plant unknown to him was an irresistible attraction."

Probst sponsors botanizing expeditions to Asia, seeking to discover endangered plants unknown to Western horticulture. He has traveled with noted plantsmen Tony Avent and Dan Hinkley to remote reaches of Korea and western China, collecting rare plants for use in science, propagation, and hybridizing. He brings back exotic plants and traveler's tales; during a slide lecture, he once spoke of Sichuan dishes featuring rhododendron blossoms, evergreen needles, wasp larvae, and french fries. Last we heard, he was taking a class in conversational Chinese.

Plant hunters are driven by passion, and Probst's passion is for the genus *Epimedium*. Garden Vision is the small nursery through which he offers rare epimediums to collectors and gardeners, seeking, as he puts it, "preservation through cultivation." A member of the Barberry family, epimedium is still something of a horticultural discovery. Known in the vernacular as barren-wort, bishop's-caps, and fairy wings, epimedium is a woodland perennial groundcover, hardy at least to Zone 5, which forms loose clumps and has the airy, delicate appearance of columbine. Its heart-shaped foliage spans three seasons, and in springtime its dainty flowers are suspended on wiry stalks like tinted spiders. Its virtuosity, beauty, and effortless care have won this enchanting shade plant a burgeoning popularity in garden circles. Probst has one of the most extensive collections in the world.

Garden Vision offers nearly 100 kinds of epimedium for sale by mail order, along with a few choice iris and bloodroot supplied by Joe Pye Weed's Garden (MA). Many epimediums are Chinese and Korean varieties never before seen in the West. In addition to nursery-propagated wild epimedium from Asia and America, Garden Vision grows rare hybrids from the collection of the late Harold Epstein, and exciting new cultivars from Japanese hybridizers and from Probst himself.

The epimedium's delicate flowers come in yellow, white, and rose, while its leaves are bright green, rose-tinted, or variegated. Choices range from tiny, hard-to-find 'Nanum' to rare, mottled *E. brachyrrhizum* and showy pink-and-white *E. epsteinii*. Although Garden Vision guarantees its cultivars true to name, iron-clad identities are not always possible in this genus. Even the expert Probst, who discovers many rare epimediums on his botanical expeditions, cannot always state their names or hardiness characteristics with certainty.

The Garden Vision catalog provides informative plant descriptions and an entrancing sheet of flower photographs. (Because of their rarity, some epimediums are of limited availability in order to preserve supply.) Generous gardeners who contribute to Probst's Expedition Fund receive a rare plant gratis. Probst has discontinued his Epimedium newsletter in favor of writing a book on the genus for Timber Press.

Garden Vision operates exclusively by mail order. Forget about dropping in on Probst at his nursery or attempting a garden tour. You can visit Garden Vision's production beds on a couple of weekends in bloom season, and that's it. If you want to meet the fascinating Darrell Probst, send him a letter or e-mail, or sign up for one of his slide lectures at the Arnold Arboretum in Boston.

GASKILL'S GARDEN SHOP AND NURSERY

43 Race Point Road, Provincetown, MA 02657
(508) 487-4855; fax (508) 487-3959
Eve Archer

Rare and unusual annuals, perennials, and vines.
Antique roses. *Small specialty nursery and greenhouse.*
Open daily 9–5, March 15 through October. Open
Christmas. No catalog or mail order.
E-mail: sylvaneve@mediaone.net

You could easily miss this fascinating nursery,
wedged like a secret onto a side road in
Provincetown, just off the Mid-Cape Highway (Route 6). That would be a
shame, for Gaskill's Garden Shop and Nursery is a tantalizing source of garden and container plants. Lovers of the unusual and experimental should
choose a weekday (being mindful of Cape traffic) and make their way out
here, regardless of the nursery's small size and remote location.

The *genius loci* of Gaskill's is Eve Archer, a self-confessed plant fanatic
who spends her waking hours in pursuit of rare and unusual specimens.
Single-mindedness, drive, curiosity, wanderlust—Archer has everything in
common with the world's great botanical explorers. Even in the present age,
plants exist that are unknown to horticulture, and we had the pleasure of
acquiring just such a plant from Archer at her nursery. Called *malacatillo* by
the Zapotec Indians of Mexico (a mountain-dwelling tribe who use it for
garlands and cut flowers), this plant lacks a botanical name and is normally
unavailable in the trade. Seeds were brought to the United States by J.L.
Hudson, a plant-collecting bounty hunter who claims to be on the "bleeding
edge" of horticulture. Nobody quite knows how tall a *malacatillo* gets in New
England, how hardy it is, or whether it will agree to flower here. We bought
it anyway, if only for its handsome foliage and rhubarb-colored stems.
Archer's adventurous attitude is contagious; we figured we would just grow it
as an annual and see what happened. (It grew to 5 feet, bloomless, and died
in a hard frost.)

The choice of plants at this small nursery is necessarily limited by its
space. That being said, the longer we spent here, the more excited we became
by the sophistication and singularity of the plant choices. We first glimpsed
Archer, outfitted in a flowered skirt and high-top sneakers, blaspheming,
struggling to bring in a pair of Australian tree ferns, which are genetically
programmed to grow 30 feet. A customer, whose garden was soon scheduled
for a tour, announced that this was his favorite nursery and deftly spirited off

a box full of striking mallows, pink with chocolate markings. Of Gaskill's impressive annual salvia offerings, we coveted two unusual Turkish salvia that are all but unobtainable—one a variety of clary ("clear eye") sage that Jesus purportedly used to cure the blind. We also admired a Himalayan indigo with pealike foliage and purple flower spikes; a huge, spiny *Solanum autopur-pureum;* and an unruly, colorful *Polygonum orientale* that looked suspiciously like pokeweed. Gaskill's Nursery is the only place we have seen the original wild petunia from China (another plant-hunter's trophy); *Cerinthe major* 'Kiwi Blue' (extolled in the garden press for its sky blue terminal foliage, but devil-ish to find in nurseries); and hardy cactus. One of Archer's favorite plants was a common New England weed known as Indian paintbrush *(Asclepius tuberosa),* which had been sent to finishing school in England to improve its flower color. Hard-to-find antique and species roses (beloved by Archer for their "history, beauty, scent and toughness") round out the nursery's offerings.

Gaskill's Nursery occupies a small, fenced lot under shade trees, next to a parking lot. Its office, an eccentrically shaped wood-and-glass shed, is surrounded by a welter of plants: in containers, on tables, on stone walls, and on the ground. Some perennials are grown by Gaskill's; others come from small specialty growers. No catalog or mail order is available. The labels being of erratic quality, visitors need guidance to find the best things. This is an absorbing, ever-changing nursery, the product of much ongoing thought and effort on the part of its owner. Instead of Gaskill's, we wish it were called The Outermost Nursery, so that gardeners could tell what intriguing things Eve Archer is up to here on the Outer Cape.

Directions: Take Route 6/Mid-Cape Highway to Provincetown and exit onto Race Point Road; the nursery is 0.2 mile on the right.

Nearby attractions: Next door, Nelson's Farm Market sells sandwiches, bike rentals, fish-ing tackle, and bug repellent; bathrooms are picturesquely sited in a converted outhouse. Beech Forest Trail, 0.25 mile inland on Race Point Road, is a graded walking trail through a native woodland that remains, as it appeared to Pilgrims who stopped here in the early 1600s, "encompassed about to the very sea with oaks, pines, junipers, sassafras, and other sweet woods" (Mourt's Relations, A Chronicle of Plymouth Colony). This mile-long trail affords an easy walk around a wild pond and through a surviving beech forest that represents the final stage of native forest development on Cape Cod.

HARDWICKE GARDENS

254A Boston Turnpike (Route 9 east), Westborough, MA 01581
(508) 366-5478, 366-5630; fax (508) 836-4539
Paul Trudeau

Aquatic plants. Specialty nursery and garden center. Open April 1 to Christmas Eve, Monday to Saturday 9–6, Sunday 12:30–6. Greenhouse open mid-May to November 1. Free plant catalog. Shipping and delivery available. Pond-supplies catalog $2. Garden statuary and fountains. Free seminars; write for schedule.

Located on busy Route 9 in Westborough, Hardwicke Gardens is a nursery specializing in aquatic plants and pond supplies. Established as a garden center decades ago by owner Paul Trudeau, a trained architect and horticulturist, Hardwicke now devotes itself exclusively to water gardening. Here gardeners with ponds and pools can find water lily hybrids worthy of Claude Monet, and all the floating plants and marginals needed for a naturalistic water garden. Plumbing supplies include well-selected liners, fountains, tubs, pumps, and filters. Intriguing paraphernalia include Japanese stone basins, bamboo dippers, koi (ornamental Japanese fish), bird-attraction kits, and 16-inch handcrafted wooden sailboats made to drift lazily around the pond.

Hardwicke Gardens is best known for its hardy water lilies, available as standard and dwarf hybrids in beautiful shades of red, pink, white, and yellow; some are enhanced by mottled foliage and intense fragrance. Hardwicke Gardens also grows tropical water lilies in day- and night-blooming varieties, and a few hardy lotus. We can report from experience that a sky blue tropical water lily called 'Pamela' will grow in a whiskey barrel on a city street, to the delight of children. Water gardeners can also find oxygenating plants; surface plants such as floating fern and water clover; leafy uprights such as forget-me-not and pickerelweed; and numerous grasslike sedges and bamboos that enjoy having wet feet. We enjoy seeing water-loving native iris such as yellow flag, blue flag, and blue-eyed grass (a tiny iris) set among the showy Siberian and Japanese iris hybrids.

Most of Hardwicke Gardens' aquatic plants are grown in greenhouse pools on the premises. While aquatic plants are commonly sold bare-root, Hardwicke Gardens sells potted lotus and water lilies with established root systems that will bloom the first season, an important selling point for flower lovers. The catalog provides good plant descriptions, and both Trudeau and his intelligent sidekick, Gary Rivers, willingly provide expert advice on the cultivation and winterizing of aquatics. Frequent free seminars lure water-garden enthusiasts; one popular course shows how to build tabletop fountains.

As a sideline, Hardwicke Gardens creates instant "indoor parks," complete with fountains, urns, and benches, for weddings, fund-raising parties, and Hollywood movies. An assembly of concrete garden statues imprisoned behind cyclone fencing imparts an uncanny air to the nursery's statuary yard, once the site of a full-service retail garden center.

Directions: From I-90/Mass. Pike, take exit 11A onto Route 495 north, then exit 23 onto Route 9 west. In 4 miles, at the second light, make a U-turn onto Route 9 east; the nursery is 0.2 mile on your right (next to R.G. Shakour Beauty Supplies & Equipment).

Nearby attractions: Founded in 1961, Windy-Lo Nursery, 309 Eliot Street (Route 16), South Natick, MA 01760 (508-655-0910) is a retail garden center known for annuals and geraniums, with an expanding perennial yard full of exciting new stock.

HERMIT MEDLARS WALK

3 Pierce Street (Route 140), Foxborough, MA 02035
(508) 543-2711
Bill and Ada Godfrey

Bearded iris. *Hybridizer's nursery. Open daily from mid-April through June, and by appointment. Catalog $1. Mail order. Display beds. Bloom season late April through June. E-mail: hmwalk@ici.net. Web site: http://home.ici.net/~hmwalk.*

Hermit Medlars Walk is a small hybridizer's nursery specializing in dwarf bearded iris. Owners Bill and Ada Godfrey, British natives who named their nursery after a famous garden in England, appear to be having a wonderful time breeding and growing bearded iris cultivars. The Godfreys are active members of the Iris Society of Massachusetts and well connected in the iris world. Their home-based nursery is a trove of bearded iris hybrids in amazing colors, with strong emphasis on miniatures and dwarfs.

These days, bearded iris breeders are producing rococo innovations rivaling those seen in the daylily world: patterns, bicolors, ruffles, frills, gilding, stitched edges, wire edges, bubble ruffling, and repeat bloom—all on plants proven hardy to northern gardens. Hermit Medlars Walk propagates and grows iris hybrids produced by the Godfreys, New England breeders, and well-known hybridizers across the country. The Godfreys test all new iris plants in their garden before introducing them to customers, ensuring against pretty faces that do not survive in the ground. Guests are welcome to visit the nursery and tour its popular display and trial beds, which are in bloom from late April through June.

Like many obsessions, dwarf bearded iris breeding possesses a unique vocabulary. Hermit Medlars Walk's catalog lists more than 60 miniature dwarf bearded iris hybrids (called MDBs) and over 150 standard dwarf bearded iris (called SDBs) in all imaginable states of color and ornament. The Godfreys' dwarf bearded iris collection is strong in "luminatas" (white edges and beards, with marbled or washed centers) and "plicatas" (stitched edges on a white ground).

These diminutive iris bloom in May and love New England's cold winters and rocky soil. Recent Godfrey introductions, pictured on the cover of the plant catalog, include 'Lemon Curd' (a frilly butter-cream), 'Glebe Brook' (sky blue with green vein-ing), 'Wimple' (a frilly lavender crested number, named for a medieval headdress), and 'Plymouth Hoe' (a nautical navy on white, named for the British harbor where Sir Francis Drake "played bowls" before going to defeat the Spanish Armada.)

FLOWER OF BEARDED IRIS, SHOWING PARTS.

Other MDBs favored by members of the Iris Society include ruffled white 'Pure Allure', violet and ruby-black 'Jeweler's Art', purple-veined white 'Snow Tree', and yellow-bearded cream/violet plicata 'Rebus'. Some MDBs are so complex that they must be seen to be evaluated. Among the simpler iris, we noticed a warm brown dwarf by Paul Black called 'Spot of Tea' and a vivid carrot-colored dwarf by the late Bee Warburton (famous for her Siberian iris) called 'Orange Caper'.

The MDBs so beloved by the Godfreys are charming in small gardens and indispensable in rock gardens; we're going to try them in a roof garden. In addition to miniature dwarf bearded iris, the nursery's catalog lists intermediate and tall bearded iris and beautiful hybrids of the Louisiana iris, a hardy native iris that thrives at the edge of ponds and streams. (The stream where they are planted at Hermit Medlars Walk is called the River Kwai, on account of its having an improvised bridge.) Personal net worth is not a barrier to entry here, as many ornate iris in Hermit Medlars' collection sell for just a few dollars, and samplers offer a dozen iris for about $1 a plant.

Directions: From I-95, take the Foxborough/Route 140 exit onto Route 140 west. After Foxborough center, go past the Dairy Queen. In 1 mile, the driveway is on the right, opposite the ROUTE 1 BOSTON sign on the left.
From Route 495, take the Wrentham/Route 1 exit onto Route 1 north. Take the first right immediately after the Foxborough State Trooper barracks; at the bottom of the hill, go straight across Route 140 into the driveway.

Nearby attractions: Norway Farms, 33 Medway Street, Norfolk, MA 02056 (508-528-0107; www.norway-farms.com) specializes in specimen-size woody ornamentals and unusual conifers.

HillBilly Acres

196 Old Oaken Bucket Road, Scituate, MA 02040-0253
(781) 545-6621
Douglas W. Litchfield

Annuals, tropicals, and container plants. Aquatic plants. Perennials. Bedding plants. Small specialty greenhouse nursery. Open Easter to Labor Day, daily 9–5 and by chance. No catalog or plant list. Plant picture book. Pet rabbits. Tool sharpening. Chimney sweep services.

HillBilly Acres is an unconventional hippie greenhouse operation incongruously sited on a pleasant road in coastal Scituate, south of Boston. For more than 20 years, owner Doug Litchfield had experimented with growing interesting and unusual plants in an old bathtub, a pond, and three greenhouses outside his home in the suburbs. The disorderly creativity with which he assembled this livelihood prompted neighbors to mutter about "hillbillies," a moniker he delightedly adopted as the name of the nursery. Long-haired, mustachioed, and clad in jeans and a worn straw cowboy hat, Litchfield gives every appearance of enjoying his role as resident hillbilly. Any gardener tempted to take the joke seriously, however, has only to scrutinize the resident plant material to discover a connoisseur's treasury of rare and uncommon annuals, tropicals, and aquatics, grown inside and outside the greenhouses.

Litchfield has excellent horticultural contacts and gets his plants from sophisticated sources. His best-selling coleus, for example, is 'Amazon', a gorgeous gold-green–mahogany foliage plant obtained from Roger Swain of PBS's *The Victory Garden*. The black duckfoot coleus is an original from Conway's Nursery (RI). A giant papyrus, whose seed Litchfield obtained through a British supplier, is descended from viable seed discovered in an ancient Egyptian tomb.

Although HillBilly Acres once grew a bit of everything, the nursery increasingly emphasizes unusual annuals and tropicals that excel as container plants. We noticed fine collections of coleus, fuchsia, tender salvia, tender geranium (or pelargonium), succulents, and dahlias; a spectacular red-gold dahlia with variegated foliage was bred at the nursery. We bought magenta ice plants for added color in a window box succulent garden, and admired the sky blue clerodendron, variegated hops, and weird geranium with hairy purple stems. Spring hanging baskets, uncommon perennials (such as wild phlox), unusual fall mums, cut flowers, and a few choice trees and shrubs round out the nursery's offerings.

Grown from seed and cuttings, plants are sold in small pots in the greenhouses, reached by a narrow path enveloped in tropical flora. In the absence of a catalog, gardeners can consult on–site volumes of plant photographs; the annuals and tropicals grow quickly to resemble their photo likenesses.

Much of the nursery stock can be seen blooming profusely in containers lining the driveway, where they interweave riotously to form a colorful hedgerow jungle. 'Gold Giant' coleus grows in a hollowed tree stump; tropical blue pickerelweed inhabits a bucket of spackling compound; huge variegated canna lilies and zebra grass engulf an unseen fountain. We noticed black taro sharing the bathtub with a blue water lily. Something resembling yellow fuchsia sprouted from the head of a ceramic frog. A derelict carriage, an old wooden rowboat, and rusting farm equipment also function as container gardens. The nursery does a sideline in live bunnies.

HillBilly Acres begins to sell seedlings at Easter and is always open by chance, but its main season (described as "frenzied") is from Memorial Day to July. Litchfield believes in following the wisdom of the seasons, and resists selling tender annuals and tropicals until, as he says, "after the last full moon of May." Visitors in doubt about open hours can consult the nursery's fully functional stoplight, suspended above the driveway. When the green light is on, HillBilly Acres is open. In fall and winter months, when the stoplight is red (nursery closed), Litchfield, under the enterprise name of SootBusters, occupies himself as a tool sharpener and chimney sweep.

Directions: From Boston, take either Route 93 or Route 95/128 to Route 3 south, and then exit 13 onto Route 53 north. At the first light, turn right onto Route 123 east. At the junction of Routes 123 and 3A, turn sharply left onto Old Oaken Bucket Road; the nursery is 1 mile on your right.

Nearby attractions: Doug Litchfield's wife, Anne, takes comic engagements as "Hannah," a professional magician and clown (781-545-2303). Note the commercial cranberry bogs on Old Oaken Bucket Road (formerly Old Satuit Trail, an Indian path), near the nursery; they make an interesting comparison with a nearby Audubon Society bog, which offers habitat for endangered pitcher plants—Litchfield can provide directions. Kennedy's Country Gardens, 85 Chief Justice Cushing Highway (Route 3A), Scituate, MA 02066 (781-545-1266) is a friendly, professional, family-owned garden center that has been serving Boston's south shore since 1960.

HUNTING HILLS FARM

Route 63, Montague, MA 01351
(413) 367-2667
Suzanne Kretzenger

Organically grown fruit trees; ornamental woody plants. Open Tuesday to Saturday 7–6, Sunday 6–5, all year. No catalog or mail order. Farm-raised plants, vegetables, and meat.

At first glance, a less promising resource for hard-to-find plant material would be hard to conjure. Hunting Hills is a dilapidated former dairy farm in the upper Connecticut Valley, now functioning as a tree and shrub nursery. It has the disorderly quality of a failed 19th-century farmstead, a visual reminder of why so many New England farmers went West during the Gold Rush or left for factory jobs. Owner Suzanne Kretzenger inherited Hunting Hills from her father in 1965 along with the occupation of farmer, which requires hard 12-hour days, seven days a week.

Surprisingly, the farm's collection features uncommon and rather sophisticated plants, all raised organically at the farm or by local growers. Gardeners come here seeking regionally adapted plants that cannot be found elsewhere. Hunting Hills Farm specializes in fruit trees and ornamental woody plants hardy to Zone 4. The farm once had a plant list, but Kretzenger says she got too busy to update it; "We could be open more than year-round."

Hunting Hills Farm focuses on deciduous ornamental trees such as Eastern redbud, tree lilac, flowering plum and pear, weeping elm and cherry, shadblow, cutleaf birch, contorted hazel, and katsura. Among the apple and fruit trees, older varieties suited to New England conditions predominate. Flowering shrubs include buddleia, rose-of-Sharon, shrub dogwood, and various rhododendrons and azaleas, including a native swamp azalea and the ultra hardy Northern Lights azalea cultivars developed at the University of Minnesota. Hunting Hills carries no needled conifers, only deciduous and broadleaf evergreens. Attractive, organically raised perennials and herbs, including pink lavender and some older varieties of peony, are available at good prices. All the plants are well acclimated to New England conditions.

A decade ago, a large farm stand was added to the property, where Kretzenger's mother, Anne, minds the store. In the tradition of family farms, Hunting Hills operates year-round, offering farm-grown meat, fresh vegetables, raw honey, hay-bale mulch, thistle seed, fall pumpkins, and Christmas wreaths.

Directions: From the Boston area, take Route 2 west to Millers Falls. Turn left onto Route 63 South; the farm is 4 miles on your left.
From Route 91, take exit 27 to Route 2 east. Turn right onto Route 63 south; the farm is 4 miles on your left.

Nearby attractions: The Mohawk Trail, a 63-mile stretch of Route 2 between Orange and Williamstown, is a pre-Columbian Indian trail surrounded by 50,000 acres of state parks and forests, justifiably popular for fall foliage tours (413-664-6256). Williams Farm, Main Street, Deerfield, MA 01342 (413-773-5186), has been growing corn on conservation land for decades, and now operates a garden center offering quality shade trees, ornamental shrubs, and perennials. In Millers Falls village on Route 63, Yield House/Renovator's Supply (413-659-2654) has an outlet for closeouts.

JOE PYE WEED'S GARDEN

337 Acton Street, Carlisle, MA 01741
(978) 371-0173
Jan Sacks and Marty Schafer

Siberian iris; interspecies iris hybrids. *Hybridizer's nursery. Open by appointment. Catalog $2. Mail order only. Display gardens.*

Joe Pye Weed's Garden is a wonderful nursery, but it has no joe-pye weed. It specializes in Siberian iris cultivars, most of which are bred by the owners, hybridizers Jan Sacks and Marty Schafer. In addition to Siberian iris, this nursery offers unusual cultivars of the native blue flag *(Iris versicolor)* and rare species and interspecies iris hybrids. All are sophisticated plants of great beauty and horticultural interest to iris lovers throughout the region.

The Schafer-Sacks team opened Joe Pye Weed's Garden in 1984 and started breeding Siberian iris in 1985. They are professional gardeners who make their living growing unusual cut flowers for the florist trade and arranging flowers for weddings; serious iris breeding is their vocation. Their fascination was first ignited by the late Bee Warburton of Westborough, a noted iris hybridizer who was their mentor and mother hen in the art of iris breeding. They claim she took them under her wing and instructed them "until she didn't worry about us anymore." Since then, the Schafer-Sacks team has moved to the forefront of Siberian iris breeding in New England, having been passed the baton by Dr. Currier McEwen (see *Eartheart Gardens,* ME).

Joe Pye Weed's Garden offers more than 85 Siberian iris cultivars by mail order, including some excellent Schafer-Sacks hybrids, Warburton hybrids, and combined efforts of the Warburton/Schafer-Sacks team. A number of these are American Iris Society award winners. The Schafer-Sacks's goal with Siberian iris is to develop superior yellows, true blues, colorful overlay patterns, decorative style arms, amoenas (iris lingo for a flower with white signals and colored falls), and upright habit. We were smitten by their nautical, blue-and-white-ruffled 'Ships Are Sailing'; the award-winning cobalt 'Trim the Velvet'; and a pastel floozie called 'Careless Sally' (described as an "unusually fertile" iris that "makes a good parent"). Other intriguing offerings are a fragrant *Iris carthaliniae* called 'Georgian Delicacy' (native to the Georgian Republic), and an unusual dark iris with maroon leaves called 'Dark Aura' (often collected for its foliage). The nursery was first to introduce to America a unique black-flowered *Iris versicolor* called 'Mysterious Monique.' The nursery also carries a dozen iris from Dr. Thomas Tamberg, a German hybridizer specializing in interspecies iris cultivars, which are notoriously difficult because of discrepant gene counts. We admired Tamberg's yellow-and-brown-veined 'Berlin Tiger' and delicate white *Iris setosa* 'Norris 1', which appears like a flight of seabirds in the evening light.

Located in Carlisle on the site of old farmland, Joe Pye Weed's Garden contains enchanting cottage and rock gardens leading down to a vast, rectangular growing bed. The admirable display gardens contain colorful and rare plants, including unusual forms of *Iris cristata,* hellebore, peony, thalictrum, and some plant-hunting trophies donated by Darrell Probst (see *Garden Visions,* MA). Rich soil fairly bounces underfoot, and cultivation practices are excellent. The initial rows in the trial beds contain recent Schafer-Sacks hybrids that are still under assessment. Farther down are Siberian iris hybrids that have passed muster and await sufficient stock increase, including some coveted yellows. To the vexation of collectors, none of these can be purchased until they are properly registered and introduced for sale—a process that can take several years. As evidenced in the catalog, Schafer and Sacks have an amusing habit of naming their Siberian iris hybrids after country dance and fiddle tunes. We rather hoped they would name an anonymous, pale, oyster-colored iris in the trial beds 'Foggy Mountain Breakdown', after the legendary Flatt and Scruggs bluegrass tune.

Visiting Joe Pye Weed's delightful display gardens and growing beds can be enormous fun when the Siberian iris are in flower, between the first and third weekends of June. Because this is a small nursery with busy owners, respectful visitors should be content with a self-guided tour. Do not expect on-site digging, for all orders are placed through the catalog and shipped by mail. Plants come as fresh, recently divided plant stock, with (as they say) "no old clumps."

Directions: From Route 95/128, exit onto Route 4/225 west and follow Route 225 when the roads diverge. In Carlisle, pass the small rotary and turn left onto Acton Street; the nursery is on your left at #337.

LYMAN ESTATE GREENHOUSES

185 Lyman Street, Waltham, MA 02154
(781) 891-7095
SPNEA Horticulturist Lynn Ackerman

Greenhouse plants; herbs and fruit trees. *Historic greenhouses dating to the 18th century. Open Monday to Saturday 9:30–4. No catalog or mail order. Periodic plant sales. Gardening workshops. Historic house and grounds. Web site: www.spnea.org/lymangreenhouse.*

The Lyman Estate's historical greenhouses are a living continuation of the Boston Brahmins' early fascination with horticulture. The Lyman Estate dwelling, called The Vail, was built in 1793 by Salem architect Samuel McIntyre in the English style, and is now a house museum owned by the Society for the Preservation of New England Antiquities (SPNEA). The estate is a hidden oasis in Waltham, seemingly impervious to the industrial city that now surrounds it. The 39-acre estate grounds (under restoration) reflect English 18th-century landscape design and feature five antique glasshouses, the oldest greenhouses still standing in New England. Visitors should take a moment to appreciate the estate collection of camellias dating to 1820, and the magnificent festooning grapevines, taken as cuttings from vines at Britain's Hampton Court in the 1870s. (The grape varietals are 'Black Hamburg' and 'Green Muscat'; these days the raccoons usually eat them.)

The Lyman Estate Greenhouses still produce conservatory plants, herbs, and potted plants for sale throughout the year. Much of the stock is raised from seed and cuttings by the SPNEA horticultural staff, who do their best to combat whitefly, that ancient scourge of greenhouse nurseries. (Gardeners often quarantine their purchases to prevent transmission of this pest.) On peaceful weekdays, visitors may wander undisturbed among orchids, hibiscus, citrus trees, tropical and subtropical plants, and flowering container plants. Only the herbs (115 varieties) are winter hardy. Plant selection varies, and no written catalog is available. Ask about desired varieties not on exhibition, for the estate's collection exceeds its display space, and the staff will custom-propagate plants on request.

The Lyman Estate Greenhouses host a number of well-known plant sales during the year: camellias in January or February; orchids in March and October; herbs and topiary in April or May; and hosta and shade perennials in May or June. Proceeds go to support this distinguished and lovely memorial to 18th-century naturalism.

Directions: From Route 95/128, take exit 27A and follow Totten Pond Road east to the end. Turn right at the light onto Lexington Street. At the next traffic light, turn left onto Beaver Street. At the far side of the rotary, the estate entrance is between stone pillars.

Nearby attractions: The Arnold Arboretum in Boston (617-524-1718) is famous for its exceptional trees and 530 varieties of lilac; Lilac Sunday is celebrated in mid-May, and a prestigious plant sale is held in September.

MAHONEY'S GARDEN CENTERS

242 Cambridge Street (Route 3), Winchester, MA 01890
(781) 729-5900; fax (781) 721-1277
The Mahoney family

Satellite locations:
880 Memorial Drive, Cambridge, MA 02139; (617) 354-4145
958 Main Street, Route 28, Falmouth 02536; (508) 548-4842
Edgartown/Vineyard Haven Roads, Oak Bluffs, MA 02557; (508) 693-3511
2929 Route 28, Osterville, MA 02655; (508) 420-4428
1069 Main Street, Route 38, Tewksbury, MA 01876; (978) 851-2712
115 Boston Post Road, Route 20, Wayland, MA 01788; (508) 358-7333
Growing Division, 100 Bedford Road, Woburn, MA 01801; (781) 932-9327

Perennials. Grasses, geraniums, and hanging baskets. *Large retail garden center in many locations. Open daily, 9–6, Friday 9–8. No catalog or mail order. Garden supplies, pots, lattice, outdoor structures. Seasonal plants.*

Mahoney's Garden Centers is a family-owned, second-generation business that caters to the needs of affluent gardeners in greater Boston and on Cape Cod and Martha's Vineyard. Regarded as a "Boston institution," it has won Boston magazine's "Best of Boston" award for many years in succession. Mahoney's specializes in fine container-grown perennial plants in more than 1,500 varieties. Also available are hanging baskets, geraniums, vines, grasses, and other ornamental garden plants. Mahoney's at Rocky Ledge, the flagship store in Winchester, has been in business for 30 years and sells three million plants per year. In combination with eponymous garden centers in seven other locations, Mahoney's ranks among the country's top 50 nurseries in volume of sales. Old-timers may remember Mahoney's at Arrowhead in Wayland as the former Arrowhead Nursery, in its day a noted source of garden plants.

Mahoney's contracts with 20 different growers to ensure quality and a large selection of perennial stock. On random visits during the growing season, we found an excellent selection of upscale garden perennials, wonderful ornamental grasses, good herbs, more than 30 kinds of sedum, and winsome offerings of white tradescantia, variegated Jacob's ladder, pink anemones, stoloniferous blue phlox, bearberry, lovely ferns, and Japanese kirengeshoma, a graceful yellow-flowering shade plant. By August, native shade plants such as trillium and trout lily may look severely stressed, but these are ephemerals that die back after spring bloom. On the whole, we found Mahoney's stock to be surprisingly well grown for an organization of this size and volume. All plants are intelligently labeled and described, and the staff is helpful.

Mahoney's is perpetually crowded on weekends with gardeners who are short of time and willing to pay for convenience. In the absence of a plant list or catalog, even gardeners who normally prefer to plan their purchases must visit Mahoney's to find out what is available. While this may not be the most thoughtful or cost-effective way to acquire plants, we cannot deny that Mahoney's is accessibly located and well stocked with stylish plant varieties that appeal to urban-area gardeners. The perennials at Mahoney's are supplemented with annuals and vegetable flats in the spring, and ornamental trees and shrubs throughout the growing season. Seasonal plants and Christmas trees are sold at the holidays, and hanging baskets of rosebud impatiens whisk out the door for Mother's Day. Mahoney's is a comprehensive resource for garden supplies, containers, lattice panels, garden furniture, outdoor structures, and all manner of Christmas items.

Directions to Mahoney's at Rocky Ledge (Winchester): From Route 95/128, take exit 33A. Turn off the ramp onto Route 3 east. In 3.5 miles, Mahoney's is on your right.

NEW ENGLAND BAMBOO COMPANY

5 Granite Street (Route 127), Rockport, MA 01966
(978) 546-3581; fax (978) 546-1075
Christopher DeRosa

Bamboo. Ferns and grasses. *Specialty nursery. Open Tuesday to Friday 9–4; winter hours by appointment only. Catalog $2. Mail order. Display beds. Design-build landscaping. E-mail: info@newengbamboo.com. Web site: www.newengbamboo.com.*

New England Bamboo Company is the region's premier source of exotic bamboo plants. Owner Chris DeRosa is a seasoned design-build landscaper who has long participated in the New England Flower Show in Boston. One year in the later 1980s, his exhibit featured a Japanese-style garden, and the trouble it took to come up with exotic bamboo inspired him to found a bamboo nursery. Now New England Bamboo is one of the largest bamboo growers in the country, serving wholesale and retail customers mostly by mail order.

Bamboos are, of course, elegant woody grasses long used in Asia for tools, weapons, building materials, food, and landscape plants. New England Bamboo imports original stock directly from Asia, after which it spends months in quarantine before being propagated in the greenhouses and released for sale. Visitors are welcome to purchase bamboo plants at the nursery, situated on a picturesque street in Rockport, a quaint seaside village (formerly a fishing village and artist colony) near Gloucester, on Boston's north shore. The nursery's location is made apparent by restless stands of tall bamboo, half hidden behind an Oriental fence. Bamboo's success in coastal areas made us wonder why New England sea captains did not import graceful, rustling, clump-forming bamboos long ago, during the China trade.

New England Bamboo carries more than 150 evergreen bamboos hardy to Zones 5 and 6, many quite rare, as well as a number of tender bamboos (Zone 8) that must be treated as annuals or houseplants by northern gardeners. Virtually all these bamboos originate in Asia and the Himalayas, with the exception of one bamboo from South Africa and another called canebrake, which is native to the Ozarks. (Of the 700 species bamboos, only two are American, used mainly for fishing poles and cattle fodder.)

Bamboos have two growth habits, clump-forming and "running"—that is to say, invasive. Within these categories, the diversity of bamboo hybrids is astounding. New England Bamboo has 8-inch midgets; 70-foot giants; tropical-looking bamboos with 2-foot leaves; bamboos that weep, creep, and zigzag; and bamboos with silver stripes, yellow grooves, red margins, blue culms, and purple shoots. The nursery carries hedge bamboo, fountain bamboo, arrow bamboo, black bamboo, snakeskin bamboo, and Tonkin cane bamboo. 'Beautiful' bamboo is used by Asian bamboo artists; 'Sweet Shoot' bamboo appears in Chinese stir-fry. One spectacular 35-foot species bamboo *(Phyllostachys aureosulcata spectabilis)* has chartreuse foliage and a kink near the base of its canes; a rare 'Swollen Node' bamboo has strange, saucerlike internodes.

Many of the nursery's bamboos are unique varieties collected in remote regions of China. A few rare ornamentals are imports from Japan, evoking perfectly the sensibility of Japanese gardens. New England Bamboo carries several "new-generation" hybrids of the famous Muriel bamboo *(Fargesia murielae),* a graceful mountain clump-former that blooms on a genetically fixed cycle every 100 years and then dies. (The original American specimen, which was collected by the Arnold Arboretum's 1907 China expedition, bloomed and died in 1998, along with all the other Muriel bamboos in the world; the new Muriel hybrids are seedlings from the mother plant.) Original bamboo hybrids developed or discovered by New England Bamboo are a dwarf form of 'David Bisset', and one touted as "the only bamboo in the world with a variegated and ribbed stem." In keeping with its bamboo theme, the nursery offers fine ornamental grasses and a good selection of ferns for the shade garden.

New England Bamboo sells bamboo in many sizes, from small pots to huge specimens. Given the unstoppable vigor of running bamboos, a small plant will normally do. In the case of costly rare and collector's bamboos, first-year plants represent a relative bargain and often sell out in spring. The staff knows its business and will educate visitors on the plant's fine points. (We planted a running 'Yellow Groove' bamboo in a half whiskey barrel, and were warned that it will eventually burst the barrel hoops.)

Gardeners seeking a tranquil relationship with bamboo should stick to the clump-forming varieties. Because all the so-called running bamboos, according to Wyman's Gardening Encyclopedia, "can become vicious spreading pests if not rigidly restrained in the garden," the nursery sells containment barriers and advises on effective control strategies. For an alternative garden screen that does not involve submerging 3-foot plastic barriers or mowing 25-foot margins around a running bamboo plant, rustic Oriental fencing crafted from dried bamboo stalks is available in 8-foot lengths.

Directions: Take Route 95/128 north, stay on Route 128 when the roads split, and follow to its end in Gloucester. At the second rotary, turn left onto Route 127 north. In Rockport, bear left at the ROUTE 127 PIGEON COVE sign; the nursery is on Route 127 (where it becomes Granite Street) on the right.

Nearby attractions: Further north on Route 127, turn right at Old Farm Inn to visit Halibut Point State Park (978-546-2997), an old granite quarry with magnificent ocean views to the Isles of Shoals and the coast of Maine. Stay on Route 127 north for a scenic ride circling back to Route 128. The town of Essex, a former shipbuilding community off Route 128 at exit 14, is known for its antique shops.

NEW ENGLAND WETLAND PLANTS

820 West Street, Amherst, MA 01002
Mailing address: 800 Main Street, Amherst, MA 01002
(413) 256-1752; fax (413) 256-1092
Julie Marcus

Conservation-grade wetland plants. Native plants and seeds. Wattles and tubelings for erosion control. *Native-plant nursery. Open by appointment. Free catalog. No mail order. Erosion-control products. Wetlands engineering services. Web site: www.newp.com*

New England Wetland Plants (NEWP) is an ecological nursery specializing in wetland plants native to the northeastern United States. Founded by Julie Marcus in 1993, it is run by wetlands scientists out of a wooden barn on a boggy site near Hampshire College in the Pioneer Valley. The nursery propagates conservation-grade plant material used in erosion control and wetlands restoration projects. State agencies and conservation groups frequently turn to NEWP when they want to restore a disturbed wetland. This is an excellent resource for native-plant enthusiasts who need or want to enrich the biology

of a disturbed swamp or woodland. Because NEWP is basically a wholesale nursery selling wetland natives in quantity, gardeners should not bother it with small orders; this resource is suited to those seeking a significant number of plants.

The plant mix at New England Wetland Plants replicates the species growing naturally in native wetlands. The catalog reads like a walk in the woods. Wetlands are divided into plant zones progressing through open water, marsh, and wet meadow to scrub and damp forest. NEWP identifies each plant by its growth habit, its place in a wetland, and its value as food or cover for wildlife. Plants suited to open water include native water lilies and various pond weeds. Marsh-loving plants include bulrushes, pickerelweed, arrowhead, and (we love this name) common three-square. Plants often found in wet meadows are cat's tail grass, blue flag, vervain, wool grass, and joe-pye weed. Scrub plants include various shrub dogwoods and willows, highbush blueberry, arrowwood, and fragrant shrubs such as spicebush and sweet pepperbush.
Wet forest and upland buffer plants include red maple, black gum, white pine, Eastern hemlock, serviceberry, gray birch, lowbush blueberry, and sweet fern. Many of these plants, such as black huckleberry and unusual rushes, are impossible to obtain from commercial sources.

New England Wetland Plants propagates its stock in irrigated greenhouses, producing small plants in large quantities. Herbaceous specimens come in 50-plant flats, everything else in quart and gallon pots. Although most commercial orders require plants by the thousand, NEWP is willing to sell smaller quantities of wetland plants to retail customers engaged in landscape enrichment. Needless to say, no plants are taken from the wild.

The nursery's aim is to replicate wild native wetlands, not to meet nursery standards for ornamental landscape plants. As a result, most NEWP plants are described as "conservation-grade," having the irregular habit of uncultivated natives, like the ones you see in damp woods and meadows.

In addition to potted plants, New England Wetland Plants sells specialty seed mixes suitable for wetland conservation, erosion control, wildflower meadows, and wildlife support. "Fascines," or wattles (unrooted dormant cuttings of readily rooted species, such as dogwoods and willows), are sold in large bundles. Also available are "tubelings" (rooted plants in 8-inch soil tubes, used in soil stabilization) and products to assist erosion control, water quality, and soil bioengineering. Plant material must be ordered in advance and picked up at the nursery. Trucking and installation services are available for large jobs.

NEWP will advise customers on plant selection, site plans, and erosion-control materials; gardeners in deep trouble can hire a NEWP wetlands engineer. An appointment is necessary.

Directions: From the I-90/Mass. Pike, take exit 4 onto Route 91 north. Take exit 19/Northampton and turn right onto Route 9 east. In Amherst, turn right onto Route 116 south. In 3 miles, the nursery is on your left, in the barn behind the brick Cape.

NEWBURY PERENNIAL GARDENS

65 Orchard Street, Byfield, MA 01922
(978) 462-1144
Richard and Patricia Simkins

Perennials. Small, family-owned garden center. Open daily mid-April through June 8–5, and July through mid-September 10–5. Closed July 4 and Labor Day. Catalog $3. No mail order. Custom orders. Display gardens open for a nominal charge May through August, Thursday through Monday 10–4, closed Tuesday, Wednesday, and some Saturdays after 1 P.M. No picnics or animals allowed on the grounds.

Located in Byfield on the verge of a river meadow, Newbury Perennial Gardens seems like a Virginia tidewater plantation transported to Massachusetts. Its owners, Richard and Patricia Simkins, live in a large brick Colonial Revival house backed by extensive formal gardens sweeping down to the Parker River. Just beyond the house, adjacent to a gray shed, is a small, choice garden center with a wonderful selection of perennials and other plants. Ornamented with arbors and container displays, the garden center is open from April to mid-September. Byfield may be only 45 minutes north of Boston, but it seems like another world.

The main focus of Newbury Perennial Gardens is ornamental perennials. This being a garden center, not a nursery, all plants are bought in from reliable growers. What makes Newbury Perennial Gardens special is its innovative plant selection, which includes handsome old favorites, choice new cultivars, and plants you may not have heard of before. Sure, every garden center carries daylily, hosta, and iris, but we had to crack open the garden encyclopedia to identify such novelties as phuopsis (crosswort), phlomis, phyteuma (horned rampion), sarcococca (sweet box), and leontodon (hawkbit; it looks like a novelty dandelion). Even more useful to normal gardeners are refreshing choices in plant categories that have become a bit dowdy—asters (Japanese varieties and nine new New England asters); chrysanthemum (new daisies and heirloom mums); campanula (30 kinds); dianthus (pretty carnations, mountain pinks, and wild sweet william); hellebore (including *Helleborus foetidus* and *H. lividus*); and Oriental poppy (28 kinds). The phlox tribe alone embraces 71 cultivars of Carolina, Canadian, and summer phlox, stoloniferous phlox, and various phlox species (our favorite is a rebloomer called 'Blue Eyes').

Although perennials are the main attraction, Newbury has a bit of everything. We found well-selected ferns and grasses, roses and clematis, and choice vines, shrubs, and trees. We also liked the herbs of character, with evocative names such as self-heal, skullcap, mountain mint, catchfly, and spleenwort. In spring the exotic annuals betray a taste for "tropicalismo" container gardening, what with all the daturas, coleus, cannas, and bananas.

Newbury Perennial Gardens abuts elaborate display gardens that were started in 1976 on a 12-acre hayfield surrounding the Simkins residence. These formal estate gardens contain 24 individual theme gardens connected by a signposted path. It is hard to tell whether the formal gardens support the garden center or the other way around. Most of the plants in the formal gardens are for sale in the retail area. Given the Simkinses' consuming passion for gardening, it is quite possible that the retail area exists just to stock the beds. We loved the theme gardens housing collections of gentians, succulents, grasses, alpines, and bog plants, as well as the Waterfall Garden (a cascade of low, white-flowering shrubs that "flow" only in spring) and the Weeping Garden (the dearest little pet cemetery, planted with weeping trees). Most impressive are the Grotto, a self-confessed "cross between Italian Romantic Garden period and Tom Sawyer nostalgia," and the formal Allée, a tree corridor framing a view of terraces leading down to the Parker River. The garden can be rented for weddings, so be sure to call ahead for open garden hours on any Saturday in summer.

Directions: Byfield is 35 minutes north of Boston. From I-95 north, take exit 55 and go east off the ramp onto Central Street. In 0.7 mile, turn sharply left where the street divides onto Orchard Street; the nursery is 1.2 miles on your right.

Nearby attractions: Backtracking 0.5 mile on Orchard Street, Great Meadow Farm (signposted) is conservation land containing high rolling meadows that resemble England's Oxfordshire downs; a path leads to the Parker River through open fields, bordered by copses of oak and hickory. Syringa Plus, 14R Old Point Road, Newbury, MA 01951 (978-352-3301), is a small nursery growing lilacs, rhododendrons, and azaleas in varieties not common in the nursery industry; most plants are one- to two-year seedlings. Historic Newburyport, north on I-95, is a renovated seaport jumping with good cafes and restaurants; in June, the annual Newburyport Garden Tour (978-462-2681) opens period homes and gardens to benefit the local Historical Society.

NOR'EAST MINIATURE ROSES

P.O. Box 307, 58 Hammond Street, Rowley, MA 01969
(978) 948-7964; fax (978) 948-5487; orders (800) 426-6485
John Saville

Miniature roses. Business hours: all year, Monday to Friday, 8–4:30. Free color catalog. Mail and phone order. Greenhouses open daily, call ahead. Display garden. Lectures and workshops. E-mail: nemr@shore.net Web site: www.noreast-miniroses.com.

Nor'East Miniature Roses is the largest mail-order nursery in the country devoted to miniature roses. It carries more than 100 varieties, including sweethearts, minis, micro-minis, climbers, tree roses, and cascading roses in hanging baskets. The nursery was founded as a hobby by Harmon Saville, owner John Saville's father, who hybridized more than 90 varieties of miniature roses, many of them prizewinners. Nor'East Miniature Roses grew to encompass two large greenhouse operations, in Massachusetts and California, and recently consolidated all operations in Massachusetts. The nursery has continued hybridizing, and its roses now hold 19 American Rose Society awards and two AARS awards. The nursery breeds and propagates all its own roses, and ships them year-round to any U.S. destination.

Miniature roses are dwarf tea roses that reach 12 to 24 inches in height, grow on their own roots, and are as hardy as ordinary roses once established; micro-minis are even smaller. First discovered in Switzerland, dwarf roses require the same care as other hardy roses. Due to Nor'East's relentless breeding efforts, miniature roses come in many colors, including some startling pigment combinations. (The catalog provides color photographs of each hybrid offered.) Nor'East's best-selling rose is 'Rainbow's End', a lurid red-and-yellow bicolor, now also available as a climber. Awardwinners include neon tangerine 'Little Flame', velvety crimson 'Black Jade', butter yellow 'Little Tommy Tucker', fragrant white 'Pacesetter', and pink-edged porcelain 'Child's Play'.

Dwarfism in roses is an acquired taste, but gardeners who love the itty-bitty will appreciate 'Sarachild', a 3-inch micro-mini with the tiniest pink flowers we have ever seen. In connection with a science experiment of the effects of gravity on fragrance, the nursery's 'Overnight Scentsation' became the first rose in space; it accompanied U.S. Sen. John Glenn on the space shuttle Discovery in 1998. (It wasn't the first plant in orbit, though; the Soviets sent an orchid into space years ago.) Purchases of 'Amy Grant', a miniature pink tea rose named for the Christian pop singer, go to support a children's hospital in Memphis.

Nor'East sells miniature roses in 2½-inch pots, singly and in collections. Hanging baskets and tree roses (which resemble the talking roses in Alice in

Wonderland) are also available. Almost all sales are accomplished by mail order; a shipping frenzy occurs around Mother's Day. Interested visitors are welcome to stroll through Nor'East's greenhouses and small display gardens in Rowley, but it is best to call ahead and confirm that someone is there.

Directions: Rowley is 45 minutes northeast of Boston. Take Route 95/128 north and when the roads split, continue on Route 128. Take exit 20 onto Route 1A north. In Rowley center, turn right onto Hammond Street; the greenhouses are on your left at #58, behind a gray ranch house.

NOURSE FARMS

4 River Road, South Deerfield, MA 01373
(413) 665-2658; fax (413) 665-7888
Tim Nourse

Strawberry and raspberry plants. Asparagus, rhubarb, and horseradish. *Large specialty grower. Open all year, Monday to Friday, 8–5. Free catalog. Mail and phone order. Live plants available April 1 to May 31. Plants sold on the premises Monday and Tuesday in season. Lab tours by appointment. Pick-your-own berries from mid-June, daily 8–4 (413-665-2650). E-mail: info@noursefarms.com. Web site: www.noursefarms.com.*

Nourse Farms is a global agricultural operation growing tissue-culture strawberry and raspberry plants on alluvial farmland bordering the Connecticut River. Owner Tim Nourse is a ninth-generation New England farmer who grew up on his family's dairy farm in Westborough; he now operates Nourse Farms in the bucolic landscape of South Deerfield, on land that has been dedicated to agriculture for 350 years.

Hardly a traditionalist, Nourse has been, for decades, an energetic standard-setter in the commercial propagation of strawberry plants. Nourse Farms uses a state-of-the-art lab to clone fruit plants and ensure that all breeding stock is virus-free. The operation is sited in a brick laboratory building surrounded by 400 acres of growing fields in South Deerfield, the epicenter of the Pioneer Valley. The farm sells 20 million strawberry plants per year from seven green-houses. Though geared to commercial growers, Nourse Farms serves home gardeners and pick-your-own farms seeking high-quality plants for the berry patch. An illustrated catalog (also published on the Web site) gives planting advice and suggests berry cultivars best suited to home gardens.

The backbone of Nourse Farms' business is strawberry plant stock (called "nuclear stock" by the U.S. Department of Agriculture). Nourse Farms offers 24 tissue-culture strawberries in early-, middle-, and late-season varieties.

'Jewel', 'Sparkle', and 'Allstar' are seasonal strawberries well suited to home gardens. A 1995 introduction, 'Northeaster', thrives in heavy soil and promises to rival 'Earliglow', the current early-season favorite. For gardeners not interested in staggering their crops, Nourse Farms carries everbearing strawberries that produce fruit from June to October. All are large-fruited, disease-resistant hybrids that come in flats of 25, 50, and 100. Large orders are charged an extra dollar per 1,000 plants, a kind of campaign contribution for grower-supported strawberry research.

Nourse Farms' other specialty is plant stock for 20 varieties of disease-resistant raspberries bearing red, yellow, black, and purple fruits. The most popular everbearing raspberry, 'Heritage', can be mowed to the ground after the fall crop, allowing gardeners to avoid the chore of pruning thorny canes. Two yellow raspberries, 'Goldie' and 'Kiwigold', are extra-sweet everbearing sports of 'Heritage'. Raspberry brambles are sold in quantities of 5, 10, and 50 as bare-root canes, tissue-culture plugs, or nursery-grown plants; gardener's choice, the price is the same for each.

Nourse Farms also offers eight varieties of highbush blueberry (sold as 18- to 30-inch plants), two kinds of asparagus, two kinds of rhubarb, and a horseradish. Any gardener who has tried to eradicate horseradish will appreciate the catalog's caution that "a few roots will last a lifetime." Plants are normally sent by mail order, but can be picked up at the farm on Monday and Tuesday during spring shipping season (closes June 1). Nourse Farms also runs a pick-your-own berry farm that opens in mid-June for berries, rhubarb, shell peas, and snow peas.

Directions: Deerfield is north of Springfield. From Route 91, take exit 24 onto Route 5 north. Turn left at the light onto Route 116. In 1 mile, turn right onto Sugar Loaf Extension and continue on merging with River Road; Nourse Farms is 3 miles on your right.

Nearby attractions: The 17th-century house museums of Historic Deerfield (413-774-5581), built when the town was the northwest frontier of New England, are considered one of the region's great treasures. "Not long before the break of day, the enemy came in like a flood upon us," wrote Rev. John Williams of the 1704 Indian attack; the John Sheldon House still bears the marks of tomahawks. Old Deerfield village was described by the poet Conrad Aiken as "not so much a town as the ghost of a town, its dimness almost transparent, its quiet almost a cessation ... It is saying 'I dared to be beautiful, even in the shadow of the wilderness'; but it is also saying, 'And the wilderness haunts me, the ghosts of the slain race are in my doorways and clapboards, like a kind of death.'" (Excerpted from The WPA Guide to Massachusetts, *1932.)*

OLD STURBRIDGE VILLAGE

1 Old Sturbridge Village Road, Sturbridge, MA 01566
(508) 347–3362; fax (508) 347-0369

Heirloom seeds and plants. *Nonprofit outdoor history museum. Garden center open May through October. Museum open all year, daily 9–5, November through March 10–4; closed January except weekends. Free catalog. Mail order for seeds only. Web site: www.osv.org.*

Old Sturbridge Village (OSV) is a re-created New England farming village of the early 19th century, a period of rapid economic change when food-crop cultivation began making way for ornamental gardening. OSV's display gardens, planted with historically accurate flowers and vegetables, exhibit the styles and practices of gardening common to New England in the 1830s. Seeds and plants of the kind grown in the museum's period herb and wall gardens (some propagated on the premises) are sold to gardeners through OSV's seed catalog and through plant sales in the gift shop.

Many of OSV's heirloom flower and vegetable seeds are still familiar to modern gardeners, but others are little known or hard to obtain from commercial sources. Examples of now uncommon flower seeds are OSV's scarlet tassel flower, tall mallow, and pre–1860 'Connecticut Tavern' columbine collected from an abandoned garden in Connecticut. Heirloom vegetable seeds include 'Jacob's Cattle' bush bean, 'Dwarf Gray' sugar pea, 'Wethersfield' onion, 'Soldier' bush bean (good for Boston baked beans), and a rare Connecticut field pumpkin provided to early settlers by Native Americans. This is one of the few sources for salsify, or vegetable oyster, a pre–1800 root vegetable with a flavor resembling that of oysters. OSV's heirloom seed list includes fuller's teasel (once used for carding wool), motherwort (for female "hysteria"), and an odd, parsniplike root called Hamburg parsley.

In addition to seed, more than 100 historic OSV plants are cultivated in the museum's greenhouses. These include black hollyhock, maiden pink, Roman chamomile, clary sage, and antique dyer's herbs such as weld and woad. Apple trees propagated from the museum's Preservation Orchard are also available, along with a few historic roses.

Directions: The museum entry is on Route 20 in Sturbridge. From Route 90/Mass. Pike, take exit 9 onto Route 20 west; the entrance is shortly on your left. From Route 84, take exit 3B onto Route 20 west; the entrance is shortly on your left.

Nearby attractions: A similar re-created historic village, Plimoth Plantation, P.O. Box 1620, Plymouth, MA 02362 (800-262-9356), publishes a free mail-order catalog for historic seed and heirloom vegetables derived from New England's American Indian tribes; the seed list includes a cornfield pole bean planted by Wampanoag women when the oak leaves were the size of a mouse's ear.

PARADISE WATER GARDENS

14 May Street (Route 18), Whitman, MA 02382
(781) 447-4711; fax (781) 447-4591
Paul W. Stetson

Aquatic plants; water lily and lotus cultivars. Aquatic plant nursery. Open all year, Monday to Friday 8–6, Saturday 8–5, Sunday 1–5. Free color catalog. Mail order. Visitors welcome. Web site: www.paradisewatergardens.com.

Paradise Water Gardens has been growing and selling aquatic plants since 1950, well before the current craze for water gardening. Located in Whitman, in a rundown rural pocket oddly close to Boston yet reminiscent of inland Maine, Paradise Water Gardens is a family operation owned and run by Paul Stetson. Although this aquatic plant nursery has few pretensions, it carries sublime water lily and lotus hybrids and does a banner business in all manner of aquatic plants and water-garden supplies. The nursery welcomes visitors. Aquatic plants are sold bare-root in plastic baggies; gardeners can save considerably on shipping by picking up orders at the nursery.

Paradise Water Gardens combines the evolved aesthetics of a Japanese Zen garden or Monet's Giverney with the down-and-out rural clutter of backwoods New England. Its main concrete-based greenhouse sounds like a leaky cellar; old pond foundations are fractured; and outdoors, jumbled mounds of disused pots are scattered on concrete rubble. When we first visited the nursery in early spring, we wondered if it was still in business. It was, and we found its plant selections (propagated at a separate Bridgewater location) surprisingly sophisticated. The Stetsons know quite a bit about aquatic plants. Paradise Water Gardens sells out of water lily and lotus hybrids briskly each year (the hardy lotus are gone within two weeks). In fact, water gardening by definition requires a strong stomach for muck and stagnant water, which is just what aquatic plants want and need. Whatever one thinks of the housekeeping, from the standpoint of an aquatic plant, this place really is paradise.

The nursery propagates and grows nearly all its hardy aquatic plants in warm and cold greenhouses. Hardy water lilies and lotus undergo the rigors of New England winter before being broken up for sale in the spring—just like terrestrial plants. The nursery has an extensive collection of perennial water lilies (*Nymphaea* spp.), which occupy 14 pages of the mail-order catalog. These beautiful plants come in a rainbow of warm colors and provide spectacular summer bloom display in the nursery ponds. Most popular are dwarf and pygmy varieties, suitable for small pools and tubs. Most of the hardy water lilies developed by hybridizers Perry Slocum and Kirk Strawn (some in limited quantity) are available here; the nursery displays those it considers outstanding. Paradise Water Gardens also offers magnificent hardy lotus (*Nelumbo* spp.), which, being invasive, must be restricted or grown in containers. Exquisite Japanese lotus hybrids are reminiscent of tree peonies; as a religious icon, the lotus is much prized by Buddhists.

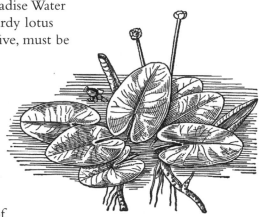

In addition to hardy aquatics, Paradise Water Gardens grows dazzling tropical water lilies, many of them heavily perfumed or night-blooming—the equivalent of tropical plants here on earth. Tropical water lily hybrids come brilliantly colored in raspberry, scarlet, fuchsia, peach, lemon, purple, and turquoise. The nursery also offers Japanese, Siberian, and Louisiana iris; shallow-water marginal plants such as pickerelweed and watermint; canna and calla lilies; rushes and ornamental grasses; and various floating and oxygenating aquatic plants. Gardeners scrutinizing the bottom of the plant list will find some queer things indeed, tiny aquatics that "grow rapidly" and could be an environmental felony to flush into the public water supply. Check with your local scientist; aquarium use only, please.

Paradise Water Gardens makes its own vinyl, rubber, and plastic pools and pool liners, and offers an extensive line of plumbing products such as pumps and filters that make artificial water gardening possible. Fountain sprays, waterfall mechanisms, and aquarium needs are included in its supply list. The nursery keeps humming in winter by breeding and purveying Japanese koi, Chinese goldfish, and various aquarium fauna, including live "scavengers" that eat fish sewage. Our favorite is the Japanese trap-door snail, which reportedly "brings forth their young alive," right there in the tank.

Directions: Whitman is south of Boston, near Brockton. From Route 3 south, take Exit 16B onto Route 18 South/Weymouth; the nursery is 8 miles on your right. From I-95, take exit 17 onto Route 27 east. In Whitman, turn right onto Route 18 south; the nursery will be on your right.

Nearby attractions: A mile south on Route 18, Peaceful Meadows Dairy Farm sells fresh ice cream made on a still-active farm that has been in the same family since the 1920s. The ice-cream stand, a period piece from the 1950s, still makes that unique New England concoction, the frappe. The cow barn is open to visitors.

PLEASANT VALLEY GLADS AND DAHLIAS

P.O. Box 494, 163 Senator Avenue, Agawam, MA 01001
(413) 786-9146 and (413) 789-0307
Roger and Gary Adams

Bulbs for gladiolus, dahlia, and tuberose. *Hybridizer's bulb farm. Open all year. Mail-order catalog. Minimum order $20. Wholesale cut flowers. Groups and visitors welcome by arrangement. E-mail: gary@gladiola.com. Web site: www.gladiola.com.*

Located south of Springfield, in the old tobacco-growing country of the Connecticut Valley, Pleasant Valley Glads and Dahlias is the region's foremost grower of gladiolus, dahlia, and tuberose bulbs (technically not bulbs at all, but corms and tubers). All three plants are tender in New England, requiring fall digging and winter storage in the cellar or refrigerator; but they remain popular for verve and color in floral borders, containers, and cutting gardens.

Pleasant Valley is essentially a rural bulb farm, selling by mail order around the world, with a sideline in wholesale cut flowers for the florist trade. Commercial bulb growing (almost never done around here anymore) involves a backbreaking round of hand-digging, dividing, planting, weeding, irrigating, cutting, sorting, inspecting, heat-treating, cataloging, and order filling. Owner Gary Adams does this work with the help of his father, Roger Adams Sr., a lifelong farmer and champion hybridizer who was born in the farmhouse on the property and has grown gladiolus since 1948.

Known nationwide for its prizewinning gladiolus hybrids, Pleasant Valley grows its own unique "show glads." These include numerous champions and medalwinners; hybrid gladiolus developed by other breeders; and rare and unusual gladiolus imported from Czechoslovakia, Canada, and elsewhere. The owner continues his father's tradition of breeding show glads that have a tendency to sweep the championship awards at national and regional plant shows; two acres of the farm are devoted to its breeding program. (The other Adams son, Roger Jr., an associate dean in the University of Connecticut's agriculture program, also contributes original gladiolus hybrids.) All corms and tubers are grown on the farm's five large production fields, formerly in tobacco, which have been in the Adams family for more than a century.

Gladiolus are iris relatives prized (especially by florists) for their large, sword-shaped stalks of showy flowers. Like daylilies, gladiolus have been extensively hybridized. While their popularity has varied over the years, they remain widely grown as summer flowers; succession planting can keep them going for three months.

Pleasant Valley's annual catalog describes its remarkable collection of 300 gladiolus hybrids and 120 miniatures. Variations in the color, pattern, texture, and size of the gladiolus hybrids found here almost defy description. Adventurous gardeners will be tempted to find a place for "black" glads, "blue smoke" glads, or glads tinted salmon, peach, royal purple, white-green, copper-cream, and crimson with smoke overtones. In texture velvety or silky, these gorgeous flower spikes come ornamented with colored throats, blotches, and lip petals. Many corms are inexpensive, making them a spectacular, minimal-care floral bargain with almost no downside for the busy gardener, other than simple winter bulb storage. (If waste is no object, gladiolus can be treated as annuals, and not even dug up in the fall.)

Pleasant Valley also grows unique dahlia tubers, including many new hybrids. Dahlias are bright Mexican flowers with a dashing history: They were collected from Mexican gardens in the 17th century (the Aztecs called them *Cocoxochitl*) and grown in King Philip's garden at Escorial in Spain. The dahlias made their way to Napoleon's garden at Malmaison, where Empress Josephine tended them by hand, until an envious handmaid attempted to filch some tubers by persuading her lover, a Polish nobleman, to bribe a gardener; stung, the empress exiled the pair from court and had the entire dahlia collection chopped with hatchets. Royal rage did not prevent the dahlia's swift entry into European gardens and a prime place in Victorian bedding schemes. As with other plants from grandmother's garden, dahlia cultivation underwent a neglectful pause before enjoying a modern revival.

Pleasant Valley's terrific dahlia collection offers every color but blue; growth from 2 to 8 feet; and profuse bloom on flowers that are large, small, collared, incurved, or formed to resemble a water lily, cactus, peony, orchid, ball, or pompon.(We're unsure what lacinated and fimbrated mean, but Pleasant Valley has them, too.) According to writer Verlyn Klinkenborg, modern gardeners are "likely to be attracted and repelled in equal measure by such outlandish blossoms, some of which—the pompons especially—look like preposterous vegetative fictions." The best dahlias seem to be small and black-red, though Pleasant Valley grows some extraordinary yellows, pinks, bicolors, oranges, and whites—more than 170 kinds in all. We were intrigued by the new, heat-resistant scarlet 'Emperor' and blood red 'Zorro' (1991 Dahlia of the Year); curiously, though, the crimson 'Bishop of Llandaff' so valued by British gardeners is not on the list.

Pleasant Valley also propagates Mexican tuberose bulbs. Tuberose flowers are so perfumed that, according to the grower, "one stem will fragrance a room." Where else can you think of finding double pearl tuberose—especially on a New England farm?

Pleasant Valley asserts that each of the flower bulbs packs a "show flower, cut flower, decorative, or all in one." Its superb flower bulbs may be more common in the florist industry than in gardens these days, but they have inspired such historic passion, and their form and color are so marvelous, why shouldn't modern gardeners give them a whirl?

Directions: Call for an appointment and confirmation of directions. From I-91 south, take exit 13/West Springfield onto Route 57 west. At the end, turn left onto Route 187 south into Suffield, Connecticut. Call for local directions.

ROCK SPRAY NURSERY

P.O. Box 693, 1 Depot Road, Truro, MA 02666
(508) 349-6769; fax (508) 349-2732
Kate D. Herrick

Heath and heather. *Specialty Nursery. Garden shop open late April through Columus Day, daily 9–5. Catalog $2. Mail or phone order. Display garden. E-mail: kherrick@rockspray.com. Web site: www.Rockspray.com.*

Begun in 1980, Rock Spray Nursery is a large wholesale and retail nursery, run by founder Kate Herrick, specializing in heaths and heathers hardy to New England. Heather thrives in sun on poor acid soil and grows wild on the moors and mountains of Europe (where it is native) by the square mile. Colorful flower spikes, evergreen foliage, fall and winter color, and easy care make it a hospitable ground cover for New England gardens, which have plenty of poor acid soil and low maintenance requirements. Rock Spray Nursery carries more than 100 varieties and nine species of heath and heather, all greenhouse propagated in 2½-inch pots. Once established in the garden (the first year out of the greenhouse is tricky), Rock Spray's plants are hardy to Zone 5 and colder.

More that half of Rock Spray Nursery's plants are cultivars of summer-blooming Scotch heather *(Calluna vulgaris),* chosen for its mauve and pink flowers and diverse, colorful foliage. 'Finale', for example, has amethyst flowers on gray and plum foliage; 'Winter Chocolate' has lavender blooms on gold, chocolate, and red foliage; and 'Darts Hedge Hog' has pink and lime green foliage, wintering to burnished orange. Anyone who has hiked in Ireland will recognize 'County Wicklow', a mounding green heather with double shell pink flowers. We once won seven years' good luck by discovering wild white heather on a crag in County Wicklow; Rock Spray carries 10 cultivated whites, with foliage ranging from yellow–gold to green–silver (no mention of luck, however). Rock Spray's hardy spike heath *(Bruckenthalia spiculifolia)* bears pink blossoms on the tips of its branches.

The rest of Rock Spray's plants are members of the heath family (Erica), which includes winter heath, bell heather, cross-leaved heather, Cornish heath, Watson's and William's heaths, and winter-flowering hybrids. Although botanically distinct, these heaths look very much like Scotch heather. Most numerous in cultivation is winter-flowering heath *(Erica carnea)*, whose pink, rose, and lilac flowers really do bloom (we swear) in winter, beginning in December. Rock Spray's winter-flowering heath hybrids *(Erica x darleyensis)* are hardy to Zone 3, and their green foliage is often cream-tipped. Many other heaths carry charming flowers, such as the pink-and-white 'Eden Valley', salmon 'Pink Pearl', pale 'Apple Blossom', cherry-red 'Mrs. Maxwell', and large, rosy 'Truro'—taken not from Cape Cod but from the Cornish moors in Truro, England.

Rock Spray will customize heath and heather mixtures, and has assembled hundreds of collections for gardeners over the years. Rock Spray also offers "theme" collections for year-round bloom, summer or winter bloom, foliage color, rock gardens, and cold (Zone 4) gardens. The propagating greenhouses (run by an all-woman crew) are, unfortunately, not open to visitors. However, Rock Spray's Garden Shop in Truro provides an attractive retail outlet for its plants, supplementing an extensive mail-order business.  Stunning rock-curbed display beds surround the Garden Shop, illustrating the garden uses of heath and heather and their appearance in maturity. The Garden Shop carries choice companion plants not listed in the catalog—we found dwarf evergreens, many-colored thymes, herbs, roses, and white wisteria standards—as well as books on heather, hand pruners, tufa planters, hanging baskets, and garden pots.

Gardeners seeking virtual heather gardens can download a screensaver of blooming heather from the nursery's Web site.

Directions: Take Route 6 east onto Cape Cod. Pass the Orleans rotary. In 17 miles, take the Truro Center exit. Bear right, under the highway, and turn left and then imme-diately right onto Depot Road (toward the harbor); the garden shop is on your right.

Nearby attractions: Crocker Nurseries, Route 37, Brewster (508-896-5060) is a good garden-center resource for perennials, trees, shrubs, and bedding plants; free garden clinics are held in summer.

ROSELAND NURSERY

247 Main Street, Acushnet, MA 02743
(508) 995-4212; (800) 777-2292; fax (508) 998-2972
Fred Reuter

Hardy roses. Fruit trees. *Specialty nursery. Open April to Thanksgiving, daily 7–8. Free rose and fruit tree catalogs. No mail order. Small display garden. Florist.*

Roseland Nursery carries 300 varieties of hardy roses and sells more than 300,000 of them each year. Founded in 1952 and located in Acushnet, just north of Fairhaven and New Bedford, Roseland claims to be the largest supplier of potted roses in the Northeast. Roseland sells its plants regionally, and focuses on the kind of roses that grow well in New England. Its plants are container-grown in 2-gallon pots from bare-root cuttings custom-propagated by a California grower; they are then kept in cold greenhouses until ready for sale in the spring. Most Roseland roses are hardy 2-year-old plants that can be planted directly outside. Roses usually cost about $10 per pot, unless you buy 100 or more plants. Roseland carries a sideline of fruit trees in 5-gallon containers imported from New York and Oregon. The nursery is a favorite haunt of landscapers.

Roseland carries the gamut of hardy roses. Each pot is stamped with a plastic picture label for ready identification. The pots are also color coded to indicate awardwinners and new introductions (brown pots); patented roses such as David Austin's English roses and Meidiland landscape roses (black pots); and non-patented roses, such as old garden roses and hybrids whose patents have expired (green pots). Roseland is a great source of AARS winners such as the shocking-pink 'Fame' (1998), scarlet 'Opening Night' (1998), and demure pink 'Carefree Wonder' (1996), a rose that lived up to its name by growing successfully in a whiskey barrel in Boston.

Roseland's list includes antique roses, hybrid teas, miniatures, grandifloras, and landscape classics such as 'Sea Foam', 'The Fairy', 'Betty Prior', 'New Dawn', and 'Dorothy Perkins' (often called "the Cape Cod Rambler"). Some of Roseland's expired-patent roses sound really fun to try, such as the snow-white gold-hearted ground cover 'Jeepers Creeper'; the salmon-pink shrub (perfect for teenage girls) called 'Boy Crazy'; and our absolute favorite from the 1960s, 'Mister Lincoln' (a garnet velvet 1965 AARS winner with an intense citrus perfume). Not listed in the catalog, but available at the nursery, is Meidiland's Romantica line of updated old landscape roses.

Gardeners seeking particular roses known in childhood will do well to peruse Roseland's catalog, which continues to list roses that were popular decades ago but have not made their way onto anyone's heirloom list.

Besides roses, Roseland offers cut flowers and garden plants grown from plugs and cuttings, including herbs, shrubs, and flowering perennials. Containerized fruit trees include apple, peach, nectarine, apricot, pear, sweet and sour cherry, plum, prune plum, crab apple, ornamental pear, and weeping cherry. A rose-embowered gazebo presents a popular photo opportunity to visitors.

Directions: From Providence, take Route 195 east to exit 13B, then take Route 140 north to exit 4 and turn left at the ramp; the nursery is 2.3 miles on your left. From Boston, take Route 24 south to exit 12. Take Route 140 south to exit 6, bear left at the second light, and turn left at the next light; the nursery is 1 mile on your left. From Cape Cod, take Route 195 west to exit 20, then take Route 105 north. In 3 miles, bear left in Rochester center onto New Bedford Road. In 4.3 miles, at the T-junction, turn left onto Main Street; the nursery is 1.7 miles on your right.

F.W. SCHUMACHER CO.

36 Spring Hill Road, Sandwich, MA 02563-1023
(508) 888-0659; fax (508) 833-0322
David and Donald Allen

Seeds for trees and shrubs. *Specialty seed house. Business hours: Monday to Friday 8:30–4. Free catalog. Mail and phone orders. Germination information available with order. No nursery visitors; seed pickup by advance appointment.*

F.W. Schumacher Co. is a wholesale supplier of tree and shrub seed to the nursery industry. More than 1,000 types of seed are available, most grown locally. Schumacher's stated intention is to provision "competent plantsmen, for research and breeding work," but nonprofessionals may also order seed on a retail basis—only if they "confine correspondence to the most necessary" and provide stamped, self-addressed envelopes for return correspondence. Seed is available in inexpensive trial packets, by the ounce, and by the pound.

Growing trees and shrubs from seed can be a great horticultural adventure for the patient gardener. We know of a beautiful garden containing handsome trees and shrubs, some quite rare, grown from seed over a 15-year period; the Polly Hill Arboretum on Martha's Vineyard was grown almost entirely from seed. Schumacher's 20-page catalog lists a mind-boggling assortment of ornamental trees and shrubs whose seed is available. A specialty is native plant seed, virtually unobtainable elsewhere. Seed for beloved varieties of lilac, elm, pine, oak, maple, and dogwood is supplemented with rarer seed for Kentucky coffee tree, Carolina silver-bell, golden-rain tree, golden-chain tree, northern Osage orange, white mulberry, and Amur cork tree. Exotic European and Asian species are represented, including the Japanese maple. The catalog prints special lists of azalea and rhododendron seed, fruit stock, and seed for newly introduced plants. Schumacher also buys rare woody-plant seed, and publishes its wish list in the catalog.

While Schumacher seeds are harvested from specific tree and shrub cultivars, these seeds may not produce the same varieties of plants. This is because seed taken from named hybrids, while often superior, does not necessarily breed true. (Apples, for example, are notoriously unstable to grow from seed, having been intensely hybridized for centuries.) Germination information should be requested with each order. Absent propagation experience, we also recommend Schumacher's introductory booklet, *How to Grow Seedlings of Trees and Shrubs.*

Directions: Seed pickup is by appointment only. From Route 6 east, pass over the Sagamore Bridge to Cape Cod and take exit 3 / Sandwich / Quaker Meetinghouse Road. Turn left off the ramp, cross Route 6A and the railroad tracks, and turn right at a bend in the road into the nursery's driveway, marked by green gates and stone pillars; the office is on the left.

Nearby attractions: Heritage Plantation, Grove Street, Sandwich (508-888-3300), is a 76-acre park planted with 35,000 rhododendrons bred in the 1930s by noted hybridizer Charles Dexter. Plantation gardens containing 1,000 varieties of trees and shrubs, an extensive heather collection, and 550 daylilies surround a museum devoted to Americana; peak rhododendron bloom is in May and June.

R. SEAWRIGHT

P.O. Box 733, 201 Bedford Road (Route 225), Carlisle, MA 01741-0733
(978) 369-1900; fax (978) 369-0915
Bob and Love Seawright

Daylilies and hostas. *Hybridizer's nursery. Open daily, May 1 to September 1, and by appointment. Hours in May 10–5, June to September 9–5. Catalog: $2. Mail order. Advance orders accepted. Display gardens. Peak daylily bloom July 15 to August 5. Group tours by arrangement. E-mail: Seawright@aol.com.*

R. Seawright is a hybridizer's nursery located in an old hayfield in Carlisle, a pleasant, leafy town northwest of Boston. Bob Seawright is a former computer systems programmer who founded the nursery in 1977 after his hobby—hybridizing daylilies—overwhelmed him. Seawright is a lifelong aficionado who began collecting daylilies at age 12 in Mississippi, saving his money to buy 50-cent plants. In midlife he decided to change careers and pursue daylily breeding. (We heard an amusing story about the transition, when he attended a technology conference and described his occupation as "plant design"; his high-tech listeners thought he meant industrial design, not daylily breeding.)

The nursery specializes in growing "fine daylilies and exotic hostas," including original daylily hybrids from Seawright's breeding program. Both daylilies and hostas are superior low-maintenance garden plants that have attracted intense hybridizing interest in recent years, with spectacular results. The Seawright collection includes more than 700 hardy daylilies and 200 hostas, emphasizing the superior performers, awardwinners, and new and classic introductions of both plants.

Seawright's primary concern is with daylilies. Its field-grown plants, adapted to northern conditions, offer up-to-the-minute color and style from major breeders, including Bob Seawright and his mentor, the late Don Stevens. Among the more flamboyant Stevens-Seawright hybrids are 'Beulah Stevens' ("a real Arizona sunset"); 'Clif Hayes' (apricot with a yellow sunburst and lavender midrib); 'Cynthia Page Platais' (fluted grape with a plum halo and poison green throat); and 'Don Stevens' (yellow with a bam! black eye). More demure Stevens-Seawright creations are 'Penelope Weld White' (pale porcelain pink); 'Claiborne Watkins Dawes' (ruffled deep rose); 'Rachel's Hope' (tall, graceful, flared near-white); and 'Leola Fraim' (said to look like a colossal daffodil). Seawright's new 'Red Landscape' is a vibrant scarlet daylily that would look wonderful massed against an unpainted wooden barn; his exquisite 'Love' series is, of course, named for his wife. One of Don Stevens's most popular solo hybrids, an exquisite, September-blooming, lemon yellow daylily called 'Sandra Elizabeth', is priced here quite reasonably.

Seawright also grows daylily hybrids from recognized New England breeders such as the Barths (see *Barth Daylilies,* ME), Dr. Currier McEwen (see *Eartheart Gardens,* ME), and the Lachmans of Amherst, Massachusetts. For connoisseurs, the nursery offers Patrick Stamile's 'Candy' series (all yummy, especially 'Strawberry Candy', a Stout Medal winner); 16 plants from the Marsh 'Chicago' series; 37 of Pauline Henry's celebrated 'Siloam' hybrids; and some

stunning plants developed by hybridizers Moldovan, Sellers, Childs, and Peck.

Although plants are available by mail order, visitors to the Seawright garden can select plants in the growing fields and have them freshly dug on the spot. A four-volume photograph album permits gardeners to evaluate daylilies that are not then in bloom. A separate plant list organizes daylilies by color, fragrance, duration, and bloom season. Nocturnal gardeners will value Seawright's lengthy list of evening-blooming daylilies, perfect for overworked professionals and romantics with moon gardens.

Seawright offers its "exotic hosta" collection not as an afterthought but as a complementary perennial that does for the shade garden what daylilies do for sun. Plantsman Tony Avent has called hosta "the Timex of the plant world" on account of its maintenance-free reliability as a foliage plant. Seawright's hostas are sold as potted plants in all shapes, sizes, and colors: gold, blue, moss, and emerald; striped, variegated, stitched, and edged; crinkled, cupped, puckered, and corrugated; lush giants and tiny dwarfs. The nursery seems to favor pedigreed showstoppers such as 'Great Expectations', 'Green Piecrust', 'Sea Lotus Leaf', 'Zounds', and 'Pizzazz'. Some hostas, being members of the lily family, produce a bonus of elegant, perfumed flowers. A few Seawright hostas are stoloniferous plants (spreading by creeping rhizomes) that do well as ground cover. This being a nursery run by daylily fanatics, all mail orders, including hostas, come with a bonus daylily plant.

Directions: From Route 95/128, take exit 31B onto Route 4/225 west, staying on Route 225 west when the roads diverge. In 6.1 miles, pass Kimball's Ice Cream; the nursery is 0.3 mile on your right. Turn in and park on the grass.
From Route 495, take Route 2 east. In 7 miles, go three-quarters of the way around the Concord rotary and exit right onto Barrett's Mill Road. In 1.8 miles, turn left onto Lowell Road. In 0.3 mile, in Carlisle center, take Route 225 east/Bedford Road; the nursery is 0.3 mile on your left. Turn in and park on the grass.

Nearby attractions: Green Acre Sales, 36 Elaine Road, Sudbury, MA 01776 (978-443-8222; E-mail: SHGreene@aol.com) is a small nursery specializing in hosta and daylilies (catalog $1; minimum order $20); owner Steve Greene publishes The Hosta Finder, *a guide to hosta cultivars at 45 nurseries around the country. Greywood Farm, 85 River Road, Topsfield, MA 01983-2110 (978-887-7620; E-mail: GreywoodMA@worldnet.att.net) is a small grower of daylilies, hostas, and Japanese iris, run by daylily hybridizer Darlene Springer Wilkinson (mail-order catalog $1.50; minimum order $25); the hobbyist hybrids from members of the New England Daylily Society are inexpensive and loads of fun.*

SHADY GATE GARDENS

P.O. Box 258, Lumbert Cross Road, Mill River, MA 02144
(413) 229-8633
Martha Bryan

Distinctive annuals and container plants. *Small specialty nursery. Open May through July, Thursday to Sunday 8:30–4:30 and by appointment. Free plant list. No mail order. Display garden.*

Shady Gate Gardens is a self-described "nursery for the adventurous gardener," operated out of the side yard and barn of its owner, Martha Bryan, in the southern Berkshires. Shady Gate is a small operation with a short season; its specialty is uncommon annuals and tender perennials, grown from seed or cuttings—most make excellent container subjects. Practically every plant in this interesting little nursery will make a connoisseur salivate. We know of horticultural celebrities who send their gardeners here to shop. Come early and beat the pros.

Shady Gate Gardens has charm and a sense of fun. Its zesty selection of ornamental annuals, supplemented with hardy perennials, is altered every season in pursuit of the new. Shady Gate carries ornamental vegetables such as snake gourd, smoky fennel, 'Afro' parsley, and 'Mini Sky Blue' sweet potato vine. It grows a dozen flowering tobaccos, three castor beans, and five amaranths, including one called 'Hot Biscuits'. It has two British introductions, bupleurum (green–gold) and *Cerinthe major purpurascens,* both touted in the garden press but nearly impossible to locate. It offers yellow cosmos, cherry red clarkia, variegated honeysuckle vine, angel's-trumpets, a tiny white thyme called 'Highland Cream', and the odd little eyeball plant *(Acnella spilanthes).* Shady Gate grows a blue-flowered shoofly *(Nicandra physaloides)* that was a star in our container garden until it killed off its competitors; it has a rose-flowered *Rhodochiton atrosanguinium* that other nurserymen hoarded for their friends. It carries plants with outlandish Latin names: Quamoclit, Zaluzianskya, Tolpis.

Shady Gate is a focused nursery producing exotic plants that add annual color to flower borders and containers. Visitors who wonder what these plants really look like can see many of them cascading from display pots or artfully climbing the walls of the barn: variegated hops intertwining with moonflowers, Oriental oregano paired with painted tovara and duckfoot coleus. Its plant list, referencing uncommon plants solely by Latin nomenclature, will send normal gardeners off to the library to consult *Hortus III.* Less studious gardeners can just show up at the nursery and buy whatever is intriguing. The latter course will appeal to Martha Bryan, who exhorts her customers to "have fun with what's new, underused, and worth the experiment." Visit Shady Gate Gardens, take a ride on the zoom.

Directions: Shady Gate is 20 minutes south of Stockbridge, near the Connecticut border. From Stockbridge, take Route 7 south for 2.6 miles and turn left onto Monument Valley Road. In 4.6 miles, cross Route 23 and continue straight onto Lake Buel Road. In 2.8 miles, bear right at a fork in the road. In 1.9 miles, bear left at the fork. In 1.8 miles, in Mill River, turn left at the Mill River General Store. In 1 mile, turn left onto Lumbert Cross Road; the nursery is 0.2 mile on the left.

Nearby attractions: Chesterwood, 4 Williamsville Road, Stockbridge (413-298-3579; www.nthp.org), is the turn-of-the-century summer studio and garden of Daniel Chester French, sculptor of the Lincoln Memorial; the property is maintained as a gentlemen's estate graced with formal sculpture gardens, woodland walks, and mountain views. The Berkshire Botanical Garden, Routes 102 and 183, Stockbridge (413-298-3926), is the area's 15-acre botanic garden; open May through October, daily 10-5. Eastern Native Seed Conservancy, P.O. Box 451, 222 Main Street, Great Barrington, MA

01230 *(413-229-8316; E-mail: natseeds@aol.com) is a nonprofit mail-order source for heirloom vegetable seed; its Native Seed Project attempts to preserve the region's oldest food crops, domesticated by American Indians.*

STONEHEDGE GARDENS

54 Richardson's Corner Road, Charlton, MA 01507
(508) 248-5502
Barbara and Paul Rogers

Unusual houseplants and annuals. Tomato seedlings. Herbs. Succulents and cactus. *Family-run greenhouses. Open all year, daily 8:30–4:30. No catalog or mail order. Seasonal and holiday crops. Display garden.*

For more than 20 years, broadcaster-horticulturist Paul Rogers has hosted *The Gardener's Calendar,* a gardening show on WTAG in Worcester that functions as a Master Gardener hotline for radio listeners. Behind the scenes, Rogers's wife, Barbara, has been running a small greenhouse operation out of their home in Charlton, where appreciative gardeners can purchase some of the interesting plants that her husband describes on the radio. Stonehedge Gardens specializes in houseplants, annuals, herbs, holiday plants, and spring tomato seedlings. Some are popular greenhouse subjects, others are new or outlandish varieties that Rogers has heard about on his travels and gets to play around with at night, for fun and enjoyment, just to keep his hand in horticulture.

The Rogerses raise what they sell from seed and cuttings, and have developed quite a following among gardeners seeking innovative plants that are hard to obtain from commercial sources. Their latest passion is for fragrant, night-blooming angel's trumpets and unusual alliums. Past obsessions with parti-colored coleus and scented geranium account for unusual assortments in the greenhouse. Barbara Rogers is a self-described "cactus nut" who keeps an array of tropical cacti and succulents along one whole wall. The Rogerses' regular customers would have a fit if they did not find, each year, the huge, creamy 'Pink Marshmallow' fuchsia in hanging baskets; 'Grandpa Ott's' rampant heirloom morning glory; and 'Gartenmeister Bonstedt' tree fuchsia with narrow, salmon flowers beloved by hummingbirds. Delightful dish gardens crammed with miniature houseplants are also justly popular.

Tomato seedlings include rare varieties such as the heritage 'Brandywine', a wine red Russian tomato called 'Black Krim', and various potato-leaved and low-acid hybrids. Our favorite, at least in theory, is a supersize plum tomato called 'Vatican', pilfered by a neighbor from the Pope's garden in Rome. We noticed popular petunias, annual vines, and interesting herbs such as Vietnamese coriander, Texas marigold, salad burnet, and toothache plant.

In December, the greenhouse is filled with seasonal poinsettia and

Christmas cactus brought in for the occasion. A charming garden is sand-wiched between the greenhouses and the Rogerses' antique farmhouse.

Directions: Charlton is 10 miles southeast of Worcester. From Route 90/Mass. Pike, take the Auburn exit onto Route 290 south, then take the first exit onto Route 20 west. After passing Route 56, go 3 miles and turn left at the light onto Richardson's Corner Road; the nursery is 0.5 mile on the right.

Nearby attractions: On Route 20 west in Charlton, follow signs to Charlton Orchards (508-248-7820) for apples and Christmas trees, and to Fay Mountain Farm (508-248-7237) for fresh-pressed cider. Architecture buffs may note Charlton's restored 1840 Greek Revival schoolhouse and handsome 18th-century Rider Tavern, open by appoint-ment (508-248-3202). Travelers heading north may stop for prehistoric fast food at Hot Dog Annie's, Route 56, Leicester (508-892-9059), a local institution serving hot dogs with legendary barbecue sauce for nearly 50 years (three for $2.55 at our last check; 30 years ago it was eight for $1).

SYLVAN NURSERY

1028 Horseneck Road, Westport, MA 02790-1392
(508) 636-4573 and 636-5615; fax (508) 636-3397
Neil Van Sloun, Chairman
James McBratney, President

Landscape-grade trees and shrubs. Seashore plants. Heath and heather. *Large commercial nursery. Business hours: March to November, Monday to Saturday 7:30–4; December to February, Monday to Friday 8–4:30. Closed Sunday and holidays. Small display garden. No retail catalog. Orders by fax, phone, mail, or in person. Plant lists on the Web site. Delivery services on 48 hours' notice. No children allowed on the premises. E-mail: sales@sylvannursery.com. Web site: www.sylvannursery.com.*

Sylvan Nursery, a wholesale nursery founded 30 years ago by Neil Van Sloun, is a major player in the national horticulture industry that burgeoned with the development of the interstate highway system following World War II. Sylvan occupies 120 acres in coastal Westport, possibly the warmest micro-climate in New England. Its sales area alone comprises 50 acres. Favored by design professionals for its vast selection of landscape-grade trees and shrubs, Sylvan is open to adult retail customers who are prepared to sidestep UPS trucks, forklifts, and heavy motorized equipment. For safety reasons, no children are allowed on the premises, and we personally would not risk the family dog.

This is no place for a leisurely stroll. Come prepared with a shopping list, sun-shielding hat, and comfortable walking shoes. Everyone, professionals included, must check in at the front desk before going anywhere. Here retail customers can orient themselves, borrow an umbrella, use the rest room, and consult the Retail Price List, a huge computer printout of all the plants available, listed alphabetically in botanical Latin. The busy office staff is efficient and quick with directions. We asked about fastigiate European hornbeam and were briskly directed to the right side of Greenhouse 18, where we found several large specimens. Customers in the looking stage may foray out alone on foot. Customers in the tagging and buying stage may travel with an outside sales representative in one of Sylvan's jaunty vehicular transports (akin to flatbed golf carts). Shipping can be arranged for large items.

Sylvan's principal attraction is its immense collection of ornamental trees and shrubs in landscape sizes. These plants are trucked in from nurseries all over the country. Many specimens are available in multiple sizes, ranging from medium to huge. As with all trees and shrubs, the bargains are in smaller-size plants. Most professionals personally inspect each specimen before tagging the ones they want, and you should, too. The range of ornamental trees, woody shrubs, evergreens, ground covers, perennials, and topiary available at Sylvan defies easy summary. The nursery boasts of being a "Horticulturist's Candy Shop," which accurately captures some of its colorful and bewildering variety. We counted 58 maple cultivars and 17 kinds of boxwood. Sylvan basically has everything. Seaside plants are a specialty, as are heaths and heathers, the only plants propagated on the premises. Potted perennials come from an esteemed local source. Sods of lowbush blueberry, hay-scented fern, and bunchberry are available at reasonable prices by the square foot.

Depending on your energy level, Sylvan Nursery can be exhausting or exhilarating. If you are up for it, this is a terrific place to survey a huge range of ornamental trees and shrubs. This is for serious gardeners only. From the standpoint of physical endurance, we recommend bringing water and treating a visit like a day hike.

Directions to Sylvan Nursery: Westport is on the Massachusetts coast near the Rhode Island border. From I-195 (east from Providence or west from Cape Cod), take exit 10 onto Route 88 south. In 17 miles, when the road ends, turn left onto East Beach Road, which becomes Horseneck Road; the nursery is 2 miles on the right.

Nearby attractions: Westport retains its beautiful coastal farmland. Horseneck Beach, a public beach on a magnificent stretch of ocean, is a mile down Horseneck Road from the nursery. Fresh local produce is sold at farm stands 2 miles up Horseneck Road in the other direction. Vineyard tours and wine tasting can be had at the 200-acre Westport Rivers Vineyard and Winery, 417 Hixbridge Road, Westport (508-636-3423). Locals and summer folk frequent Bayside Restaurant, 1253 Horseneck Road, Westport (508-636-5882), for seafood and ocean views.

TOWER HILL BOTANIC GARDEN

P.O. Box 598, 11 French Drive, Boylston, MA 01505-0598
(508) 869-6111
Worcester County Horticultural Society

Heirloom apple scions. *Nonprofit botanic garden. Open Tuesday to Sunday, 10–5. Free scion list. Mail order, spring only. Peak orchard bloom mid-May. Spring plant sale. Horticultural display gardens. Garden tours. Entry fee; free to members. Web site: www.towerhillbg.org.*

Tower Hill Botanic Garden maintains a flourishing garden on a 132-acre hill farm in central Massachusetts, east of Worcester. Tower Hill is home to the Worcester County Horticultural Society, the third oldest active horticultural society in America, founded in 1842 by the same fruit-growing farm community that produced Johnny Appleseed (a native of nearby Leominster). Many years ago, the society inherited a collection of 119 heirloom apple trees collected by S. Lothrop Davenport in the 1940s, when old varieties were being lost to commerce. The Davenport collection spent years at Old Sturbridge Village (MA) before being replanted in the Harrington Orchard on the south slope of Tower Hill.

Many apples in the Davenport collection are heirlooms developed by farmers in New England and New York; some even hark back to the Middle Ages. Every March, scion wood from the collection is sold for $2.50 per stick (each stick producing two or three scions) to gardeners who want to propagate heirloom apple trees; grafting is necessary because apples do not breed true from seed. Seminars on grafting, with rootstock provided, are held in the Stoddard Education and Visitors Center, which enjoys spectacular views west over the Wachusett Reservoir.

Tower Hill offers a year-round display of fine garden plants suited to cultivation in New England. A brainchild of the society is the Cary Award, given annually to distinctive, season-extending woody plants suitable to northern gardens, many of which can be seen in Tower Hill's gardens. A new 18th-century-style Orangerie exhibits tender exotics readily grown in a northern greenhouse. The New England School of Gardening, a joint effort of the society and Clark University, offers a certificate in horticulture and other lectures and classes. Tower Hill's popular spring plant sale offers many unusual perennials and woody plants (including Cary Award shrubs); exotic annuals and container plants; specialty plants at plant society booths; and for lunch, "hort dogs."

Directions: Tower Hill is in central Massachusetts, 8 miles east of Worcester. From Route 90/Mass. Pike, take exit 11 onto Route 495 north, then exit 25 onto Route 290 west. Take exit 24 and turn right off the ramp. In 3 miles, pass through Boylston center and turn right at the blinking yellow light; Tower Hill is the first driveway on your left.

Nearby attractions: Established in 1915, Bigelow Nurseries, 455 West Main Street (Old Boston Post Road), Northboro, MA 01532 (508-845-2143), is a large, family-owned nursery maintaining one of the largest tree and shrub inventories in the country, on 400 acres in Worcester County; retail customers can make an appointment to select specimen-size trees and shrubs in the growing fields, just as professionals do. Davis Mega-Maze (978-422-8888) is New England's largest field maze, designed in England by master maze designer Adrian Fisher on a century-old family farm in Sterling; a unique labyrinth is created each year in the cornfield, affording dazed visitors an opportunity to get truly lost (open from July through September, 10–5; allow several hours).

TRANQUIL LAKE NURSERY

45 River Street, Rehoboth, MA 02769-1395
(508) 252-4002; fax (508) 252-4740; (800) 353-4344 (orders)
Warren Leach and Philip Boucher

Daylilies. Japanese and Siberian iris. Perennials. *Open May through October, Wednesday to Sunday 10–5; open daily 10–5 in July and August. Catalog $1. Visitors welcome. Japanese Iris Society and American Hemerocallis Society display gardens. Peak bloom for Siberian iris June 1, Japanese iris July 7, daylilies July 20. July open house. Lectures and demonstrations. Garden design. E-mail: dchogan@sprynet.com. Web site: www.tranquil-lake.com.*

Tranquil Lake is a specialty nursery known for its immense collection of field-grown daylilies, amassed over three decades on a pleasant meadow in south-eastern Massachusetts. No other flowering plant has undergone as many transformations as the carefree daylily, and no other nursery in New England carries so many varieties, from old-fashioned classics to bright new hybrids. Tranquil Lake's mail-order catalog lists 400 daylilies, but the nursery grows 3,000 varieties in its 10-acre production field; it is the largest supplier in the

Northeast. Tranquil Lake is also known for its fine collections of Japanese and Siberian iris, planted in moist soil on the silted oxbow of a river running on the far edge of the production fields.

In recent years, a superb collection of pot-grown perennials has made an appearance at the nursery, along with embellished display gardens. Tranquil Lake's 22-acre nursery occupies bottomland that was once an Indian camp; ancient artifacts and arrowheads sometimes surface during cultivation of the fields.

Tranquil Lake daylilies span the open rainbow: The list is long and includes, in addition to classic tangerines and yellows, some gorgeous pinks, creams, melons, apricots, lilacs, roses, black-reds, and plums. (The only colors lacking are pure white and the impossible true blue.) The nursery has large-flowered daylilies with big faces; delicate small-flowered daylilies; miniatures; doubles; long-stalked "altissimas," and spiders. Some have long continuous bloom; others rebloom in the same growing season; still others are nocturnal, wonderful in evening gardens. On viewing the new introductions, we practically wanted to eat the Lachmans' luscious 'Violet Shadows' (a grapey gilt-edged plum with a chartreuse throat) and Sobel's delicious 'Strawberry Time' (like strawberry ice cream, streaked with vanilla). In fact, many daylilies are edible; Tranquil Lake's catalog promotes the use of daylily pods as vegetables (according to the nursery, "they taste like peapods"), and encourages their use in appetizers and desserts.

For all their delicious color and ornament, Tranquil Lake's daylily hybrids seem chosen to retain their dignity without overindulging in fussy bustles and ruffles. Every year, owners Warren Leach and Philip Boucher introduce distinguished daylily hybrids from their own breeding program and from other noted New England breeders. We were stopped in our tracks one evening by a huge, luminous, butter yellow, night-blooming daylily called 'Alna Pride', from hybridizer Nick Barth (see *Barth Daylilies, ME*). Such introductions are often expensive, but for the economical gardener, Tranquil Lake's plant list includes many older, award-winning classics that are quite affordable. For $6, for example, a gardener can acquire dainty pink 'Decatur Jewel', miniature apricot 'Siloam Sugar Time', lavender 'Grape Ice', or evening-blooming 'Butter Pat'.

Collections of easy, short, miniature, and edible daylilies are offered, as well as customized assortments for particular situations or gifts. One clever way to acquire a daylily garden is to buy and transplant them in flower, a practice daylilies will tolerate. An award-winning gardener we know enjoys a wonderful daylily display at her summer home in August, the time she and her family are there to enjoy them. Daylilies are shipped bare-root in freshly dug double fans or clumps (four or five fans), with bonus plants accompanying orders that allow substitutions.

Tranquil Lake's admirable collection of beardless iris (called apogons) thrives in growing beds at the wet end of the nursery. The catalog offers 50 Siberian iris, 15 Japanese iris, and a number of species iris, but this represents only a fraction of the collection. Of the Japanese iris, Tranquil Lake offers both American and Japanese hybrids, greedy dazzling plants that gardeners with moist spots find irresistible and everyone else despairs of growing. Of the elegant Siberian iris, Tranquil Lake carries many fine old cultivars (a number are awardwinners) at quite reasonable prices. This nursery sometimes reminds us of a good wine cellar that does not mark up prices on old bottles very often.

Tranquil Lake is an official show garden for the Japanese Iris Society and the American Hemerocallis Society, and its gardens are in high color in June and July. Iris and daylilies are shipped by mail all over the country, but local customers enjoy much greater selection of hybrids than do mail-order customers. Nursery visitors can also purchase excellent potted perennials and grasses, set out near the house, where ice water and daylily lists are distributed. Owner Warren Leach is an accomplished garden designer, and graceful examples of his work can be seen in the mixed perennial borders threading through the nursery—note the stunning combinations of low-maintenance and drought-tolerant plants. We love Leach's bog garden and thyme-covered seat (fragrant to sit upon), but our sentimental favorite is the scarecrow-guarded kitchen garden, planted by Leach and his wife, Debi, each summer at the entry to the daylily beds.

Directions: Rehoboth is 8 miles east of Providence. From Providence, take Route 195 east, and take exit 1 in Massachusetts (not Rhode Island). Turn left off the ramp onto Route 114A north and go straight to a stop sign. After 2 lights, turn right onto Route 44 east. In 3.7 miles, turn left onto River Street; the nursery is signposted on the right. According to the owners, "during bloom season the fields of flowers light the way."

Nearby attractions: In the 17th century, Rehoboth and Swansea were the site of important conflicts between early settlers and Americans Indians during King Philip's War. Anawan Rock, where a Wampanoag chief was captured in 1676, is 100 yards south of Route 44 on New Street; a footpath leads from a small parking lot. In Fall River, bored family members can amuse themselves at Battleship Cove (508-678-1100; 800-533-3194) by touring a World War II battleship, submarine, destroyer, PT boat, helicopter, and Japanese suicide boat; an antique carousel operates seasonally.

TRIPPLE BROOK FARM

37 Middle Road, Southampton, MA 01073
(413) 527-4626; fax (413) 527-9853
Stephen R. Breyer

Native perennials. Ground covers. Hardy bamboos, grasses, and cacti. Wildlife garden plants. Small specialty nursery. Open by appointment. Free catalog. Mail order. Display garden growing beds. No chemical pesticides used. Visitors must call ahead. E-mail: info@tripplebrookfarm.com. Web site: www.tripplebrookfarm.com.

Stephen Breyer—ecologist, plant farmer, and self-described stick-in-the-mud—has operated Tripple Brook Farm as a mail-order nursery since 1983. He works with the help of an indolent family dog, Amber, and, he says, "anyone in the family without a valid alibi." Tripple Brook Farm is a weathered ranch house set on a wooded hillside bordering the Pioneer Valley in western Massachusetts. It is surrounded by self-engineered plastic greenhouses, small display gardens, and a few wooden chicken coops from the days when Breyer's parents operated Tripple Brook as a poultry farm.

Tripple Brook Farm specializes in growing unusual, attractive, and productive landscape plants that do not require much maintenance. Many are hardy native plants that support wildlife and are rarely available in nurseries. Of particular interest is the farm's collection of native ground cover deserving wider garden use: hog peanut, Canada mayflower, groundnut, wild ginger, barren strawberry, partridgeberry, and pussy-toes. We chose native pachysandra, which is three times the size of the overused Japanese variety, and a tiny creeping potentilla with glossy foliage *(Potentilla tridentata)* that was being grown for a private botanical garden in New York. Bamboos are also a specialty, including tiny dwarfs, huge giants, and a running ornamental Japanese variety called 'Yellow Groove', which has a tendency to bend at the knee or, in bamboo parlance, genuflect.

The plant collection at Tripple Brook Farm includes interesting native grasses, sedges, ferns, and mosses; some are marsh plants adaptable to aquatic gardens. Native plants that are edible as well as ornamental include sassafras, wild sarsaparilla, wild rice, papaw, and Jerusalem artichoke. Cooks may enjoy culinary lemongrass and a horsetail known as giant souring rush, formerly used as a pot cleaner. Also available are fragrant native herbs such as mountain mint and wood nettle, and tough rock garden plants such as hardy tiger jaws, shinleaf, and fire pink. Ornamental native perennials include hardy plumbago, wild phlox, blue-stemmed goldenrod, Allegheny thermopsis, and our favorite substitute for veronica, blue-flowered anise hyssop, which makes a good tea. Near the pond we saw a native verbena called simpler's joy, a medicinal herb whose dense floral seed spikes seem to be crafted from needlepoint.

Well before the current fascination with tropical plants, Tripple Brook Farm began carrying a banana plant that survives in Zone 5B, hardy pomegranate and fig trees, hardy cacti (prickly pears with armed Mickey Mouse ears), and a narrow-leaved yucca known as Adam's needle, whose seed was collected 20 years ago by Breyer's sister on a roadside in the Southwest. Yucca and cactus plants are grown in an amusing display garden that looks like a scene from the Arizona desert, complete with sun-bleached cattle skulls left over from Tripple Brook's beef-farming days.

To the casual visitor, colonies of weeds and native plants (at times indistinguishable) may give Tripple Brook Farm a certain hardscrabble 19th-century appearance, but this should not be confused with poor farming practices. Many native plants are propagated in wild marshy patches or woodland colonies, using ethically responsible methods that are distinguishable from wild-digging. Because they are unpampered, the farm's plants transplant easily and have a good survival rate. Plants can be ordered by mail or freshly dug at the nursery. Because Tripple Brook Farm uses no chemical herbicides, its weed-battling arsenal is limited to simple remedies such as cooking potting soil in the oven and dousing weeds with boiling water. The catalog contains dense, opinionated, and informative plant descriptions far exceeding industry norms, and makes fun winter reading.

Directions: From I-91, take exit 16/Holyoke onto Route 202 west. One mile after entering Westfield, turn right onto Old Stage Road, then turn left at the first stop sign onto Middle Road; the nursery is 1.5 miles on the right, a green ranch house on a hill behind an older Cape. Visitors must call ahead.

UNDERWOOD SHADE NURSERY

P.O. Box 1386, North Attleboro, MA 02763-5152
(508) 222-2164; fax (508) 222-0386
Russ Bragg and Connie Wick

Woodland perennials. Hardy ferns. Native woodland plants. Grasses and ground covers. Pulmonaria, primrose, and violet. Open by appointment. Catalog $2. Mail order. Visitors welcome. E-mail: info@underwoodshadenursery.com. Web site: www.underwodshadenursery.com.

Underwood Shade Nursery was founded by Russ Bragg and Connie Wick after they became interested in shade plants in the usual way: They built a home on a wooded lot in North Attleboro, and tried to figure out what would grow in the woods. Wick is a librarian and Bragg is a certified arborist and horticulturist who works in the tree business. They joined the New England Wild Flower Society, and learned to grow shade-tolerant perennials for their own use. Then one day Bragg the arborist had a "duh" moment and realized that people with shade trees need plants to go under them. Together the couple began propagating uncommon shade plants in the woods behind their house, and selling overstock to gardeners seeking what they call "solutions for shade." Today their small nursery is one of the region's most intriguing sources of unusual shade plants for the woodland garden. It is the only nursery we know with a thorough understanding of dry shade and the plants that will grow under maple trees.

Underwood Shade Nursery is small, specialized, and in a sense experimental; its focus is on native, hybrid, and exotic woodland shade plants. The nursery is adventurous in testing seed for uncommon shade perennials (including unnamed varieties from China); Bragg boasts of rescuing from oblivion worthy plants that are "exiles from the garden press." A number of nursery offerings are horticultural unknowns that are unobtainable in the trade due to obscurity, "weed" status, or the time and effort (sometimes years) required for germination. The nursery acquires and grows native plants in an ethical manner, and propagates its own trillium. Because of its naturalistic approach and interesting plant list, the nursery sells shade plants to The Garden in the Woods (MA), various native plant societies and restoration projects, and appreciative shade gardeners throughout New England.

The nursery lists nearly 300 varieties of woodland perennials in its catalog, but due to growing demand and the vagaries of hard weather, constant availability is not guaranteed. Recently introduced (as "new ferniture") is the Mickel Collection of hardy ferns, unique ferns ranging from 3-inch miniatures to 6-foot fronds developed by Dr. John Mickel, of the New York Botanical Garden. (Mickel's book, *Ferns for American Gardens,* reflects 35 years of fern research and cultivation.) Underwood has adopted pulmonaria, or lungwort, as a specialty; its catalog lists 14 varieties (more are grown at the nursery), including the only one that has ever appealed to us, with azure flowers and pox-free foliage. Chrysogonum, or green-gold, is one of the nursery's excellent native ground covers; others include woodland phlox, yellowroot, twinleaf, miterwort, partridgeberry, Allegheny spurge (our native pachysandra), Meehan's mint, and, dear to our hearts, unusual violets (15 kinds).

Underwood Shade Nursery is a reliable source of native jack-in-the-pulpit, heart-leaved wild ginger, yellow alexander, blue-stemmed goldenrod, wild wood aster, low meadow rue, and rattlesnake weed. Its charming spring wildflowers include varieties of shooting star (*Dodecatheon* spp.), blue-eyed grass (*Sisyrinchium* spp.), and the exquisite Massachusetts state flower *(Epigaea repens),* known, of course, as the mayflower. The nursery also grows interesting hellebores, cranesbill geraniums, and ornamental grasses, including sedge and wood rush. A number of "worts" appear on the plant list: leadwort, toothwort, dropwort, and barrenwort. One spring visit we spied Asian toad lilies, a very dwarf potentilla, Japanese false anemone, Siberian bluebells, and a variegated tovara with chocolate chevrons (reclassified as persicaria, it deserves to be grown more). Our gardening companion acquired a white Himalayan primrose of great purity (*Primula denticulata* 'Alba') for her woodland garden. Listed in the catalog but not yet incarnate were a blue corydalis discovered in China, a green-flowered foxglove, and a costly prize, a native wood lily *(Lilium philadelphicum)* that the nursery has been propagating from seed for years.

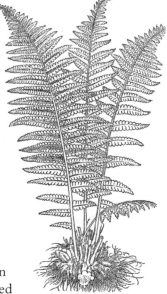

The nursery's plant stock comes in 4-inch-square quarts, though larger plants are available. Some are taken as divisions from stock plants, some are grown from seed, and some—the ones that look great in April—are bought in from reputable growers in Connecticut. Most plants are propagated on-site and must tough out the winter unprotected. However scruffy such a plant may look in early spring compared to its hothouse cousin, though, its survival tells you that it will grow in shade, in the ground, under trees, in New England. Deer-resistance is a bonus trait noted in the catalog.

Although acquiring plants by mail order is easier, nursery visitors are rewarded with the pick of the litter and a chaperoned tour by the personable Russ Bragg. This is a home-based nursery, so visitors must call for an appointment. In its sparse suburban woodland carpeted in leaf litter, this nursery is not intended to make a spectacular visual impression on the visitor. Yet what is going on here is worthy work, more serious than it looks.

Directions: North Attleboro is southwest of Boston, not far from Providence. From I-95, take exit 5/North Attleboro. Call in advance for local directions.

Nearby attractions: New England Bonsai, 914 South Main Street, Bellingham, MA 02019 (800-457-5445), is one of the region's largest growers and importers of bonsai (free mail-order catalog). Briggs Nursery, 295 Kelley Blvd. (Route 152), North Attleboro, MA 02760 (508-699-7421; www.briggsgarden.com), is an attractive garden center with a good collection of blue-blooded perennial plants at reasonable prices.

WALTER K. MORSS & SON

RFD 2, Lakeshore Road, Boxford, MA 01921
(978) 352-2633
Stanwood Morss

Farm-grown raspberry, strawberry, and blueberry plants. *Organic farm nursery. Open daily. Free catalog. Mail order or pickup. Live plants shipped April, May, October, and November. Pick-your-own raspberries from July to frost.*

Walter K. Morss & Son is an old-fashioned farm nursery growing small fruit seedlings for truck farmers and home gardeners. Founded on family farmland in Boxford cultivated since 1690 (now conservation land), Morss & Son has, since 1923, specialized in northern-grown raspberries, strawberries, and blue-berries—"selling only the varieties we know will give the best results" in cold-climate gardens, says owner Stanwood Morss.

Gardeners are welcome to visit the farm and see firsthand how the plants are grown. According to Morss, the farm operates "as organically as possible"; recycles 90 percent of its boxes and packaging; and uses more than 3,000 cords of horse manure per year from a local racetrack. The farm hardens off all its seedlings and hand-trims its strawberry plants because, Morss says, they work best that way. Despite this horticultural handwork, Morss & Son plants are all modestly priced.

Morss grows 20 raspberry hybrids on a 30-acre patch of conservation farmland. Raspberry cultivars include thornless 'Canby Red'; delicious yellow 'Amber' and 'Fall Gold'; and two-crop-a-year 'September', developed by the now defunct New York State Experiment Station (a victim of cold-blooded tax cuts). Two everbearing raspberry hybrids developed by the University of

New Hampshire, 'Durham' and 'Fall Red', are capable of being mowed to the ground in lieu of hand-pruning. Morss's own favorites are 'Boyne' and 'Killarney', both productive, ultra-hardy hybrids developed in Manitoba and often requested by pick-your-own farms. For variety, Morss sells raspberry collections chosen "for family gardening and long picking season." Gardeners wishing to sample the farm's raspberries can pick their own from July to frost.

The farm also grows 21 strawberry hybrids on 8 acres of conservation land, mostly on virus-free foundation stock from Canada. Morss strawberries comprise old and new varieties, including large-fruited 'Raritan', frost-free 'Premier', popular new 'All Star', and flavorful 'Sparkle'. Strawberries are sold as freshly dug plants, packed carefully, and accompanied by plainspoken farmerly advice from the owner: "The most important single thing in growing strawberries is to set plants early. With no other crop is early-spring setting so important. We set ours in March and April when possible, and try to have them all set by April 20."

Finally, Morss offers 15 hardy blueberry hybrids, sold as 12- to 18-inch plants; these include 'Northland', which reportedly produces "not a big berry, but can stand down to 10 to 20 below zero." Several hardy grapevines are available, along with a large, flavorful rhubarb called 'Canada Red'. Order early, for these farm-grown seedlings are popular and the stock sometimes runs out.

Directions: From Boston, take Route 495 north to exit 43. Turn right onto Route 125, and right again onto Route 133. Take your first left onto Lakeshore Road and pass Kingsbury Avenue; the farm will be on your left.

WAQUOIT HEATHER NURSERY

P.O. Box 3214, 131 Carriage Shop Road, Waquoit, MA 02536
(508) 548-6979
George and Edna MacKinnon

Heath and heather (Ericaceae). *Small specialty nursery. Open all year. Visitors welcome, call ahead. Catalog $2. Mail order, $10 minimum. Shipping April through September. Display beds.*

Waquoit Heather Nursery is a small specialty nursery located next to the MacKinnons' home in Waquoit, a village in the town of Falmouth on Cape Cod. George and Edna MacKinnon have been gardening here for 25 years, growing heath and heather, two delightful moorland shrubs that are fellow members of the Ericaceae family. The couple carry more than 250 varieties, collected over the years from such sources as the English Heather Society, the

Arnold Arboretum, and the late H.V. Lawrence, a noted landscaper who first brought heather to Cape Cod. Edna MacKinnon, who grew up on an English dairy farm, claims she was "pitchforked into this" by her Scottish-American husband. She does the propagation and potting, and he handles the heavy work. Their fine heath and heather collection blooms year-round, even in the depth of winter.

Though heaths and heathers may vary in cold hardiness, the MacKinnons' selections of heather *(Calluna vulgaris)* and heath *(Erica carnea)* are well suited to northern gardens: Most are hardy to 30 degrees below zero (Zone 4) with wind protection. The nursery grows more than 200 varieties of heather and 33 of heath. Together these plants make a remarkable carpet of woven color that appears bright and subtle in all seasons, much like an herb-dyed tartan or a Harris tweed. On a December visit, with only the evergreens providing color in other gardens, we were amazed to see the MacKinnons' winter-flowering heathers in profuse bloom: clusters of tiny white, pink, lilac, and heliotrope flowers, set off against rich dark and light green foliage. The heather's autumn foliage display still blazed in shades of salmon (*Caluna vulgaris* 'Hamlet Green'), citron (*C. vulgaris* 'Gold Haze'), pink-tipped gold (*C. vulgaris* 'Winter Chocolate'), and tomato-tipped green (*C. vulgaris* 'Firefly'). It was nearly Christmas, and the plants were dusted in snow. We fell in love with the whole collection on the spot. The summer bloom display is supposed to be just as beautiful, and includes some lucky white heather, which the Scots say can be found only by Gypsies in the wild.

The MacKinnons are experts in heath and heather culture and can advise gardeners on proper planting, care, and garden use. Waquoit Heather Nursery sells plants purchased on-site in all sizes; mail-order plants are sold in small sizes only. Visiting gardeners may dig their own clump of heather from the growing beds for just $10, an amazing bargain if the plant is handled properly.

The nursery's well-labeled display gardens are marked by stone paths near a greenhouse, separated from the growing beds by whirligigs and a small arboretum of unusual trees. Heaths and heathers interweave well with lavender, herbs, dwarf conifers, and English box. Be sure to ask Edna MacKinnon to show you her "bit of Scotland," consisting of a large stand of escaped heather occupying the verge of a nearby scrub pine forest; the plants sprouted from seed blown from the greenhouse, and were pollinated by wild bees.

Directions: From Route 495, take Route 28 south over the Bourne Bridge to Cape Cod, and exit onto Route 151. Turn right. In 3 miles, after a light, take the next right onto Currier Road/Falmouth Airport. In 3 miles (bearing left at any perceived forks and passing two stop signs), the road becomes Carriage Shop Road. The nursery is on your left at #131, in the small shed and greenhouse behind a yew hedge.

Nearby attractions: Ashumnet Holly and Wildlife Sanctuary, 286 Ashumnet Road, Falmouth, MA 02536 (508-563-6390), is a holly arboretum planted by Wilfred Wheeler ("the Holly Man") to preserve hollies against fire damage and wild collecting; it is now a bird sanctuary owned by the Massachusetts Audubon Society.

WESTON NURSERIES

P.O. Box 186, East Main Street (Route 135), Hopkinton, MA 01748-0186
(508) 435-3414; fax (508) 435-3274; (800) 322-2002 (orders)
Wayne and Roger Mezitt

Trees and shrubs. Rhododendron and azalea hybrids. Conifers; maples; crab apples, and magnolias. Perennials. *Large, family-owned nursery and garden center. Open Monday to Saturday, April to June 8–6, July to October 9–6, November to March 9–5. Christmas shop November 28 to December 24, Monday to Saturday 9–5, Sunday 10–5. Free catalog. No mail order. Phone orders accepted. Delivery and landscaping services. Display gardens. Lectures.*

Established by the Mezitt family in 1923, Weston Nurseries is a 900-acre horticultural preserve that claims to be "New England's largest grower of landscape-sized plants, shrubs, and trees." With 650 acres of growing fields, 30 acres in container production, 21 greenhouses, and 220 acres of sales area, display gardens, and woodland, the sheer size and scope of Weston's operation preempts counterclaims.

Weston Nurseries is known for growing thousands of superior tree and shrub cultivars, particularly flowering crabs and conifers, and for its celebrated rhododendron and azalea hybrids. In recent years Weston has developed a good stock of roses and container-grown perennials. For a New England nursery of these proportions to be propagating and growing 90 percent of its own plants is a testament to the professional achievements of the Mezitts, now in their fourth generation of nurserymen.

The Mezitt family has long been known for its shrewd eye in selecting superior strains of nursery stock. The nursery was founded by Peter Mezitt, a Latvian farmer who studied agriculture near Moscow before immigrating to Massachusetts and working on Weston's Case Estates. After opening their nursery, the Mezitts prospered by producing thousands of plants specially suited to New England conditions, and survived the Great Depression by catering to a post-Victorian craze for rock gardens. In 1939, Ed Mezitt, son of the founder, tried his hand at hybridizing small-leaf rhododendrons to achieve earlier spring bloom. His first attempt at "pollen-dabbing" produced the famous 'PJM' hybrid, named on the spot for his father, who called it "the most spectacular rhododendron of our time." Another noted rhododendron hybrid, 'Olga Mezitt' (known as the pink PJM) was named for Ed Mezitt's mother. Since then, Weston Nurseries has introduced dozens of original rhododendron and azalea hybrids to the nursery trade. Its best-known achievements are with early-flowering small-leaf rhododendrons, dwarf azaleas, and summer-flowering azaleas. Today, Weston offers more than 70 original rhododendron and azalea hybrids. All are the result of Ed Mezitt's interest in breeding smaller hybrids that lengthen the bloom season in cold-climate gardens.

Weston Nurseries' annual catalog, listing hundreds of tree and shrub cultivars, is a more informative resource than most retail garden books. Erudite but readable, it runs to 288 pages and has the feel of a midsize paperback. The catalog uses icons to indicate plants that have won awards or are nursery introductions—the easiest way we know to figure out if a plant is an AAS winner, a Perennial Plant of the Year, a Cary Award winner, a Pennsylvania Horticultural Society Gold Medal winner, or (like the Hopkinton white cedar and midget boxleaf yew) a unique cultivar introduced by Weston. The catalog prints useful "Flowering Calendars" showing bloom times for perennials and rhododendrons; "Tree Calendars" charting the flower, fruit, and foliage seasons of trees; a "Maple Fall Color Calendar" charting maple foliage; and similar calendars for ornamental shrubs and vines. When spring orders are finished, we always put this catalog in the bookshelf rather than the wastebasket. Weston's catalog is required reading for gardeners old and new.

Weston Nurseries is a comprehensive source of specimen-size ornamental trees and shrubs suited to northern gardens. Its field-grown stock is wide-ranging and hard to summarize. Deciduous trees, for example, include 40 kinds of maple, 11 beeches, nine birches, 25 magnolias, 19 flowering crabs, and many intriguing items such as ruby honeylocust, pink silver-bell, fruitless weeping mulberry, and seedless ash. Weston's shrub selection embraces buckeyes, shadblows, quinces, dogwoods, brooms, witch hazels, chokecherries, and all the hydrangeas and viburnums anyone could want. Its collection of evergreen trees and shrubs is equally broad.

Most plants are sizable, mature specimens, and priced accordingly. Customers can select plants at the nursery, or call and have them dug to order; delivery and planting are available for an extra charge. We hear reports that Weston's field-grown plants occasionally come with a pernicious weed (with a chrysanthemum-like leaf) that is intractable if not immediately routed; thankfully, this is not our experience. We once bought a Weston-bred copper beech and had the nursery's landscape crew plant it on our property; although beeches resent transplanting, the tree flourished.

Weston Nurseries' goal, apparent everywhere, is to develop the Hopkinton site as a recreational and educational destination for regional gardeners. The horticultural staff is intelligent and helpful. Plants are well labeled with markers interspersed along walkways. The outside sales area is interwoven with display gardens (designed by Joseph Hudak) to inform and delight strollers. Weston maintains a hypnotizing outdoor train garden, in which a miniature garden railway wends its way through a bonsai landscape. At a nearby animal pen, children can feed corn to two gentle pygmy goats for a quarter.

Weston's huge presence occupies an entire open valley and wooded hillside in Hopkinton, its terraced growing beds networked by miles of buried drainage tiles. From the road, gardeners can view Weston's entire nursery operation and the growing fields that occupy this impressive, much altered, horticultural landscape.

Directions: From Route 90/Mass. Pike, exit onto Route 495 south and take exit 21A/West Main Street. Follow West Main Street as it feeds into Route 135; the nursery is on your left, about a mile past the second light.
From Framingham, take Route 135 east for 7 miles; the nursery is on the right.

NEW HAMPSHIRE

NEW HAMPSHIRE

1. Bodacious Blossoms
2. Edgewater Farm
3. The Fells Nursery
4. Lake Street Garden Center
5. Lowe's Roses
6. Meredith Country Gardens
7. The Mixed Border Nursery
   and Gardens
8. Murray Farms
9. Perennials From Susan
10. Rolling Green Nursery
11. Spider Web Gardens
12. Uncanoonuc Mt. Perennials
13. Wayside Farm

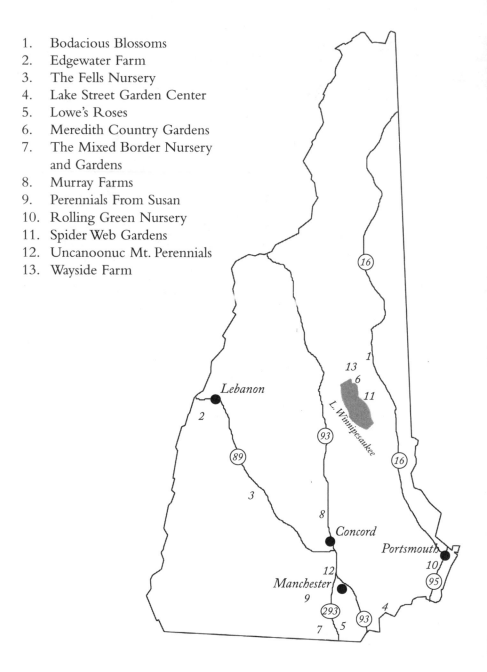

BODACIOUS BLOSSOMS

P.O. Box 242, 1297 Chocorua Road, Chocorua, NH 03187
(603) 323-7557; fax (603) 323-7790
Nancy M. Cavalieri

Perennials, annuals, and herbs. *Small specialty nursery. Open May through Labor Day, daily 9–5; evenings and autumn by chance or appointment. No catalog or mail order. Orders may be called ahead.*

Established in 1996, Bodacious Blossoms is situated northeast of Lake Winnipesaukee, in the pretty town of Chocorua, not far from the town's milldam. This micro-nursery is housed in a new wooden dwelling surrounded by bouncing blossoms deservedly called bodacious. Owner Nancy Cavalieri is a part-time bookkeeper and longtime plant lover who is known locally as the Flower Lady. We can't tell if that's because she jump-started a garden out of nothing, madly propagates plants in her living room and basement, or is Chocorua's only local source of interesting and unusual plants. (We're pretty sure she will custom-grow plants if you give her enough notice.) Her energy and enthusiasm inspire confidence that she will defy the odds of solo nurserymen and stay in business, a boon to gardeners in New Hampshire and beyond.

Bodacious Blossoms specializes in classic and unusual perennials, annuals, and herbs. The owner propagates many plants by seed during the winter, though some of her perennials are purchased as plugs and pot-grown in the spring. The perennial yard features decorative garden plants such as pink platycodon, blue indigo, ruby cardinal flower, red lupine, and golden Marguerite. Indispensable classics include boltonia, mildew-resistant bee balm, and veronica 'Crater Lake'. Shade plants feature uncommon woodlanders such as leopard's-bane, heart-leaf alkanet, woodland phlox, Japanese painted fern, and hosta hybrids. Also available are superior cottage-garden plants, easily cared for by summer people, such as pretty white mallow, scented geranium, hardy lavender, fern-leaved yarrow, clematis, and handsome perennial phlox. All perennials come in generous gallon pots and are well tended. The nursery also offers woody shrubs that go well with perennials, such as lilac, scarlet quince, dwarf euonymus, and red-osier dogwood.

Bodacious Blossoms grows a terrific flock of uncommon annuals, including tricolor salvia, wild monarda, annual aster, tropical datura, creeping zinnia, and interesting varieties of nasturtium, annual phlox, and cosmos. We were especially intrigued by the uncommon herbs, both culinary and medicinal. Gardeners in rural New Hampshire must not find it easy to locate anise hyssop (a soothing tea), vervain and valerian (both soporifics), elecampane (roots used as a sweetener), astragalus (an immune-system strengthener known as huang qi in Chinese medicine), and skullcap (a nervous-system tonic, potentially useful as a divorce alternative). Given the country location of this nursery, its plant selection is bountiful, bold, and adventurous—bodacious, in fact. Gardeners who want to keep it that way should come by for plants, or call in their orders in spring.

Directions: From I-95 in Portsmouth, New Hampshire, take the Spaulding Turnpike/Route 16 north, and continue on Route 16 when the turnpike ends. In Chocorua, turn left onto Route 113; the nursery is a mile on your right. From I-93, take exit 24, and turn left onto Route 113 east; the nursery is on your left, just before the town of Chocorua.

Nearby attractions: The town of Chocorua is dominated by the legend of Chocorua, a Pequawket chief who was killed by a white settler on the summit of the cone-shaped mountain that looms over the area. Summer estates and antique houses occupy the region, now free of Indian raids. Chocorua Lake, north on Route 16, offers a delightful spot to picnic and swim in sapphire water. Famous among botanists are the Ossipee Pine Barrens, east on Route 113, just past Madison center; this fascinating plant community consists of white, red, and pitch pine populating a sandy glacial outwash. On Route 113, 2.7 miles farther east, the Madison Boulder (signposted) is one of the world's largest glacial erratics, an immense block of granite weighing 4,662 tons, equivalent in mass to two World War II naval destroyers. The boulder is colonized by lichens (called rock tripe) which once provided a backup food supply to American Indians.

EDGEWATER FARM

99 River Road, Plainfield, NH 03781
(603) 298-8391 and (603) 298-5764
Lockwood and Anne Sprague

Unusual annuals, herbs, and perennials for container and cottage gardens. Spring vegetable flats. *Small, family-run horticultural farm. Open for plant sales from late April to mid-October, daily 10–5:30. Plant list. No mail order. Farm stand on Route 12A, Plainfield, open mid-June through October. U-pick strawberries, mid-June to early July. Farm stand on Route 202/9, Hillsboro, open mid-May through September. E-mail: Lockwood.Sprague@valley.net. Web site: www.edgewaterfarm.com*

Edgewater Farm is a diversified horticultural farm, energetically run and beautiful to look at, that is committed to producing high-quality garden plants and vegetables from its own greenhouses and fields. Owners Lockwood and Anne Sprague (he is known as Pooh) grew up on area dairy farms; after flirting with careers in music and teaching, they started Edgewater Farm in 1974 as a vegetable and U-pick strawberry farm. In the late 1970s they began growing ornamental plants and herbs around their

antique farmhouse in Plainfield, on rich rolling land bordering the
Connecticut River. They now operate 10 greenhouses (comprising an
acre of greenhouse space) and several large production fields. Their nursery
is a committed friend of regional horticulture, having supported The Garden
Conservancy's restoration of The Fells gardens on
Lake Sunapee (NH).

Edgewater is a wonderful resource for
regional gardeners, producing diverse and
imaginatively chosen annuals, herbs,
perennials, and vegetable transplants for
container and cottage gardens. Most plants
have been field-tested, which means that
expert growing advice is available on virtually
every specimen. Edgewater Farm takes pride in being "a working farm
committed to producing high-quality plants," using responsible, sustainable
agricultural practices. Plants are sold in pots and containers from greenhouses
at the home farm, as well as from two stylish farm stands in Plainfield and
Hillsboro, colorfully ornamented with hanging plants and display beds
from spring to frost.

The Spragues are tireless horticultural farmers who have clearly been
bitten by the exotic-plant bug; their plant list contains many "new and
unusual" offerings from British and American seed houses. Their greenhouses
are brimming with the kind of cutting-edge plants gardeners compete for in
spring: dashing annuals, tropicals, and foliage plants; heirlooms and herbs;
pretty cottage-garden perennials; vegetable seedlings suited to northern
gardens; and wonderful mixed hanging baskets and live herb wreaths.
Edgewater Farm's container plants are intriguing and sophisticated, far
exceeding the norm of typical rural greenhouses. The farm grows fine
fuchsias, including several bronze-leafed, heat-tolerant triphyllas that look
simply wonderful in containers. Its unusual coleus are vegetatively propagated
and therefore uncommonly large, showy, and sun tolerant. Tender salvias
come in peach, cobalt, azure, purple, yellow, and white.

The farm claims to grow "the latest, fanciest, industrial-strength
geraniums from national propagators" alongside subtler scented and
heirlooms geraniums (actually pelargoniums). The Spragues' "personal fave"
is a nutmeg-scented pelargonium with white flowers and lacy variegated
foliage. Our parents grow 'Patricia Andrews', a showy heirloom geranium
with salmon flowers that remain, even in full bloom, curiously budlike.

Edgewater Farm also stocks superior white petunias; showy hibiscus;
miniature browallia; variegated Society garlic; a blood red irisene called
'Chicken Gizzard' ("a tad loud for our taste," say the Spragues); and peanut

butter plant *(Melianthus major),* a foliage plant with a weird odor that not everybody can stand. These exotics are supplemented with good garden perennials that go on sale in September, and, in springtime, with vegetable seedlings for the home gardener. Few greenhouses in New England offer such an attractive combination of state-of-the-art horticulture and old favorites freshly grown on an environmentally sensitive working farm. Gardeners traveling from a distance can check the plant list (available by mail or Internet) and call ahead for particular items. Those seeking plants not listed are encouraged to ask. June visitors may want to pick their own strawberries, for we agree with the owners that "there is no prettier or more scenic place to pick berries than our fields, which border the Connecticut River." After stocking up with fresh, tax-free, New Hampshire–grown plants, we recommend stopping at one of Edgewater's two farm stands for an armful of fresh vegetables and strawberries, local cheese, raw honey, and milk in glass bottles from the dairy farm down the road.

Directions: From Route 89, take exit 20, turn onto Route 12A south. In 4 miles, turn right onto River Road at the Riverbend Veterinary Clinic (owned by Anne Sprague's sister) and go 0.25 mile to the farm and greenhouses, which are on your left. Edgewater Farm's main farm stand is on Route 12A, just south of River Road in Plainfield. A satellite stand is on Route 202/9 in Hillsboro (Lockwood Sprague's home town).

Nearby attractions: Owned by Ann Sprague's brother, McNamara Dairy—"Mac's Happy Acre"—313 River Road, Plainfield, is a working dairy farm and source of fresh milk in glass bottles (603-298-MOOO/6666); the chocolate milk is terrific. Anichini, an Italian maker of expensive bed linens, has an outlet store in the Powerhouse Arcade, Route 12A, Lebanon (603-298-8656), that sells its goods at half price.

THE FELLS NURSERY

John Hay National Wildlife Refuge, Route 103A, Newbury, NH 03255
(603) 763-4789
Ann Loeffler, Gardener

Perennials, alpines, and wildflowers. Native ground cover. *Nonprofit wildlife refuge and estate garden. Self-service nursery open daily, May to September, dawn to dusk. Annual plant sale. No catalog or mail order. Refuge and garden open year-round. House tours on weekends, May to October. Special events and educational programs all year.*

The Fells, one of New Hampshire's most beautiful garden estates, is located on the shores of Lake Sunapee, on the grounds of the John Hay National Wildlife Refuge. The Fells gardens, developed by the Hay family between 1909 and the 1940s as a showplace country estate, were rescued from neglect in the 1990s by staff and volunteers of The Garden Conservancy. As a result of this infusion of interest and energy, The Fells has become a regional centerpiece for horticultural education and activity in the state.

The Fells gardens comprise a 100-foot perennial border, a hidden walled garden, a rose terrace, rhododendron and azalea shrubberies, and an important rock garden cascading down to a series of Japanese pools. The surrounding woodlands are preserved as a wildlife refuge spliced by 5 miles of carriage roads and hiking trails. The refuge protects delightful native flora and fauna, including woodland plants and a population of rainbow smelt that run up Beech Brook in spring.

At the entry to The Fells, a small gatehouse contains a self-serve nursery offering many plants found in the estate gardens and refuge. These include woodland plants, garden perennials, peonies, rock-garden plants, and companion shrubs, many of which are hardly seen in commerce. The emphasis is increasingly on woodland natives found on the refuge grounds, such as northern beech fern, a native yellow foxglove *(Digitalis ambigua),* and a mauve-pink cardinal flower *(Lobelia siphilitica)* that appeared as a natural sport in the woods. The nursery also offers the virtually deathless ornamentals that survived in The Fells gardens from the 1930s through the present. These heritage plants include a wonderful tough heather, a hardy boxwood, and a "great little veronica" that is a staff favorite.

Nearly all the nursery's plants are field-grown on the estate. No plants are wild-collected. The working end of the nursery is situated in an old dog pen beside the main house. The effort is manned by a single part-time gardener and a group of dedicated volunteers who come in twice a week and reportedly "pot their brains out."

The Fells plant sale, held on the third Saturday of August, is a convivial event attracting many local and regional friends of horticulture who support restoration of The Fells gardens. For the sale, nursery output is supplemented with unusual plant material brought in from accomplished outside vendors. The Fells sponsors classes, guided walks, exhibits, and special events all year. Its summer lecture series on gardening and natural history usually includes an evening with John Hay, the award-winning environmental writer who spent childhood summers at The Fells, back when it was his family's private Lake Sunapee retreat.

Directions: From the south and east, take Route 89 north to exit 9/Route 103 and go west to Newbury. Take Route 103A north for 2.2 miles; The Fells is on the left.

From the north, take Route 89 south to exit 12/Route 11. Turn go right at the ramp and immediately left onto Route 103A south. In 5.6 miles, The Fells is on the right. Visitors are asked to park in the lot and walk down the driveway to the house and gardens.

Nearby attractions: Designated a Farm of Distinction in 1996, Spring Ledge Farm, 220 Main Street, New London, NH 03257 (603-526-6253), runs a superior farm stand specializing in gourmet vegetables, perennial and herb plants, spring annuals, hanging baskets, and pick-your-own flowers and herbs. Enfield Shaker Museum (603-632-4346) preserves the buildings and landscape of a 19th-century Shaker community, including a re-created Shaker herb garden; a fieldstone dormitory has been sensitively converted to an inn whose restaurant serves Shaker cuisine. Rhododendron State Park in Fitzwilliam, New Hampshire (603-532-8862), protects a 16-acre grove of rosebay rhododendrons (R. maximum) growing wild near the northern edge of their range. Peak bloom is said to be in mid-July, but many locals agree with Henry David Thoreau, whose 1853 journal reported that the Fitzwilliam rhododendrons were "in perfection" around the Fourth of July.

LAKE STREET GARDEN CENTER

37 Lake Street, Salem, NH 03079
(603) 893-5858
Frank Wolfe

Annuals and container plants. Perennials. Native ground cover. Roses. Nursery stock. *Family-owned garden center. Open all year, daily 9–5; closed major holidays and the first Monday in August. No catalog or mail order.*

Lake Street is a well-known, family-owned garden center that grows much of its own extensive stock of perennials, annuals, shrubs, grasses, and aquatics. Its healthy plants, extensive selection, and good prices have made this a favorite resource for area gardeners. We know of Boston-based gardeners, too, who sneak over the border to buy plants here, perhaps to escape the state sales tax. Owner Frank Wolfe and his family, who have operated Lake Street Garden Center for years, can be counted on to stock "something special and unusual" alongside the mainstays of ornamental gardening. The nursery has for years provided show-quality spring stock to the Boston Flower Show.

Lake Street Garden Center is one of those compact, well-run businesses that may not carry everything, but always seem to have what you want. Even in September (an unfair time to judge a nursery, we admit), the selection included inspiring choices of ground cover such as variegated pachysandra, silky-leaved woodwaxen, and miniature cranberry. Among the temptations of our last visit were lime trees, exotic thymes, an immense potted rose arch, an Ayurvedic herb called Indian ginseng, lead urns, and Japanese snow-viewing lanterns *(yakumi)* carved in solid granite.

Visitors are greeted by masterful container gardens and seasonal displays that illustrate the decorative uses of Lake Street's plants: for summer, an immense flowering entry arch composed entirely of impatiens; for fall, a cornstalk tepee and container gardens deftly combining orange and yellow flowers with chartreuse foliage plants. The garden center is open daily (except for a few holidays) all year long, making it a steady resource for seasonal plants and a great ally in horticultural emergencies. At checkout, customers are given curious little hard candies with green rims that say LAKE STREET GARDEN CENTER, not printed, but embedded in the candy like Venetian glass.

Directions: From I-93, take exit 3 onto Route 111 east. At the junction of Routes 111/28 go straight onto the road that goes between U.S. Gas and the Honda dealer. In 1 mile, turn right onto Lake Street and proceed to the garden center.
From Route 495 in Massachusetts, take exit 50 onto Route 97 west into Salem, New Hampshire. At the second full light, turn right onto School Street; in 2 miles, the garden center is on your left.

LOWE'S ROSES

6 Sheffield Road, Nashua, NH 03062
(603) 888-2214
Malcolm (Mike) Lowe

Custom-propagated old garden roses. *Open by appointment. Catalog $3. Mail order. Display garden; peak bloom second and third week of June. Visitors welcome by arrangement. Consultation services. Slide lectures. Please include SASE with inquiries. Web site: www.loweroses.com.*

Mike Lowe, a retired Raytheon engineer with a passion for roses, began Lowe's Roses (formerly Lowe's Own-Root Roses) in 1979, custom-growing old garden roses from his home in a suburban neighborhood in Nashua. Lowe, who is renowned for his expertise with heirloom roses, is a lifetime certified judge of the American Rose Society. He first determined to grow roses after hearing of a great-uncle's 19th-century rose nursery in Nottingham, England, also called Lowe's Roses. Mike Lowe's personal collection of some 4,000 rose plants contains many forsaken varieties that are unobtainable from commercial breeders.

An early champion of "own-root" roses, Lowe began propagating old roses on their own roots in the late 1970s at the request of gardening friends seeking non-grafted plants. (Because the practice is cheaper and less time-consuming, commercial growers since World War I have propagated hybrid roses by grafting them onto hardy rootstock.) Due to Lowe's success and the burgeoning interest in hardy antique roses, the "own-root" movement has now affected even big commercial breeders such as Weeks and Jackson & Perkins. Nevertheless, Lowe's Roses remains popular among rose aficionados drawn by Lowe's skill as a rose propagator and his willingness to custom-grow even the rarest and most forgotten old garden roses.

What roses! Lowe's Roses sells 130 kinds of antique and modern plants expertly bred from the Lowe collection. Most of the antique roses are 19th-century hybrids—irresistible, fragrant, tough old roses from great-grandmother's garden. Among the Bourbon roses are lavender 'Omar Pacha' and vigorous pink 'Capitaine Dyel'. The centifolia "cabbage" roses include the crimson 'Duc de Fitzjames' and lilac-pink 'Petite Orleanaise'. We have never seen, in any other nursery, an Ayrshire rose (Lowe grows creamy blush 'Splendens'); a hybrid setigera climber, bred from native prairie roses (Lowe grows 'Long John Silver'); or a hybrid nitida rose, a race of ultra-hardy dwarfs bred from a native New England rose (Lowe grows bushy little 'Corylus'). The nursery offers many old China roses, damasks, Portlands, hybrid perpetuals, polyanthas, moss roses, hybrid spinosissimas, hybrid rugosas, sweetbriers, and wild species roses.

The Lowe collection has many old Gallica roses (dating to 1200 B.C.), including the ancient, perfumed apothecary rose. Modern large-flowered climbers and rambling roses of the 20th century form a scrambling maze of choices, including such resurrected classics as 'American Pillar' (scarlet, of course), 'Evangeline' (veined cameo pink), and 'The Gift' (single and double, white and pink, on the same rambler).

Among its many shrub roses, the nursery grows two original Mike Lowe hybrids that incorporate extraordinary old-rose quality. These are a fruity apricot/yellow climber called 'Autumn Sunset' (Lowe's personal favorite) and a fragrant rose with summerlong repeat bloom called 'Mike's Old-Fashioned Pink'—an instant classic introduced in the year 2000.

Lowe's Roses grows 2,000 plants each year for gardeners willing to wait up to 18 months for custom-propagated specimens. Rose orders must be received by August 1 to meet budding dates. The resulting plants are not ready until October of the next year—nor is the outcome guaranteed. While most are grown own-root, roses that are too difficult or refuse to strike on their own roots must be grafted. A backup crop is available to fill in for truculent plants. Despite the effort, Lowe's roses cost no more than commercially bred plants. While some rose varieties are now available from some commercial growers, most are rarities derived from private collections and arboreta. From the viewpoint of regular gardeners, such roses are nowhere else to be found.

Directions: Call ahead for an appointment. Take Route 3/Everett Turnpike to Nashua. There take Exit 4/FAA Center/E. Dunstable Road, and go west on East Dunstable Road. Take the seventh right onto New Searles Road; at the end turn right onto Searles Road. Take the second left onto Sheffield Road; Mike Lowe's home-based nursery at #6 and #10, on your left.

MEREDITH COUNTRY GARDENS

314 Sheridan Road, Moultonboro, NH 03254
Mailing address: RR 1, P.O. Box 233, Center Harbor, NH 03226
(603) 284-7709
Rink and Dottie DeWitt

Daylilies. Geraniums. Annuals, perennials and herbs. Fruit plants. Vegetable seedlings. Country greenhouses. Open mid-April to Columbus Day, and by chance or appointment. No catalog or mail order. Reference library. Daylily lectures. Peak bloom July 20 to August 8. E-mail: rinkinthegarden@aol.com.

Meredith Country Gardens (renamed Sheriden Gardens in 2001) caught our eye years ago, traveling down a rural road near Lake Winnipesaukee, when we glimpsed some country greenhouses surrounded by tables of lush potted plants and vegetable flats. Long owned *in absentia* by the Price family, Meredith Country Gardens is now in the hands of New Hampshire native Rink DeWitt, a former bank executive. DeWitt's wife, Dottie, is an expert gardener and sometime hybridizer known for her superb private collection of more than 730 cold-hardy daylily varieties, all of which are now available throught the nursery.

Under DeWitt's energetic direction (he runs the business, drives the tractor, and pilots the airplane that whisks off the couple to visit daylily breeders), Meredith Country Gardens is continuing its tradition of growing ornamental annuals, perennials, and herbs. These are supplemented with companion shrubs, fruit plants (such as raspberries and blueberries), and vegetable flats in spring. Local gardeners and visitors from urban areas will appreciate the good plant material sold here at reasonable prices.

Meredith Country Gardens has a knack for stocking intriguing newcomers and genial old favorites that are welcome in anyone's garden. The nursery grows much of its perennial stock from seed, including such mainstays as delphinium, perennial flax, sea holly, cottage pinks, hollyhocks (single and powderpuff), and foxglove (mixed, apricot, and Grecian). Good assortments of astilbe and hosta are on hand. We also noticed grape-leaf anemone, gold pachysandra, and interesting native plants such as leopard's-bane, Carolina thermopsis, and marsh marigold.

The herb section has traditionally been excellent, combining common culinary herbs with exotics such as costmary, cumin, perilla, lemongrass, epazote, breadseed poppy, fern-leaf dill, sweet mace, safflower, and scented mints. (Useful household herbs include patchouli for perfume, soapwort for laundry, and pennyroyal for repelling insects.) Best of all are the ornamental herbs that hold their own in a low-maintenance perennial bed: white mignonette, blue woodruff, clary sage, gold and silver oregano, many-colored thymes, and all the lavenders—French, fringed, fern-leaf, sweet, and variegated.

For the summer gardener, Meredith Country Gardens creates attractive mixed baskets and offers wonderful zonal and scented geraniums (35 kinds in all). Shrubs and trees, bought in from outside growers, are well selected for ornament and wildlife support. Highbush blueberries can be specially ordered. Daylilies can be had in starter pots or freshly dug as mature plants. Under DeWitt management, we expect the daylilies to grow ever more wonderful, including new varieties and (we hope) new introductions from the DeWitt daylily garden.

Directions: From I-93, take exit 23 onto Route 104 east. At the T, turn left onto Route 3. At the next light, turn right onto 25 east. In 5 miles, go through Center Harbor. In another 4 miles, turn left onto Sheridan Road; the nursery is 1.5 miles on your right.

Nearby attractions: A local institution open 8–6 daily in summer, Moulton Farms, Route 25, Center Harbor (603-279-3915), is a founding-family farm (Moultonboro was named for them) selling fresh vegetables, meadow bouquets, local milk and cream, and divine pies; for gardeners, Moulton Farms has pretty hanging baskets, preplanted containers, and bedding plants. Ledgewood Farms, Route 171, Moultonboro (just past Route 109), is another local source of fresh farm vegetables and cut flowers, open daily except Wednesday.

THE MIXED BORDER NURSERY AND GARDENS

363 Pine Hill Road, Hollis, NH 03049
(603) 882-5538
Douglas and Kathy Gagne

Perennials and select nursery stock. *Small specialty nursery. Open May 1 to September 30, Tuesday to Sunday 9–5. Plant list on web site. No mail order. Plant displays. Garden design services. Web site: www.themixedborder.com.*

The Mixed Border is a small, sophisticated nursery on the outskirts of Nashua, in the pretty country town of Hollis. Owner Doug Gagne opened for business in his side yard in 1994, after earning his stripes as a professional horticulturist and landscape designer. The genial Gagne maintains good professional contacts, and contributed to the restoration of The Fells garden on Lake Sunapee (NH). With his wife, Kathy, Gagne specializes in growing fine perennials intermixed with interesting shrubs, trees, vines, and a few exotic annuals. The Mixed Border is a small nursery where visitors gladly catch what is available, and expect some sellouts late in the season.

If the owner had his druthers, the Mixed Border would focus on rare and curious plants of the kind that fascinate horticulturists. Bowing to customer demand, Gagne mixes popular and proven classics with connoisseur plants not commonly available from commercial sources. On our visit, we admired the white candelabra primrose, dwarf thalictrum, white crambe (a British favorite), blue-eyed grass (actually a tiny iris), stokesia 'Silver Moon', and a superior nepeta (or catmint) called 'Dawn to Dusk'. Outsized ornamentals rarely seen in the perennial border are 'Elephant Ears' rudbeckia, a 4-foot native with bluish foliage and curious brown flower cones that look like erect acorns; and a 5-foot, stunning, coarse-leaved yellow daisy (*Inula* spp.), a sentimental favorite given to the owner by a colleague. This was the first place we ever saw *Plectranthus argenteus*, a sleek silver foliage plant that (as all the world now knows) is superb in containers, especially with annual salvia. Exotic as they seem, all perennials at the Mixed Border are hardy to Zones 4 and 5; the annuals and tender perennials, needless to say, grow only for a season.

The Mixed Border's stock is ingeniously arranged so that from a distance it actually looks like the mixed perennial border for which it is named. The owner's artistry as a designer is evident in dashing plant combinations and stylish display gardens woven through the nursery. In response to harassment from admiring customers, the nursery plans to publish its plant list on the web site. The Mixed Border buys finished plants from good sources, and plans to propagate more in the future. No chemical sprays are used, in deference to the beehives in the adjoining field. This, along with good cultivation practices, must account for the welcome profusion of otherwise-scarce honeybees, humming in the flower beds.

Directions: Hollis is on the outskirts of Nashua. From Route 3/Everett Turnpike, take exit 6. Turn right at the ramp, then right onto Route 130. Turn left after the light onto Blue Hill Avenue, which passes the Municipal Airport and becomes Pine Hill Road. The nursery is 1.75 miles on your left.

Nearby attractions: In Mason, an old-fashioned herb restaurant called Pickety Place (603-878-1151) has three luncheon seatings daily; call for reservations. This restaurant, herb garden, shop, and bookstore surrounds a picturesque antique farmhouse that inspired the illustrations for a 1948 edition of Little Red Riding Hood.

MURRAY FARMS

115 River Road, Penacook, NH 03303
(603) 753-6781
Dave and Don Murray

Annuals, perennials, and seedlings. Seasonal plants. *Seasonal greenhouses and growing fields. Open late April to Father's Day for annuals, perennials, and seedlings; mid-August to early October for mums and some perennials; Thanksgiving to Christmas for poinsettias; and Easter week for lilies and spring bulb plants. Variable hours, generally Monday to Friday 9–6, weekends 9–5. No catalog or mail order.*

Murray Farms is a seasonal, family-run operation that occupies 50,000 square feet of greenhouse space just outside Concord. Dave and Don Murray inherited the business from their parents, who founded it in 1963 on the site of the family's former dairy and poultry farm. Murray Farms grows all its own plants and sells them cheap, straight out of the greenhouses and growing fields, which are open periodically during the year.

In spring the Murrays offer annuals and perennials; in autumn, mums; at Christmas, poinsettias; and at Easter, lilies and flowering bulbs. Customers hail from all over the Northeast. We hear of people coming from Manhattan to stock up on spring plants for urban deck gardens. A Vermont lady fills her station wagon twice each fall with hanging baskets of chrysanthemums. Exact open days and hours are variable, and the stock sells fast, so call ahead if you are traveling far.

Gardeners flock here in spring, when Murray Farms sells annuals, perennials, grasses, flower seedlings, and hanging baskets. Most plants are improved forms of tried-and-true classics, but the Murrays are not afraid to try newer varieties that are durable and have good ornamental value. Among the annuals, gardeners can typically find nice petunias, impatiens, zonal geraniums, and colorful window-box plants such as scaveola, bidens, sweet potato vine (several colors), and helichrysum. We spied some 'Balcon' ivy geraniums among the annual hanging baskets.

For perennials, Murray Farms carries garden mainstays such as delphinium, lupine, yarrow, hosta, and lamb's ears. Perennials with established roots come in gallon containers, and first-year seedlings are sold in six-packs, all at very reasonable prices. One September we bought field-grown, gallon-size Russian sage plants for $6, and variegated grass for a dollar more.

From time to time Murray Farms carries a few woody plants such as contorted hazel, grafted willow, and Japanese maple. These are bought bare-root from Oregon, finished in the greenhouses, and sold to early birds at excellent prices. As with bargains the world over, plant hunters must buy anything fetching on the spot, for the entire stock may vanish in a day.

Murray Farms operates on a highly seasonal basis and sells exclusively to retail customers. After its extensive spring and summer stock is cleared, its autumn stock include mums in pots and in hanging baskets. For Christmas there are poinsettia hybrids in fashionable colors such as salmon and white; 'Winter Rose' is lovely. Murray Farms grows more than 20,000 Easter lilies, along with other flowering bulbs, for the Easter holiday. When they run out of plants grown in their own fields and greenhouses, the Murrays just shut the doors and start propagating for the next season.

Directions: From I-93, take exit 15W (west) and turn right at the second light onto Main Street/Route 3 north. In 3.2 miles, turn left onto Bog Road. In 2.2 miles, at the bridge, turn right on River Road; the greenhouses are 0.5 mile on your right.

PERENNIALS FROM SUSAN

58 Seaverns Bridge Road, Amherst, NH 03031-2114
(603) 424-2300
Susan Kierstead

Field-grown perennials. Woodland wildflowers. *Small specialty nursery. Open late April to mid-September, Thursday to Saturday 10–4. Free catalog at the nursery. No mail order. Discount on advance orders. Display gardens. E-mail: SKiers2808@aol.com.*

Perennials From Susan is a godsend for gardeners in southern New Hampshire, where proprietor Susan Kierstead offers some 1,000 perennials from organic growing beds surrounding her home in Amherst, just west of Nashua. Kierstead has good horticultural contacts and the ability to source unusual plants. The owner, who says that "gardening is a way of life," founded the nursery 20 years ago by planting a long field next to her home with perennials for sun and shade.

Many unique and lovely perennials are offered here, especially woodland plants that are scarce in commerce. Since retirement, Susan's husband, Ronald Kierstead, plays a supporting role in the nursery, just for the fun of it. Because the Kiersteads winter elsewhere and tire of spending their summers pulling weeds in the hot sun, they are gradually transforming the nursery to a shade garden, with increasing emphasis on shade-loving perennials and woodland plants. On the verges of the nursery, meandering display gardens support more than 2,000 plant species and contain ornamental grasses,

a heather garden, shady woodland gardens, and a
sandy hillside sheathed in ground cover.

Perennials From Susan is an excellent
resource for tough, mature plants that have
survived the rigors of at least one New
Hampshire winter. We wasted a whole
year trying out different ground covers in
an urban tree pit (all failed), only to have
this nursery provide us with a dwarf
white creeping potentilla that proved
tough as iron. We were impressed with
the nursery's trove of single and double
bloodroot; its prized double pink rue anemone
caused quite a stir among woodland gardeners.

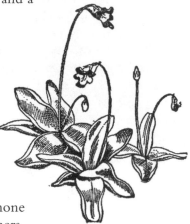

Special plant collections include native wild-
flowers, Asian wildflowers, more than 300 daylily hybrids, and hardy Japanese
iris that can be dug while in bloom. Good assortments of aster, ornamental
grass, cranesbill geranium, heuchera, and hosta are also available. It's nice to
see someone in the nursery business wake up to variegated tovaria, a delightful airy ground cover (we first spied it in California) that tolerates the driest
shade.

Perennials From Susan grows plants in organic soil, digs to order, and
offers plants bare-root or potted. The nursery's stock and plant list can be
obtained only on the premises; no mail order is offered. Discounts encourage
ordering in advance; this permits plants to be dug and ready when you
arrive. (As a special incentive to early birds, even unlisted plant treasures are
for sale if ordered in April, provided you can spot them in the display beds.)
All these conditions are a boon in disguise, for they force gardeners to visit
the nursery and discuss plants with its engaging owner, who is wise in the
virtues and habits of all her plants. She welcomes visitors (Kierstead can
usually be found in the fields, wearing a bleached sunbonnet), and maintains
that her gardens are happiest when visited by other plant enthusiasts. In
spring, the sun-dappled gardens, ornamented with double bloodroot and rare
woodland wildflowers, are well worth the trip.

*Directions: The nursery is located off Route 101A, north of Nashua. From Route
16/Everett Turnpike, take exit 11, and go west on Continental Boulevard. At the intersection of Route 101A, turn right. At the next light, turn right again onto Seaverns
Bridge Road; the nursery is 1.4 miles on your left at #58. The driveway is on
Woodbine Road, just after the house. Support civility: Do not turn around in the
neighbors' driveway.*

ROLLING GREEN NURSERY

64 Breakfast Hill Road, Greenland, NH 03840
Mailing address: P.O. Box 4093, Portsmouth, NH 03802-4093
(603) 436-2732; fax (603) 436-2309
Rick and Beth Simpson

*Perennials. Hardy seacoast plants. Ornamental trees and shrubs. Fruits.
Container plants and topiary. Small, family-run landscaper's nursery and garden
center. Open April 15 through December, Monday to Saturday 9–5, Sunday 10–4;
closed for major holidays. Plant lists $3. No mail order. Lectures and seminars. Display
gardens. Seasonal plants. Christmas greens. Landscaping and design services.*

Rolling Green is a compact, well-stocked nursery just off I-95 in coastal
New Hampshire, readily accessible to out-of-state gardeners bound for Maine
or crossing the border from Massachusetts. The nursery was founded in 1976
by landscaper Rick Simpson, who started, he says, with "a degree from UNH
and a lawn mower in the back of my Datsun pickup." Simpson and his wife,
Beth, now grow about 80 percent of their extensive inventory from liners,
and buy in the rest (mostly trees and shrubs) to fill any holes in the
inventory.

The nursery is set on level ground near the highway. Its diverse stock is
pleasantly laid out, well labeled, and orderly—a blessing for landscapers and
home gardeners with want lists. Rolling Green Nursery specializes in perennials but offers a full panoply of garden plants, including herbs, vines, fruits,
ornamental trees and shrubs, conifers, container plants, and topiary.

Rolling Green prides itself in stocking a colorful palette of more than 500
cream-of-the-crop perennials suited to the demands of fine gardening.
Whole rectangles of outdoor display space are devoted to phlox, sedum,
Montauk daisy, echinacea, and fall asters (including long-blooming double
Japanese asters). Perennial ground covers are sheltered under a large
evergreen, among them pink wood anemone, rose epimedium, sweet
woodruff, 15 kinds of cranesbill geranium, and all the ajugas one could
possibly want. Salt-tolerant perennials, such as sea lavender and lamb's ears,
are well suited to coastal growing conditions. Others are cleverly arranged to
encourage companion planting: gray artemisias next to drought-tolerant
yarrows, fall chrysanthemums beside ornamental kales. Rolling Green also
carries attractive foliage perennials (ferns, hostas, and grasses) and a few
woodland exotics such as Japanese toad lily and bronzeleaf rodgersia.

Besides perennials, Rolling Green offers a good range of "woodies"
(deciduous trees and shrubs), with emphasis on Japanese maples, flowering
crabs, hydrangeas, and lilacs. The nursery stocks attractive shrubs indigenous

to coastal conditions, such as leucothoe, elderberry, and beach rose. Among the evergreen shrubs are good azaleas, rhododendrons, and dwarf conifers. Small ornamental trees include paperbark maple, variegated box elder, shadblow, and Carolina silverbell. In the fruit tree section, we discovered Asian pear, Japanese golden plum, and unique apple trees called '5 on 1 Antique' and '5 on 1 Modern', in which five apple varieties are grafted onto a single tree. (As in any nursery, gardeners buying trees or shrubs late in the season should scrutinize foliage and root ball, so as to avoid buying a stressed, stale, or poorly rooted plant.)

Early in the season, Rolling Green carries fashionable annual container plants such as chocolate cosmos, flowering maple, and black coleus—terrific in a pot with 'Tango' New Guinea impatiens. Admirable ornamental herbs include annual salvias, scented geraniums, and fruit-scented mints (one was coconut-scented, and another had incredible velvet foliage). If this were not enough, the nursery grows its own topiary and carries fresh seasonal plants, Christmas greens, and salt-marsh hay. The cash register staff may not always be on the ball, but the Simpsons provide expert cultivation advice, informative plant lists, plant care brochures, and topical lectures and seminars. Attractive display and container gardens serve to emphasize the diversity and usefulness of Rolling Green's inventory, as convenient as a truck stop off the Interstate.

Directions: Rolling Green is near coastal Portsmouth just off I-95. From I-95, take exit 3 to Route 33 west. At the second light, take Route 151 south. In 1.5 miles, turn left onto Breakfast Hill Road. Under the overpass, the nursery is on your right. From Route 495 in Massachusetts, go north to its end in Amesbury, merge onto I-95 North, and follow directions above.

Nearby attractions: Each June, the Unitarian South Church in Portsmouth (603-436-4762) sponsors an annual walking tour of the historic gardens at Strawberry Banke; vendors sell plants and other garden-related items. The inland town of Stratham is a small farming community that raises a diversity of fresh agricultural products. Barker's Farm, 218 Portsmouth Avenue, Stratham, NH 03885 (603-778-1039), sells fresh vegetables, bedding plants, and herbs. Bunker Hill Orchards and Nursery, 97 Bunker Hill Avenue, Stratham (603-772-3748), sells fresh apples, cider, and bedding plants ("It's Always Apple Time"). Coppal House Station, 163 Winnicut Road, Stratham (603-772-4026), offers hay, sleigh rides, pumpkins, dried flowers, and organic meats ("Horse-Powered Farming").

SPIDER WEB GARDENS

P.O. Box 150, 252 Middle Road (Route 109A)
Center Tuftonboro, NH 03816
(603) 569-5056; fax (603) 569-3608
William L. Stockman

Annuals, perennials, houseplants, and nursery stock. Retail garden center and nursery. Open daily, 8–5, all year. No catalog or mail order. Small display area. Visitors welcome. Christmas greens. E-mail: spider@landmark.net.

Founded in 1938 and still a mainstay of northern gardeners, Spider Web is the best-known source of garden plants in the Lake Winnipesaukee area. The great majority of its annuals, perennials, and nursery stock are grown in the green-houses and fields behind the garden center shop. Owner Bill Stockman, grandson of the original owner, has maintained Spider Web's virtues as a nursery, while broadening its products and amenities to include those of a full-service garden center. Although the enterprise offers no plant list, staff help is available if you know what you want. A small garden and hosta bed are main-tained for display, but Spider Web Gardens is basically an attractive, self-supplied garden center, complete with containers, garden supplies, and purple martin houses fashioned by a local craftsman.

In late spring, Spider Web Gardens breaks the spell of winter by offering vivid hanging baskets: flowering maple, salvia, mallow, fuchsia, geranium, marigold, double impatiens, and anything else that thrives in pot culture. In summer, jumbo annuals and potted perennials are set outside near a weathered gray barn, backed by more field-grown perennials in the nursery yard. All the classic perennials are represented here—hosta, daylily, phlox, coralbells.

Spider Web Gardens is strong in ornamental shrubs and patio plants, some grown here and some bought in. Our canvass of the shrub yard found small-leaved Chinese lilac, Japanese kerria, Sargent cranberry, buttonbush *(Cephalanthus occidentalis)*, top-grafted weeping pea shrub, and a ghostly grey dogwood *(Cornus racemosa)*. They all looked pretty good, considering it was August. In addition to viburnums and hydrangeas, shrub roses abound at Spider Web Gardens, mostly the beautiful, tough rugosas most in demand for country gardens and second homes. (We even spied our favorite species rose, the blue-leaved *Rosa rubrifolia*.)

Spider Web runs a year-round greenhouse full of houseplants and indoor foliage plants such as peperomia and the universe of ivy. Seasonal plants include Easter lilies, forced bulbs in spring, and Dutch bulbs in fall. For the winter holidays, the enterprise carries excellent poinsettias and mail-order Christmas wreaths—fresh wreaths fashioned in partridgeberry and balsam are a specialty.

Directions: Spider Web Gardens is located on scenic Route 109A, on the east side of Lake Winnipesaukee. From Route 16/Spaulding Turnpike, turn left onto Route 109 in Sanbornville, then left again onto Route 28. In 7 miles, turn right onto Route 109A; the nursery is 7 miles on your left.

Nearby attractions: Castle in the Clouds, Route 171, Moultonboro (603-476-2352; 800-729-2468), is a turn-of-the-20th-century dream castle set in the Ossipee Mountains, open for daily tours; the eccentric owner made a fortune, spent it on his castle and private golf course, and died broke. The Old Country Store, Moultonboro (603-476-5750), is an archetypal 1781 country store, with a little museum upstairs and a cigar-store Indian out front. The Miss Wakefield Diner, Route 16, Sanbornville (603-522-6800), is a lunch-car classic. Wild lupines can be viewed in June at the Lupine Festival in Franconia and Sugar Hill (call 800-237-9007 for schedules and a map).

UNCANOONUC MT. PERENNIALS

452 Mountain Road, Goffstown, NH 03045
(603) 497-3975
Annette Rynearson

Low-maintenance perennials. Roses. Blueberry bushes. *Specialty nursery. Open May 1 to September 30, Wednesday to Sunday 9–5. Open Memorial Day and Labor Day. Free catalog. No mail order. Preseason orders accepted. Plant picture books. Display gardens. Landscape design services. Mid-July open house.*

Located on a secluded mountain road west of Concord, Uncanoonuc Mt. Perennials is a nursery dedicated to making life easier for New England gardeners by offering attractive, low-maintenance perennials that are hardy to Zones 4 and 5. Companion plants and small fruits are also available. The nursery was founded in 1980 by Annette Rynearson, a Cornell-trained horticulturist married to a landscape architect. A pastoral clearing in front of the Rynearsons' home contains 2½ acres of colorful, field-grown perennials.

Uncanoonuc Mt. Perennials specializes in plants suited to the gardens of summer-home dwellers, busy mothers, and guys who would rather watch the ball game—modern gardens, in short, whose owners want them to look good without having to kill themselves doing yard work. Some 650 varieties of sun and shade perennials are represented in Uncanoonuc's collection, along with companion shrubs. The plant stock is set out in orderly beds, some in fibre pots, some field dug on request. (Local gardeners may prefer field-digging, which produces a generous shovelful of plant material—a boon if you are not traveling far.) Customers confirm that Uncanoonuc's stock transplants easily to area gardens.

The nursery prides itself on selling top-quality plants at reasonable prices. Every year brings new introductions. While not rare and exotic, these carefree plants have been shrewdly chosen for their health, good looks, and stylish flair. We saw interesting herbs, doughty rambling roses, soft-colored daylily collections ("no orange, no red"), four kinds of pachysandra, and lovely peonies. (The nursery also sells well-made peony rings.) We especially liked the nursery's 'Dark Pink' daylily, the pink bee balm called 'Marshall's Delight', the magenta knapweed 'John Coutts', and some delightfully queer sempervivum (hens-and-chickens) with ruby flower spikes. Luscious Oriental poppies in shades of peach, rose, and salmon sell out briskly in spring, along with the stock of blueberry bushes.

The nursery yard is embraced by landscaped display gardens that showcase the Rynearsons' design talents, cleverly crafted from the same plants offered at the nursery. These enchanting gardens demonstrate the artistry that can be achieved with low-maintenance plants. Granite-lined paths lead through an ornamental rock garden, a "hot garden" of yellow- and orange-flowering plants, and, behind the shade tents, an evocative woodland garden containing shade perennials and a robust bed of snakeroot that looks quite menacing in bloom. Wild hedgerows bordering the nursery display the ultimate in low-maintenance perennials: oxeye daisy, yarrow, and Queen Anne's lace. Many customers return especially to view the gardens, which offer the elusive hope of a home garden that is both undemanding and gorgeous.

The amenities at this mountain nursery are appealing and innovative. A plastic box near the entry holds bug spray, extra pens, notepaper, and catalogs for customers. The canvas tent offers shade, ice water, information sheets, and a five-volume picture book showing plants in bloom. You can buy cut flowers by the bunch or bucket, large bags of potting soil, and fresh-grown rhubarb, asparagus, and berries in season. Horticultural advice is enthusiastically provided with all purchases. Best of all, you can admire the bionic staff of nubile young women, in cutoff jeans and hot pink company-logo T-shirts, strong as deer, who do the heavy lifting and exuberantly answer all questions. In response to our query about the meaning of *Uncanoonuc*, we were told that in the Algonquian language it refers to twin mountains, North and South Uncanoonuc, representing the bosom of a mountain goddess.

Directions: From I-93, exit onto Route 293. In Manchester, exit onto Route 114. Go straight onto Route 114 west to Goffstown Center, then turn left at the Exxon station onto Mountain Road. Follow Mountain Road (staying left at the Y) for 2.5 miles; the nursery will be on your right.
From Route 3, take exit 3 onto Route 101/114, then Route 114 west to Goffstown Center and proceed as above.

Nearby attractions: Scenic Route 13 between Goffstown and New Boston follows the Piscataqua River, a fast-moving salmon and trout stream flowing brown as root beer. In New Boston, Dodge's General Store (603-487-2241) sells fresh sandwiches in a creaky wooden interior; kids sit on the porch licking Popsicles. In Peterborough, Rosaly's Farmstand, Route 123 south of Route 101, grows fresh organic produce and chic cut flowers in a beautiful country setting.

WAYSIDE FARM

507 Whiteface Road, North Sandwich, NH 03259
(603) 284-6886
Ben and Lisa Shambaugh

Unusual annuals, vines, and container plants. Perennials. Native plants. Daylilies. *Small, family-run greenhouse and nursery. Open daily, April to June 8–5, July and August 9–5, September by appointment. Plant list $1. No mail order. E-mail: Wayside@LR.net.*

Wayside Farm is a small family-run greenhouse nursery on a country road east of Lake Winnipesaukee. Owners Ben and Lisa Shambaugh (who are both town selectmen) work hard to provision New Hampshire gardeners with distinctive flowering plants, propagating all their own stock by cutting, seed, or division. The nursery grows some 1,200 plant varieties, including perennials, vines, native plants, and uncommon annuals. Wayside Farm has a bit of everything, in the way of country greenhouses. Its adventurous plant collection includes sophisticated items more commonly found in urban settings. The farm's location in a rough, hand-cut woodland clearing, with long views to the peaks of the Sandwich Range, reminds one of the early homesteaders who settled this region of New Hampshire, intent on bringing civilization to the wilderness.

The Shambaughs' ambition as plant pioneers is most apparent in their collection of annuals and tender perennials. Besides petunias and sunflowers, Wayside Farm grows exotic coleus, variegated begonias, trailing snapdragons, sweet potato vine, and Chinese forget-me-not. Gardeners interested in the flora of South Africa can find Cape marigold, African daisy, dill-leaf ursinia, and Monarch Namaqualand-daisy (*Venidium* spp.). Salsa lovers can spice up their container gardens with Chilean monkey flower (*Mimulus* spp.), Chilean bellflower (*Nolana* spp.), Chilean glorybush (*Tibouchina* spp.), and Peruvian mask flower (*Alonsoa* spp.). Ambitious gardeners can dazzle their neighbors with little-grown trophies—flax-leaf pimpernel, red-hot cattail, blue Italian alkanet, clove-lip toadflax, meadow foam, and something called blue lips. Wayside also offers colorful annual vines such as scarlet runner bean, cup-and-saucer vine, morning glory, moonflower, lotus vine, and Chilean glory flower (*Eccremocarpus* spp.).

The nursery's perennials, though necessarily less exotic than the annuals, offer well-selected specimens from an extensive plant list. We warmed to finding—this far north—ornamental sea pink, globe thistle, helenium, snakeroot, knautia, and sea kale. Wayside Farm carries native ground covers such as baneberry and bearberry; native perennials such as amsonia, joe-pye weed, goldenrod, rodgersia, and Jacob's-rod (*Asphodeline* spp.); and native shrubs such as chokecherry (*Aralia* spp.) and shrubby dogwood. A large population of hanging baskets (25 kinds) rounds out the display.

As with any greenhouse nursery, plant selection and stock are best early in the season. Knowing customers visit Wayside Farm for bedding and container plants in May and June, before the summer crowds. August visitors are rewarded with discounts (normally 20 percent) and an annual bare-root daylily sale, in which 75 daylily cultivars are divided and sold at half price. By then, Wayside Farm's containers may be a bit weedy, but the plants don't seem to suffer. Frugal gardeners have long recognized the value of fall-planted perennials. Wayside Farm also sells its own organic compost, called Wayside Gold, along with bagged bark mulch and cocoa shells.

Directions: Wayside Farm is 65 miles from Concord, and 1.5 hours from Durham, New Hampshire. From I-93, take exit 23/Meredith onto Route 104 east to Meredith. Take Route 25 east, and in about 10 miles, turn left onto Route 113 north. In 4 miles, in North Sandwich, turn right onto Route 113A; the nursery is 2.4 miles on your right. From Route 16/Spaulding Turnpike, go to West Ossipee and take Route 25 west. In about 5 miles, turn right at the second sign for Route 113 north, and follow directions above.

Nearby attractions: Sandwich and Tamworth are among the region's prettiest towns. In North Sandwich, DiFilippe Farm & Greenhouse (603-284-6482), is a roadside stand, open year-round, doing brisk sales in greenhouse-grown annual and vegetable flats, perennials, and seasonal plants. South Tamworth's Community School Gardens, 1164 Bunker Hill Road (603-323-7000), offers fresh organic vegetables, berries, fresh organic eggs, and scenic trails; open to the public daily 9–6, from late June to early September.

RHODE ISLAND

RHODE ISLAND

1. Conway's Nursery
2. Kinney Azalea Gardens
3. Meadowbrook Herb Garden
4. Peckham's Greenhouse
5. Schartner Farms
6. Umbrella Factory Gardens

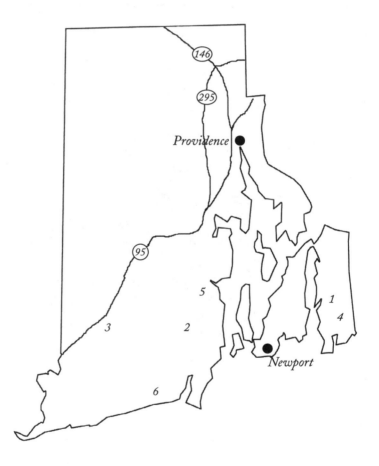

CONWAY'S NURSERY

3941 Main Road (Route 77), Tiverton, RI 02878
(401) 624-8222 phone and fax
Sean Conway

Annual and container plants. Salvia, coleus, and agapanthus. Perennials. Small *specialty nursery. Open May through September, Friday to Sunday 9–5. No catalog or mail order. Display containers. E-mail:sway44@aol.com.*

Sequestered down a gravel drive near Tiverton Four Corners, Conway's is a small nursery specializing in unusual annuals, perennials, and container plants, sprinkled with a few desirable trees and shrubs. Its proprietor, Sean Conway, is a talented landscaper with a degree in what he calls "creative biology"; he began propagating specialty plants for clients and then opened this "micronursery" in an idyllic meadow behind his home. He is now the national garden consultant for Target Stores, soon to introduce the Sean Conway Collection of preplanted container gardens.

Despite such demands on his energy, Conway plans to keep the nursery going as a kind of "studio" where he can keep an active hand in the garden arts. The beguiling setting evokes the charm of a French landscape painting. The young Conway children occasionally spill across the lawn toward the nursery, where visitors shop for garden plants near a picturesque stone-and-shingle barn, with a glimpse of the Sakonnet River through the trees.

Conway's is best known for its uncommon annuals and container plants, mostly propagated at the nursery. These include some original Conway hybridizing efforts with coleus (including a black duckfoot coleus) and agapanthus (especially miniature and bicolor varieties). Particular treasures are the coleus standards (retailed through New York florists) and the superb collection of annual salvia, arguably the finest in New England. With help from Conway's agreeable staff, we once counted more than 100 varieties of annual salvia (or ornamental sage), each one an excellent border and container subject. Our favorites were *Salvia greggii,* with plum, white, or apricot flowers; *S. discolor,* with black flowers on sticky gray stems; *S. leucantha,* with purple blossoms and felt gray leaves; and *S. Mexicana,* with blue flowers and chartreuse foliage. Four stunning hybrids are 'Indigo Spires', 'Argentine Skies', 'Purple Majesty', and 'Sierra San Antonio'. We used two blue-flowered salvia trailers *(S. chamedryoides and S. sinoaloaensis)* in a window box, to general applause from passersby.

In addition to tender container plants, a selection of pot-grown garden perennials is set out beside Conway's stone barn. The perennials combine unusual novelties with well-loved classics. Conway's grows perennial salvia that is hardy to New England, including a white-flowered *Salvia patens* discovered at the nursery. In a kind of horticultural joke, certain impostor plants that look like salvia are intermingled with the collection, such as various nepetas (ornamental mint) and an apricot-flowered lamb's ears *(Stachys hidalgo)*. We noticed a cream California poppy; a hardy nasturtium; a tall, blue-leaved black-eyed Susan; a black-flowered dianthus called 'Sooty', and some excellent cranesbill geraniums. Some of the nursery's choicest ornamentals are virtually unknown in these parts, such as the flowery pink *Rhemania angulata* (no common name), reportedly hardy to southern New England, and a variegated sedge called 'Sparkler'. Dwarf conifers and select trees and shrubs round out the nursery's collection of uncommon hardy plants.

Flanking the gravel path to the greenhouses are flower borders and several large, tropical-looking jardinieres brimming with showy annuals and tender perennials. These dramatic container gardens are grouped by color: white flowers with gray foliage, maroon with black, yellow with chartreuse, and blue with blue. Elsewhere, ornamental pools and jars are filled with lush, moisture-loving plants such as angel's-trumpets, variegated canna lilies, and marginal aquatics. The tones and textures of these inspiring container gardens testify to Conway's design skill, and offer a superb creative resource for the visiting gardener.

Our only complaint is the deficiency in plant labels, surely the bane of every small nurseryman. (We spent more than an hour trying to decipher the tender salvias in the greenhouse, one of which was unhelpfully labeled PURPLE.) In the absence of signage, a catalog, or a plant list, the container gardens at Conway's Nursery at least function as a partial inventory of the plants sold here. Visitors just have to poke around and pester the staff to find the best things. (Ed Brown is a mainstay when Conway is away.)

Once a well-kept secret of local garden connoisseurs, Conway's Nursery now attracts visitors from faraway places. Perhaps this is what comes of performing horticultural stunts on Martha Stewart's television show and introducing private-label plant collections through a hip mass retailer. We ourselves can hardly complain, having once received an extraordinary sedum sphere from Conway's Nursery as a wedding gift. We only hope that the discreet charm of this small nursery will not one day be ruined by the smell of the greasepaint, the roar of the crowd.

Directions: Tiverton is just over an hour from Boston, on the coast, near the Rhode Island/Massachusetts border. From I-195, take Route 24 South to exit 5. Turn left at the ramp, then right under the flashing yellow light. At the stop sign, turn left and follow Main Road for 6 miles. Just past Tiverton Four Corners, the nursery driveway is immediately on your right, marked with an obscure sign.

Nearby attractions: For lovers of the lurid arts, a chainsaw artist is at work across Route 77/Main Street just south of the nursery. Tiverton Four Corners hosts an annual Garden and Herb Festival on Memorial Day weekend (401-624-2600); vendors sell plants, herbs, garden antiques, and hand-painted garden tools. Visitors to Tiverton Four Corners can graze at Provender (401-624-8084), a gourmet deli with great sandwiches, and at Gray's Ice Cream (401-624-4500), a local institution. The seaside town of Little Compton, south on Route 77, is one of the loveliest in Rhode Island. Green Animals, Cory's Lane (off Route 114), Portsmouth, RI 02840 (401-847-1000; www.newportmansions.org) is one of the oldest topiary gardens in the country. Dating to 1872, it houses a menagerie of 80 topiary animals, birds, arches, spirals, and geometric blocks on a bayside estate. The garden also grows hardy fig trees.

KINNEY AZALEA GARDENS

2391 Kingstown Road, Kingston, RI 02881
(401) 783-2396
Dr. Sue Gordon, Horticulturist

Azalea hybrids. Broad-leaved evergreen shrubs. *Hybridizer's garden collection. Nursery open by appointment. No catalog or mail order. Free information sheet. Gardens open to the public all year until dusk. Bloom period mid-April to early June. Peak bloom in mid-May. Fall foliage.*

A garden historian once asserted that all gardens are attempts to regain paradise. This was our experience one luminous evening in June when we first visited Kinney Azalea Gardens (formerly Kingstown Hill Azalea Gardens), a privately owned garden behind a house in Kingston. The moon was up, the sky still blue, and the garden was radiant, on fire with azalea blossoms. Against a stately backdrop of evergreens, masses of naturalized azaleas blazed— magical, incandescent—with an almost unbelievable brilliance: pure white, tangerine, yolk yellow, glowing rose, vermillion, and purple. These mature bushes (some reaching tree size) grew freely, intermingling in natural, dynamic postures. A maze of curved pathways, leading to vistas in every direction, gave the 5-acre garden a sense of mystery and immensity. Everywhere a spicy perfume lingered on the air. Intriguing little side paths led to hidden treasures: a stand of wildflowers, a mature pepperbush, a clump of leucothoe, a white dogwood. Fellow visitors, awed by the display, were families, lovers, and solitary gardeners; we overheard one mother hiss, *"Chrissy, don't run";* another remarked quietly, "I've never seen anything so beautiful."

A stone marker at the entrance to Kinney Azalea Gardens honors its founder, the late Dr. Lorenzo F. Kinney Jr., who first began cultivating azaleas behind his family home as a retirement hobby in 1956. Kinney's aim was to trial southern azaleas (not then considered hardy in Rhode Island) and to develop robust hybrids in honor of his wife, a Virginia native who loved the splendor of southern azaleas. Original plant stock came from southern gardens and from Kinney's father, a botany professor whose own azalea hybrids were already appreciated on estates around Rhode Island. Over the years, with help from local college students, Kinney planted more than 500 azalea hybrids in his garden, including many of his own creations. These Kinney hybrids, called the K-Series, still adorn the garden's K Path. Kinney Azalea Gardens is now owned by Tony and Betty Kinney Faella, who maintain the family's interest in horticulture. The gardens are managed by Dr. Sue Gordon, a botany professor at the University of Rhode Island who worked closely with Lorenzo Kinney for many years and now continues his trial and hybridizing work.

Kinney Azalea Gardens grows more than 800 rhododendron and azalea hybrids, most of which can be purchased as mature specimens straight from the garden; some are also sold as seedlings. Because they have been allowed to assume their distinctive natural forms, mature azalea plants come in unique, striking shapes not commonly found in the nursery trade: tall and upright, horizontal and spreading, layered and procumbent, dwarf and bonsai.

The diversity of the Kinney azalea collection is enchanting. We loved 'Reddy', a layered, glossy, lipstick red azalea; 'Gold Peace' with striking cup-shaped gold flowers; 'Flame Creeper', an evergreen, salmon-flowered ground cover azalea; and 'Peureka', a mutation found at the nursery, its pale pink flower speckled red. Kinney Azalea Gardens grows the best variegated azalea, 'Gerard's Silver Sword'; the best double pink azalea, 'Rainbow'; and many excellent small-leaved hybrids from Weston Nurseries (MA). Demure white azaleas include 'Snow' and its cousins. Plants named for the garden's founders are 'Lorenzo Kinney' (pale pink) and 'Elizabeth Kinney' (peach with a green throat).

The Kinney azaleas have multiseasonal interest. Some bloom in autumn, such as 'Indian Summer', and others have extraordinary fall foliage, such 'Hino Crimson', which turns blazing red. The garden grows hard-to-find species, such as the original "yak" rhododendron *(Rhododendron yakusimanum)* and the native pinkshell azalea *(R. vaseyi)*. Besides the azalea/ rhododendron collection (azaleas are, of course, botanically classified as rhododendrons), Kinney Azalea Gardens sells a few broad-leaved evergreen shrubs such as holly, mountain laurel, coast leucothoe, and Japanese andromeda, which also thrive here.

The shrubs sold at Kinney Azalea Gardens are freshly dug to order, balled and burlapped, year-round. Plants range in size from 60-year-old mature specimens to 4-year-old liners (grown from seed and cuttings). With their diversity of form, bloom color, and foliage, the Kinney azaleas have character and distinction that are unobtainable in standard nursery stock ("no flowering meatballs!"). Considering the plants' maturity, prices are reasonable. While large quantities of any one plant are usually not in stock, similar hybrids can be combined to provide mass effects and extended bloom.

Sue Gordon, who can recite the name and characteristics of every azalea in the garden, is available for free consultation on plant selection. Spring visitors can inspect her favorite azalea, number K-23, under evaluation for the last 10 years. Autumn visitors may admire the extraordinary fall foliage of the azaleas, and with luck discover the path leading to the exquisite Franklin tree, which blooms in October.

Directions: From Providence, take I-95 to exit 9/Route 4 south. Follow Route 4 after it becomes Route 1 south, and exit right onto Route 138/URI. Turn left at the next light onto Route 108. At the sixth house on your left, turn down a gravel drive to a parking area; if you reach a gas station on the right, you went one house too far.

Nearby attractions: Kingston is a pretty 18th-century town housing the University of Rhode Island (URI), whose East Coast Experiment Station maintains research collections of conifers, crab apples, dogwoods, blueberries, rhododendrons, grasses, apples, and unusual trees. The URI Cooperative Extension runs the area's Master Gardener Hotline (800-448-1011), Monday to Thursday 9–2. In early June and late September, the Rhode Island Wild Plant Society, P.O. Box 114, Peace Dale, RI 02883 (401-783-5895) holds plant sales in early June and late September at the URI Greenhouses, Flagg Road, Kingston. A farmer's market occupies the URI parking lot on Route 138, Kingston, Saturdays 9-2 in season. An open wooden tower at the junction of Routes 138 and 1 offers panoramic views of the Rhode Island coast.

MEADOWBROOK HERB GARDEN

93 Kingstown Road, Wyoming, RI 02898
(401) 539-7199; (888) 539-7603
Heinz Grotzke

Organically grown herbs. *Small certified organic herb grower. Open year-round, Monday to Saturday 9–5, Sunday noon–4. No catalog or mail order of live plants. Display garden. Herb shop. Books. Mail-order catalog for dried herbs, spices, and herb products.*

Something about an herb garden transports us to the Middle Ages, when healing and culinary herbs were a necessary part of every garden; even Charlemagne's palace garden at Aix-la-Chapelle was devoted largely to roses and herbs. "The summer has been hectic with planting, composting, weeding, mulching, and harvesting. The drying houses have been steadily humming, as the cheerful helpers hand harvest, chop, and spread crop after crop of beautiful fragrant herbs." This record derives, not from a Carolingian monastery, but from Meadowbrook Herb Garden, which has been cheerfully growing fresh herbs for more than 30 years.

Founder Heinz Grotzke, a lifelong herb grower, operates the nursery with his daughter Ingrid and her husband, Jamie, out of an herb shop and green-houses located on a scenic byway in southern Rhode Island. Using organic methods, the nursery grows more than 300 kinds of culinary, ornamental, and medicinal herbs. These are offered in the form of live plants, dried herb mixtures, and freshly made herbal products.

Meadowbrook grows its herb stock in beautifully kept beds worthy of a medieval monk. Small and tender herbs are propagated in greenhouses extending between the nursery's herb shop and wooden barn. Visible through a hedge opening are extensive beds of field-grown herbs, backed by a diminutive orchard. The overall effect is of charm and simplicity on a small scale, what our Irish friends call a "dote." Meadowbrook Herb Farm grows tarragon, lemon balm, comfrey, and lovage along with parsley, sage, rosemary, and thyme. It grows chamomile and fruit-scented mints for tea; fennel and calendula for salads; lavender for linens; catnip for cats; hollyhocks for heirloom 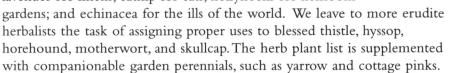 gardens; and echinacea for the ills of the world. We leave to more erudite herbalists the task of assigning proper uses to blessed thistle, hyssop, horehound, motherwort, and skullcap. The herb plant list is supplemented with companionable garden perennials, such as yarrow and cottage pinks.

Meadowbrook's old-fashioned roadside herb shop (as well as its mail-order catalog) carries a fascinating array of wildcrafted dried herbs and imported spices—along with Meadowbrook's own tea blends, an animal herb supplement, herbal oils, and natural skin-care products from Europe. The shop is a source for illustrated books (herbals) and wooden garden furniture (one chair has birdhouses cleverly inbuilt as arms). Visitors should be sure to stroll through the small garden beside the shop, whose rows of herbs are neatly segregated and labeled. The evergreen hedge sheltering this little garden captures and holds its sweet, almost sacramental herbal perfume.

Directions: From I-95, take exit 3 onto Route 138 east; the herb shop is about a mile on the right.

Nearby attractions: Kenyon Corn Mill Company (401-783-4054; 800-753-6966) operates a historic grist mill on the Queen's River, just off Route 138 in Usquepaugh; its signature product, stone-ground white cornmeal, is an essential ingredient in traditional Rhode Island johnnycakes.

PECKHAM'S GREENHOUSE

200 West Main Road, Little Compton, RI 02837
(401) 635-4775; fax (401) 635-2752
Rick Peckham

Perennials, annuals, shrubs, and trees. Zonal geraniums. Seasonal plants. Tropical houseplants. Family-owned greenhouses founded in 1865. Open all year: May and June daily 9–5; July and August, Monday to Saturday 9–5; September to April, Tuesday to Saturday 9–5, Sunday 11–5. No catalog or mail order. Gardening supplies.

Located on the Rhode Island shore, Peckham's Greenhouse is the garden center standby most frequented by area gardeners for their horticultural needs. Visitors are greeted by a bright roadside display garden, bursting with colorful zinnias, hollyhocks, marigolds, and salvias. This popular greenhouse was founded in 1866 by the Peckham family, hereditary potato farmers who once owned most of the local landscape, and still operate large farms in the area. Its dozen greenhouses, still in family hands, are managed and run by horticulturist Rick Peckham. If it can claim a specialty, Peckham's is well-chosen "plants, pots, and paraphernalia" for home gardeners. Peckham's is an enduring resource, open year-round, supplying gardeners with spring flats, summer perennials, fall mums, winter evergreens, and tropical houseplants through the seasons. As the locals say, "Peckham's is Peckham's."

Peckham's Greenhouse grows most of its own annuals and potted perennials, and buys in its trees and shrubs. The glory of Peckham's is its extensive spring selection of tender geraniums (actually pelargoniums), supplemented by begonias and other colorful annuals for the container or window box. The perennial yard, organized in the fashion of a simple knot garden, holds attractive varieties of pot-grown perennials. A number of these are seaside plants, such as sea lavender, well suited to the coastal climate. A few choice woodland plants include primroses, variegated vinca, and sweet violets. Peckham's shrub yard, small but select, includes good hardy shrub roses, hydrangeas, late-blooming azaleas, and clematis (we bought our first small-flowered blue clematis here). Among the trees are good selections of apple and ornamental fruit trees. Fall chrysanthemums come in attractive varieties, and the tropical greenhouse holds hibiscus and orchids among the leafy houseplants.

Peckham's Greenhouse prides itself on offering quality garden plants year-round. Questions about the cultural requirements of its plants can be addressed to the Peckhams, who know what they are doing and, like their farming ancestors, were born to the work. Before leaving, notice the bucolic view, across Main Road, of cattle grazing on Peckham farmland overlooking the Sakonnet River and the sea.

Directions: Little Compton is located on the coast, near the Rhode Island/Massachusetts border. From Route 195, take Route 24 south to exit 5 and turn left at the ramp. Go right under the flashing yellow light, then left at the stop sign. Follow Main Road/Route 77 south past Tiverton Four Corners for another 3 miles, then turn left onto Peckham Road; the nursery is immediately on your left.

Nearby attractions: Windy Hill Nursery, 69 Old Main Road/Route 77, Little Compton (401-635-4888), is a superior garden center and landscape design/construction firm that grows many of its own trees and shrubs, including an excellent selection of lilacs. Walker's Roadside Stand, 261 West Main Road/Route 77, Little Compton (401-635-4719), sells fresh farm-grown vegetables; its resident coffee bar, Olga's Cup and Saucer, is run by food artists with an accomplished hand at sweet pastry. The Commons, located on The Common in Little Compton (401-635-4388), is a classic town lunchroom with johnnycakes on the menu; the day's newspapers are passed around among patrons. Sakonnet Vineyards, 162 West Main Road, Little Compton (401-635-8486), offers wine tastings, tours, picnics, and vineyard walks.

SCHARTNER FARMS

Route 2, Exeter, RI 02822-9717
(401) 294-2044; fax (401) 295-1004
The Schartner family

Field-grown shrubs and trees. Nursery stock. *Wholesale grower's garden center. Open daily 8–6, March to December. No retail catalog or mail order. Seasonal plants. Pick-your-own berries and Christmas trees. Group tours.*

Rhode Island is the epicenter of large-scale horticulture in New England, but most of its horticultural farms—often third-generation affairs established 50 or 100 years ago on hundreds of acres—remain wholesale operations that are virtually invisible to the retail public. Schartner Farms is the exception: a large, family-owned wholesale grower that operates a retail garden center within sight of its original production fields (once a dairy farm). Schartner Farms is a well-run, traditional horticultural enterprise that has not only resisted the temptation to sell farmland to developers, but has also actually increased its acreage with production land in New Hampshire.

The Schartner Farms retail garden center, a gray-shingled shop on a level roadside in Exeter, is well provisioned with nursery-grown shrubs and trees, supplemented with perennials and other stock. Seasonal offerings include spring annuals, vegetable flats, fall mums, and poinsettias grown in the greenhouses behind the garden center. Pick-your-own berries and Christmas trees are sold in season, attracting school tours and family outings.

Like many local growers, Schartner Farms sells shrubs and trees off a plant list that is not overly broad or cutting-edge, but has good stock that does well in the region. The garden center describes its offerings as "fruits, flowers, shrubs, and vegetables with character." A small roadside display garden, with white annual salvia and pink mandevilla vine, seems determined to prove the point. Among the shrubs and trees, only the balled-and-burlapped specimens are Schartner-grown.

The shrub yard contains good viburnums, such as the classic Korean spice viburnum *(V. carlesii)* and native arrowwood *(V. dentatum);* well-selected lilacs, such as 'Pocahontas' and 'Assessippi' (on the Arnold Arboretum's top 50 list); native hollies such as inkberry and winterberry; oak-leaf and variegated hydrangea; aronia, a native shrub commonly known as chokecherry; and some nice variegated weigela and white wisteria. The trees are mainly standard shade and street trees, such as red oak and little-leaf linden, but include evergreens and some lovely ornamentals such as serviceberry and Japanese stewartia.

We're pretty sure customers can have trees and shrubs field-dug by special order from the production area, which is a great way to ensure fresh plants and minimize transplant shock. The landscape on which Schartner Farms produces its field-grown plant stock is as flat as a Dutch bulb farm. The region's longstanding desirability as farmland is attested by the alacrity of 17th-century settlement (the area is riddled with "treaty stones" marking early land deals with the Narragansett Indians) and the enduring quality of its horticultural products.

Directions: From Providence, take I-95 south to exit 9/Route 4. Take Route 4 south, and then exit 5B onto Route 102 north. Turn left onto Route 2 south; the garden center is 0.75 mile on your right.

Nearby attractions: G.A. Decoster, 200 Ten Rod Road/Route 102, Exeter (401-294-2852), is a grower of specialty hostas; the Decosters sell plants to individual gardeners out of their 2-acre garden from June through September—call for an appointment and plant list. Bald Hill Nurseries in Exeter (401-884-0001) is an old family farm selling field-grown ornamental shrubs and trees (including boxwood, hollies, and Japanese maples) through a retail outlet on Route 2; be sure to insist on freshly dug stock. To the east, the historic village of Wickford, a seaside community dating to 1674 on Scenic Route 1A, North Kingston, is on the National Register of Historic Places.

UMBRELLA FACTORY GARDENS

4820 Post Road (Route 1A), Charlestown, RI 02813
(401) 742–0045; gift store (401) 364-6616
Patrick Shellman

Hardy and old-fashioned perennials. Annuals and container plants. Daylilies. Custom-planted hanging baskets. *Small specialty nursery. Open April 15 through September, daily 9–5. No catalog or mail order. Cut flowers. Customized containers.*

The Umbrella Factory is a weird name for it: a rambling antique farmstead, in continuous use since 1760, now housing a series of funky gift emporia and a terrific plant nursery. The main gift bazaar, incongruously called the Fantastic Umbrella Factory, carries Betty Boop magnets, rubber snakes, Japanese paper lanterns, and retirement crying towels (but no umbrellas). Nursery visitors enter the complex through a cedar arbor, pass under a white wisteria pergola, skirt the gift emporia, and proceed through a small atmospheric garden to the five hoophouses that comprise the Umbrella Factory Gardens nursery. Under the discerning eye of its owner, horticulturist Patrick Shellman, Umbrella Factory Gardens (in business here since 1980) specializes in old-fashioned perennials, spring annuals, and ornamental hanging baskets for sun or shade.

We are not the first container gardeners to appreciate the quality of plants at Umbrella Factory Gardens. For years, well-heeled gardeners from Providence and the Rhode island shore have had their hanging baskets custom-planted here every spring. Umbrella Factory Gardens produces the most gorgeous moss baskets we have seen in any nursery, crammed with colorful, durable annuals in the highest style. During our visit, we noticed one luscious moss basket filled to abundance with pink verbena, gray helichrysum, white and purple superfina petunias, and Swan River daisies ... an exquisite all-pink basket combining tiny 'Tom Thumb' fuchsia, double rose impatiens, and dwarf pink Cobbitty daisy ... and a basket brimming with brilliant, scarlet-flowered tuberous begonias paired dramatically with cascading chartreuse ipomoea. An unusual doughnut-shaped basket, planted entirely in white million bells, looked like a fairy wreath. Among the potted annuals, we found blue anagallis and a stunning zonal geranium with ruby flowers and near-yellow foliage, aptly named 'Persian Queen'; both were reserved for a customer. Our visit occurred in June and we learned our lesson: Arrive early for annuals and hanging baskets or, better yet, bring in containers in April for custom planting; the wonderful annuals are mostly gone by Memorial Day.

If the moss baskets at Umbrella Factory Gardens pay the bills, the pot-grown perennials are, according to the owner, "like chocolates." The nursery carries a handful of rarities, such as a hot red pitcher plant *(Sarracenia purpurea)* described in the garden press as "horticulture's 'It' girl"; the only hardy cactus native to New England *(Opuntia humifusa);* and a graceful yellow wood lily *(Lilium canadense)* that is nursery-propagated, and no longer grows wild in Rhode Island. In the main, though, the perennials at Umbrella Factory Gardens are well-known plants that gardeners still love: cranesbill geranium, bottle gentian, old-fashioned iris, white phlox, and delicate meadow rue. The nursery's fine collection of field-grown daylilies includes the best near-whites (such as 'Gentle Shepherd') and a pretty pink called 'Bamba Music', all at reasonable prices. Cut flowers grown for the florist trade, such as gladiolus and sunflowers, are available to retail customers through the season. On the way out, visitors can stop at the exotic rooster cage (FEED ZEE ANIMALS 25 CENTS) and at Dave's Den for black lights, bead curtains, hemp twine, and hula hoops.

Directions: From Providence, take I-95 south to exit 9/Route 4 south and continue when it changes to Route 1. Take the Ninigret Park/Tourist Info exit, make a U-turn onto the Post Road (Route 1A North); The Umbrella Factory is a mile on your right. From the south, take I-95 north to exit 3, then take Route 138 east, Route 2 south, and Route 1 west to the Ninigret Park exit, and follow directions above.

Nearby attractions: On Umbrella Factory grounds, Spice of Life Natural Foods Café (401-364-2030) serves lunch and cappuccino under the shade of an immense maple. Scenic Gardens, 4909B Old Post Road/Route 1A, Charlestown, RI 02813 (401-364-6580), is a nursery known for unusual trees and shrubs and for its large collection of roses. The town of Charlestown has the darkest night skies in southern New England; every clear evening just after sunset, the Frosty Drew Nature Center and Observatory, Ninigret State Park, Route 1A (401-364-9508), allows visitors to view the heavens through a large modern telescope. The Ninigret National Wildlife Refuge is home to the region's only native cactus, Opuntia humifusa.

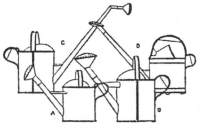

DIFFERENT FORMS OF WATER-POT.

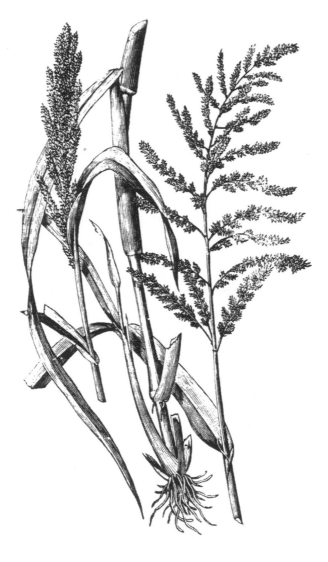

VERMONT

VERMONT

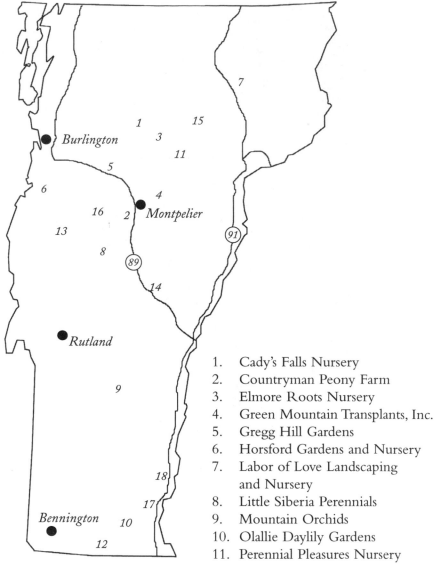

1.   Cady's Falls Nursery
2.   Countryman Peony Farm
3.   Elmore Roots Nursery
4.   Green Mountain Transplants, Inc.
5.   Gregg Hill Gardens
6.   Horsford Gardens and Nursery
7.   Labor of Love Landscaping and Nursery
8.   Little Siberia Perennials
9.   Mountain Orchids
10. Olallie Daylily Gardens
11. Perennial Pleasures Nursery
12. Raising Rarities
13. Rocky Dale Gardens
14. Standing Stone Perennial Farm
15. Vermont Daylilies
16. Von Trapp Greenhouses
17. Walker Farm Garden
18. Windham Wildflowers

CADY'S FALLS NURSERY

RD 3, Box 2100, 637 Duhamel Road, Morrisville, VT 05661
(802) 888-5559
Don and Lela Avery

Hardy perennials. Unusual conifers. Native woodland and wetland plants.
Alpines, roses, heathers, grasses. Family-operated nursery. Open May and June,
Tuesday to Sunday 10–6. Open July to season's end, Tuesday to Saturday 10–6. Free
catalog. No mail or phone order. Display garden. Best bloom late June and early July. E-
mail: averycfn@sover.net.

Founded by Don and Lela Avery in 1980 on a 19th-century farm, Cady's
Falls is a family-owned nursery operated by self-confessed "plant nuts" who,
they say, are "winning the struggle to remain abnormal." The Averys offer
hardy, sophisticated plants for cold-climate gardens: perennials, rock-garden
plants, native plants, ferns, vines, grasses, dwarf conifers, shrubs, and trees.
Nearly all these plants are propagated and grown at the nursery, an almost
unheard-of feat when their range and variety is considered.

The Averys are committed to keeping their nursery small and personal,
and do all the work themselves. They declare, "We have no gift shop, no
landscaping crew, no propagation manager, no sales staff, no credit cards, and
no chemicals." Their nursery, operated out of a monumental dairy barn in
the Northeast Kingdom, is a tour de force of rural horticulture.

The backbone of Cady's Falls Nursery is its fine collection of hardy perennials and rock-garden plants. The cultivar list is uncommonly interesting and
deep, featuring many beautiful daylily, hosta, iris, phlox, and primrose varieties,
as well as bee balm, bellflower, poppy, cranesbill geranium, monkshood,
saxifrage, and peony. We loved the pink lily of the valley; the huge ornamental rhubarb; the tiny creeping campanula; the many-tiered white candelabra
primrose; and the 9-foot purple snakeroot (*Cimicifuga* spp.). Showy, seldom-
seen plants include rattlesnake orchid (*Goodyera* spp.), Japanese jack-in-the-
pulpit, Welsh red poppy, and Himalayan blue poppy (gardeners kill for this
plant). Some species grown here are sufficiently unusual to lack common
names: bolax, globularia, jasione, jovibarba, lespidezia, orostachys, and sidalcia.
The nursery also offers good pond plants and water lilies; heaths and heathers;
grasses; and shrub roses. Among the ornamental vines are hardy clematis,
which northern gardeners are recommended to grow "on hog fencing."

Cady's Falls carries many desirable native plants (all nursery grown), such
as baneberry, blue cohosh, bog rosemary, pussy-toes, and panax ginseng.
Spring ephemerals include double bloodroot, red toad shade trillium *(T.
sessile),* and *Hepatica acutilobia,* a tiny 3-inch Vermont wildflower with blue,

pink, and white flowers. Woodland gardeners will hanker after the nursery's unusual ferns, pitcher plants, double marsh marigolds, and lab-propagated lady's slipper orchids brought in from an outside grower.

A distinction of Cady's Falls Nursery is its extensive conifer collection tailored to rock gardeners and collectors with a taste for dwarf, weeping, and unusual evergreens. The focus here is on small, well-established plants. Some are one-year plants in gallon containers (billed as "small plants at small prices"), while others are specimen size. Deciduous trees include an unusual maple described as "a telephone pole with sugar maple leaves" and several varieties of dwarf elm. Among the new shrubs, we loved *Salix integra* 'Hakuro Nishiki', an arching, red-stemmed shrub willow with green foliage splashed white and pink (reportedly native to "England through Siberia"). A few exquisite container gardens feature bonsai trees and miniature rock gardens in hypertufa.

The driving force at Cady's Falls is Don Avery, a gifted nurseryman whose intelligence and stamina reflect a dual family heritage in farming and medicine. Avery provides informed cultivation advice and will actually stop you from buying plants that will not thrive in your conditions. The Averys screen plants for Zone 3 hardiness by paying close attention to performance in the ground. As a result, the nursery's vibrant, well-rooted stock transfers readily to New England gardens. Cady's Falls is a chemical-free nursery that sells organic fertilizers and recycles reusable plastic pots, by both accepting them and giving them away. Cultivation practices are excellent, as is the nursery's informative catalog.

Cady's Falls is a picturesque horticultural farm, intelligently run and fully meriting repeat plant-buying visits made necessary by the absence of mail order. Display gardens weave gracefully around the Averys' antique farmhouse, including a 150-foot water garden and elegant perennial, dwarf conifer, and rock gardens. An orderly sales yard surrounds the wooden barn, with long vistas over the growing fields. Visitors are welcome to stroll the gardens, inspect the propagation beds, and take a pleasant walk to a woodland pool, fed by a cascading waterfall that seems irresistible to local boys on summer afternoons.

Directions: From Route 89, take exit 10/Waterbury, then take Route 100 north through Stowe. Just after the Foxfire Inn, turn left onto Stagecoach Road. In 7 miles, at a T-junction, turn left onto Cady's Falls Road. Go left over the bridge onto Duhamel Road; the nursery is 0.5 mile on your left.
From Route 15 west, pass Route 100 and immediately turn south onto Needle Eye Road. Turn left at the end and pass over the bridge onto Duhamel Road; the nursery is 0.5 mile on your left.

COUNTRYMAN PEONY FARM

RD 1, Box 990, Northfield, VT 05663
(802) 485-8421 (evenings); fax (802) 485-8422
Bill and Anne Countryman

Herbaceous peonies. Small specialty nursery. Open daily in June, 10–dusk. Free catalog. Mail order. Display beds.

Bill Countryman got involved with peonies the way most of us get into trouble: He fell in love. His sister gave him a peony, he planted it in the garden, and when it bloomed the next year, it was, as he says, "love at first sight." He then expanded the peony bed, one thing led to another, and now Countryman and his wife, Anne, aided by their son Chris, maintain one of the largest collections of herbaceous peonies in the country—embracing more than 1,000 varieties. One stock bed contains all 36 Gold Medal winners recognized by the American Peony Society over the past 75 years. Other beds hold a good portion of the herbaceous peony cultivars known to man. In real life, Countryman runs an environmental consulting firm, but his heart is clearly with his peony farm on a steep hillside in central Vermont.

Countryman Peony Farm is a small specialty nursery offering a rotating group of 40 peony hybrids selected from its collection each year, depending on supply. Regularly included are a dozen Gold Medal winners–excellent singles, doubles, whites, pinks, reds, some spotted varieties, and a glorious yellow Ito hybrid called 'Golden Treasure' whose grandmother *(P. lutea)* is a yellow tree peony from Tibet. The nursery offers "Victorian" peonies, consisting of luscious old favorites and 19th-century heirlooms, and "Classic" peonies, consisting of worthy 20th-century hybrids. The Countryman catalog, brief but informative, describes the origin, habits, color, and bloom time of each variety, along with planting instructions. Questions can be addressed to the owners, who are walking encyclopedias on the subject of peonies.

The gardens are open daily in June, when the peonies are in glory; their bloom peaks on the summer solstice (June 21). Lucky visitors may be taken on a guided tour of the propagating beds in the Countrymans' nifty motorized golf cart. Don't miss the ornamental fowl; the chicks were hatching from their shells on our visit.

Gardeners who cannot visit the peony farm can order from the catalog and expect a three- to five-eye peony root (bigger than normal) delivered in a plastic bag (the routine method) at the appropriate planting time (autumn). Herbaceous peonies are robust aristocrats of the perennial border—hardy to Zone 2, deer-proof, and extremely long-lived. Since a properly planted herbaceous peony can easily survive for more than a century, a peony is almost certain to outlive the gardener who plants it. It's a great gift for weddings and birthdays: Think of it as a gift to the future.

Directions: From Route 89, take exit 5 onto Route 64 west. Cross straight over Route 12 onto a dirt road. At the T-junction, turn left onto Route 12A and quickly left again onto Winch Hill Road; the farm is 1 mile on your right.

ELMORE ROOTS

631 Symonds Mill Road, Wolcott, VT 05680
(802) 888-3305; fax (802) 223-1485; Vermont tollfree (800) 42-PLANT
David Fried

Hardy fruit trees. Berry plants. Flowering crabs and shrubs. Lilacs. Hedgerow plants. Nut and yard trees. Small organic nursery. *Open from late April through October, daily except Saturday, 10–5:30. Open by appointment in early April and November. Call ahead if coming far. Free catalog. No mail order. Display orchard. Tools, supplies, and organic fertilizer. Web site: www.elmoreroots.com.*

Elmore Roots is a small, family-run orchard nursery specializing in organically grown fruit trees, flowering shrubs, and berry plants, intended "for the coldest hillsides in Vermont." Located on a remote dirt road in the Northeast Kingdom, the nursery offers orchard trees and flowering shrubs that have grown to maturity on its own cold hillside (Zone 3). Since 1979, owner David Fried has propagated and grafted nursery stock from cuttings taken from this 5-acre orchard. When he runs out of stock, organic field-grown plants are brought in from cold-climate family farms.

Elmore Roots guarantees cold hardiness with a boast painted on its entry arbor: IF IT GROWS AT ELMORE, IT WILL GROW WHERE YOU ARE. One early spring, we received an irresistible postcard from the nursery depicting a flowering plum tree and a singsong message: "For berries, flowers, nuts, and fruit / We're growing them at Elmore Roots / The plants we have are not in stores / They grow in a climate just like yours." The nursery's bragging rights are confirmed by its customers; one wrote, "I live in Lincoln, and Lincoln is one of the coldest places in Vermont, and I live in one of the coldest parts of Lincoln, and your plants flourish here."

The nursery's plants are freshly hand dug and potted in an organic mix, making them easy to transport and plant. Elmore Roots' propagation practices resemble 19th-century methods: no slick 21st-century labels or regulation stock sizes here. Customers do get the benefit of a two-year guarantee on all plants, however—a more generous warranty than any other tree and shrub nursery we can think of.

Although New England once produced its own orchard trees, today's gardeners are hard pressed to find regionally grown fruit trees that continue the old growing traditions. Elmore Roots is the exception, offering 31 varieties of Vermont-grown apple trees, including heirlooms such as 'St. Johnsbury Sweet' (a sweet yellow-red keeper), 'Elmore Sweet' (small and flavorful), and 'Yellow Transparent' (said to be famous for sauce). Other fruit trees include hardy plums (one is a true greengage), pears, pie cherries, bush cherries, and Manchurian apricots. A prolific assortment of hardy fruits features blueberries, elderberries, mulberries, currants, lingonberries, and lowbush and highbush cranberries. Hardy vines and briers are also offered, such as raspberries, blackberries, Juneberries, seeded grapes (seedless grapes are too tender), kiwis, hops, and clematis.

Besides fruit trees, Elmore Roots grows wonderful flowering crab apple and own-root lilac trees. One Memorial Day, David Fried showed us his favorite small tree, a beautiful flowering crab called 'Bechtel', with silvery bark and perfumed blossoms that looked like tiny roses. The nursery's lilacs include a late villosa lilac, a Japanese tree lilac, blue 'President Lincoln', and classic French hybrids such as 'Ludwig Spaeth' and 'Mme. Lemoine'. Finally, Elmore Roots is a source for nursery-grown nut trees such as hazelnut, black walnut, nut pine, and shagbark hickory, and yard trees such as sugar maple, white birch, shadblow, and horse chestnut. A specialty here are hedgerow plants favored by the many birds and wildlife inhabiting the nursery.

Although Elmore Roots offers to "coach, design, plant, and deliver for you," delivery services are limited, and far-off gardeners should plan to pick up their plants. The nursery has a wild, sweet, almost innocent air, and is worth visiting despite its remoteness (call ahead to make sure someone will be there). A funky metal shed, merrily painted red, houses books, tools, sticky wooden apples (to foil apple predators), and organic growing supplies. Hand-potted trees and shrubs are set out under rustic arbors adorned with whimsical hand-painted signs.

Visitors are invited to picnic and take a self-guided fruit-tasting tour. In autumn, ripe apples are offered on a table under a tree, but whether for us or for visiting wildlife, we could not tell. The nursery's fragrant, overgrown orchard is loud with the sound of bees. Jungly paths lead through copses and hedgerows to hidden stands of scented lilacs, flowering crabs, and fruit trees. Wooden seats, placed strategically in dappled shade, allow visitors to sit quietly and observe the many nesting birds darting about. This wild orchard hillside has a poetic reality, melodious in the afternoon, magical in the pink air of moonrise.

Directions: From Montpelier, take Route 12 north for 19 miles. In Morrisville, by a diary farm at the bottom of a long hill, turn right at the nursery's sign (before the Elmore store). In 0.75 mile, turn left onto Symonds Mill Road; the nursery is 0.75 mile on your left (signposted).
From I-91, take exit 21 in St. Johnsbury onto Route 2 west. In West Danville, turn right onto Route 15. In Wolcott, turn left at the nursery's sign. In 2.75 miles, turn right onto Symonds Mill Road; the nursery is 1.75 miles on your right (signposted).

Green Mountain Transplants, Inc.

RR 1, P.O. Box 6C, East Montpelier, VT 05651
802-454-1533; fax 802-454-1204
Dexter R. Merritt

Vegetable and flower seedling flats. *Business hours April though June, Monday to Friday 8:30–5, Saturday 9–noon. Fax open 24 hours. Greenhouses open in June to clear stock. Free catalog. Mail order. E-mail: GMTranspl@aol.com. Web site: www.gmtransplants.com.*

Green Mountain Transplants is a seasonal nursery specializing in vegetable and flower seedlings grown in its northern Vermont greenhouses. Its seedlings (called transplants) come in 38- and 72-cell flats, shipped to customers from late April through June. Each seedling has a developed root ball and (in the 38-cell flats) soil volume about equal to a 21/2-inch pot. In effect, Green Mountain allows gardeners to oversee the last stage of seedling growth them-selves, rather than paying a retailer to finish plants for them. These seedlings transplant easily, and quickly catch up to garden center plants. The only hard part of Green Mountain's system is completing the order blank, which requires figuring out which plants come in 38-cell packs, which come in 72-cell packs, and which have a small per-plant surcharge.

While different varieties can be mixed within a single flat, glitches may occur with orders that are too complicated. To ensure timely delivery, we strongly recommend that simple, straightforward orders be placed early; remain free of alteration; and specify "no substitutions." Be warned that the green-house staff is nearly impossible to communicate with during shipping season. Within these limitations, Green Mountain offers an excellent way to acquire spring vegetable and flower gardens at a surprisingly modest cost, without the trouble and mess of sprouting seeds under grow-lights in the basement.

Green Mountain's catalog lists more than 650 varieties of vegetable and flower seedlings. Many are the kind of plants offered in six-packs by good garden centers. Vegetables include squashes, peppers, onions, tomatoes, melons, strawberries, asparagus, and more than 40 culinary herbs. Less common vegetables are also offered, such as celeriac, kohlrabi, okra, tomatillo, rhubarb, and sweet potato. The tomato list includes gold and purple tomatoes, heirlooms such as 'Brandywine' and 'Amish Paste', and a compact European variety called 'Window Box'. The chili pepper selection ranges from warm 'Hungarian Wax' to ultra-hot 'Red Habanero'. We especially liked all the lovely lettuces: red butterheads, green crispheads, frilly red Italians, and a green romaine with red freckles, called 'Freckles'.

Green Mountain seedlings also include flower varieties, old and new. Among the annuals are good choices of impatiens, fuchsia, salvia, and verbena, and some interesting trailers and vines. A number of these have won AAS awards. We particularly liked the broad selection of petunias (grandiflora, multiflora, milliflora, and trailing) and geraniums (zonal, ivy, and cranesbill), grown by the nursery from cuttings and seed. Perennial seedlings include yarrow, columbine, campanula, coreopsis, delphinium, dianthus, daylily, hosta, phlox, poppy, sedum, and veronica. An uncommon flower occasionally appears, such as the azalea-flowered snapdragon. The list includes some good ground-cover plants.

Green Mountain will custom-grow any vegetable or flower variety in a 38-cell flat (one variety per flat) if the customer provides or pays for the seed. We once tried this with a flat of *Cerinthe major purpurascens,* a dazzling container plant with blue foliage and purplish bracts. It would have worked beautifully if we had not been out of town when the plants arrived; as it was, half of the plants survived, which still made them a bargain. We recommend custom orders only to gardeners with stable schedules.

Green Mountain's catalog consists of 50 pages of newsprint, listing flowers and vegetables by common name. Besides seedling flats, the catalog offers supplies such as plastic mulch, drip-irrigation tools, and harvest baskets. Certified seed potatoes are sold in 5- and 50-pound bags, and onions and leeks in 288-cell flats or 25-plant bunches. Lily bulbs will accompany any transplant order at bargain rates. Orders are due by April 1 to guarantee spring delivery; anything later risks disappointment.

Although Green Mountain operates almost exclusively by mail-order, the greenhouses in East Montpelier are open to customers in June to clear out the remaining stock. They are located off the main highway, and getting there involves a windswept trip through dairy-farm country laced with mountain views.

Directions: Call for hours in June. From I-91, take exit 21 onto Route 2 west. In East Montpelier, turn right onto Route 114 north. In about a mile, look for greenhouses on the right, behind some apple trees. Alternatively, from Route 89, take exit 8 onto Route 2 east. Turn left onto Route 114 north and follow directions above.

GREGG HILL GARDENS

P.O. Box 1840, 3464 Gregg Hill Road, Waterbury Center, VT 05677
(802) 244-7361
Marcy Blauvelt

Perennials and alpines. Heathers. Grasses. Ornamental herbs and annuals. *Small specialty nursery. Open May 1 through October, Tuesday to Saturday 9–5, Sunday 9–5 in May and June. Free catalog. No mail order. Display gardens. U-pick cutting garden. Workshops. Garden and floral design. E-mail: ghgardens@aol.com.*

Gardeners sometimes growl about growers who don't understand garden design, and designers who don't understand plants. Marcy Blauvelt, owner of Gregg Hill Gardens, is an exception on both counts, for she is a skilled plantswoman with an exceptional eye for floral and garden design. Gregg Hill Gardens is a small, stylish nursery offering an assortment of ornamental perennials, rock-garden plants, and flowering companions, grown on the premises or bought in from Vermont growers. Gregg Hill's catalog, listing all its nursery stock, is cross-referenced to the American Horticultural Society's *A–Z Encyclopedia of Garden Plants*. The nursery operates out of a weathered barn next to Blauvelt's home, decorated with lush flowering window boxes and container gardens. The barn's interior functions as an atmospheric drying shed for everlastings cut from the garden.

The Gregg Hill property is divided by a huge, whalelike rock ledge, providing a backdrop for clever display gardens that visitors are welcome to clamber up and enjoy. Fascinating little alpine gardens sprawl enchantingly up the granite ledge; its summit supports lush perennial and production beds, contoured to the rock. Below, a woodland gale has been groomed with ferns and wildflowers. Gregg Hill opened as a U-pick flower farm in 1992, and its large cutting gardens continue to offer fresh flowers for picking throughout the season.

Given the nursery's delightful setting, it is no surprise to find plant selection governed by the same stylish flair at work in the gardens. The nursery has good collections of flowering perennials, ornamental annuals, alpines, heathers, ornamental grasses, dwarf conifers, and flowering herbs. The emphasis throughout is on ornamental value—nothing too outlandish, just beautiful plants in varieties old and new. On our visit, we admired a matlike woolly yarrow, white creeping veronica, snowdrop anemone, and cardinal flower with bronze foliage.

Attractive hanging baskets prepared at the nursery make inventive use of herbaceous perennials such as snow-in-summer, golden thyme, and the ornamental strawberry 'Lipstick'. Unlike most hanging baskets, with proper care these can be wintered over.

Blauvelt's services are in demand for custom-planted containers, garden design, and flowers arranged for weddings, inns, and special occasions. We come to Gregg Hill Gardens for its charming plants, but can never resist the ready-made fresh flower bouquets on the sales counter, pretty as a summer's day.

Directions: Waterbury Center is in north-central Vermont, south of Stowe. From Route 89, take exit 10 onto Route 100 north. In a mile or two past Waterbury Center, turn left (signposted) onto Gregg Hill Road; the nursery is on the left.

Nearby attractions: Evergreen Gardens of Vermont, Route 100, Waterbury Center (802-244-8523), is a popular local garden center stocking good plant material. The Stowe Flower and Garden Festival (800-247-8693; www.stoweinfo.com) occurs annually in late June. Ben & Jerry's Ice Cream Factory Tours, Route 100, Waterbury, 1 mile north of Route 89 (802-882-1260), offers daily plant tours, free samples in the FlavoRoom, and a "moovie" recounting "our story" ("With diplomas from a $5 correspondence course and their life savings [$8,000], they converted an old abandoned gas station in Burlington, Vermont, into the original Ben & Jerry's ..."). The Shed Restaurant and Brewery in Stowe (802-253-9311) is an award-winning pub serving six handcrafted English ales.

HORSFORD GARDENS AND NURSERY

2111 Greenbush Road (Route 7), Charlotte, VT 05445
(802) 425-2811
Eileen Schilling and Charlie Proutt

Perennials. Field-grown shrubs and trees. *Nursery and garden center. Open mid-April to December 17. Hours April through June, Monday to Friday 8–6, Saturday 8–5, Sunday 8–4; July 1 through October, Monday to Saturday 8–5, Sunday 10–4; Thanksgiving to December 17, daily 8–4:30, Sunday 10–4. Catalog $3. No mail order. Annual tree sale in April. Display garden. Landscape design services. Christmas greens.*

Established in the late 1800s, Horsford Gardens is the oldest surviving nursery in Vermont. The Horsford family left the business long ago, but owners Eileen Schilling and Charlie Proutt are intent on maintaining it as a vintage nursery, complete with antique cypress-and-glass greenhouses. A glassed-in corridor crafted from a century-old conservatory winds between the outdoor displays and propagation houses. (The old glasshouses are still functional, according to the owners: "Under glass, the environment is magical; the light is clear and true.")

Horsford Gardens grows most of its own stock, offering fresh vigorous plants, free of pesticides and fungicides, backed by a one-year guarantee. The nursery carries some of everything, in the way of full-service garden centers, but its strong suits are herbaceous perennials and hardy, field-grown shrubs and trees. The plant list retains some excellent varieties dating to the 1920s and 1930s, when the nursery provisioned the estates on Lake Champlain.

Horsford Gardens' annual catalog lists some 40 pages of perennials, herbs, and grasses for sale at the nursery. This impressive collection was accumulated over decades by Leo Roberts, an old hand at horticulture who has tended Horsford's perennials for 30 years. (He confirms his intention to return to work each spring by carving the date on the green-house wall.) Horsford's perennial tables hold excellent groups of astilbe, campanula, lily, phlox, veronica, and scented geranium. Native plants, brought in from a specialty grower, include many choice woodland perennials. The nursery's catalog is an excellent plant reference and provides good cultivar profiles, interspersed with nostalgic quotes from Horsford Gardens catalogs of 50 years ago.

A waxing selection of annuals is offered in the spring, including annual salvia, night phlox, flowering tobacco, datura, Mexican sunflower, sun-tolerant fuchsia, and various ornamen-tals with trailing, shade-loving, drought-tolerant, and night-blooming attributes. Eileen Schilling is an experienced container gardener who will help customers design window boxes and patio planters—but be warned: She is acutely partial to orange (defended as "the millennium color").

Horsford Gardens grows many flowering shrubs, roses, broadleaf ever-greens, and shade trees; we particularly admired its good selections of field-grown lilacs, flowering crab apples, and shrub dogwoods. Apple trees, blueberry bushes, and grapevines are available for the orchardist. Horsford's early spring "field tag sale" cuts 30 percent off the price of overwintered trees in the growing fields, including thousands of oaks, ashes, maples, birches, lilacs, and flowering crabs. (Late in the growing season, be sure to check shrub and tree containers carefully.) The garden shop is refreshingly gimmick-free, and carries organic compost and fertilizer, grass seed, books, tools, and fall bulbs. A Christmas shop features fresh wreaths and seasonal gifts for gardeners. Nursery customers are routinely treated to a seedling or potted plant with every purchase.

Horsford Gardens maintains a small display garden under two immense black locust trees with arresting, exquisite bark; here visitors may rest on wooden benches and ride a large tree-slung swing (tempting even to adults). Arbors, trellises, and flowering containers give Horsford an air of old-fashioned gentility; candelabras of blue lupine illuminate the garden in late May. Behind the garden center lies a fertile dale, lined out with 22 acres of trees, shrubs, and potted perennials—a heartening sight to gardeners who know the value of fresh, regionally adapted nursery stock. Be sure to enjoy Horsford's spectacular view of the Adirondack Mountains and the glint of Lake Champlain from the entry drive.

Directions: From Burlington, take Route 7 south for 10 miles to Charlotte. In 4 miles past the Shelburne Museum, turn right into the nursery's driveway (signposted).

Nearby attractions: The Shelburne Museum, Route 7, Charlotte (802-985-3346; www.shelburnemuseum.org), houses a world-class collection of American folk art in 37 historic structures; formal gardens, roses, and ornamental trees embellish the grounds, where a lilac festival is held in late May. Extraordinary farmstead cheddar is made at Shelburne Farms (802-985-8686), a 1,400-acre dairy farm whose aristocratic "cottage" on Lake Champlain is operated seasonally as an inn; its gardens were designed by Frederick Law Olmsted. The trial gardens at the University of Vermont Horticultural Research Center, Green Mountain Road (off Shelburne Road), South Burlington (802-656-2630), grow 135 varieties of flowering crab apple that bloom in May; maps and trail guides are at the central kiosk.

LABOR OF LOVE LANDSCAPING AND NURSERY

9 Sargent Lane, Glover Village (Route 16), Barton, VT 05839
(802) 525-6695
Kate Butler

Hardy perennials. Bulbs. *Small nursery. Open from April bulb bloom until hard frost, Thursday to Saturday; and by chance or appointment. Plant list. No mail order. Display gardens open daily until dark. Landscaping and garden design.*
E-mail: kkbutler@together.net.

Labor of Love Landscaping and Nursery, located in the Northeast Kingdom, specializes in perennials and bulbs that are hardy to Zone 3 (Zone 2 is tundra). This small nursery is sited in the yard of a Greek Revival house in Barton village, surrounded by hardy perennial plants in pots, raised beds, and display gardens that double as digging beds. Despite its apparent informality, this is no backyard nursery of the kind seen all over Vermont.

Kate Butler, the cheerful proprietor, is one of those relentlessly creative people who are full of surprises. She grows all her own plants from seed or division; she has a taste for unusual and "oddball stuff"; she finds amusement in growing survivors that are "not supposed to do well up here in Zone 3"; and she tries her hand at hybridizing sherbet-colored ornamental poppies and an unusual red-stemmed *Lychnis haageana*. Butler is a professional landscaper, garden designer, folksinger, weaver, and horticulturist—and she sells hand-weaving and vintage clothing out of a little shop in a front room.

Like most idiosyncratic plant collections, Labor of Love's perennials defy easy description. Distinguished hybrids grow next to experimental plants not normally found in nurseries. The nursery's main features are English cottage-garden plants, a succulent collection, and interesting alpine miniatures and rock garden plants. Among the garden plants, we noticed good cranesbill geranium, Siberian iris, mildew-free phlox, *Sedum* 'Vera Jamieson', and a pink monkshood. Among the native woodlanders are Lobelia cardinalis in three colors, Labrador tea rhododendron, and creeping Jacob's ladder. Choice shade perennials include a picotee dwarf lady's mantle, Chinese trollius, maidenhair fern, and Japanese candelabra primrose (remember, we are in Zone 3 here). The nursery's fascination with ornamental weeds produces pink and white hawkweed *(Crepis rubra* and *C. alba),* white chicory, and a red-stemmed peppermint/spearmint cross smuggled in from England—none of which we have ever seen before.

Labor of Love grows its plants in lean soil, abjuring the heavy fertilizers of commercial growers; everything looks vigorous and tough. Having survived the rigors of winter in Barton, these plants are guaranteed hardy in all but arctic conditions.

Labor of Love's nursery is open all week on the honor system, but we recommend a visit from Thursday to Saturday when you are sure to meet the redoubtable Kate Butler. She will fascinate you with a nursery tour, dig plants from her growing beds, and play her folk music CDs from the porch; in a generous moment, she may give you free poppy seed. Outdoor picnic tables are sited by a stream in sunshine for the benefit of visitors who remember to bring lunch. On the second Wednesday of the month, for a modest fee you can stay for dinner and a folk music jam.

Directions: Barton is 20 miles north of St. Johnsbury. Take I-91 north to exit 25 and follow Route 16 to Barton; the nursery is in the village on the left.

Nearby attractions: The nursery is near enough to Quebec to get French language stations on the radio.

SUSSEX OR TRUG BASKET.

LITTLE SIBERIA PERENNIALS

966 Maston Hill Road, Granville, VT 05747
(802) 767-3391 phone and fax
Vivian and Fritz Branschofsky

Hardy perennials. Heather. Succulents. Rock-garden plants. Roses, shrubs, and conifers. Small specialty nursery. Open May through September, daily 10–5, except Wednesday and Thursday. Plant list. No mail order. E-mail: siberia@sover.net.

Little Siberia Perennials is a small nursery located on a wind-scoured hillside in north-central Vermont; it specializes in hardy perennials for cold-climate gardens. Owner Vivian Branschofsky is a Virginia native who settled in Vermont after getting in a ski accident at Mad River and, as a result, meeting her husband, Fritz. The nursery she started is not called Little Siberia for nothing: It sits in a Zone 3 cold spot better suited to alpine skiing than gardening. Branschofsky's courageous response to this arctic site is to grow an innovative collection of 700 hardy perennials, including excellent rock-garden plants, succulents, and field-tested heaths and heathers (she aims to be the "Heather Queen of Vermont"). The nursery's feisty band of perennials is supplemented by a few equally cold-hardy roses, shrubs, and small conifers.

We were struck by the usefulness of these tough plants, not just for mountain and country gardens, but also for wind-scoured city rooftops and other extreme conditions. Over half the plants sold at the nursery are divisions from Little Siberia's own gardens, which comprise a series of neo-Victorian island beds contoured to its open hillside. A colorful garden island, displaying the nursery's large holdings of sedum and sempervivum, made us think of the terrific succulent gardens that could be grown in enriched roof gravel. Gardeners can study these interesting display beds by sitting on a low stone bench set in the highest garden, facing spectacular views to the Green Mountain National Forest, where we once found a half-empty bottle of champagne.

The most intriguing thing about Little Siberia Perennials is the range and depth of its hardy plant collections. Little Siberia is rich in phlox, including varieties of Canadian phlox, meadow phlox, summer phlox, creeping phlox, and mountain pinks. (Think of the living chessboards and amusing family crests that could be grown in creeping phlox!) Rock-garden plants include alpine lady's mantle, alpine hutchinsia, six rock cresses, a dozen saxifrages, four kinds of sea thrift (we know of only one growing wild on the sea cliffs in Ireland), and several charming rock jasmines, which are low-running plants with pretty little rosettes, like primroses. We also saw more than the usual number of hardy yarrows, bellflowers, gentians, bee balms, veronicas, spider-worts, cranesbill geraniums, and other unkillable perennials and alpines. Among the shade plants are good hosta and astilbe collections, and some less common native plants such as marsh marigold, rodgersia, and variegated Solomon's seal.

We suppose a nursery calling itself Little Siberia has no choice but to carry Tartarian cephalaria and Siberian bugloss. An impressive list of hardy heathers includes the winter-blooming kind that turn multicolored in autumn and burst into flower in February. Underscoring the nursery's hardiness theme are several Siberian huskies with huge thick coats, romping exuberantly in an enclosure next to the Branschofskys' chalet. Like the plants, they are mindless of the cold.

Directions: From Route 89 south, take exit 10 onto Route 100 south. Follow Route 100 (a scenic road bordering the Mad River and Green Mountain National Forest) into Granville. Turn east at the nursery's sign onto Maston Hill Road; the nursery is up the hill on the left. From Route 89 north, take exit 3 onto Route 107 west, turn onto Route 100 north, and follow directions above.

Nearby attractions: A few miles north of Granville on Route 100, Moss Glen Falls is a spectacular waterfall cascading over Green Mountain bedrock; they are approached on a composite-wood boardwalk crafted from recycled sawdust and 154,000 plastic grocery bags. Vermont Only, Route 100, Granville (802-767-4711), sells woodenware, baskets, cheese, fudge, and maple syrup.

MOUNTAIN ORCHIDS

1658 Route 100 North, Ludlow, VT 05149-9724
(802) 228-8506 phone and fax
Darrin Norton

Miniature tropical and species orchids. *Small specialty grower. Open by appointment or chance. Free catalog. Monthly specials on the Web site. E-mail: mtorchids@mail.tds.net. Web site: www.mountainorchids.com.*

Orchids comprise the largest plant family on earth, with 30,000 species and 300,000-odd hybrids. These exotic plants are pursued by legions of obsessed gardeners who find them surprisingly easy to grow in home conditions. Mountain Orchids is a small greenhouse, nestled in a vale in the Green Mountains, specializing in uncommon orchids that do well in a home greenhouse or on a northern windowsill. Darrin Norton, the nursery's youthful proprietor, has been growing tropical orchids for 20 years, and now does it well enough to rely on these plants for a living.

Although many Mountain Orchids plants originate in high tropical elevations, this greenhouse nursery is named not for Norton's orchids, but for the mountains surrounding his Vermont home. Mountain Orchids grows many miniature and wild species orchids that are rare in cultivation and almost impossible to find from other growers. (Species orchids are botanical plants as found in nature, untouched by the hybridizer's hand; only a few nurseries in the country carry wild orchids in any quantity.) Norton also breeds rare wild orchids to produce plants of equal beauty that are much easier to grow; in recent years his creations have won numerous American Orchid Society awards.

Mountain Orchids' small collection of wild and miniature orchids is diverse and decorative; a number have uncommon attributes such as fragrance, fall bloom, and variegated foliage. The nursery's strong suits are orchids of the cattleya, dendrobium, and oncidium alliances (large, loose orchid families, or tribes) and masdevallia and dracula orchids of the pleurothallis alliance. The most requested plants are Norton's own hybrids of *Dendrobium cuthbertsonii,* often bearing the 'Mountain' name; these adorable 3-inch orchids have warty foliage and long-lasting flowers in a rainbow of colors, from fuchsia to watermelon. Dendrobium orchids tend to produce beautiful sprays of flowers; our favorite, *D. victoria-reginae* 'Mountain Midnight' (another nursery hybrid), throws off a little blue-violet floral waterfall.

Mountain Orchids grows some enchanting cattleyas (popular plants known as corsage orchids). These include a cute Mexican miniature with green flowers and blue-tinted lips *(Encyclia cyanocolumna)* and a famous, perfumed white orchid called 'Lady of the Night' *(Brassavola nodosa).* The shapes of these little flowers can be amazing: those of *Haraella retrocalla* look like faces of green Scotch terriers; those of *Masdevallia* x 'Minaret' resemble tiny mosques done in peppermint. One of the nursery's showiest wild orchids, *Maxillaria pseudoeichenheimiana*, has incredible silver-spotted foliage and flowers resembling a colony of white spiders. What orchid grower can resist the wild dracula orchids, with their sinister batlike wings, or polka-dotted masdevallia orchids with yellow dorsal tails? Alluring miniature orchids from obscure alliances are grown for good measure.

Mountain Orchids grows wild and miniature orchids from all over the world; the catalog lists 160 varieties, and many more are grown in the greenhouse. Plants are sold through the nursery's mail-order catalog and its Web site, which has better color photographs. All plants are nursery-grown and responsibly sourced; CITES permits confirming legal status can be provided. Orchids usually take five to seven years to mature to first bloom, but most collectors buy seedlings; Mountain Orchids offers both seedlings and mature plants. Though rare and unusual orchids are never cheap, Mountain Orchids' seem fairly priced. Although most business is done by mail order, visitors are welcome to tour Mountain Orchid's small tropical greenhouse, surrounded by colorful rock gardens. This respite is recommended to orchid gardeners who need a lift in spring but have no time to escape to the tropics.

Directions: From I-91, take exit 6 onto Route 103 north. In 17 miles, past the town of Ludlow, turn right onto Route 100 north; the greenhouse is 3 miles on the right. Call for an appointment.

Nearby attractions: Kelley's Orchid Supplies, P.O. Box 6, Kittery, ME 03904-0006 (207-439-0922; fax 207-439-8202; E-mail: kelkos@nh.ultranet.com; www.ccsme.com/orchids/), is a popular mail-order source of orchid supplies.

OLALLIE DAYLILY GARDENS

HCR 63, P.O. Box 1, Marlboro Branch Road, South Newfane, VT 05351
(802) 348-6614; fax (802) 348-9881
Christopher S. Darrow

Field-grown daylilies. Perennials, Siberian iris, and blueberry bushes. *Small family-run organic nursery. Open May to mid-October, daily 9–5, except Tuesday. Call ahead if coming a long distance. Catalog $2. Minimum order $30. Visitors welcome. AHS Daylily Display Garden. Peak bloom late July through August. Annual daylily festival. E-mail: info@daylilygarden.com. Web site: www.daylilygarden.com.*

Chris Darrow may be living on a legacy, but he is not clipping coupons. Rather, he inherited an important collection of daylilies from his grandfather, Dr. George M. Darrow. A Vermont native, the elder Darrow was an authority on small fruits who took to hybridizing daylilies in the 1960s and 1970s, after his retirement from the U.S. Department of Agriculture as a plant geneticist. Observing a convention among daylily hybridizers, Darrow registered 59 daylily hybrids using the name of his garden as a prefix. Olallie, a West Coast American Indian word for "place where berries are found," was the Maryland farm where Darrow produced his fruit and flower hybrids. As a hybridizer, Darrow performed pioneering work with tetraploid daylilies and developed plants characterized by strong growth, extended bloom, and clear blossom color. At the end of his life, he encouraged his son and grandson to transplant his daylily collection to their Vermont farmland. In 1993, the American Society for Horticultural Science inducted Dr. Darrow into the

ASHS Hall of Fame as its eighth member, joining such distinguished plant scientists as Luther Burbank and Gregor Mendel.

Founded in 1980 with Darrow's original collection, Olallie Daylily Gardens is an organic farm growing 6 acres of daylilies in a picturesque river valley in southern Vermont not far from Brattleboro. Chris Darrow and his wife, Amelia, manage the farm with the assistance of Chris's parents, Ellen (an artist) and Dan Darrow (a Vermont State Representative). Of their 1,000 field-grown daylilies, 200 are listed in the mail-order catalog and on the Web site, and can be bought at the nursery. The Olallie collection includes Darrow and non-Darrow hybrids, early, late, and long-season bloomers, "near blues" (violets), "near blacks" (dark reds), large-flowered varieties, miniatures, and species plants.

Olallie grows 55 of George Darrow's 59 registered hybrids, including 'Olallie All Summer', which blooms for two months, and 'Olallie Christopher', named for his grandson Chris. Darrow used a special late-blooming Japanese daylily in his breeding efforts; consequently, the Darrow hybrids tend to be floriferous, late-blooming varieties, such as 'Ripe Peach', 'Antique Salmon', and 'Recurved Ruffled Red', a heavy September bloomer with 34 buds per scape. Garden-worthy hybrids bred but never registered by Darrow are designated *VT* in the catalog, indicating their availability at the Olallie farm in Vermont, alongside Chris Darrow's own hybridizing efforts. Olallie also offers unique cultivars saved from Darrow's private garden, as well as daylily collections chosen for landscape use, seasonal bloom, and flower color.

Ollalie sells field-grown hardy daylilies, "unpampered," chemical-free, and freshly dug within 24 hours of shipping. Two sizes are available, depending on whether you want a starter plant or fast bloom. Bonus plants accompany every order, and a "division sale" offering significant discounts is held over Labor Day (through September). For those who fall in love with an unlisted plant, the Darrows have a considerate practice of notifying customers by postcard when a previously unavailable daylily comes into production.

Thousands of visitors come to the farm each summer to take a self-guided tour of the daylily beds, order plants, peruse the tools and books in the garden shop, and buy farm-grown companion plants (including unusual campanula, thalictrum, and Siberian iris from the Rock Garden Society, and blueberry bushes). Most daylilies are sold right out of the fields while the plants are in bloom.

Olallie's jam-packed daylily beds, colorful and well labeled, have been officially designated an AHS Display Garden by the American Hemerocallis Society. Olallie remains a "place where berries are found"; visitors can pick fresh blueberries in Olallie's pick-your-own patch. Border collies romp the premises, and their offspring are occasionally for sale as well.

Directions: South Newfane is 9 miles from Brattleboro. From I-91, take exit 2 onto Route 9 east. Turn left at the T-intersection onto Route 5/30 north. Pass through Brattleboro and bear left at the Y onto Route 30 north. In 8.5 miles, just after what is touted as the "longest covered bridge in Vermont," turn left onto Williamsville Road. Turn left at the end, pass through a covered bridge, and turn left at the South Newfane General Store; the farm is 0.5 mile on your left.

Nearby attractions: Newfane Greenhouse & Nursery, Route 30, 2 miles north of Newfane village (802-365-4408), grows annuals in seven greenhouses, including rare begonias, geraniums, and orchids, and a shade garden of native plants. The turn-of-the-century Inn at South Newfane (802-348-7191) serves meals in a rustic setting. On Route 5 in Putney, Curtis's Barbecue (802-387-5474), standing proud as "the Ninth Wonder of the World," serves fresh-smoked pork and chicken barbecue out of an aqua school bus, parked permanently next to Rob's Mobil and Car Care (just south of town).

PERENNIAL PLEASURES NURSERY

P.O. Box 147, 63 Brick House Road, East Hardwick, VT 05836
(802) 472-5104
Rachel and Judith Kane

Old-fashioned flowers and herbs. Antique garden plants. *Open May 1 to mid-September, 9–5 daily except Monday, and by appointment. Catalog $3. Send SASE for herb list. Mail order; no phone order. Display gardens. Garden restorations. Herbal studies. English cream teas, Memorial Day to Labor Day, daily except Monday, 12:30–4:30; reservations recommended. Web site: www.antiqueplants.com*

Perennial Pleasures Nursery surrounds a Federal-period brick farmhouse (built in 1840) in a small town in the Northeast Kingdom. British owner Rachel Kane and her mother, Judith, specialize in propagating and growing old-fashioned flowers, herbs, and antique garden plants. Their collection includes more than 1,000 heirloom plants and flowering ornamentals, some hunted and dug from forgotten gardens and old cemeteries. Perennial Pleasures is an excellent source of historically accurate plants for 17th-, 18th- and 19th-century garden restorations. To assist interested customers, the Kanes have assembled plant collections for specialty garden situations: white-flowered shade-garden plants; native plants for butterflies; an 18th-century dooryard garden; and a 17th-century garden of medicinal plants called simples. The herb garden contains more than 200 kinds of ancient culinary and medicinal herbs, dye plants, and aromatics.

Anyone who thinks old-fashioned plants hold no surprises has yet to study them carefully. Because the Kanes are horticultural historians and plant sleuths, their nursery is the perfect place for gardeners to find curious and

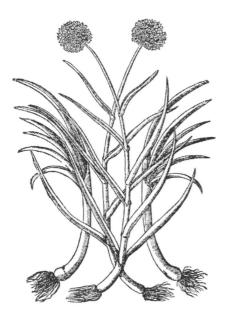

rare vintage plants alongside the relics of old cottage gardens. Perennial Pleasures is home to a 19th-century black hollyhock; an antique spotted cranesbill allegedly superior to 'Johnson's Blue'; a chocolate foxglove from the turn of the last century; Roman chamomile, the real thing, used for lawns 300 years ago; a double-flowered filipendula called honeysweet, sacred to the Druids; a 17th-century wild bergamot voted 1996 herb of the year; and a 20th-century refugee from Yugoslavia, a white mallow called kataibelia.

Among the nursery's flowering annuals, gardeners can find a double white opium poppy (17th century); a camellia-flowering balsam impatiens that was, it is said, "welcomed in the often outlandish 18th-century garden"; and a white marsh marigold (one to a customer). Cottage-garden plants seem the stuff of midsummer nights' dreams: English cowslips, eglantine roses, cottage pinks, primroses, and sweet violets.

Perennial Pleasures issues an absorbing, history-drenched catalog that documents its plants' introduction dates; describes their virtues and habits; and recounts historical vignettes that impart, by some inexpressible process, a renewed glamor to these heirlooms. The catalog reports that Napoleon sent mignonette seeds to Josephine, who christened it "little darling"; that weld was used by the Romans as a green dye, coloring the tunics of the vestal virgins; and that 16th-century ladies quilted lavender into their hats in order "to comfort the braines." We never knew that soapwort, a former laundering agent, still grows wild around old mill sites; that Welch onions come from China; that costmary tea was brewed in ancient Egypt; or that a pickle made of nasturtium seeds was used as a condiment in the 17th century (our mother still does this). The catalog not only provides such bewitching data, but also furnishes plant attribute lists, period gardening source lists, and century lists with plant introduction dates, beginning with the landing of the *Mayflower.*

Most Perennial Pleasures plants have real historical interest, and many are wonderfully fragrant. All plants are field-grown at the nursery in organic conditions, and proven hardy to Zone 3. Hand-collected untreated seed is offered for many of the nursery's plants. Seedlings are shipped in four-packs in the spring. An excellent booklist appears in the catalog.

The amenities offered at Perennials Pleasures Nursery are unusually civilized and commodious. The Kanes perform antique garden restorations. Visitors may stroll the nursery gardens and inspect the display beds, which include trellised walkways and an herb garden surrounding a standing megalith. A garden shop carries charming teapots, books, seeds, and garden ornaments. English cream teas, which have attracted a local following, are held in the flower garden or conservatory from June to Labor Day (reservations recommended).

Directions: East Hardwick is 10 miles from St. Johnsbury. From I-91, take exit 21/St. Johnsbury, and turn onto Route 2 west. In West Danville, take Route 15 north, then turn right onto Route 16. In East Hardwick village, follow signs to the nursery (the only brick house in the village), located on Brick House Road.

RAISING RARITIES

P.O. Box 405, Jacksonville, VT 05342
(802) 368-7273
Owen Robinson

Hardy native lady's slipper orchids. *Small specialty nursery. Open by appointment; call for directions. For plant list, send long SASE. Mail order.* [Wholesale only as of 2001].

Operating out of a hillside greenhouse in southern Vermont, Raising Rarities is a small native-plant nursery growing lab-cultivated hardy lady's slippers, elusive marvels of the Eastern woodlands that are now illegal to dig from the wild. Lady's slippers are, of course, elegant woodland orchids whose lips form a sexy, slipperlike pouch. Their Latin name, *Cypripedium* (or "cyps" for short), means "Venus's slipper." Raising Rarities propagates and sells four kinds of native lady's slipper, all hardy from Zones 3 to 7: the large yellow lady's slipper *(Cypripedium pubescens);* small yellow lady's slipper *(C. parviflorum);* showy lady's slipper *(C. reginae);* and a large mahogany-and-cream lady's slipper native to the southern Appalachians *(C. kentuckiense).* These hardy woodland orchids dislike cultivated gardens, but will thrive in the shade-dappled leaf mold of maple, oak, ash, and beech forests.

Owen Robinson, the nursery's owner and chief propagator, is a self-taught botanist who founded Raising Rarities after abandoning an electronics career at Raytheon to pursue a passion for native orchids. (His interest in plants was piqued at age four, when he planted a potato.) Robinson's goal is to promote and preserve lady's slippers, many of which are absent from the nursery trade due to their protected status and the perplexities of propagation. These plants are supposed to be finicky; we were surprised to learn how readily lab-propagated lady's slippers transfer to any rich woodland offering them enough space to establish colonies. Once settled, they form clumps that double in size each year.

Raising Rarities germinates lady's slipper seed in a sterile laboratory, using an artificial in vitro fertilization process worthy of a human fertility clinic. The process begins with the harvesting of minute orchid seeds from capsules that look like okra pods. In nature, these pods expel millions of tiny seed specks that float on the wind and spread to new environments, where one seed in a million will find the right conditions for growth. In Robinson's laboratory, ripe orchid seeds are hand-pollinated with a toothpick, refrigerated for several months to break dormancy, and grown out in glass flasks, hundreds of which line the walls. There they are nurtured, for periods of up to 18 months, in a unique growing medium made of pineapple juice, coconut milk, and potato extract. Sprouted seeds are eventually planted in woodland or boglike conditions that mimic their favorite habitat. Plants take from three to nine years to come into bloom.

Raising Rarities sells mature lady's slipper plants and some seedlings. All plants are guaranteed to be artificially propagated by seed or tissue culture; CITES permits ensuring their legal status can be provided on request. Prices for lady's slippers seem reasonable, considering their rarity and the time and trouble it takes to produce them. Dormant plants are shipped bare-root in spring and fall, accompanied by detailed cultural instructions.

Although Raising Rarities is predominantly a mail-order operation, nursery visits can be arranged—a special treat in May when the lady's slippers are in bloom. Robinson's tropical orchid collection perfumes the passage to the greenhouse laboratory. Outdoors, beautiful edible and ornamental gardens include a collection of exotic lady's slippers from Russia and Manchuria. Robinson experiments in crossing native lady's slippers with their Asian counterparts, an activity that is already producing stunning, easy-to-grow hybrids that will become available (we ardently hope) sometime in the new millennium. [The nursery operates wholesale as of 2001].

Directions: Jacksonville is 10 miles southwest of Brattleboro. Call for directions.

Nearby attractions: The Vermont Ladyslipper Company, 56 Leduc Road, New Haven, VT 05472 (www.vtladyslipper.com), is an alternate source for lab-propagated hardy cypripediums. The Brattleboro Farmer's Market, Route 9 west of town, May through October, Saturday 9–2, is a source for superb farm-fresh vegetables, garden plants, handcrafts, and other farm products.

ROCKY DALE GARDENS

62 Rocky Dale Road (Route 116), Bristol, VT 05443
(802) 453-2782
Bill Pollard and Holly Weir

Unusual conifers. Native species. Trees and shrubs. Perennials. *Small specialty garden center. Open April 1 to October 31, daily 9–6, closed Tuesday. Open by appointment the rest of the year. Catalog $2. No mail order. Display gardens. Guided garden walks Sunday at 10 A.M., June through September. E-mail: rockydll@together.net.*

Rocky Dale Gardens is an owner-run specialty nursery treasured by serious gardeners for its choice perennials, hard-to-find native plants, rare conifers, and unusual trees and shrubs. Owners Bill Pollard and Holly Weir are displaced Californians who have operated Rocky Dale since moving to northwestern Vermont in 1980. (Bill trained at a rare-plant nursery in California.) Rocky Dale Gardens is sited beside the owners' Victorian home in Bristol, on property that backs onto the quartzite outcroppings of Lincoln Mountain; its rich soil derives from the area's ancient history as a river valley.

Despite its small size, Rocky Dale carries an exceptional range of enticing plant material not readily found in regional nurseries and garden centers. Rare and unusual conifers—cavorting in strange shapes, splashed white or tinted blue or gold—occupy the parking lot island like an animated sculpture garden. Among them we once found a standard-form golden dwarf Hinoki cypress; a rare gold-tipped spruce; and several tree-form bird's-nest spruces of intense blue. Deciduous trees include a tropical-looking castor aralia; a locust called 'Twisty Baby' with weird irregular branches; and the dwarf green ash 'Leprechaun', with branches pruned to resemble a candelabra.

Rocky Dale offers classic ornamental trees, too, such as Eastern redbud, hardy catalpa, yellow dogwood, and the latest varieties of maple, beech, and flowering crab, tweaked by hybridizers to afford multiseasonal interest. We particularly admired 'Crimson Frost' birch, with exfoliating white bark and purple leaves, and a blazing shrub dogwood called 'Midwinter Fire', with red, orange and yellow stems.

Crossing all plant categories is a notable selection of native plants such as American hornbeam, witch hazel, swamp pink azalea, elderberry, bulrush, wood poppy, and a shiny native ground cover called twinleaf *(Jeffersonia diphylla)*. Wonders of the Orient include Asian jack-in-the-pulpit, variegated Japanese petasites, a huge ornamental rhubarb from China, and contorted flowering quince (billed as "one of those kinky and twisted bizarre plants that we love"). Among the woody shrubs were ghost bramble, fern-leaf buckthorn, dwarf arctic willow, golden raspberry (as a ground cover in shade, it seems crafted of sunlight), and lots of attractive rhododendrons, hydrangeas, and roses.

Rocky Dale offers hardy perennials in normal garden-center categories— daylily, hosta, iris, and other stalwarts of the perennial border—but little of its stock selection is ordinary. The more intriguing perennials betray, we suspect, an expert process of hunting down cutting-edge plants through horticultural contacts around the country. New on our visit were a pale pink cardinal flower; a turtlehead hybrid called 'Hot Lips'; a near-black daylily, 'Root Beer'; mandragora (last heard of in Shakespeare); and a blue-and-gray Asiatic bluebell that does not go dormant. Rocky Dale's collections of campanula, hosta, sedum, garden pinks (*Dianthus* spp.), and ornamental grasses are also impressive. Some classic perennials have been given new piquancy by an unusual color or texture: lamb's ears with gold foliage; catmint with pink flowers; a glossy pachysandra. Perennial herbs include hard-to-find ginseng and unusual ornamental thyme. Among the tiny alpines were pretty edelweiss, draba, and saxifrage. We were glad to see some new plants of regional origin, such as cranesbill geranium 'New Hampshire Purple' and iris hybrids from a local breeder.

Rocky Dale publishes a superior plant catalog, and the absence of mail order does little to reduce the nursery's popularity with gardeners from New England and beyond. Plant stock is organized in convenient groupings of conifers, deciduous trees and shrubs, perennials, annuals, herbs, and alpines. The nursery's stunning 3-acre display garden, lush even in August, is a master-piece of design deserving close inspection or, better yet, the guided tour conducted by the owners on Sunday morning.

A few perennials, such as hosta, are propa-gated at Rocky Dale, but most plants are bought in from superior outside sources. Although we generally prefer nursery-bred stock, nearly half of Rocky Dale's plants originate with local growers. Rocky Dale takes excellent care of its plants, and gets few if any complaints about tree and shrub transplant shock; even at the season's end, the large stock looks wonderful. In spring Rocky Dale offers good selections of unusual annuals and tender perennials (called "tenderennials" by a noted garden wag). Discounted plant sales begin in August and produce some remarkable bargains. During Vermont winters, Rocky Dale's owners— "tenderennials" themselves—split for California.

Directions: From Burlington, take Route 7 south to Bristol, then take Route 116 north (Rocky Dale Road); the garden center is 1.5 miles on your right.
From Route 89, take exit 12 onto Route 2A south. Turn left onto Route 116 south. Pass through several towns to the juncture of Route 17; Rocky Dale is 1.5 miles on your left.
Four-wheel-drive vehicles can take Route 89 to exit 10 and Route 100 south. Turn right onto Route 17 and cross the Lincoln Mountain gap (a dirt road, sometimes washed out). On the other side of the mountain, turn left onto Route 116. In 1.5 miles, the nursery is on your left.

Nearby attractions: Lincoln Mountain is traversed by challenging hiking trails. Green Mountain Trout Farm, Bristol (802-455-4488; 800-55-TROUT), offers catch-your-own rainbows and cob-smoked trout "raised on pure Vermont well water"; tours are held on Saturday. Famous for its gardens, the Basin Harbor Club, Route 22A, Vergennes, VT 05491 (802-475-2311; www.basinharbor.com), hosts an annual Flower Days Festival; a spring sale of unusual annuals; and a summerlong series of plant sales, garden tours, flower-arranging contests, and English high teas.

STANDING STONE PERENNIAL FARM

RFD 1, P.O. Box 83, 36 Johnson Hill Road, South Royalton, VT 05068
(802) 763-8243
Lynne Hall and David Brandau

Hardy field-grown perennials. Seedlings. Own-root roses. *Small organic perennial farm. Open mid-April to mid-September, daily 9–5, Sunday 10–4; closed Monday from July through September. Free catalog. No mail order. Volume discounts. Neolithic display gardens. Garden design services. Standing stones.*

Standing Stone Perennial Farm is a horticultural farm that grows classic garden perennials on a delightful old farmstead in central Vermont; its display gardens seem to have been designed by a neolithic farmer. Owners Lynne Hall and David Brandau are humorous intellectuals and self-taught horticulturists with a rich appreciation for the material culture of Stone Age Europe. Their organic farm/nursery, founded in the mid-1980s, is surrounded by some of the region's most intriguing display gardens.

Huge standing stones are placed throughout the perennial gardens, not just for ornament, but as calendrical and timekeeping devices; these are, in effect, prehistoric compasses and clocks. A rock-crafted sundial in the garden tells exact time. A leaning megalith is oriented to Polaris, the North Star. Such stellar alignments have been checked precisely by compass and adjusted for latitude. (Brandau, who has a graduate degree in the history of religion, assured us that the farm practices "no blood sacrifice except barbecued chicken wings.")

The owners began their horticultural career as vegetable farmers. They still attend the Norwich Farmers Market on Saturday morning, but now with perennial plants rather than potatoes. To make way for perennials, the vegetable beds were banished to the other side of the road "by agreement with the deer," says Brandau, which miraculously leave them alone. Perhaps the nursery's Buddha statues, feng shui garden alignment, and Tibetan prayer flags have as quieting an effect on animals as they do on humans. (The farm has no pacifist arrangements with woodchucks, however; according to the owners, "It's war.")

Standing Stone is an excellent source of ornamental perennials for New England gardens. An attractive catalog lists more than 650 robust perennials and own-root shrub roses. The plants are organically grown and, after spending at least one winter in the ground, completely hardy. The varieties selected are mostly proven classics with superior ornamental interest—plants you can really count on in the garden: hardy old-fashioned peonies such as 'Festiva Maxima' and 'Sarah Bernhardt'; mildew-resistant bee balm such as 'Marshall's Delight'; stalwart daylilies such as 'Mary Todd' and 'Bonnie Barbara Allen'; and hosta classics (an especially good value) such as 'Sum and Substance', 'Frances Williams', and *H. sieboldiana* 'Elegans'. The farm grows clematis, Siberian iris, bleeding hearts, bellflowers, and a populous tribe of phlox: garden phlox, meadow phlox, woodland phlox, creeping phlox, and wild sweet William. The color code extends to uncommon black hollyhocks and yellow monkshoods; we loved the little forget-me-nots in pink, blue, and white. Even the plant names evoke the summer cottage garden: sea holly, foxglove, poppy, and primrose.

Standing Stone grows native plants such as pink turtlehead, heliopsis (false sunflower), and helenium (sneezeweed), along with a good smattering of ornate grasses and ferns. Asian exotics include pink Japanese anemones and a double Japanese aster (*Kalimeris* spp.). Culinary and ornamental medicinal herbs are available: elecampane (a 6-foot yellow helenium), agastache (a lavender-flowered giant hyssop), five varieties of echinacea, and 10 kinds of creeping thyme. The garden's organic vigor is indicated by the resonant presence of bees, butterflies, and croaking bullfrogs.

The perennial plants at Standing Stone Perennial Farm are sold in big pots at reasonable prices; some, such as double feverfew, are offered in inexpensive flats in the spring. This is a terrific resource for gardeners seeking tried-and-true garden plants for cold situations. Visitors are welcome to consult photo albums showing the farm's perennials in flower and, if needed, pay a visit to its uniquely ornate outhouse.

No visitor should leave the nursery without viewing the megalithic circle across the road, past the diminutive bridge spanning a stock pond. This is the real thing, a small stone henge oriented to the spring equinox. Gardeners seeking their own standing stones can choose among the granite megaliths tilted against the wall in the parking lot: Each costs $20 if the owner can lift it into your car, $45 if he needs the tractor.

Directions: From I-89, take exit 2/Sharon to Route 14 north and cross Route 110 in South Royalton. In 1.8 miles, turn left into Royalton Village, cross the White River, and turn right at the T-intersection onto Back River Road. In 0.8 mile (crossing under I-89), bear right at the fork. The farm is at the next Y in the road: a red-trimmed white house with a big standing stone.

VERMONT DAYLILIES

Barr Hill Road, Greensboro, VT 05841
(802) 533-7155
Dave and Andrea Perham

Hardy field-grown daylilies. *Small specialty nursery. Open July 1 to Labor Day, Wednesday to Sunday noon–5, and by appointment. Free catalog. Mail order. Display beds. Visitors welcome.*

Vermont Daylilies is a small family-run nursery set on a hill in northern Vermont, specializing exclusively in hardy, field-grown daylilies. Since 1992, owners Dave and Andrea Perham have operated Vermont Daylilies out of a large plot in front of their home in the pretty town of Greensboro. The Perhams are self-confessed horticultural amateurs who "know nothing but daylilies." They began with a daylily collection purchased from Lewis and Nancy Hill, noted writers and hybridizers who live nearby, and still carry many original Hill hybrids. The nursery's collection has since expanded to encompass more than 400 named daylily hybrids. Colors span the daylily rainbow of red, pink, mango, gold, lime, lavender, orchid, purple, and burgundy. These may not be the latest high-style dazzlers, but for reliable performance in a cold climate, Vermont Daylilies' plants (which do include some ruffles, ribs, eyes, and bicolors) can still contribute to a beautiful garden.

What we like best about Vermont Daylilies is the toughness and vigor of its plants, sold at reasonable prices. (Overstock is offered on sale at just a few dollars a plant.) All daylilies are field-grown in a microclimate finger of intense cold (Zone 3) that also suffers wind exposure. The surviving plants can spend five or six days in a car, live in a pail of water for two weeks, and still transplant well into the garden. Buyers are given their choice of potted or field-grown plants, sold as double fan divisions. Mail order is available on a low-key basis, but many gardeners prefer to pick up plants at the nursery. A modest annual catalog presents a terse list of available daylilies; like other readers, we wish it were a bit more informative. A picture book is also kept at the nursery, but it is more fun to buy plants freshly dug during bloom season, so you know exactly what they look like and when they bloom.

The Vermont Daylilies display garden (also its growing bed) is open to visitors from July to Labor Day. This is a nearly perfect time to visit Vermont's Northeast Kingdom, whose towns retain the astringent charm of New England before the onset of suburban sprawl. The nursery is set between dairy farms at the base of the Barr Hill Nature Conservancy, and as a sideline sells antiques out of the barn.

Directions: From I-91/St. Johnsbury, take exit 21 onto Route 2 west. In West Danville, turn right onto Route 15 north. In Hardwick, take Route 16 north. In 4.6 miles, at Greensboro Bend, turn left at the nursery's sign. In 3 miles, at a T-junction, turn left and then immediately right at Willey's Store in Greensboro center; follow signs 1.5 miles to the nursery.

Nearby attractions: Craftsbury Common has one of the loveliest town greens in New England. Stone's Throw Gardens, East Craftsbury (802-586-2805), is a small nursery offering hardy roses, lilies, perennials, and flowering trees and shrubs; open May through August, Wednesday to Sunday 10–5. Enchanting display gardens surround its 1795 farmhouse, featuring climbing roses on old stone walls; an English tea garden; mown paths through meadows to a pond; and fields of colorful perennials against a backdrop of the Green Mountains.

VON TRAPP GREENHOUSES

208 Common Road, Waitsfield, VT 05673
(802) 496-4385
Sally and Toby Von Trapp

Annuals and perennials. Hanging baskets. *Specialty greenhouses. Open May through August: in May and June, Monday to Saturday 9–6, Sunday 10–4; in July, Monday to Saturday noon–5, Sunday noon–4. Call for hours in August. No catalog or mail order.*

Von Trapp Greenhouses is a family-owned nursery producing fresh greenhouse-grown annuals, perennials, and vegetable flats in spring and summer. Toby and Sally Von Trapp are adventurous nurserymen with a burgeoning stock of colorful ornamental plants. Their modern, well-ventilated greenhouses, located off the main road near the old common in Waitsfield, are popular with area gardeners and summer people; one gardener journeys from Cape Cod to load up with plants every spring.

Toby Von Trapp is descended from Baron Von Trapp, best known as the protagonist in *The Sound of Music,* who settled with his family nearby and founded the Trapp Family Lodge on 2,000 acres. (Locals still recall the days when convent-educated Maria had holy water founts installed in the lodge's guest rooms.) For nearly 20 years, Von Trapp Greenhouses has specialized in unusual flowering annuals and hanging baskets. The Von Trapps may not grow edelweiss, but if you are a container gardener, they are sure to have a few of your favorite things.

This is the perfect place to acquire summer color for northern gardens: lush hanging baskets, brilliant tuberous begonias, cascade petunias, and diverse ivy and zonal geraniums. A full supply of Proven Winners is on hand, along with other bright and durable container plants. The annuals included white nierembergia, brilliant-hued salpiglossis, and superior annual salvias such as clary sage, violet *Salvia viridis,* and sky blue *S. uliginosa.* Among the foliage accents we found *Plectranthus argenteus,* a silver-leaved Swedish ivy–relative providing an excellent anchor for containers and flower borders.

The Von Trapps grow everything themselves from seed and cuttings. Supplementing the annuals and hanging baskets are garden perennials in gallon pots and a good variety of short-season vegetable seedlings suited to Zone 4 conditions (including tiny currant tomatoes). The six-packs of annuals and vegetables come in biodegradable fiber packs that transplant well into northern gardens. The greenhouses are marvelously clean: We saw no weeds, no junk, no bugs, and a responsible pest management policy that favors biological controls. Visitors have access to beautiful display gardens situated between the greenhouses and the Von Trapps' home; be sure to admire the spectacular views over alpine meadows to some of the highest peaks in the Green Mountains.

Directions: Waitsfield is in north-central Vermont. Take Route 89 to exit 10 and turn onto Route 100 south. In Waitsfield, before the village, turn left onto Tremblay Road (signposted). Turn right at the T-junction, and go up the hill. At a triangular intersection, cross onto Common Road (off the paved road); the greenhouses are down the avenue of trees, 0.25 mile on your right.

Nearby attractions: The Warren Store in Warren, south of Waitsfield (802-496-3864), is a chic country store with a superior deli; outside picnic tables are sited on a deck overlooking Mad River gorge.

WALKER FARM GARDEN

RD 2, P.O. Box 556, Route 5, Putney, VT 05346
(802) 254-2051; fax (802) 254-1173
Jack and Karen Manix

Perennials. Annuals and container plants. Vegetable flats. *Open mid-April to Thanksgiving, 10–6 daily. Free plant list and newsletter. No mail order. E-mail: jacmanix@sover.net. Web site: www.walkerfarm.com.*

Located on a rural highway just north of Brattleboro, Walker Farm Garden is a roadside farm stand turned serious. A decade ago, Walker Farm sold flats of pansies to passersby out of an unattended farm stand, on the honor system. Now this once simple farm stand operates from a weathervane-capped wooden barn, where visitors can pull off the road for garden supplies, fresh produce, and an incredible trove of garden and container plants. An old sugarhouse brims with garden pots; some 20 outdoor tables are filled with unusual hardy perennials. The foremost greenhouse contains a striking assembly of annual and container plants. A black-and-white fuel tank is wittily painted to mimic a Vermont cow garden ornament. Extensive plant lists are available for annuals, perennials, specialty plants, and vegetables. Some farm stand!

Walker Farm Garden is basically a horticultural farm specializing in ornamental garden plants. Owners Jack and Karen Manix admit to getting "a little wacky every winter" doing their horticultural homework. The farm's selections get better every year, and customers now include Vermont's most noted garden writers, Wayne Winterrood and Jamaica Kincaid. Walker Farm offers some 1,400 varieties of annuals and perennials—an impressive range for a rural farm nursery. Growing fields, plastic greenhouses, and distant blue hills form the backdrop to this interesting source for sophisticated ornamental plants.

The Manixes' venturesome interest in horticulture is most evident in the perennial yard, where we found uncommon alpines, choice perennials, an expanding vine collection, and a wide range of ornamental grasses. Some delightful surprises were white flax, variegated wall germander, and wine red New Zealand lavender. Many variegated and unusual foliage plants are included in both the annual and perennial collections. Walker Farm grows most of its plants from seed or cuttings; some are brought in from The Plant Group and Sunny Border Nursery, prime regional wholesalers of distinctive perennials. Fine shrubs and alpine troughs are brought in from Pride's Corner Farm, a quality wholesaler in Connecticut.

Besides perennials, Walker Farm Garden grows an expanding list of annuals from seed. Mixed among the petunias and impatiens we found good zinnias, snapdragons, marigolds, nasturtiums, African daisies, and a whole table filled with tropical exotics. Walker Farm's overwintered pansies and violas remain popular, as do its exceptional zonal and ivy geraniums (*Pelargonium* spp.). Fancy annuals include yellow cosmos, Chinese forget-me-not, angel's-trumpets, flowering tobacco, night-blooming phlox, dahlias, and a few oddities such as peanut butter plant and shoofly plant.

Walker Farm has special collections of container plants—plectranthus, coleus, and unusual ivy, for example. We scooped up the purple velour *Gynura aurantiaca* and beet red *Iresine herbstii*, even though they were unlabeled (an occasional problem at this nursery). Exact horticultural names can be determined by checking the stock plant or consulting the garden books handily displayed on an old farm cart near the cash register—not for sale, but as an informal reference library for customers. Visitors should also check out the farm's heirloom tomato seedlings and organically grown herb and vegetable flats in spring, and cut flowers and fresh vegetables all summer.

Directions: From I-91 north, take exit 3 and go left at the lights onto Route 5 north; Walker Farm is 4 miles on your right.
From I-91 south, take exit 4 and turn left at the ramp onto Route 5 south; Walker Farm is 4 miles on your left.

Nearby attractions: Grafton Village Nursery (802-843-2442) is a tiny preorder greenhouse that buys in seedlings and has them ready by Memorial Day; it can tend them in your absence. Grafton Village Cheese Company, Grafton (800-472-3866; www.graftonvillagecheese.com), sells outstanding Vermont cheddar; its award-winning Classic Reserve Cheddar is so sharp that it makes your mouth itch. Dan Snow (802-254-2673) is a noted dry stone wall builder in Dummerston. In mid-July, the Yellow Barn Garden Tour takes place in Putney, combining self-guided private garden tours with chamber music concerts to benefit the Yellow Barn Music School, Main Street, Putney, VT 05346 (802-387-6637).

WINDHAM WILDFLOWERS

P.O. Box 207, Westminster Station, VT 05159
(802) 387–4096 and (603) 464–3935
Ruth Vroman Gorius

Natural wildflower seed. Catalog on web site. Mail order. No visiting hours. CD-ROM pictorial plant encyclopedia. Web site: www.flowerseeds.com.

Windham Wildflowers sells all–natural wildflower seed grown in the Vermont garden of Ruth Vroman Gorius, an experienced old-timer, formerly of Putney Nursery. Gorius says she began selling wildflower seed as "my answer to the many exotic wild plants Vermont would not allow us to mail." The nursery's brief "old tyme catalog" lists seed for 144 native wildflowers (for sun and shade), hybrid perennials, and alpines. Native seeds include jack–in–the–pulpit, wild leek, wild bergamot, shooting star, Bowman's-root, blue cohosh, and wild sarsaparilla, as well as many common meadow plants beloved of wildlife. Alpines include edelweiss, alpine poppy, sea pink, and a saxifrage mix.

Windham Wildflowers' seed is sold by mail or through the Web site; many varieties are unobtainable from commercial seed sources. Seed is sold in individual packets or by the ounce (enough to cover 60 square feet). The nursery concocts unique seed mixtures for perennial wildflowers, cut flowers, butterfly and hummingbird attractants, and woodland perennials native to New England.

A CD-ROM pictorial encyclopedia of 100 wildflowers is produced by the nursery. Seed orders are accompanied by homey wisdom from Ruth Gorius, including her endorsement of "scarecrows and cats" as effective plant guardians.

Nearby attractions: Alternative sources for mail-order seed in Vermont are High Mowing Organic Seed Farm, RR 1, Box 95, Derby Line, VT 05830 (802-895-4696)(heirloom and open-pollinated vegetable seed), and Le Jardin de Gourmet, P.O. Box 75, St. Johnsbury Center, VT 05863 (802-748-1446)(flower, vegetable, and herb seed; shallot bulbs). The Vermont Wildflower Farm, P.O. Box 6, Charlotte, VT 05445 (800-424-1165) keeps a signposted wildflower meadow on Route 7 in Charlotte (visitors welcome); despite its name, this seed house is affiliated with a large horticultural enterprise in Missouri and its seed orders processed by a call center in Peoria, Illinois.

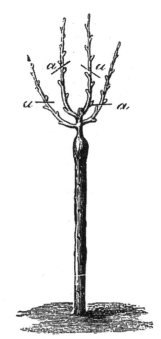

SECOND YEAR'S PRUNING OF STANDARD
WITH TWO SHOOTS.

INDEX
TO
PLANT SOURCES

INDEX TO PLANT SOURCES

Based on our far-flung travels and voracious catalog consumption, we offer some conclusions about where we think gardeners can find good plants in New England. The present index is intended to help you locate particular plants for your garden. These source lists refer only to the nurseries, garden centers, and hybridizers profiled in this book; it goes without saying that other good sources exist, both inside and outside New England.

 The source recommendations below are organized by plant name and category (such as Roses or Perennials), specialized plants (such as Seacoast Plants and Cold-Hardy Plants), and useful nursery amenities (such as Display Gardens and Organic Growers). For ready reference, each entry refers to the state chapter (such as (MA) for Massachusetts) where nursery portraits appear in alphabetical order; the same device is used in the text where nurseries are cross-referenced. We have placed a star (★) next to those offering something exceptional in each category. The sources listed here are, of course, located in New England, and generally produce plants that are well suited to the climatic and cultural conditions of the region.

AFRICAN VIOLETS
Cape Cod Violetry, *Falmouth, MA*★
Werner's Picket Mountain Farm, *Newfield, ME*

ALPINE AND ROCK-GARDEN PLANTS
Avant Gardens, *North Dartmouth, MA*★
Ashley Falls Nursery, *Ashley Falls, MA*
Beardsley Gardens, *Sharon, CT*
Cady's Falls Nursery, *Morrisville, VT*★
Comstock, Ferre & Co., *Old Wethersfield, CT*★
The Fells Nursery, *Newbury, NH*
Gregg Hill Gardens, *Waterbury Center, VT*
Hermit Medlars Walk, *Foxborough, MA*
HillBilly Acres, *Scituate, MA*
Little Siberia Perennials, *Granville, VT*★
Mainescape Garden Shop, *Blue Hill, ME*
Oliver Nurseries, *Fairfield, CT*★
Stone Soup Farm, *Monroe, ME*
Tripple Brook Farm, *Southampton, MA*
Twombly Nursery, *Monroe, CT*★
Walker Farm Garden, *Putney, VT*

ANNUALS AND TENDER PERENNIALS
Andrew's Greenhouse, *Amherst, MA*★
Avant Gardens, *North Dartmouth, MA*★
Beardsley Gardens, *Sharon, CT*
Blue Meadow Farm, *Montague, MA*★
Bodacious Blossoms, *Chocorua, NH*
Conway's Nursery, *Tiverton, RI*★
Edgewater Farm, *Plainfield, NH*★
Everlasting Farm, *Bangor, ME*★
Gaskill's Garden Shop and Nursery, *Provincetown, MA*
Green Mountain Transplants, Inc., *East Montpelier, VT*★
Gregg Hill Gardens, *Waterbury Center, VT*
Hedgehog Hill Farm, *East Sumner, ME*
HillBilly Acres, *Scituate, MA*★
Lake Street Garden Center, *Salem, NH*
Lauray of Salisbury, *Salisbury, CT*
Logee's Greenhouses, *Danielson, CT*★
Mainescape Garden Shop, *Blue Hill, ME*
Meredith Country Gardens, *Moultonboro, NH*
Murray Farms, *Penacook, NH*
North Creek Farm, *Phippsburg, ME*
Old Farm Nursery, *Lakeville, CT*
Peckham's Greenhouse, *Little Compton, RI*
Rocky Dale Gardens, *Bristol, VT*
Shady Gate Gardens, *Mill River, MA*★
Spider Web Gardens, *Center Tuftonboro, NH*
Stonehedge Gardens, *Charlton, MA*★
Umbrella Factory Gardens, *Charlestown, RI*★
Von Trapp Greenhouses, *Waitsfield, VT*★
Walker Farm Garden, *Putney, VT*★
Wayside Farm, *North Sandwich, NH*★

APPLE TREES
See "Fruit Plants and Trees"

AQUATIC AND WATER-GARDEN PLANTS
Beardsley Gardens, *Sharon, CT*
Cady's Falls Nursery, *Morrisville, VT*
Conway's Nursery, *Tiverton, RI*
Hardwicke Gardens, *Westborough, MA*★
HillBilly Acres, *Scituate, MA*
New England Wetland Plants, *Amherst, MA*★
O'Donal's Nurseries, *Gorham, ME*
Paradise Water Gardens, *Whitman, MA*★
Tripple Brook Farm, *Southampton, MA*

AZALEAS
See "Rhododendrons and Azaleas"

BAMBOO
Allen C. Haskell Horticulturists, *New Bedford, MA*
Burt Associates Bamboo, *Westford, MA*★
New England Bamboo Company, *Rockport, MA*★
Tripple Brook Farm, *Southampton, MA*★
The Variegated Foliage Nursery, *Eastford, CT*

BEGONIAS
Everlasting Farm, *Bangor, ME*
Lauray of Salisbury, *Salisbury, CT*★
Logee's Greenhouses, *Danielson, CT*★
Peckham's Greenhouse, *Little Compton, RI*
Werner's Picket Mountain Farm, *Newfield, ME*
White Flower Farm, *Litchfield, CT*

BONSAI
Cady's Falls Nursery, *Morrisville, VT*
Shanti Bithi Nursery, *North Stamford, CT*★

BULBS
The Daffodil Mart, *Torrington, CT*★
Fedco, *Waterville, ME*★
John Scheepers, Inc., *Bantam, CT*
Pleasant Valley Glads and Dahlias, *Agawam, MA*★
Schipper & Co., *Greenwich, CT*
Van Engelen, Inc., *Bantam, CT*★
White Flower Farm, *Litchfield, CT*

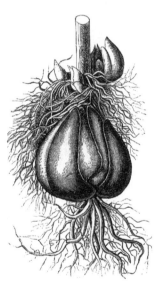

CACTUS
Lauray of Salisbury, *Salisbury, CT*★
Stonehedge Gardens, *Charlton, MA*
Tripple Brook Farm, *Southampton, MA*
Walnut Hill Greenhouse, *Litchfield, CT*★

CAMELLIA
Logee's Greenhouses, *Danielson, CT*
Lyman Estate Greenhouses, *Waltham, MA*

CHRISTMAS GREENS AND PLANTS
Allen C. Haskell Horticulturists, *New Bedford, MA*
Around the Bend Nursery, *Lakeville, MA*★
Edgewater Farm, *Plainfield, NH*
Hedgehog Hill Farm, *East Sumner, ME*★
Horsford Gardens and Nursery, *Charlotte, VT*

Mahoney's Garden Centers, *Winchester, MA*★
Murray Farms, *Penacook, NH*
O'Donal's Nurseries, *Gorham, ME*
Schartner Farms, *Exeter, RI*
Steeplebush Farm Herbs, *Limington, ME*
Stonehedge Gardens, *Charlton, MA*
Stone Soup Farm, *Monroe, ME*
Werner's Picket Mountain Farm, *Newfield, ME*

CHRYSANTHEMUMS
Bristol Mums, *Bristol, CT*★

CITRUS TREES
Allen C. Haskell Horticulturists, *New Bedford, MA*
Logee's Greenhouses, *Danielson, CT*
Lyman Estate Greenhouses, *Waltham, MA*

CLEMATIS
Bay State Perennial Farm, *Whately, MA*
Cady's Falls Nursery, *Morrisville, VT*
Completely Clematis Specialty Nursery, *Ipswich, MA*★
Standing Stone Perennial Farm, *South Royalton, VT*
White Flower Farm, *Litchfield, CT*

CLIMBING PLANTS
See "Vines and Climbing Plants"

COLD-HARDY (ZONE 3-4) PLANTS
Cady's Falls Nursery, *Morrisville, VT*★
Fernwood, *Swanville, ME*
Fieldstone Gardens, *Vassalboro, ME*★
Garden in the Woods Nursery, *Framingham, MA*
Hidden Gardens, *Searsport, ME*★
Labor of Love Landscaping and Nursery, *Barton, VT*★
Little Siberia Perennials, *Granville, VT*★
Perennial Pleasures Nursery, *East Hardwick, VT*
Perennials Preferred Nursery, *Waldoboro, ME*★
Snow Brook Gardens, *Parkman, ME*
Standing Stone Perennial Farm, *South Royalton, VT*
Uncanoonuc Mt. Perennials, *Goffstown, NH*
Valente Gardens, *North Berwick, ME*

COLEUS
Avant Gardens, *North Dartmouth, MA*
Blue Meadow Farm, *Montague, MA*★
Conway's Nursery, *Tiverton, RI*★
Edgewater Farm, *Plainfield, NH*

HillBilly Acres, *Scituate, MA*
Logee's Greenhouses, *Danielson, CT*
Stonehedge Gardens, *Carlton, MA*
Walker Farm Garden, *Putney, VT*
Wayside Farm, *North Sandwich, NH*

CONIFERS—TREES AND SHRUBS
Allen C. Haskell Horticulturists, *New Bedford, MA*
Broken Arrow Nursery, *Hamden, CT*★
Cady's Falls Nursery, *Morrisville, VT*★
Conway's Nursery, *Tiverton, RI*
O'Donal's Nurseries, *Gorham, ME*★
Old Farm Nursery, *Lakeville, CT*
Oliver Nurseries, *Fairfield, CT*★
Rock Spray Nursery, *Truro, MA*
Rocky Dale Gardens, *Bristol, VT*★
Schartner Farms, *Exeter, RI*
Sylvan Nursery, *Westport, MA*★
Twombly Nursery, *Monroe, CT*★
Weston Nurseries, *Hopkinton, MA*

CONSERVATORY PLANTS
See "Houseplants" and "Tropical and Conservatory Plants"

CONTAINER PLANTS
Allen C. Haskell Horticulturists, *New Bedford, MA*
Andrew's Greenhouse, *Amherst, MA*★
Avant Gardens, *North Dartmouth, MA*★
Blue Meadow Farm, *Montague, MA*★
Conway's Nursery, *Tiverton, RI*★
Edgewater Farm, *Plainfield, NH*★
Everlasting Farm, *Bangor, ME*★
Gaskill's Garden Shop and Nursery, *Provincetown, MA*
Gingerbread Farm Perennials, *Wayne, ME*★
Gregg Hill Gardens, *Waterbury Center, VT*★
HillBilly Acres, *Scituate, MA*★
Lake Street Garden Center, *Salem, NH*★
Lauray of Salisbury, *Salisbury, CT*
Logee's Greenhouses, *Danielson, CT*
Meredith Country Gardens, *Moultonboro, NH*
Murray Farms, *Penacook, NH*
North Creek Farm, *Phippsburg, ME*
Peckham's Greenhouse, *Little Compton, RI*
Rocky Dale Gardens, *Bristol, VT*★
Rolling Green Nursery, *Greenland, NH*
Shady Gate Gardens, *Mill River, MA*★
Spider Web Gardens, *Center Tuftonboro, NH*

BOSTON FERN.

278

Umbrella Factory Gardens, *Charlestown, RI*★
Von Trapp Greenhouses, *Waitsfield, VT*★
Walker Farm Garden, *Putney, VT*★
Walnut Hill Greenhouse, *Litchfield, CT*
Wayside Farm, *North Sandwich, NH*★
Werner's Picket Mountain Farm, *Newfield, ME*
White Flower Farm, *Litchfield, CT*

DAFFODIL BULBS (NARCISSUS)
The Daffodil Mart, *Torrington, CT*★
John Scheepers, Inc., *Bantam, CT*
Schipper & Co., *Greenwich, CT*
Van Engelen, Inc., *Bantam, CT*★

DAHLIAS
Fedco, *Waterville, ME*
Green Mountain Transplants, Inc., *East Montpelier, VT*
HillBilly Acres, *Scituate, MA*
Pleasant Valley Glads and Dahlias, *Agawam, MA*★

DAYLILIES (HEMEROCALLIS)
Barth Daylilies, *Alna, ME*★
Bloomingfields Farm, *Gaylordsville, CT*★
Hedgehog Hill Farm, *East Sumner, ME*
Meredith Country Gardens, *Moultonboro, NH*★
Olallie Daylily Gardens, *South Newfane, VT*★
Perennials From Susan, *Amherst, NH*
Plainview Farm Fine Perennials, *North Yarmouth, ME*
Rock Oak Gardens, *Gray, ME*★
Rocky Dale Gardens, *Bristol, VT*
R. Seawright, *Carlisle, MA*★
Standing Stone Perennial Farm, *South Royalton, VT*
Stone Soup Farm, *Monroe, ME*
Sunnyside Gardens, *Turner, ME*
Tranquil Lake Nursery, *Rehoboth, MA*★
Umbrella Factory Gardens, *Charlestown, RI*
Uncanoonuc Mt. Perennials, *Goffstown, NH*
Valente Gardens, *North Berwick, ME*★
Vermont Daylilies, *Greensboro, VT*★
Wayside Farm, *North Sandwich, NH*
White Flower Farm, *Litchfield, CT*

DISPLAY GARDENS—BOTANICAL
Broken Arrow Nursery, *Hamden, CT*
Garden in the Woods Nursery, *Framingham, MA*★
Logee's Greenhouses, *Danielson, CT*
Perennials Preferred Nursery, *Waldoboro, ME*

Tower Hill Botanic Garden, *Boylston, MA*★
Tripple Brook Farm, *Southampton, MA*

DISPLAY GARDENS—ORNAMENTAL
Allen C. Haskell Horticulturists, *New Bedford, MA*★
Ashley Falls Nursery, *Ashley Falls, MA*
Cady's Falls Nursery, *Morrisville, VT*★
Gregg Hill Gardens, *Waterbury Center, VT*
Hillside Gardens, *Norfolk, CT*★
Kathleen Nelson Perennials, *Gaylordsville, CT*★
Kinney Azalea Gardens, *Kingston, RI*★
Newbury Perennial Gardens, *Byfield, MA*★
Plainview Farm Fine Perennials, *North Yarmouth, ME*★
Resourceful Judith Designs, *Woodstock, CT*★
Rocky Dale Gardens, *Bristol, VT*★
Standing Stone Perennial Farm, *South Royalton, VT*★
Stone Soup Farm, *Monroe, ME*
Sunnyside Gardens, *Turner, ME*
Twombly Nursery, *Monroe, CT*★
Uncanoonuc Mt. Perennials, *Goffstown, NH*

EPIMEDIUM
Avant Gardens, *North Dartmouth, MA*
Blanchette Gardens, *Carlisle, MA*
Garden Vision, *Hubbardston, MA*★
Twombly Nursery, *Monroe, CT*
Underwood Shade Nursery, *North Attleboro, MA*

EVERGREENS
See "Conifers—Trees and Shrubs" and "Shrubs—
Broadleaf Evergreen"

EVERLASTINGS (DRYING FLOWERS)
Gregg Hill Gardens, *Waterbury Center, VT*
Hedgehog Hill Farm, *East Sumner, ME*★
Perennial Pleasures Nursery, *East Hardwick, VT*
Stone Soup Farm, *Monroe, ME*

FERNS
Bay State Perennial Farm, *Whately, MA*
Beardsley Gardens, *Sharon, CT*
Blanchette Gardens, *Carlisle, MA*
Cady's Falls Nursery, *Morrisville, VT*
Fernwood, *Swanville, ME*★
Garden in the Woods Nursery, *Framingham, MA*
Hedgehog Hill Farm, *East Sumner, ME*
Kathleen Nelson Perennials, *Gaylordsville, CT*

Logee's Greenhouses, *Danielson, CT*
New England Bamboo Company, *Rockport, MA*★
Plainview Farm Fine Perennials, *North Yarmouth, ME*
Underwood Shade Nursery, *North Attleboro, MA*★
Weston Nurseries, *Hopkinton, MA*
White Flower Farm, *Litchfield, CT*

FRAGRANT PLANTS
Logee's Greenhouses, *Danielson, CT*
Perennial Pleasures Nursery, *East Hardwick, VT*★
Select Seeds, *Union, CT*
Shepherd's Garden Seeds, *Torrington, CT*

FRUIT PLANTS AND TREES
Elmore Roots, *Wolcott, VT*★
Fedco, *Waterville, ME*★
Green Mountain Transplants, Inc., *East Montpelier, VT*
Hedgehog Hill Farm, *East Sumner, ME*
Hunting Hills Farm, *Montague, MA*
Logee's Greenhouses, *Danielson, CT* (citrus)
Meredith Country Gardens, *Moultonboro, NH*
Nourse Farms, *South Deerfield, MA*★
O'Donal's Nurseries, *Gorham, ME*★
Peckham's Greenhouse, *Little Compton, RI*
Rolling Green Nursery, *Greenland, NH*
Roseland Nursery, *Acushnet, MA*★
Tower Hill Botanic Garden, *Boylston, MA* (apple scions)★
Twombly Nursery, *Monroe, CT*
Walter K. Morss & Son, *Boxford, MA*★

GERANIUMS (CRANESBILLS)
Avant Gardens, *North Dartmouth, MA*★
Bay State Perennial Farm, *Whately, MA*
Blue Meadow Farm, *Montague, MA*
Hedgehog Hill Farm, *East Sumner, ME*
Hillside Gardens, *Norfolk, CT*
Mahoney's Garden Centers, *Winchester, MA*
Peckham's Greenhouse, *Little Compton, RI*
Plainview Farm Fine Perennials, *North Yarmouth, ME*
Rocky Dale Gardens, *Bristol, VT*★
Stone Soup Farm, *Monroe, ME*
Underwood Shade Nursery, *North Attleboro, MA*

GERANIUMS (PELARGONIUMS)
Avant Gardens, *North Dartmouth, MA*
Blue Meadow Farm, *Montague, MA*
Edgewater Farm, *Plainfield, NH*★

Everlasting Farm, *Bangor, ME*
Green Mountain Transplants, Inc., *East Montpelier, VT★*
HillBilly Acres, *Scituate, MA*
Logee's Greenhouses, *Danielson, CT*
Mahoney's Garden Centers, *Winchester, MA*
Meredith Country Gardens, *Moultonboro, NH★*
Murray Farms, *Penacook, NH*
Peckham's Greenhouse, *Little Compton, RI★*
Umbrella Factory Gardens, *Charlestown, RI★*
Walker Farm Garden, *Putney, VT*
Werner's Picket Mountain Farm, *Newfield, ME*

GLADIOLUS
Fedco, *Waterville, ME*
Pleasant Valley Glads and Dahlias, *Agawam, MA★*

GRASSES
Allen C. Haskell Horticulturists, *New Bedford, MA*
Avant Gardens, *North Dartmouth, MA*
Bay State Perennial Farm, *Whately, MA*
Beardsley Gardens, *Sharon, CT★*
Blue Meadow Farm, *Montague, MA*
Cady's Falls Nursery, *Morrisville, VT*
Fernwood, *Swanville, ME*
Garden in the Woods Nursery, *Framingham, MA*
Green Mountain Transplants, Inc., *East Montpelier, VT*
Kathleen Nelson Perennials, *Gaylordsville, CT*
Mahoney's Garden Centers, *Winchester, MA★*
New England Bamboo Company, *Rockport, MA★*
Plainview Farm Fine Perennials, *North Yarmouth, ME*
Rocky Dale Gardens, *Bristol, VT*
Tripple Brook Farm, *Southampton, MA*
Walker Farm Garden, *Putney, VT*
Weston Nurseries, *Hopkinton, MA★*

GROUND COVER PLANTS
Allen C. Haskell Horticulturists, *New Bedford, MA*
Ashley Falls Nursery, *Ashley Falls, MA*
Avant Gardens, *North Dartmouth, MA*
Beardsley Gardens, *Sharon, CT*
Broken Arrow Nursery, *Hamden, CT*
The Fells Nursery, *Newbury, NH*
Fernwood, *Swanville, ME*
Garden in the Woods Nursery, *Framingham, MA*
Hillside Gardens, *Norfolk, CT★*
Kathleen Nelson Perennials, *Gaylordsville, CT*
Lake Street Garden Center, *Salem, NH*

Mainescape Garden Shop, *Blue Hill, ME* (sods)
Perennials From Susan, *Amherst, NH*★
Plainview Farm Fine Perennials, *North Yarmouth, ME*★
Rocky Dale Gardens, *Bristol, VT*
Rolling Green Nursery, *Greenland, NH*
Sylvan Nursery, *Westport, MA* (sods)★
Tripple Brook Farm, *Southampton, MA*
Twombly Nursery, *Monroe, CT*★
Underwood Shade Nursery, *North Attleboro, MA*★
The Variegated Foliage Nursery, *Eastford, CT*
Weston Nurseries, *Hopkinton, MA*★

HANGING BASKETS
See "Container Plants"

HEATH AND HEATHER
Cady's Falls Nursery, *Morrisville, VT*
Gregg Hill Gardens, *Waterbury Center, VT*
Hedgehog Hill Farm, *East Sumner, ME*
Little Siberia Perennials, *Granville, VT*★
Rock Spray Nursery, *Truro, MA*★
Sylvan Nursery, *Westport, MA*★
Waquoit Heather Nursery, *Waquoit (Falmouth), MA*★

HEIRLOOM PLANTS
The Daffodil Mart, *Torrington, CT*
Fedco, *Waterville, ME*
Logee's Greenhouses, *Danielson, CT*★
Old Sturbridge Village, *Sturbridge, MA*★
Perennial Pleasures Nursery, *East Hardwick, VT*★
Resourceful Judith Designs, *Woodstock, CT*
The Roseraie at Bayfields, *Waldoboro, ME*
Select Seeds, *Union, CT*★
Shepherd's Garden Seeds, *Torrington, CT*
Tower Hill Botanic Garden, *Boylston, MA*

HERBS
Andrew's Greenhouse, *Amherst, MA*
Bay State Perennial Farm, *Whately, MA*
Bodacious Blossoms, *Chocorua, NH*★
Edgewater Farm, *Plainfield, NH*
Fedco, *Waterville, ME*
Gilbertie's Herb Gardens, Inc., *Westport, CT*★
Green Mountain Transplants, Inc., *East Montpelier, VT*
Hedgehog Hill Farm, *East Sumner, ME*
Logee's Greenhouses, *Danielson, CT*★
Lyman Estate Greenhouses, *Waltham, MA*

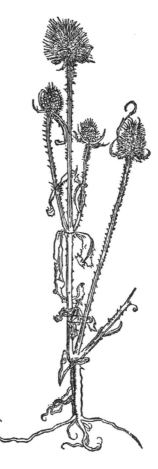

Meadowbrook Herb Garden, *Wyoming, RI★*
Meredith Country Gardens, *Moultonboro, NH*
Old Sturbridge Village, *Sturbridge, MA*
Perennial Pleasures Nursery, *East Hardwick, VT*
Shepherd's Garden Seeds, *Torrington, CT*
Standing Stone Perennial Farm, *South Royalton, VT*
Steeplebush Farm, *Limington, ME★*
Stone Soup Farm, *Monroe, ME*

HOLLY
See "Shrubs—Broadleaf Evergreen"

HOSTAS
Allen C. Haskell Horticulturists, *New Bedford, MA★*
Avant Gardens, *North Dartmouth, MA*
Bay State Perennial Farm, *Whately, MA*
Blanchette Gardens, *Carlisle, MA★*
Cady's Falls Nursery, *Morrisville, VT*
Fernwood, *Swanville, ME★*
Hedgehog Hill Farm, *East Sumner, ME*
Hillside Gardens, *Norfolk, CT★*
Kathleen Nelson Perennials, *Gaylordsville, CT*
Lyman Estate Greenhouses, *Waltham, MA*
Perennials From Susan, *Amherst, NH*
Plainview Farm Fine Perennials, *North Yarmouth, ME*
Rocky Dale Gardens, *Bristol, VT*
R. Seawright, *Carlisle, MA★*
Standing Stone Perennial Farm, *South Royalton, VT*
Valente Gardens, *North Berwick, ME*
The Variegated Foliage Nursery, *Eastford, CT★*

HOUSEPLANTS
Avant Gardens, *North Dartmouth, MA*
Blue Meadow Farm, *Montague, MA*
HillBilly Acres, *Scituate, MA*
Lauray of Salisbury, *Salisbury, CT★*
Logee's Greenhouses, *Danielson, CT★*
Lyman Estate Greenhouses, *Waltham, MA*
Peckham's Greenhouse, *Little Compton, RI★*
Spider Web Gardens, *Center Tuftonboro, NH*
Stonehedge Gardens, *Charlton, MA★*
Walnut Hill Greenhouse, *Litchfield, CT★*
Werner's Picket Mountain Farm, *Newfield, ME*

HYBRIDIZERS
Barth Daylilies, *Alna, ME* (daylily)
Blanchette Gardens, *Carlisle, MA* (astilbe)

Broken Arrow Nursery, *Hamden, CT* (mountain laurel) ★
Cape Cod Violetry, *Falmouth, MA* (African violet)
Eartheart Gardens, *South Harpswell, ME* (iris)
Fernwood, *Swanville, ME* (hosta) ★
Garden Vision, *Hubbardston, MA* (epimedium) ★
Hermit Medlar's Walk, *Foxborough, MA* (iris) ★
Joe Pye Weed's Garden, *Carlisle, MA* (iris)
Kinney Azalea Gardens, *Kingston, RI* (azalea)
Logee's Greenhouses, *Danielson, CT* (passionflower)
Rock Oak Gardens, *Gray, ME* (daylily) ★
R. Seawright, *Carlisle, MA* (daylily) ★
Valente Gardens, *North Berwick, ME* (daylily) ★
Weston Nurseries, *Hopkinton, MA* (rhododendron and azalea)

IRIS
Eartheart Gardens, *South Harpswell, ME*★
Hedgehog Hill Farm, *East Sumner, ME*
Hermit Medlars Walk, *Foxborough, MA*★
Joe Pye Weed's Garden, *Carlisle, MA*★
Perennials From Susan, *Amherst, NH*
Snow Brook Gardens, *Parkman, ME*
Tranquil Lake Nursery, *Rehoboth, MA*★
White Flower Farm, *Litchfield, CT*

KALMIA
See "Mountain Laurel"

LADY'S SLIPPERS—HARDY
Cady's Falls Nursery, *Morrisville, VT*
Fernwood, *Swanville, ME*
Raising Rarities, *Jacksonville, VT*★

LILACS
Broken Arrow Nursery, *Hamden, CT*
Elmore Roots, *Wolcott, VT*★
Fedco, *Waterville, ME*★
Fox Hill Nursery, *Freeport, ME*★
Hedgehog Hill Farm, *East Sumner, ME*
Horsford Gardens and Nursery, *Charlotte, VT*★
Old Farm Nursery, *Lakeville, CT*
Rolling Green Nursery, *Greenland, NH*
Twombly Nursery, *Monroe, CT*
The Great Plant Company, *New Hartford, CT*
The Variegated Foliage Nursery, *Eastford, CT*
Weston Nurseries, *Hopkinton, MA*

LILIES
(For Hemerocallis, see "Daylilies")
Bay State Perennial Farm, *Whately, MA*
The Daffodil Mart, *Torrington, CT*
Hedgehog Hill Farm, *East Sumner, ME*
John Scheepers, Inc., *Bantam, CT*
North Creek Farm, *Phippsburg, ME*
Stone Soup Farm, *Monroe, ME*★
Underwood Shade Nursery, *North Attleboro, MA*
Van Engelen, Inc., *Bantam, CT*
White Flower Farm, *Litchfield, CT*★

MOUNTAIN LAUREL (KALMIA)
Broken Arrow Nursery, *Hamden, CT*★
KinneyAzalea Gardens, *Kingston, RI*
Oliver Nurseries, *Fairfield, CT*★
Twombly Nursery, *Monroe, CT*★
Weston Nurseries, *Hopkinton, MA*★

NARCISSUS
See "Daffodil Bulbs"

NATIVE PLANT SEEDS
Fedco, *Waterville, ME*
Garden in the Woods Nursery, *Framingham, MA*★
Johnny's Selected Seeds, *Albion, ME*★
F.W. Schumacher Co., *Sandwich, MA*★
Windham Wildflowers, *Westminster Station, VT*★

NATIVE PLANTS AND WILDFLOWERS
Bay State Perennial Farm, *Whately, MA*
Blanchette Gardens, *Carlisle, MA*
Blisscapes Nursery and Wildlife Sanctuary, *South Dartmouth, MA*★
Broken Arrow Nursery, *Hamden, CT*★
Cady's Falls Nursery, *Morrisville, VT*
Fedco, *Waterville, ME*
The Fells Estate Nursery, *Newbury, NH*
Fernwood, *Swanville, ME*
Garden in the Woods Nursery, *Framingham, MA*★
Hillside Gardens, *Norfolk, CT*
Kathleen Nelson Perennials, *Gaylordsville, CT*
Mainescape Garden Shop, *Blue Hill, ME*
New England Wetland Plants, *Amherst, MA*★
Perennials From Susan, *Amherst, NH*★
Rocky Dale Gardens, *Bristol, VT*
Sylvan Nursery, *Westport, MA*
Tripple Brook Farm, *Southampton, MA*★

Twombly Nursery, *Monroe, CT*★
Umbrella Factory Gardens, *Charlestown, RI*
Underwood Shade Nursery, *North Attleboro, MA*★
Wayside Farm, *North Sandwich, NH*
Weston Nurseries, *Hopkinton, MA*

ORCHIDS
A&P Orchids, *Swansea, MA*★
The Great Plant Company, *New Hartford, CT*
J&L Orchids, *Easton, CT*★
Lauray of Salisbury, *Salisbury, CT*
Logee's Greenhouses, *Danielson, CT*
Lyman Estate Greenhouses, *Waltham, MA*
Mountain Orchids, *Ludlow, VT*★

ORGANIC GROWERS
Blanchette Gardens, *Carlisle, MA*★
Blisscapes Nursery and Wildlife Sanctuary, *South Dartmouth, MA*
Bloomingfields Farm Seeds, *Gaylordsville, CT*★
Butterbrooke Farm, *Oxford, CT*
Cady's Falls Nursery, *Morrisville, VT*★
Elmore Roots, *Wolcott, VT*★
Fedco, *Waterville, ME*★
Fernwood, *Swanville, ME*★
Hedgehog Hill Farm, *East Sumner, ME*★
Hidden Gardens, *Searsport, ME*★
Meadowbrook Herb Garden, *Wyoming, RI*
Olallie Daylily Farm, *South Newfane, VT*★
Standing Stone Perennial Farm, *South Royalton, VT*★
Stone Soup Farm, *Monroe, ME*
Tripple Brook Farm, *Southampton, MA*★
Walter K. Morss & Son, *Boxford, MA*★
Windham Wildflowers, *Westminster Station, VT*

PEONIES
Bay State Perennial Farm, *Whately, MA*
Beardsley Gardens, *Sharon, CT*
Cady's Falls Nursery, *Morrisville, VT*
Cricket Hill Garden, *Thomaston, CT*★
Countryman Peony Farm, *Northfield, VT*★
Fedco, *Waterville, ME*
Gingerbread Farm Perennials, *Wayne, ME*
Hedgehog Hill Farm, *East Sumner, ME*
Standing Stone Perennial Farm, *South Royalton, VT*
Uncanoonuc Mt. Perennials, *Goffstown, NH*
White Flower Farm, *Litchfield, CT*

PERENNIALS—SEEDLINGS

Green Mountain Transplants, Inc., *East Montpelier, VT*★
Hedgehog Hill Farm, *East Sumner, ME*★
Murray Farms, *Penacook, NH*
Standing Stone Perennial Farm, *South Royalton, VT*

PERENNIALS—SHADE

Allen C. Haskell Horticulturists, *New Bedford, MA*
Ashley Falls Nursery, *Ashley Falls, MA*
Avant Gardens, *North Dartmouth, MA*
Bay State Perennial Farm, *Whately, MA*★
Beardsley Gardens, *Sharon, CT*
Blanchette Gardens, *Carlisle, MA*★
Cady's Falls Nursery, *Morrisville, VT*★
Conway's Nursery, *Tiverton, RI*
The Farmer's Daughter at Hillcrest Farm, *Auburn, MA*
The Fells Estate Nursery, *Newbury, NH*
Fernwood, *Swanville, ME*★
Fieldstone Gardens, *Vassalboro, ME*
Garden in the Woods Nursery, *Framingham, MA*★
Gingerbread Farm Perennials, *Wayne, ME*
Green Mountain Transplants, Inc., *East Montpelier, VT*
Hedgehog Hill Farm, *East Sumner, ME*
Hidden Gardens, *Searsport, ME*
Hillside Gardens, *Norfolk, CT*★
Kathleen Nelson Perennials, *Gaylordsville, CT*
Labor of Love Landscaping and Nursery, *Barton, VT*
Lake Street Garden Center, *Salem, NH*
Little Siberia Perennials, *Granville, VT*
Lyman Estate Greenhouses, *Waltham, MA*
Mahoney's Garden Centers, *Winchester, MA*
Mainescape Garden Shop, *Blue Hill, ME*
Meredith Country Gardens, *Moultonboro, NH*
The Mixed Border, *Hollis, NH*
Newbury Perennial Gardens, *Byfield, MA*
Olallie Daylily Gardens, *South Newfane, VT*
O'Donal's Nurseries, *Gorham, ME*
Peckham's Greenhouse, *Little Compton, RI*
Perennial Pleasures Nursery, *East Hardwick, VT*
Perennials From Susan, *Amherst, NH*★
Perennials Preferred Nursery, *Waldoboro, ME*★
Plainview Farm Fine Perennials, *North Yarmouth, ME*★
Rocky Dale Gardens, *Bristol, VT*
Rolling Green Nursery, *Greenland, NH*
Standing Stone Perennial Farm, *South Royalton, VT*
Twombly Nursery, *Monroe, CT*★
Uncanoonuc Mt. Perennials, *Goffstown, NH*

Underwood Shade Nursery, *North Attleboro, MA*★
The Variegated Foliage Nursery, *Eastford, CT*★
Wayside Farm, *North Sandwich, NH*
Weston Nurseries, *Hopkinton, MA*
White Flower Farm, *Litchfield, CT*

PERENNIALS—SUN

Allen C. Haskell Horticulturists, *New Bedford, MA*★
Ashley Falls Nursery, *Ashley Falls, MA*
Andrew's Greenhouse, *Amherst, MA*★
Avant Gardens, *North Dartmouth, MA*★
Bay State Perennial Farm, *Whately, MA*
Beardsley Gardens, *Sharon, CT*
Blanchette Gardens, *Carlisle, MA*
Bodacious Blossoms, *Chocorua, NH*
Cady's Falls Nursery, *Morrisville, VT*
Comstock, Ferre & Co., *Old Wethersfield, CT*★
Conway's Nursery, *Tiverton, RI*
Edgewater Farm, *Plainfield, NH*
Everlasting Farm, *Bangor, ME*
The Farmer's Daughter at Hillcrest Farm, *Auburn, MA*
Fedco, *Waterville, ME*
Fernwood, *Swanville, ME*
Fieldstone Gardens, *Vassalboro, ME*★
Garden in the Woods Nursery, *Framingham, MA*
Gaskill's Garden Shop and Nursery, *Provincetown, MA*
Gingerbread Farm Perennials, *Wayne, ME*★
Green Mountain Transplants, *East Montpelier, VT*
Gregg Hill Gardens, *Waterbury Center, VT*
Hedgehog Hill Farm, *East Sumner, ME*
Hidden Gardens, *Searsport, ME*★
Hillside Gardens, *Norfolk, CT*★
Kathleen Nelson Perennials, *Gaylordsville, CT*★
Labor of Love Landscaping and Nursery, *Barton, VT*
Lake Street Garden Center, *Salem, NH*
Little Siberia Perennials, *Granville, VT*
Mahoney's Garden Centers, *Winchester, MA*★
Mainescape Garden Shop, *Blue Hill, ME*
Meredith Country Gardens, *Moultonboro, NH*
The Mixed Border, *Hollis, NH*★
Murray Farms, *Penacook, NH*
Newbury Perennial Gardens, *Byfield, MA*★
North Creek Farm, *Phippsburg, ME*
O'Donal's Nurseries, *Gorham, ME*★
Olallie Daylily Gardens, *South Newfane, VT*
Old Farm Nursery, *Lakeville, CT*
Peckham's Greenhouse, *Little Compton, RI*

Perennial Pleasures Nursery, *East Hardwick, VT*
Perennials From Susan, *Amherst, NH*
Perennials Preferred Nursery, *Waldoboro, ME*★
Plainview Farm Fine Perennials, *North Yarmouth, ME*★
Rocky Dale Gardens, *Bristol, VT*
Rolling Green Nursery, *Greenland, NH*
Standing Stone Perennial Farm, *South Royalton, VT*★
Stone Soup Farm, *Monroe, ME*
Sylvan Nursery, *Westport, MA*
Tranquil Lake Nursery, *Rehoboth, MA*
Twombly Nursery, *Monroe, CT*★
Uncanoonuc Mt. Perennials, *Goffstown, NH*★
Umbrella Factory Gardens, *Charlestown, RI*
Von Trapp Greenhouses, *Waitsfield, VT*
Walker Farm Garden, *Putney, VT*
Wayside Farm, *North Sandwich, NH*
Weston Nurseries, *Hopkinton, MA*★
White Flower Farm, *Litchfield, CT*

PERENNIALS—TENDER
See "Annuals and Tender Perennials"

POTATO TUBERS
Fedco, *Waterville, ME*
Green Mountain Transplants, Inc., *East Montpelier, VT*
Shepherd's Garden Seeds, *Torrington, CT*
Wood Prairie Farm, *Bridgewater, ME*★

PRIMROSES (PRIMULA AND OENOTHERA)
Avant Gardens, *North Dartmouth, MA*
Bay State Perennial Farm, *Whately, MA*
Kathleen Nelson Perennials, *Gaylordsville, CT*
Perennials Preferred Nursery, *Waldoboro, ME*
Twombly Nursery, *Monroe, CT*
Underwood Shade Nursery, *North Attleboro, MA*★
White Flower Farm, *Litchfield, CT*

RHODODENDRONS AND AZALEAS
Broken Arrow Nursery, *Hamden, CT*★
F. W. Schumacher Co., *Sandwich, MA*
Kinney Azalea Gardens, *Kingston, RI*★
O'Donal's Nurseries, *Gorham, ME*
Oliver Nurseries, *Fairfield, CT*
Rolling Green Nursery, *Greenland, NH*
Sylvan Nursery, *Westport, MA*★
Twombly Nursery, *Monroe, CT*★
The Variegated Foliage Nursery, *Eastford, CT*

Weston Nurseries, *Hopkinton, MA*★
York's Hardy Rhododendrons, *Bath, ME*★

ROCK-GARDEN PLANTS
See "Alpine and Rock-Garden Plants"

ROSES
Allen C. Haskell Horticulturists, *New Bedford, MA*
Bay State Perennial Farm, *Whately, MA*
Beardsley Gardens, *Sharon, CT*
Cady's Falls Nursery, *Morrisville, VT*
Fedco, *Waterville, ME*
Gingerbread Farm Perennials, *Wayne, ME*
Lake Street Garden Center, *Salem, NH*
Lowe's Roses, *Nashua, NH*★
Nor'East Miniature Roses, *Ipswich, MA*★
North Creek Farm, *Phippsburg, ME*★
Old Farm Nursery, *Lakeville, CT*
Resourceful Judith Designs, *Woodstock, CT*★
Roseland Nursery, *Acushnet, MA*★
The Roseraie at Bayfields, *Waldoboro, ME*★
Spider Web Gardens, *Center Tuftonboro, NH*
Standing Stone Perennial Farm, *South Royalton, VT*
Twombly Nursery, *Monroe, CT*
Uncanoonuc Mt. Perennials, *Goffstown, NH*
Weston Nurseries, *Hopkinton, MA*

SEACOAST PLANTS
North Creek Farm, *Phippsburg, ME*
Peckham's Greenhouse, *Little Compton, RI*★
Rock Spray Nursery, *Truro, MA*
Rolling Green Nursery, *Greenland, NH*★
The Roseraie at Bayfields, *Waldoboro, ME*
Sylvan Nursery, *Westport, MA*★
Waquoit Heather Nursery, *Waquoit (Falmouth), MA*

SEDUM AND SEMPERVIVUM
See "Succulents—Hardy"

SEEDLINGS
See "Vegetable Seedlings" and "Perennials—Seedlings"

SEEDS
Allen, Sterling & Lothrop, *Falmouth, ME*
Butterbrooke Farm Seeds, *Oxford, CT*
Comstock Ferre & Co., *Old Wethersfield, CT*

Fedco, *Waterville, ME*★
Garden in the Woods Nursery, *Framingham, MA*
Johnny's Selected Seeds, *Albion, ME*★
New England Wetland Plants, *Amherst, MA*
Old Sturbridge Village, *Sturbridge, MA*
Perennial Pleasures Nursery, *East Hardwick, VT*
Pinetree Garden Seeds, *New Gloucester, ME*
F.W. Schumacher Co., *Sandwich, MA*★
Select Seeds, *Union, CT*★
Shepherd's Garden Seeds, *Torrington, CT*
Windham Wildflowers, *Westminster Station, VT*

SHRUBS—BROAD-LEAF EVERGREEN
Ashley Falls Nursery, *Ashley Falls, MA*
Broken Arrow Nursery, *Hamden, CT*★
Garden in the Woods Nursery, *Framingham, MA*
Horsford Gardens and Nursery, *Charlotte, VT*
Hunting Hills Farm, *Montague, MA*
Kinney Azalea Gardens, *Kingston, RI*★
O'Donal's Nurseries, *Gorham, ME*★
Old Farm Nursery, *Lakeville, CT*
Oliver Nurseries, *Fairfield, CT*★
Rocky Dale Gardens, *Bristol, VT*
Rolling Green Nursery, *Greenland, NH*
Schartner Farms, *Exeter, RI*
Sylvan Nursery, *Westport, MA*★
Twombly Nursery, *Monroe, CT*★
The Variegated Foliage Nursery, *Eastford, CT*
Weston Nurseries, *Hopkinton, MA*★
York's Hardy Rhododendrons, *Bath, ME*★

SHRUBS—DECIDUOUS WOODY
Allen C. Haskell Horticulturists, *New Bedford, MA*★
Beardsley Gardens, *Sharon, CT*
Blisscapes Nursery and Wildlife Sanctuary, *South Dartmouth, MA*
Broken Arrow Nursery, *Hamden, CT*★
Fedco, *Waterville, ME*
Garden in the Woods Nursery, *Framingham, MA*
Hedgehog Hill Farm, *East Sumner, ME*
Horsford Gardens and Nursery, *Charlotte, VT*★
Hunting Hills Farm, *Montague, MA*
Mainescape Garden Shop, *Blue Hill, ME*
O'Donal's Nurseries, *Gorham, ME*
Old Farm Nursery, *Lakeville, CT*
Oliver Nurseries, *Fairfield, CT*★
Rocky Dale Gardens, *Bristol, VT*
Rolling Green Nursery, *Greenland, NH*

Schartner Farms, *Exeter, RI*
F.W. Schumacher Co., *Sandwich, MA* (seed)
Spider Web Gardens, *Center Tuftonboro, NH*
Sylvan Nursery, *Westport, MA*★
Twombly Nursery, *Monroe, CT*★
The Variegated Foliage Nursery, *Eastford, CT*
Weston Nurseries, *Hopkinton, MA*★

SHRUBS—EVERGREEN
See "Conifers—Trees and Shrubs"

SHRUBS—STANDARDS
Allen C. Haskell Horticulturists, *New Bedford, MA*★
Old Farm Nursery, *Lakeville, CT*★
Sam Bridge Nursery & Greenhouses, *Greenwich, CT*★

SUCCULENTS—HARDY
Andrew's Greenhouse, *Amherst, MA*★
Avant Gardens, *North Dartmouth, MA*★
Bay State Perennial Farm, *Whately, MA*
Blue Meadow Farm, *Montague, MA*
Conway's Nursery, *Tiverton, RI*
Hillside Gardens, *Norfolk, CT*
Little Siberia Perennials, *Granville, VT*★
Rocky Dale Gardens, *Bristol, VT*
Uncanoonuc Mt. Perennials, *Goffstown, NH*
Weston Nurseries, *Hopkinton, MA*

TOPIARY
Allen C. Haskell Horticulturists, *New Bedford, MA*★
Around the Bend Nursery, *Lakeville, MA*★
Sam Bridge Nursery & Greenhouses, *Greenwich, CT*

TREES—FRUIT
See "Fruit Plants and Trees"

TREES—SHADE AND ORNAMENTAL
Allen C. Haskell Horticulturists, *New Bedford, MA*★
Bay State Perennial Farm, *Whately, MA*
Blisscapes Nursery and Wildlife Sanctuary, *South Dartmouth, MA*★
Broken Arrow Nursery, *Hamden, CT*★
Fedco, *Waterville, ME*★
Garden in the Woods Nursery, *Framingham, MA*
Horsford Gardens and Nursery, *Charlotte, VT*★
Mainescape Garden Shop, *Blue Hill, ME*
O'Donal's Nurseries, *Gorham, ME*★
Old Farm Nursery, *Lakeville, CT*

Oliver Nurseries, *Fairfield, CT*★
Rocky Dale Gardens, *Bristol, VT*★
Rolling Green Nursery, *Greenland, NH*
Schartner Farms, *Exeter, RI*
F.W. Schumacher Co., *Sandwich, MA* (seed)
Sylvan Nursery, *Westport, MA*★
Twombly Nursery, *Monroe, CT*★
The Variegated Foliage Nursery, *Eastford, CT*
Weston Nurseries, *Hopkinton, MA*

TROPICAL AND CONSERVATORY PLANTS
Avant Gardens, *North Dartmouth, MA*
Blue Meadow Farm, *Montague, MA*
HillBilly Acres, *Scituate, MA*
Lauray of Salisbury, *Salisbury, CT*★
Logee's Greenhouses, *Danielson, CT*★
Lyman Estate Greenhouses, *Waltham, MA*
Peckham's Greenhouse, *Little Compton, RI*
Stonehedge Gardens, *Charlton, MA*
Walnut Hill Greenhouse, *Litchfield, CT*★
Werner's Picket Mountain Farm, *Newfield, ME*
White Flower Farm, *Litchfield, CT*

TULIP BULBS
See "Bulbs"

VEGETABLE SEEDLINGS
Andrew's Greenhouse, *Amherst, MA*★
Edgewater Farm, *Plainfield, NH*★
Everlasting Farm, *Bangor, ME*
Green Mountain Transplants, Inc., *East Montpelier, VT*★
Hedgehog Hill Farm, *East Sumner, ME*★
Johnny's Selected Seeds, *Albion, ME*★
Meredith Country Gardens, *Moultonboro, NH*
Nourse Farms, *South Deerfield, MA*
Shepherd's Garden Seeds, *Torrington, CT*
Stonehedge Gardens, *Charlton, MA*★
Von Trapp Greenhouses, *Waitsfield, VT*★
Walker Farm Garden, *Putney, VT*
Walnut Hill Greenhouse, *Litchfield, CT*

VINES AND CLIMBING PLANTS
Allen C. Haskell Horticulturists, *New Bedford, MA*
Ashley Falls Nursery, *Ashley Falls, MA*
Avant Gardens, *North Dartmouth, MA*★
Bay State Perennial Farm, *Whately, MA*
Completely Clematis Specialty Nursery, *Ipswich, MA*★

WATER-GARDEN PLANTS
See "Aquatic and Water-Garden Plants"

WILDFLOWERS
See "Native Plants and Wildflowers"

WINTER-INTEREST PLANTS

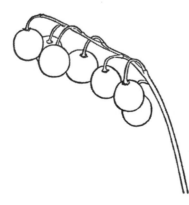

ALPHABETICAL INDEX OF NURSERIES

THE FREEMAN.

About the Author

Ruah Donnelly is an attorney and Massachusetts native with a lifelong interest in New England gardens—especially other people's. Her first plant, acquired at age 11, was a white iris rescued from a derelict rock garden. Childhood chores included vegetable gardening in New Hampshire and early trial-testing of 'Butter and Sugar' corn. She has planted a tree on every property she has owned, including white dogwood, golden weeping willow, river birch, copper beech, and variegated pagoda tree.

She is an active supporter of the Worcester County Horticultural Society, which owns the 132-acre Tower Hill Botanic Garden in Boylston, Massachusetts. Her urban container gardens have won *Making Boston Grow* awards for several years. She lives with her husband in Boston.

NOTES